D0205250

The Jacobin Clubs in the French Revolution

The Jacobin Clubs in the French Revolution

The Middle Years

Michael L. Kennedy

Princeton University Press
Princeton, New Jersey

To the Archivists of France

Contents

Preface

THIS IS the second of a proposed trilogy of works on the Jacobin clubs during the French Revolution. The first volume, covering the period of the Constituent Assembly (1789–September 1791), was published by Princeton University Press in 1982. A third volume, dealing with the Terror and the Thermidorean Reaction, looms ahead. If health permits, and if my interest does not flag, I hope to finish it by the early 1990s.

The "middle years" of Jacobin history are framed by the opening of the Legislative Assembly on October 1, 1791, and a decisive coup which occurred in Paris on June 2, 1793. In between are several dramatic events, including the outbreak of the Revolutionary Wars; the overthrow of the monarchy; the September Massacres; the convocation of a National Convention; and the trial and execution of Louis XVI. During the last eight months of this span, the Jacobin club network was deeply divided by a schism between two groups of republicans in Paris, the Girondins and Montagnards.

Volume two, like volume one, is "less a thesis than a narration, more a picture than an analysis." My foremost concern has been to recount what happened, to present the evidence. I have consciously sought to avoid pure theorization. Confident of facts, I have also been chary of dogma. Too many histories of the Revolution have been distorted by partisanship or by trying to force data into some rigidly preconceived mold.

As in the first volume, I have focused my attention upon the provincial clubs. The Jacobin Society of Paris, or the "mother society," as it was called by affiliates, seems to me to be a subject unto itself. Besides, its history is relatively well known. A good recent synthesis that centers primarily on the Paris club is Gérard Maintenant's *Les Jacobins* (Paris, 1984), in the series "Que sais-je."

The vast number of provincial clubs, and the multiple interests and activities of their members, complicated my task. At times, I well-nigh drowned in seas of data. Nonetheless, I did not use a computer, save in the final stages of typing. Old-fashioned methods of recording, cataloguing, and writing, in my opinion, still have much to say for them. Indeed, I believe that I stumbled across certain things that I would never have been able to program a computer to find.

Because of the limits of space, I have had to compress into brief chapters some topics on which book-length manuscripts could be written. I apologize to readers in advance for short-changing a few subjects. Little is said, for example, about local politics. My history concentrates on issues and events of national import. I have also chosen in this volume not to write a chapter on women in the clubs. The story of the distaff side of Jacobinism will be continued in book three.

Two monetary units are mentioned frequently. The "livre" was not a coin but a standard of value used for reckoning wealth or income. It was equal to twenty "sous," or "sols." Just exactly what purchasing power a livre would have today is hard to compute. In 1979, an economist friend and I calculated that it would be worth a little more than three American dollars. But I now think that this figure was too low; and to be frank, I can no longer remember how we arrived at it. Four or five dollars might be more accurate.

Some readers may be unfamiliar with the administrative divisions of Revolutionary France. The largest was the department, of which there were eighty-three in 1791. The departments were divided into districts, districts into cantons, cantons into communes, and communes into sections. Each department and district had an elected council and a permanent executive committee called a directory. The communes had a general council and a permanent municipal corps presided over by a mayor. Throughout the text I have employed a kind of shorthand and referred to these governing bodies as simply the "department," the "district," and the "commune" (or municipality).

This volume is based on data accumulated over a long period. The initial spadework was done in 1968–69 while researching my thesis on the club of Marseille. Since then, I have done research in France on four occasions (1972, 1977–78, 1982, and 1984) and personally examined archival holdings in sixty-six departments. My last trips were sponsored by the American Council of Learned Societies and the American Philosophical Society.

In the intervals between these research trips, I have read hundreds of monographs and articles and ordered much primary source material on microfilm. This would not have been possible without grants from the Winthrop College Research Council and the efficient work of the Interlibrary Loan staff of the Winthrop Library. I express my special appreciation to two librarians, Adelaide Williams and Dorothy Berry. I cannot begin to thank the scores of French archivists and historians who have assisted me.

Portions of the chapters on network fluctuations and the press appear as articles in the *Journal of Modern History* and *French Historical Studies*. I acknowledge my debt to the editors of these journals. I also wish to thank Hans Schmitt, Owen Connelly, Pierre Laurent, and Isser Woloch for recommending me for grants and fellowships. Jean Morse typed portions of the manuscript, taught me how to use a word processor, and solved numerous technical problems. As always, my wife, Adele, has been very supportive and understanding.

Abbreviations

AD	Archives départementales
AHRF	*Annales historiques de la Révolution française*
AM	Archives municipales
AN	Archives nationales
AP	*Annales patriotiques*
ArchP	*Archives parlementaires*
BM	Bibliothèque municipale
BN	Bibliothèque nationale
CD	*Courrier des 83 départements*
COR	Correspondance (This symbol is always followed by the name of a French town. It refers to the correspondence of the clubs of the town. The locations of the dossiers and registers of correspondence are given in the "Essay on the Sources of Jacobin History in the Departments.")
JC	*Journal de la correspondance de Jacobins*
JD	*Journal des débats des Jacobins*
JDM	*Journal des départements méridionaux*
M	*Moniteur*
PF	*Patriote français*
PV	Procès-verbaux (This symbol is always followed by the name of a French town. It refers to the minutes of the clubs of the town. The locations of these minutes are given in the "Essay on the Sources of Jacobin History in the Departments.")
RF	*Révolution française*

PART ONE

The Clubs and Their Members

I

Fluctuations of the Network

I N THE twenty months from October 1, 1791, to June 2, 1793, clubs functioned in a minimum of 1,544 French communes, and perhaps as many as 2,000. The loss of Jacobin archives, orthographical errors in surviving records, and the multiple use of certain place names guarantee that some societies will remain forever unidentified.

All departments had clubs, but the distribution was uneven (see Appendix A). Generally speaking, societies did not thrive in remote and thinly populated areas. In the Midi, for example, there were pockets of low activity in the western Pyrénées, the Cevennes, and parts of the Alps. In the Gard, the populous eastern plain fairly bristled with clubs; the mountainous districts of the west were underrepresented. Any attempt to correlate geographical distribution strictly with topography, population statistics, or number of communes, however, runs into pitfalls. The Hautes-Alpes and Basses-Alpes had *four* and *forty* societies respectively, but were not vastly dissimilar in population (120,000 vs. 169,000) or in degree of isolation. The Bouches-du-Rhône and the area termed today the Vaucluse were relatively poor in terms of numbers of communes, but fabulously rich in clubs.

The highest concentrations of clubs occurred in the south, in a belt from the Gironde to the Var. At each end of this Jacobin galaxy were the powerful societies of Bordeaux and Marseille. Their gravitational pull was felt in many departments. But all the Midi did not whirl about Bordeaux and Marseille. The clubs of Toulouse, Montpellier, Montauban, Nîmes, and Perpignan, to name only a few, were quite significant. And certain small-town societies, such as Tonneins, were astonishingly active and independent.

Burgundy, Normandy, the Paris region, the Nord and Pas-de-

Calais, and the frontier departments of the northeast had moderate to high densities of clubs. But in the north as a whole, numbers were much lower. We know not why this was so. Perhaps the disparity was due to the temperament of southerners, who loved to socialize.[1] What the north lacked in quantity, it compensated for in quality. In zeal and industry, such societies as Brest, Strasbourg, Clermont-Ferrand, Besançon, Auxerre, Beaune, Dijon, Chalon-sur-Saône, Versailles, and Lorient yielded in no respect to their southern sisters.

Clubs also functioned in at least nine overseas, colonial settlements: Port-au-Prince and Le Cap François (Haiti); Pointe-à-Pitre, Ste.-Rose, and Moule (Guadeloupe); Cayenne (Guiana); Tobago (Tobago); St.-Pierre (St.-Pierre et Miquelon); and St.-Louis (Mauritius). Most secured affiliation from the Paris Jacobins and corresponded with societies in the French Atlantic ports. The vast distances separating them from the mother country, however, precluded them from playing a significant part in network affairs.[2]

In the category of historical curiosities one must likewise place the predominantly French "Jacobin" societies that appeared in Genoa, Aleppo, Constantinople, and other foreign commercial entrepots. The United States had two such clubs before June 1793, and six by the end of that year. The first, and certainly the most active, was founded at Charleston on January 14, 1792. It was affiliated with Paris and Bordeaux, and its members gloried in being called "Jacobins." The gunsmith François Desverneys, who had been a Charlestonian since 1780, always wore a Phrygian bonnet, and to his signature affixed the words: "French patriot until death."[3]

Up to August–September 1792, the bulk of the clubs called

---

[1] See M. Agulhon, *La Sociabilité méridionale*, 2 vols. (Aix, 1966).

[2] Cf. J. Saintoyant, *La Colonisation française pendant la Révolution* (Paris, 1930), II, 120, 273, 286, 330–333. H. Prentout, *L'Ile de France sous Decaen* (Paris, 1901), pp. 83–84. ArchP, June 11, 1793. JC, Feb. 20, Oct. 18, Dec. 15, 1792. JD, Dec. 14, 1791, June 16, 1793. COR, Bordeaux, 12 L 29–33. PV and COR, Lorient, June 26, 1791, Jan. 2, 8, Apr. 23, June 11, Dec. 31, 1792. PV, Le Havre, Dec. 25–26, 1792.

[3] M. Kennedy, "Le Club Jacobin de Charleston," *Revue d'histoire moderne et contemporaine* (1977), pp. 420–438, and "La Société française des amis de la liberté et de l'égalité de Philadelphie," *AHRF* (1976), pp. 614–628.

themselves "Societies of Friends of the Constitution." At that date most changed their names to "Societies of Friends of Liberty and Equality" or, less frequently, "Societies of Friends of the Republic." Rules regarding affiliation also remained unaltered until the end of 1792. Applicants were required to submit formal petitions to the Paris Jacobins, along with membership rosters, copies of their by-laws, and character references from two previously affiliated societies. In the interests of local concord, the Paris club limited the number of affiliates to one per city.

Before the Feuillant schism, about 439 clubs received certificates of affiliation from the Paris Jacobins. The number of nonaffiliates exceeded 500. It is impossible to determine whether the ratio improved in 1792 and 1793, for the Paris society, in spite of many entreaties from provincial clubs, discontinued the practice of publishing lists of affiliates. Lack of accreditation by Paris did not necessarily mean that a society was doomed to hang in limbo. The nonaffiliated Society of Surveillants of Bordeaux established formal ties with about twenty clubs of *province*.[4]

In the "middle years," as during the Constituent Assembly, the clubs usually communicated through the post. Some carried on a prodigious correspondence. Poitiers got 757 pieces of mail in 1792, most from sister societies. It was not uncommon for secretaries at the club of Marseille, in 1792–93, to open fifteen letters and packages per day. Beauvais spent roughly 10 percent of its budget on postage. The Récollets Society (Society of Friends of the Constitution) of Bordeaux was in touch with individuals and political groups in England, Belgium, Ireland, the Caribbean, and the United States.[5]

A HARD core of perhaps one hundred societies operated continuously from October 1791 to June 1793. In the remainder, periods of liveliness alternated with comatose states. Clubs in every region experienced hard times in the early Legislative Assembly. Twenty-nine former affiliates shut down and, to my knowledge,

---

[4] R. Dubos, "Une Société populaire bordelaise, les Surveillants de la Constitution," *Revue historique de Bordeaux* (1935), p. 118.

[5] COR, Poitiers, S 1, S 23–26. *JDM*, 1792–93. PV and COR, Marseille. PV, Bordeaux (Récollets). PV, Beauvais, Dec. 29, 1791. COR, Bordeaux, 12 L 29–33.

never reopened. The societies of Guéret, Magnac-Laval, Lourdes, Durtal, and Tain disbanded, for all practical purposes, until 1793.[6] Allassac closed for about one year. Pau, Tulette, Bourbonne, Cholet, Hyères, Bapaume, Tarbes, Combes, Embrun, Eymoutiers, Colmar, Delle, and St.-Tropez went into eclipses ranging from six weeks to six months.[7] At Castres, Gaillac, St.-Affrique, and Senlis meetings became perfunctory. New enrollment ceased at Grignols and Villandraut. Honfleur and Versailles were weakened by resignations.[8] Nearly everywhere, attendance dropped. In great clubs like Toulouse the absenteeism was merely worrisome. Compiègne, however, shrank to half a dozen members; Châtillon-sur-Chalaronne had to lower its quorum to seven. Lectoure pleaded with and threatened delinquents. No one seemed to care.[9]

Budgetary shortfalls went hand-in-hand with truancy. Balancing of expenditures with receipts was a perpetual problem in the clubs, but never more acute than in the early autumn of 1791. Le Mans, which was 887 livres in arrears, devoted several meetings to finances. Shaken by the resignation of its treasurer, who was tired of begging members for their dues, Provins issued an ultimatum to the guilty parties: "Are you going to pay, yes or no? If the answer is . . . no, you will be expelled. You have until November 1 to mull it over."[10] Provins had to close, but other clubs clung to life through austerity measures. At least twenty-two

[6] R. and L. Chervy, "La Société populaire de Guéret, 1791–1794," *Mémoires, Société des sciences de la Creuse* (1962), p. 434. PV: Magnac-Laval, Sept. 25, 1791, Apr. 11, 1793; Lourdes, Sept. 1791, May 6, 1793; Tain, Oct. 23, 1791, May 27, 1792, Sept. 1, 1793; Durtal, Sept. 25, 1791.

[7] A. Ulry, "Les Clubs révolutionnaires de Donzenac et Allassac," *Bulletin de la Société de la Corrèze* (1921), p. 176. PV: Pau, Oct. 15, 1791, Dec. 2, 1792; Tulette, Sept. 24, 1791, Jan. 20, 1792; Bourbonne, Aug. 28–Dec. 11, 1791; Eymoutiers, Aug. 10–Dec. 16, 1791, May 6, 1793. L. Testut, *La Ville de Beaumont pendant la période révolutionnaire* (Bordeaux, 1922), pp. 744–802. P. Leuilliot, *Les Jacobins de Colmar* (Strasbourg, 1923), pp. xvi–xvii. See also *JC*, Mar. 22, Apr. 22, 1792. *CD*, Apr. 1, 1792. COR, Bordeaux, 12 L 30, 38.

[8] Abbé Raylet, "Procès-verbaux de la Société . . . de St.-Affrique," *Mémoires de la Société des lettres de l'Aveyron* (1942), pp. 297–515. PV: Castres, Gaillac, Senlis, Honfleur, Versailles. AD, Gironde, 12 L 38, 40.

[9] PV: Châtillon, Oct. 2–Nov. 7, 1791; Lectoure, Oct. 7–Nov. 29, 1791.

[10] PV: Pau, Oct. 15, 1791; Le Mans, Oct. 23–Nov. 7, 1791. J. Bellanger, *Les Jacobins peints par eux-mêmes; . . . la Société populaire de Provins (1791–1795)* (Paris, 1908), pp. 28–29.

proclaimed in October that they would no longer pay postage on incoming letters and packages, except those of the "mother society." By November 1791, network correspondence had plummeted to critically low levels.[11]

The great autumn slump may be ascribed, in part, to the lingering effects of the "Feuillant schism," the mass secession of moderates from the "mother society" on July 15–16, 1791. The schismatics had formed a new society at a former Feuillant convent and had appealed to the departmental clubs for their support. After an initial wave of defections, and considerable indecision, most of the clubs had rallied to the Paris Jacobins by early September. But Montfauçon, Commercy, Honfleur, and Neuville waited until October to seek reconciliation with the Jacobins. November came before St.-Hippolyte returned to the fold. Vienne "at last rid itself of Feuillants" in February 1792. Melun abjured its errors in March; Negrepelisse, Figeac, and Cholet in April; Port Ste.-Marie and Loudun in May. The issue was not settled at Châteauroux and Espalion until pro-Jacobin minorities seceded from the Feuillantist societies in April and June and formed new clubs.[12]

Boredom and complacency also contributed to the recession. With the enactment of the Constitution in September, members at Condrieu thought that the Revolution was over and returned to "business as usual." The clubbists of Monpazier were struck by "Revolutionary fatigue" and convened on only eight occasions in the next five months. At Foix the president declared that "indifference" threatened the existence of the society. A clubbist at Boulogne candidly observed that chronic absenteeism was due to the "peu d'importance" of subjects under discussion. Anesthetized by the "tranquility" of the Hérault, Lodève felt no need to correspond with Paris. Villamblard stopped writing to the Paris Jacobins because of "a lack of interesting matters to communicate." Lannion did not want "to weary the mother society with

[11] *AP*, Oct. 12, 14, Nov. 3, 1791. *M*, Oct. 4, 7–8, 14, Nov. 3, 6, 1791.
[12] PV: Honfleur, Oct. 20, 1791; Neuville, Oct. 1791; St.-Hippolyte, Oct. 28, Nov. 27, 1791; Châteauroux, Aug. 11, 1791. E. Noiriel, "La Société . . . de Melun," *RF* (1904), pp. 323–345. M. Jouet, "Un club jacobin en province," *Revue du Berry* (1896), p. 35. *JD*, Nos. 80, 88. *JC*, Mar. 10, Apr. 16, 18, 21, May 5, 17, June 2, 1792.

its petty concerns." "Uninteresting times" lulled Rostrenen into a sleep that lasted until April 1792.[13]

Another blow was the loss of key leaders. That the life of a small society often depended on one man was made abundantly evident in the fall of 1791. The departure of zealous Jacobins to the Legislative Assembly left a void. Falaise dissolved and Revel became dormant when prominent members joined volunteer battalions bound for the frontiers. The "voice of the people" called the leaders of the Muret society to local administrative posts and reduced the club to inanition. The Sierck club almost always vegetated when the future Conventionnel, Nicolas Hentz, was out of town.[14]

Temporary damage was also inflicted by the law of September 29, 1791. The result of a backlash against the clubs in the Constituent Assembly, this law precluded them from meddling in the affairs of government agencies, petitioning collectively, or appearing as a unit in public ceremonies. When the spokesman for the constitution committee, Le Chapelier, proposed this measure, he added, as was customary, some "instructions." Had they been adopted, it would have become unlawful for clubs to affiliate, correspond, print their debates, or hold public meetings. Fortunately for the network, Robespierre's vigorous opposition caused the "instructions" to be deleted. The decree stood alone, without specifically banning affiliation and correspondence.

The Club National of Bordeaux was openly defiant of the law of September 29, vowing to sever correspondence with any club that admitted Le Chapelier or one of his "clique." Rennes and Neuville went to extremes of submission, inscribing the law on tablets in their assembly halls, lest anyone deign to forget its provisions. Bewilderment and alarm were the most common reactions. A member at Thionville moved that the club should dissolve. In a letter to the Paris Jacobins an unidentified society bespoke its fear that the law might destroy the network. At Gail-

---

[13] PV: Monpazier, Foix. G. Arnaud, *Histoire de la Révolution dans . . . l'Ariège* (Toulouse, 1904), pp. 267–268. J.-B. Holuigue, *Les Promoteurs de la Révolution en Boulonnais* (Boulogne, 1892), p. 216. *JC*, May 7, 14, 19, June 11, 1792.

[14] PV: Falaise, Oct. 24, Dec. 2, 1791. *JC*, May 14, 17, 1792. N. Dicop, *Le Club des Jacobins de Sierck* (Metz, 1975), p. 12.

lac it led to numerous resignations. According to E. Gautheron, it briefly muzzled the club of Le Puy.[15]

The truth is that some newspaper accounts of the debates in the Constituent Assembly left the impression that Le Chapelier's "instructions" had been approved. To counteract this notion, the Paris Jacobins, in early October, published and circulated a *Discours sur l'utilité des sociétés patriotiques* of Brissot, and an *Eclaircissement sur le décret du 29 septembre 1791*, written by Robespierre and Pétion.[16] These *imprimés* stiffened club resolve. When conservatives at Le Havre and Niort moved that the decree and instructions of Le Chapelier be read aloud, opponents maneuvered so that the speech of Brissot would be heard also. At Beauvais the Constitutional Bishop, Massieu, compared the doctrines of Le Chapelier and Brissot and concluded that clubs were "schools of civic virtue" that could only be opposed by "deranged or evil men." Strasbourg published Brissot's discourse in French and German. Lorient read it every week for three consecutive weeks and mailed printed copies to affiliates. After listening to the *Eclaircissement*, Condrieu judged that the utility of clubs could not be doubted, and Blaye decided that the law "impaired in no way the existence of the society."[17]

Meanwhile, the decree itself was being undercut by the Legislative Assembly. On October 17 deputies friendly to the clubs diverted a motion to censure the society of Amiens for sending an address in which it vowed, ironically, to uphold the constitution. Two days later, when questions were raised about the legality of a similar address from Lisieux, the legislators recognized the right of citizens to assemble peacefully and to sign their names individually to petitions. Although this resolution was challenged on November 29, December 5, and again on February 4

<hr />

[15] *JD*, No. 71. E. Gautheron, "Un club de Jacobins de province. La Société . . . du Puy," *Bulletin historique . . . du Puy* (1934), p. 85. PV: Gaillac, Oct. 15, 21, 1791; Thionville, Oct. 5, 1791; Neuville, Oct. 9, 1791. COR, Montpellier, L 5547.

[16] *JD*, No. 71. *PF*, Oct. 1, 1791. COR, Poitiers, S 20; Reims.

[17] H. Labroue, *La Société populaire de Bergerac* (Paris, 1915), p. 181. F.-C. Heitz, *Les Sociétés politiques de Strasbourg* (Strasbourg, 1863), p. 166. PV: Blaye, Oct. 15, 20, 1791; Niort, Oct. 5, 12, 1791; Condrieu, Oct. 23, 1791; Beauvais, Dec. 11, 1791; Le Havre, Oct. 6, 10, 1791; Versailles, Oct. 21, 1791; Lorient, Oct. 17, 1791; Falaise, Oct. 16, 1791; Thionville, Oct. 28, 1791.

by strict constructionists, it was consistently reaffirmed. Henceforth, to petition the Legislative Assembly legally, the clubbists merely had to call themselves "the active citizens of the city of _____."[18]

The first great surge of club petitions came in late November and early December following the king's veto of a decree on the émigrés. Moreover, the prospect of war caused the society of Beaune, in a circular of December 1, to cry out for more network correspondence. Lille and Niort notified Beaune of their "absolute concurrence." Marseille and Montpellier published analogous addresses. Lorient voted to pay postage on all mail from affiliates and persuaded the journalist Carra to entreat others to do the same "in this time of crisis." Toulouse, which had anticipated Beaune's appeal, circulated its own plea for "more communication of thoughts and ideas" to which Lauzun, Munster, St.-Affrique, Orléans, Montpellier, and Lyon responded affirmatively.[19] In December and January, correspondence swelled to a fortissimo chorus.

The correspondence committee of the "mother society" had been so abnormally quiet in the early autumn of 1791 that St.-Amand (Nord) and Lorient sent alarmed inquiries to Paris. Perhaps their letters had an effect; for, in late November, the committee apologized for the break-off of communications and produced its first circular since October 7. This circular asked affiliates to assess the performance of local officials, describe conditions in the armed forces, and note "anything else affecting order, tranquility, and public security in their regions." The Paris club promised to collate the data and forward the information to the "good deputies" in the Legislative Assembly.[20]

A few societies looked askance at this circular. Amiens turned it over to its departmental administration. Vienne, which was still dominated by "Feuillants," accused the Paris Jacobins of inquisitorial tactics. Auray drew up a reply, but then pigeonholed

[18] *ArchP*, Oct. 17, 19, Nov. 29, Dec. 5, 1791, Feb. 4, 1792.

[19] PV: Niort, Dec. 14, 1791; St.-Affrique, Dec. 23, 1791; Lille, Nov. 27, Dec. 1, 1791; Toulouse, Nov. 19, 1791, Feb. 1, 1792; Montpellier, Dec. 19, 1791; Périgueux, Dec. 15–20, 1791. *AP*, Dec. 27, 1791, Jan. 6, 1792. COR, Montpellier, L 5549; Niort, 3001; Reims; Lorient.

[20] PV: Lorient, Dec. 26, 1791; Niort, Nov. 27, 1791. *JD*, Oct. 21, 1791.

it when a member charged that it was a violation of the law of September 29. At Niort, the committee assigned to prepare the report procrastinated for three weeks, feeling that it might be "dangerous for the society" to draw up a detailed response.[21]

Opposition and foot-dragging seem to have been the exception rather than the rule. By February the Paris society had received more than fifty reports, which collectively are a kind of thermometer of public spirit in the departments. Of more immediate importance, the process of conducting the inquest rejuvenated several societies. Bourbonne awakened from a two-and-a-half-month slumber. Saverne shook off the inertia that had gripped it. Sète spent three weeks discussing its response. Tulle and Agen contacted all the clubs of their departments seeking information.[22]

The success of this probe inspired the Paris club, in January, to adopt a policy of sending out bi-monthly encyclicals on contemporary issues. Had this experiment worked, it might have resulted in more network unity. Lamentably, the circulars became a political football kicked about by the factions in the "mother society." In the sessions of February 22, 24, Billaud-Varenne and Robespierre accused the correspondence committee of overstepping its authority by saying in one of the encyclicals that the society favored war. Further dissension erupted on February 26, 27, when a spokesman for the committee read the texts of the circulars of February 15 and March 1. Although both were sanctioned, they proved to be the last in the series.[23]

In the first of these circulars (January 17, 1792), the correspondence committee advocated the "multiplication of village and small-town clubs," and the maintenance of "active communications between them and the principal societies in each depart-

[21] F.-J. Darsy, *Amiens . . . pendant la Révolution* (Amiens, 1878–1883), I, 177. PV: Niort, Dec. 2, 25, 1791; Auray, Nov. 30, Dec. 25, 28, 1791.

[22] *JD*, Nos. 120–121. *JC*, Nos. 2–28. A. Galland, "La Société populaire de Cherbourg," *Bulletin du Comité des travaux historiques* (1906), p. 339. D. Fischer, "La Société . . . de Saverne," *Revue d'Alsace* (1969), pp. 73–75. V. Forot, *Le Club des Jacobins de Tulle* (Tulle, 1912), p. 160. PV: Montauban, Dec. 9, 1791; Fécamp, Jan. 1, 1792; Tonneins, Dec. 2, 1791; Sète, Dec. 5–29, 1791; Le Mans, Nov. 27, Dec. 4, 1791; Bourbonne, Dec. 11, 1791; Castres, Dec. 6, 1791; Honfleur, Nov. 27, 1791.

[23] *JD*, Nos. 148–150.

ment." Besançon, on February 2, fired back copies of speeches pronounced by its commissioners at the installation of societies in Serre and Franois. "We foresaw your wishes," it boasted, "since we are already propagating societies in the countryside." On February 21, Besançon announced the formation of five more societies. Wissembourg, on February 3, notified Paris of the establishment of clubs at Woerth, Kaudel, and Lembach. Montréjeau pledged on February 6 to create new societies.[24]

The club foundations in February, while spotty, heralded a renaissance. The number of functioning societies soared in March, April, and May. This ascent may be attributed, in part, to the end of winter. Every spring, in spite of the pressures of field work, the population of clubs increased. Jacobin societies first issued forth in large quantities, in April–May 1790. April–June 1791 marked the zenith of the network during the Constituent Assembly. In March–May 1793, the total of societies was only slightly inferior to May 1792. More clubs existed in the spring of 1794 than at any other time.[25]

The great thaw of 1792 set in shortly after the publication of the circular of March 1, which reiterated, in stronger terms, the need for new clubs. As though freed from a spell that had held them in thrall, Chalon-sur-Saône, Tonneins, Bourbonne, and the Surveillant Society of Bordeaux voted to dispatch "missionaries" into the countryside. Nîmes wrote to affiliates urging the multiplication of clubs. St.-Hippolyte determined to ask "known patriots" in nearby towns to institute societies. Le Mans approved a plan designed to generate clubs in the Sarthe. By the end of March, Bazas, Luçon, and Juilly had also vowed to follow the advice of Paris.[26]

The proselytizing fire, once ignited, burned for weeks. Felletin

[24] *JC*, Feb. 3, 22, Mar. 3, 8, 1792; A. Aulard, *La Société des Jacobins*, III (1889–1897), p. 328, PV: Quingey, Mar. 7, 1792; Ornans, Feb.–Mar. 1792.

[25] There are exceptions to every rule. Pellagrue and Bergues died in April. Lauris's sessions temporarily halted on May 27. Saverne also experienced a spring "swoon." PV: Pellagrue, Lauris. Fischer, *Saverne*, pp. 75–76. L. Moreel, *Les Jacobins flamands* (Dunkerque, 1926), pp. 101–102.

[26] PV, Chalon-sur-Saône (hereafter Chalon), Mar. 15, 1792; Toulouse, Mar. 12, 1792; Bourbonne, Apr. 1, 25, 1792; Tonneins, Mar. 16, 1792; St.-Hippolyte, Mar. 18, 1792; Le Mans, Mar. 29, Apr. 5, 1792. *JC*, Mar. 24–Apr. 18, 1792. *PF*, Mar. 27, 1792. *AP*, Mar. 26, 1792. Dubos, *Surveillants*, p. 128.

proclaimed, on May 3, that in response to Jacobin wishes, it was propagating Revolutionary ideals in the Creuse. A "congress" of clubs at Clermont-Ferrand (May 8–10) resolved to augment the number of societies in the Puy-de-Dôme. Epinal, on May 20, exhorted "country folk" to form more clubs. Toulon (June 2) gloated that its commissioners were speeding to all parts of the Var to found popular societies. Lisieux and Lorient (June 10–11) called for clubs to be formed in all the towns of their districts.[27]

In certain departments, opposition was encountered. Lons-le-Saunier moaned to Paris on March 24 that it had tried to institute clubs in its district. "But everywhere, charges of sedition, ridicule, criminal prosecutions, and inquisitions worse than the Spanish, have annihilated them." Digne expressed grave doubts about implementing the program of the March 1 circular in the Basses-Alpes: "Moderates and egoists have wiped out public spirit here. . . . Our own society is reduced to fifteen patriots." According to Apt and St.-Saturnin, prospects were equally dim in the Vaucluse.[28]

Lons-le-Saunier received no outside assistance, but such was not the case in the Basses-Alpes and Vaucluse, where much depended upon the will of Marseille. From February to April, national guardsmen from Marseille, acting on orders of the club and municipal government, brutally eliminated counterrevolutionary elements at Aix, Arles, and Avignon. Henceforth, the Marseillais were the virtual masters of Provence. When citizens at Valernes, Apt, and other small towns appealed for help in founding clubs, Marseille decided to act, even if it meant flouting the law. On April 2, it boasted to Paris that its "army" was about to make a sweep of four or five departments. "Clubs! Clubs! The tiniest hamlets will have them. Our missionaries are currently preparing halls, registers, and podiums."[29]

From March to June, commissioners from Marseille, accompanied by armed national guardsmen and representatives from sister societies, crisscrossed the southeast. The success of this cru-

---

[27] AN, DXVI, 81. COR, Poitiers, S 26. PV and COR, Lorient. *JC*, May 11, June 18, 1792.

[28] *JC*, Mar. 31, Apr. 18, 1792. PV, Apt.

[29] AN, F⁷ 3659²·³. *JDM*, Mar. 6–Apr. 14, 1792. *AP*, Apr. 13, 1792. *JC*, Apr. 14, 1792.

sade partially explains the great number of clubs in this region. At least seventeen (Villelaure, Saignon, Cucuron, Roussillon, Ansouis, Bastidonne, La Tour-d'Aigues, Le Cadanet, Beaumont, La Motte, Bedarrides, Châteauneuf-du-Pape, La Bastide-des-Jourdans, Vaison, Ste.-Cecile, St.-Martin, and Peipin-d'Aigues) popped up in the Vaucluse at this time.[30] Two Marseillais claimed to have sired sixty clubs in the Basses-Alpes in forty days. Valernes, Castellane, Riez, Sisteron, Senez, Moustiers, Seyne, Cereste, Vaumeilh, Volonne, Villeneuve, Oraison, Malijai, Pierrerue, Valensoles, and Forcalquier may definitely be counted among their offspring.[31] Commissars from Marseille also ventured into the Var, implanting a club at St.-Zacharie on April 14.[32]

As early as 1790 Lille had proposed the creation of a national governing body in Paris composed of delegates from affiliated clubs. But this scheme died aborning. Up to the end of the Constituent Assembly, the Jacobin network remained an association of more or less sovereign entities. Only on the regional level was progress made beyond simple affiliation and correspondence. In early 1791, "congresses" of clubs were convened in several departments, and Jacobins in the Vendée formed an "Ambulant Society" which shifted its meeting place from town to town.[33]

During the depressed days of the early Legislative Assembly, such activity nearly ceased. Cognac, for example, refused to send deputies to a congress planned at Blanzac, believing it to be a violation of the law of September 29. By 1792, however, as the realization dawned that France faced a national emergency, attitudes changed. After a long hiatus the Vendée Ambulant Society convened at Pallicau in January, and then at Sables-d'Olonne,

[30] PV: Courthézon, Apr. 28, May 3, 16, 1792; Grambois, Mar. 10, 12, 25, May 23, 1792; Vaison, Apr. 10, 1792. *JDM*, Mar. 20–June 30, 1792.

[31] PV: Riez, May 14, 1792; Castellane, May 4, 1792; Valernes, Apr. 11, 1792; Volonne, May 20, 24, 1792. COR, Marseille, L 2075–2076. AM, Marseille, I₂, carton 1792. C. Cauvin, "La Formation de la Société populaire de Sisteron," *Annales des Basses-Alpes* (1901), pp. 71–79, 139–152.

[32] COR, St-Zacharie.

[33] Musée Calvet (Avignon), Fonds H. Chobaut, 5992, "Les Congrès et les comités centraux des sociétés populaires, principalement dans le sud-est, 1790–1793." PV, Cognac, June 10, 1791. AN, C 130. *CD*, Mar. 24, Apr. 9, 19, 1791. *Mercure universel*, Apr. 3, 1791. *Journal des amis de la constitution*, May 10, 1791.

St.-Gilles-sur-Vie, La Mothe-Achard, and Talmal. The club of
Tournus, on February 17, suggested that all the principal societies
dispatch delegates to a general assembly in the capital. About the
same date a convention of eight clubs took place at St.-Paul-
Trois-Châteaux.[34]

On February 29, Carra printed an account of the St.-Paul affair
in his immensely popular *Annales patriotiques*, simultaneously ap-
pealing for monthly conventions of clubs in each department.
From these gatherings, he suggested, two to three envoys could
be selected to go to biennial Parisian synods, which "men of good
will" from other European lands might be induced to attend.
After the appearance of this visionary article, conventioneering
became a nationwide fad. In March and early April departmental
or regional meetings of club representatives were held at Niort,
Autun, Bourg, Valence, Lyon, Strasbourg, and Moulins. The societies of Montauban and Périgueux discussed the feasibility of
departmental "federations." Ste.-Foy notified Bordeaux of its
readiness to confer with its counterparts in the Gironde. La
Tremblade lobbied at Saintes for an assemblage of societies of the
Charente-Maritime. Nevers conceived the grandiose idea of
hosting a twelve-department conference.[35]

The project of national synods advocated by Carra was debated in the convention at Moulins and on May 15 in a congress
of clubs of the Aude at Carcassonne. The Aude societies proclaimed that they were "waiting expectantly for a solemn reunion of deputies of the kingdom and of friendly foreign nations."
Although Carra's dream was unrealizable, some deputations
were sent to Paris. Strasbourg told the "mother society" to expect the arrival of emissaries from the federation of the Haut- and
Bas-Rhin. Conventioneers at Lyon voted to dispatch two permanent legates to Paris, on the grounds that only two of the fif-
teen-member legislative delegation of their department spoke for
the "parti du peuple."[36]

[34] PV, Cognac, Oct. 18, 1791. *JC*, Feb. 27, 1792. COR, Niort, 3005.

[35] *JC*, Apr. 9, 18, 23, 1792. COR, Niort, 3003. *JDM*, Apr. 28, 1792. PV: Valence, Mar. 25, Apr. 9, 1792; Montauban, Mar. 7, 10, 1792; Périgueux, Mar. 27,
1792; Chalon, Mar. 18, Apr. 15, 1792; Niort, Mar. 10, 1792; Neuville, Apr. 21,
1792; Condrieu, Mar. 25, 1792.

[36] *JC*, Apr. 9, 14, 23, 1792. COR, Bordeaux, 12 L 30.

The congress of the Tarn at Castres on May 2 was a mere pep rally where delegates listened to poetry, testimonials, and inspirational speeches, while musicians played "melodious and patriotic airs." Many of the assemblies, however, tackled serious issues. The federation of the Côte-d'Or at Dijon (early June) petitioned the Legislative Assembly to deport nonjuring priests, raze monasteries, and disarm well-known aristocrats. Chalonsur-Saône invited representatives of twenty-seven clubs to its convention and carefully planned the agenda. Questions discussed in the meetings (June 1–5) included: "How to end vices and insure full participation in elections?" "What is the best means to convince the people of the wisdom of the laws ordering the free circulation of grains?" And "how can poverty be abolished and aid given to the needy?"[37]

Although most congresses were one-time affairs, they became staple fare in certain departments. I count thirteen conventions, of varying sizes, in the Vaucluse and Drôme between February 1792 and June 1793. In the Saône-et-Loire, in addition to those of Autun and Chalon, federations occurred at Louhans (October 1792) and Mâcon (January 1793). The "assemblée patriotique centrale" of the Puy-de-Dôme met at Clermont, Ambert, and again at Clermont (May to early July).[38] The most extraordinary experiment was attempted in the west. On May 10–11, 1792, representatives of the clubs of Niort, Nantes, La Rochelle, and the Ambulant Society of the Vendée gathered at Luçon. Each society agreed to host one congress per year. They also asked Angers to join their association, and the latter concurred. The five-department consortium held its first meeting at Fontenay on June 24, 1792. It was an "imposing spectacle." Fine weather permitted participants to meet in the open air. A second conclave was scheduled for August 24, 1792, at La Rochelle. The third meeting took place in Niort on February 7, 1793. Angers excused itself, citing diminished enrollment, but three clubs of the Vienne de-

---

[37] *JC*, June 23, 1792. AD, Saône-et-Loire, 4 L 1. M. Henriot, *Le Club des Jacobins de Semur* (Dijon, 1933), pp. 130–131. PV: Vitteaux, May 27, 1792; Nuits, May 27, 1792; Castres, May 2, 1792; Chalon, Apr. 25, May 2, June 1–4, 1792.

[38] *JC*, May 29, 31, July 16, 21, 1792. COR, Niort, 3005. *M*, June 4, 1792. *AP*, June 5, 1792. *PF*, June 15, 1792. H. Libois, *Les Délibérations de la Société populaire de Lons-le-Saunier* (Lons-le-Saunier, 1897), p. 57.

partment sent observers. The date for the fourth conference was set for April 24 at Nantes.[39]

At the height of the "federation" movement of the spring of 1792, the network, for the first time, got a boost from the executive branch of government. On April 4, shortly after his surprise appointment as minister of finance, Etienne Clavière made a triumphal appearance at the Paris Jacobins and gave a speech urging tax compliance. Printed copies of his oration were soon speeding to provincial clubs, together with covering letters bearing Clavière's signature. These letters must have been written by secretaries of the Paris club, for they reminded long-silent societies of the dates of their last correspondence, asked if they had disbanded, and encouraged them to resume communications.[40]

A few societies were miffed or puzzled by the passages regarding correspondence. Rabastens and Lorient produced evidence showing that they had written to the Paris club numerous times since the dates given in the letters. Tourcoing and Auvillars also said that mistakes had been made and worried that their mail was being intercepted. Bourg tried to brazen its way out of an embarrassing situation. "If we have said nothing about our frontiers," it blustered, "it is because we fear nothing." Compiègne attributed its incommunicative behavior to disgust over the "scandalous" divisions in the "mother society." The Antipolitiques of Eguilles found it ironic that after several fruitless attempts to win affiliation from Paris, they were reproached for not corresponding.[41]

More often than not, however, the clubs recognized the "justice" of Clavière's censures. At least twenty-six apologized for their past behavior and promised to write more often. Six (Château-Thierry, Provins, St.-Tropez, Billom, Pontlevoy, and St.-Aignan) announced that they had been closed and were reopening. Villeneuve-le-Roy and Fécamp, which were suffering from terminal illnesses, went into temporary periods of remission.[42]

---

[39] COR, Niort, 3001–3006. *ArchP*, Feb. 22, 1793.

[40] *PF*, Apr. 21, 1792. PV, Perpignan, Apr. 20, 1792.

[41] *JC*, May 10, 17, June 2, 9, 11, 1792. PV and COR, Lorient, Apr. 26–May 6, 1792.

[42] *JC*, Apr. 23–June 11, 1792. Bellanger, *Provins*, p. 33. M. G. Prévost, "La Société de . . . Villeneuve-le-Roy, 1790–1792," *Bulletin, Société des sciences historiques de l'Yonne* (1913), pp. 508–523. PV: Auray, Apr. 27, 1792; Honfleur, Apr. 29,

The Declaration of War, on April 20, was a far more potent stimulant. Once-roomy assembly halls overflowed with citizens bringing donations for the war. In Alsace, where the attrition rate for societies had been high, several reopened briefly. The frantic desire for news caused marked increases in the correspondence of frontline clubs. Metz was the choice of many societies that wanted updates on the fighting, because, in a circular dated May 5, it had promised to pay postage on all incoming letters and had advised its sisters to adopt the same practice. And in another circular of June 6, it designated three members to whom clubs of the interior could address their queries. "War is upon us!" it wrote. "Rumors are flying! We must have accurate communications."[43]

Apparently Metz had no trouble in processing its mail, but Lille and Châlons-sur-Marne were not so fortunate. After the initial French defeats on April 29, Lille in particular was inundated with requests for battlefield reports. At first it replied to each query, but the burden proved to be too great for its small membership. In a circular of late May it advised affiliates who wanted daily news from the front to subscribe to the *Argus patriote*, a newspaper to be published at Valenciennes.[44]

The king's dismissal of the Jacobin ministers Roland, Clavière, and Servan on June 13 and the invasion of the Tuileries (the royal residence) by a mob on June 20 touched off a political crisis that culminated in the overthrow of the monarchy on August 10. The network fairly throbbed with activity throughout this period. But some societies experienced problems, and the number in operation may have declined slightly. Saddened by the events of June 20, Confolens and Neuville (Rhône) closed. Boulogne, Vaison, and Fécamp expired in July from unknown causes. Auray, St.-Affrique, Lauris, and Compiègne recessed for two months. Le Havre and Rouen were diminished in size by the resignation of royalist sympathizers.[45]

1792; Aire, May 13, 1792; Lectoure, Apr. 27, 1792; Fécamp, Mar. 26–May 10, 1792.

[43] *JC*, May 31–June 6, 1792. PV: Vannes, May 15, 1792; Blaye, May 17, 1792; Aire, May 17, 1792; Périgueux, May 16, 1792; Toulouse, May 9, 1792. COR, Montpellier, L 5544; Colmar.

[44] COR, Lille. *JC*, May 10, 15, 1792.

[45] PV: Rouen, July 21–31, 1792; St.-Affrique, June 27, Aug. 16, 1792; Vaison,

A fascinating epiphenomenon of the summer of 1792 was the appearance of "central committees" in the departmental seats composed of deputies from the departmental societies. This new system of club governance had first been proposed by the "mother society" in the circular of March 1, 1792. But it was not instituted at that time, save perhaps in the Yonne,[46] because of concerns about its constitutionality. By June, however, the days of the monarchical constitution were numbered, and the clubs were willing to take extraordinary measures.

On June 21–22, after receiving news of the king's latest vetoes and the dismissal of the "Jacobin ministers," Castillon-sur-Dordogne and Ste.-Foy asked the Récollets Society of Bordeaux to form a central committee. Two days later Bordeaux published an address to the clubs of the Gironde and the departmental *chefs-lieux*. It called for the foundation of central committees in every department. The duties of these bodies, Bordeaux stated in a circular of July 5, would be "to gather intelligence, transmit it to the other central committees, and recommend appropriate actions." From the ranks of the departmental committees, Bordeaux hoped, men could be chosen to sit on a national bureau in Paris.[47]

The central committee of the Gironde commenced operations on July 1 and was quite active for several weeks, corresponding with member societies, issuing manifestos, and dispatching bulletins to the "other central committees of France." Bordeaux claimed that all the societies of the Gironde were represented. But La Réole hung back, fearing that the committee might become "a power against the state" and the "pure, virgin" constitution, and Comps refused to participate because its members could not afford to leave their work for an indefinite period. Providing for the subsistence of two deputies in Bordeaux was indeed a problem. Libourne had to conduct a fund-raising drive. Blaye was

---

July 22, 1792; Fécamp, July 17, 1792; Neuville, June 23, 1792; Le Havre, June 23–July 31, 1792. Holuigue, *Boulogne*, pp. 285–288, 296. *JC*, July 26, 1792. Babaud-Laribière, *Etudes historiques et administratives* (Confolens, 1863), I, 95.

[46] PV, Villeneuve, Apr. 13, 1792.

[47] *JC*, July 9, 30, 1792. COR: Bordeaux, 12 L 38, 40; Poitiers, S 26. Dubos, "Surveillants," p. 79. P. Flottes, "Le Club des Jacobins de Bordeaux," *RF* (1916), pp. 357–358.

more practical, designating as its representatives two members who were then residing in Bordeaux.[48]

Clubs like La Réole and Comps could be found in almost every department. Agen characterized the committees as "political heresy" and the Bordelais as "dupes of perfidious men who want to destroy royal authority." Bergerac, for unknown reasons, refused a summons from Périgueux to send representatives to a central committee of the Dordogne. Honfleur demurred to a similar proposal from Caen because of doubts about its constitutionality. Brive had no delegates on the central committee of the Corrèze because those it would have designated for this "honorable endeavor" were busy on "burdensome and dangerous" assignments. Loudun elected two deputies to the committee of the Vienne, but only over the objections of its president who argued that it should respect the constitution and brush aside "republican" ideas.[49]

Despite resistance that their organizers encountered, central committees functioned for brief periods in at least eight departments besides the Gironde. Toulouse adopted Bordeaux's plan on June 25, and by July 12 had formed a committee on which four other societies of the Haute-Garonne are known to have been represented. Montpellier announced on June 29 that it was about to start a central committee that would speak for the twenty-five "truly patriotic" societies of the Hérault. It was still functioning in August. Besançon jumped on the bandwagon between July 5 and 15, founding a *comité central* for "the Doubs and neighboring departments." At least one club outside the Doubs, Lons-le-Saunier, sent delegates. Tulle accepted Bordeaux's proposal on July 15 and had instituted a central committee by July 25. Fourteen societies assisted in the creation of the central committee of the Var at Toulon on July 18–19. Thereafter, most of its business was conducted by a five-man executive board. It was finally suppressed on November 28 because it had "outlived its usefulness and was too costly to maintain." The central committee of the Pyrénées-Orientales, founded on July 24, was composed almost

[48] *JC*, July 28, Aug. 11, 1792. *ArchP*, July 10, 1792. COR, Bordeaux, 12 L 38. M. Besson, *Histoire de la Révolution à Libourne* (Libourne, 1968), pp. 174–176.

[49] COR: Bordeaux, 12 L 29; Poitiers, S 23. Forot, *Tulle*, pp. 209–214. PV: Périgueux, July 16, 1792; Honfleur, July 24, 1792.

entirely of members of the Perpignan society; each departmental affiliate was asked to designate one person to be its "special correspondent." By October, when its minutes ceased, it had become simply an internal organ of the Perpignan club. Twenty-five clubs had delegates at the inaugural session of the central committee of the Gard in Nîmes on August 19. Tours (August 27) proclaimed that it had instituted a central committee in the Indre-et-Loire.[50]

FROM the late summer and early autumn of 1792 come a jumble of conflicting signals. The rebirth of societies at St.-Claude, Craponne, Foix, Givet, Etampes, Ganges, St.-Vallery, and other locales where the fall of the monarchy broke the power of "aristocrats" was, for Jacobins, certainly a cause for optimism.[51] Increases in enrollment in some societies after August 10 must, with some reservations, also be counted as a plus factor. Sallies, which had been reduced to a "small number," saw its benches filled by the return of "wayward brothers." Saverne granted admission to fifty "converts." But Gisors was frightened when twenty "aristocrats" asked for membership. And St.-Jean-du-Gard expressed concern that "all the Feuillants, royalists, and moderates of the Midi" were flocking to the clubs.[52]

That many clubs operated at high speeds was also an indicator of continuing network vitality. Marseille held morning and evening sessions. Lauris, just returned from a two-month recess, declared its sessions to be "permanent" after August 10, and convened thirty of the next sixty days. Auray, which had closed from June 21 to August 26, met thirteen times in September. Tulette averaged only 1.5 sessions per month from January 20 to August 3, but twenty-six are recorded in August–September. Honfleur, near death in July–August, had twenty-four meetings in October alone. The frequency of assemblies at Nuits doubled

[50] *JC*, July 14, 21, Aug. 2, 18, 30, Nov. 5, 1792. COR, Poitiers, S 26. Forot, *Tulle*, p. 201. C. Brelot, *Besançon révolutionnaire* (Paris, 1966), p. 91. PV: Toulouse, June 25–July 24, 1792; St.-Hippolyte, Sept. 3, 1792. AD, Pyrénées-Orientales, L 1450. E. Poupé, *Le Département du Var, 1790–an VIII* (Cannes, 1933), p. 334. F. Rouvière, *Histoire de la Révolution française dans le Gard* (1887–89), II, 275, 420, 429–430.

[51] *JC*, Aug. 30, Sept. 22, 24, 29, Oct. 6, 8, 1792. Arnaud, *Ariège*, pp. 318–319.

[52] *JC*, Oct. 13, 15, 25, 1792. Fischer, *Saverne*, pp. 77–80.

in September–October. Cherbourg, Lons-le-Saunier, Eymoutiers, and Louhans also added extra sessions.[53]

The most positive sign of all was the number of new foundations. In the district of Draguignan alone, ten societies sprang up
from August to October 1792.[54] More than thirty materialized in
the Vaucluse and southern Drôme in the same period. Clubs also
came to life in significant numbers in the Yonne, Loiret, Ardèche,
Isère, Pyrénées-Orientales, and Haute-Garonne. Some of the
credit for this must be accorded to the Revolutionary Government in Paris. Commissioners of the Executive Power helped to
establish clubs at Montargis, Lorris, Boiscommun, Pithiviers,
and Mamers. Circulars of the minister of the interior, Roland, led
to the formation of societies at Eu, Carvin, and Herblay.[55] A
pamphlet of the justice minister, Danton, read at the club of Auray on September 9, inspired electors of twenty-two towns of the
Morbihan who were in attendance to pledge to create clubs on
their return home.[56]

The villagers of the northern Vaucluse and southern Drôme
seem to have acted on their own initiative. To legitimize their
clubs, however, they invited representatives from nearby societies to the installation ceremonies. Lioux was "ordained" by Jacobins from St.-Saturnin and Blanvac; Méthamis by clubbists
from Carpentras and Mazan; Violès by "brothers" from Orange,
Camaret, and Jonquières. Tulette graciously consented to send
deputies to the installations of clubs at Bouchet, Vison, St.-Ro-
man-de-Malegarde, Cairanne, Buisson, St.-Maurice, Rasteau,
Grillon, Monségur, and Beaumes.[57]

[53] *JDM*, Sept. 1792. PV: Tulette, Lauris, Nuits, Eymoutiers, Honfleur, Auray.
L. Guillemaut, *Histoire de la Révolution dans le Louhannais* (Louhans, 1879), II, 46–
48.

[54] Poupé, *Var* (Cannes, 1933), p. 334; "La Société populaire de Callas," *RF*
(1903), pp. 482–483; and "La Société populaire de Villecroze," *RF* (1901), pp.
132–135.

[55] *JC*, Sept. 24, Oct. 13, 18, Nov. 10, 1792. PV: Largentière, Oct. 20, 1792; Eu,
Sept. 21, 1792; Pithiviers, Sept. 9, 1792; Boiscommun, Sept. 22, 1792. G. Fleury,
La Ville . . . de Mamers durant la Révolution (1909–1911), III, 208–209.

[56] PV, Auray, Sept. 9–10, 1792.

[57] *JC*, Sept. 29, Oct. 6, 29, 1792. PV: Malemort-du-Comtat, Oct. 18, 1792;
Roman-de-Malégarde, Aug. 13, 17, 1792; Violès, Oct. 14, 1792; Jonquières,

Unfortunately, nearly every healthy sign in August–September 1792 was offset by symptoms of disease. The overthrow of the monarchy adversely affected a few clubs. Vienne reported to the Paris Jacobins on September 27 that it had been reduced "to a very small number of partisans of liberty since the day of August 10." In a state of apparent shock Annonay met only four times in two months. Mass resignations and severe absenteeism sapped the strength of Laval and Vire.[58]

The club movement in the north was dealt a stunning blow by the Prussian-Austrian offensive. Societies at Longwy, Roubaix, and Tourcoing disappeared during the enemy occupation. At the approach of the invaders, the clubbists of St.-Mihiel, and perhaps Nancy, cowardly burned their records. The Sierck society dispersed in fear; its chronicler, Nicolas Grégoire, was hidden by a peasant. With the city under siege, Lille ceased to meet. Maubeuge reported that it was "surrounded by enemies and losing members." Douai, Ste.-Menehould, Châlons-sur-Marne, Linselles, Thionville, Bourbourg, Dunkerque, and Metz closed for varying lengths of time.[59]

Odd though it may seem, the general elections of late August and September had a debilitating effect upon the clubs. With the bulk of their membership active in sectional and electoral assemblies, many societies could not raise a quorum. The minutes of Aire, Châteauroux, Alençon, and Perpignan break off for two or three weeks, about the date of the openings of departmental electoral assemblies. The "permanence" of the sections of Le Havre, from September 2 to December 7, delayed the recovery of the club there. Once again, the loss of newly elected deputies ren-

---

Sept. 30, 1792; Méthamis, Sept. 16, 23, 1792; Lioux, Sept. 22, 1792; Tulette, Aug. 3–Sept. 26, 1792.

[58] PV, Laval, Apr. 1, 1793. *JC*, Oct. 4, 1792. L. Rostaing, *Les Anciennes loges maçonniques d'Annonay et les clubs* (Lyon, 1903), pp. 177–191. P. Nicolle, *Histoire de Vire pendant la Révolution 1789–1800* (Vire, 1923), p. 103. M. Butet-Hamel, "La Société populaire de Vire," *Comité des travaux historiques. Bulletin historique et philologique* (1900), p. 303.

[59] *JC*, Sept. 17, 27, Nov. 15, 1792. *JD*, Sept. 30, 1792. L. Bultingaire, *Le Club des Jacobins de Metz* (Paris, 1906), pp. 32–46. A. Mansuy, "Les Sociétés populaires à Nancy," *Annales de l'Est* (1899), p. 439. PV, Thionville, Aug. 24, Nov. 12, 1792. Dicop, *Sierck*, p. 15.

dered some societies inert. The Quintin club ceased to meet after Honoré Fleury left for the Convention.[60]

There is also evidence of a psychological letdown in September. Spent energy, after a summer of abnormally heavy activity, might be the best explanation for the idleness of Bourg and Montbard. The clubbists of Castillon, Ars-en-Ré, and other small towns turned their attention to farming. Bourgoin, Aiguesvives, and the Surveillants of Valence dissolved for several weeks for unknown reasons. The Legislative Assembly, in its last weeks of existence, received almost no petitions from provincial societies. That network correspondence atrophied is apparent from published circulars of Strasbourg and Bordeaux in late September, calling for its resumption.[61]

The downturn in correspondence was made more severe by the disbandment of the correspondence committee of the "mother society" after August 10. A circular of September 12 explained that its members were busy with elections or engaged in missions for the Revolutionary Government. When nothing was done to correct the situation, Lorient rebuked the Paris club for its inertia. Provins begged not to be left in a state of "cruel uncertainty." Angoulême, Besançon, Carcassonne, Pertuis, Marseille, Bischwiller, Aigre, and Nérac also registered complaints in September and October.[62]

Nagged by its affiliates, and locked in a war of words with the Girondins, the Paris club finally undertook remedial measures. On October 1, it voted to reinstitute the correspondence committee. Three weeks later, when Chabot observed that correspondence needed to be "doubled or tripled," it added ten people to the committee and adopted new rules designed to give them more meeting time. By this date the committee was again re-

---

[60] PV: Aire, Alençon, Châteauroux, Perpignan, Le Havre.

[61] L. Fochier, *Souvenirs historiques sur Bourgoin* (Vienne, 1880), pp. 444–499. M. de Richemond, "Délibérations de la Société . . . d'Ars-en-Ré," *Société . . . de la Saintonge* (1904), pp. 29–253. E. Dubois, *Histoire de la Révolution dans l'Ain* (Bourg, 1931–35), III, 46. PV: Aiguesvives, Aug. 31, Nov. 5, 1792; Montbard, Sept. 28, Dec. 16, 1792; Valence, Aug. 5, Sept. 30, 1792; Aire, Sept. 19, 1792; Bordeaux, Sept. 21, 22, 1792. COR: Reims; Bordeaux, 12 L 38.

[62] *JD*, Sept. 14, 1792. PV and COR, Lorient, Sept. 7, 10, 12, 1792. *JC*, Sept. 22–Nov. 5, 1792.

sponding to letters of departmental clubs. "Citizens," it wrote to Niort, "our correspondence is even more necessary now because of the intrigues of the factions; let it recommence."[63]

DURING the autumn of 1792 some fifty clubs were founded in areas occupied by French military forces. However, the tempo of network activity slowed in France proper. Indeed, in late October and early November, a precipitous three-month slide commenced. As in the previous year there was much concern about empty benches and nonpayment of dues.[64] Semur, Vire, and Douai closed for several months. Vitteaux failed to meet in December. And many of the newly planted societies in the southeast began to wilt.[65]

A major cause of the recession was the factionalism in the capital. The Girondin-Montagnard schism will be considered later. Suffice it to say here that many provincial societies broke off affiliation with the Paris society or threatened to do so. With defections mounting, the Paris Jacobins approved a change in rules regarding affiliation. On November 25, it scrapped the provision requiring letters of recommendation from two nearby clubs, deciding instead that prospective affiliates should secure character references from two of its members. In early 1793, in a surfeit of egalitarian zeal, the "mother club" also determined to use the terms "fraternization" and "association" in lieu of "affiliation." The network may not have been made aware of these actions, however, for provincial clubs continued to send letters of reference for their sisters and to use the word "affiliation."[66]

The return of cold weather was also a depressant. Winter's onset always presented problems. Prudent and well-heeled clubs began preparations in the autumn, ordering stoves and loads of wood, replacing broken windows, or moving to better-insulated

[63] *JD*, Oct. 3, 23, Nov. 4, 1792. COR, Niort, 3006 bis.
[64] L. Lemaire, *Les Jacobins à Dunkerque* (Dunkerque, 1913), pp. 359–360. Galland, "Cherbourg," p. 382. PV, Beaumont, Dec. 1, 1792.
[65] Henriot, *Semur*, pp. 165, 198. Nicolle, *Vire*, p. 231. G. Aubert, "La Révolution à Douai," *AHRF* (1936), p. 531. PV: Méthamis, Vitteaux, St.-Roman-de-Malegarde.
[66] *JD*, Nov. 27, 1792.

buildings.[67] Scrimping on wood and forgoing a stove usually meant that a club was poor. For Avallon, however, it was a matter of principle not to buy a stove "since only Sybarites, and not citizens warmed by public-spiritedness, cannot endure, for an hour or two, the rigors of the season." Besides, it reasoned, a fire would attract a mob of people who would come to the sessions only to warm themselves. The experiences of other societies suggest that Avallon was right on the last score. At Bergerac, members had to be enjoined not to huddle around the stove. The clubbists at Nuits sat so close to the fire that wax from melting candles ran down on their clothes.[68]

If heated halls were often too crowded, the winter of 1791–92 had shown that unheated ones were likely to be empty. At Vannes on November 1, a shivering member pointed out that cold temperatures were hurting attendance and that something had to be done. Lille suspended some meetings in December because of frigid conditions, and in January asked for permission to move into a college hall which offered "more shelter from the rigors of winter." At Lauris, on January 26, the president adjourned all sessions until the arrival of warm weather. Three times in November the clubbists of Villeneuve debated the pros and the cons of buying a stove from the local notary, but they decided not to because it lacked *tuyaux*. It would have been wiser to have made the purchase, because February brought severe freezes. The flow of sessions was interrupted, and Villeneuve never completely recovered.[69]

The winter of 1792–93 was almost a repeat of 1791–92. At Tartas, on February 6, one of only four members who showed up expressed dismay that his "brothers" could remain at home while the Republic's soldiers were "freezing" on the frontiers. Pau's sessions ceased from December 13 until February 20 when it decided to buy a stove. At Orthez a member exclaimed in late January that the assembly hall was "deathly cold." Between Febru-

[67] PV: Grambois, Dec. 11, 1791; Le Havre, Nov. 3, 6, 1791; Nuits, Nov. 9, 1792; Neuville, Oct. 15, 29, 1791; Chalon, Oct. 27, 1791; Lorient, Dec. 13, 1791; Toulouse, Nov. 16, 1791; St.-Hippolyte, Sept. 9, 1792.

[68] M. Giraud, "La Société . . . à Avallon," *Société d'études d'Avallon* (1914–16), p. 111. Labroue, *Bergerac*, p. 189. PV, Nuits, Dec. 21, 1792.

[69] PV: Villeneuve, Oct. 15, 29, 1791; Vannes, Nov. 1, 1791; Lille, Dec. 9, 11, 1791, Jan. 13, 1792; Lauris, Oct. 16, 1791, Jan. 26, Feb. 20, 1792.

ary 3 and 17 the first gap occurs in its minutes. Lille, however, was spared the poor attendance of the previous winter when a member generously donated two large stoves.[70]

Winter weather notwithstanding, the Revolution heated up again in late January and February 1793. In the supercharged atmosphere of March–April, network activity soared to levels comparable to those of the previous spring. New societies appeared at Larche, Pézenas, Cheval-Blanc, Lezat, Ingouville, St.-Ybars, Varilhes, and Lunéville.[71] Long-sidelined clubs like Mayenne, La Teste-de-Buch, Fécamp, Verdun, Mas-d'Azil, St.-Lizier, Magnac-Laval, Artonne, Thann, Beaumont, and Bourg rejoined the "active roster."[72] The merger of the societies at Valence marked the beginning of a vigorous period in the Drôme.[73] Meetings increased at Lille, Limoges, Marseille, Lectoure, Eymoutiers, Castres, Gaillac, Eu, Largentière, and Ars-en-Ré.[74]

The execution of the king on January 21 probably helped to fuel the recovery. Many clubs felt duty-bound to issue statements of support, and the preparation of addresses to the Convention often necessitated a resumption of meetings. Toul and Belfort arose from the ashes on January 23 and February 6. Aire awakened from a short nap on January 27. Its first acts were to endorse the decisions of the deputies in Paris and to write to affiliates urging "punctual correspondence" in the "trying times" that might lie ahead.[75]

The entry of England and Spain into the war (February 1, March 7) and defeats of French forces in the Low Countries definitely energized the network. The club of Pau, in the Pyrénées,

---

[70] PV: Tartas, Feb. 6, 1793; Lille, Nov. 25, 1792; Pau, Feb. 20, 1793. A. Planté, "Les Jacobins d'Orthez," *Bulletin, Société des sciences de Pau* (1901).

[71] Arnaud, *Ariège*, p. 268. PV: Ingouville, Mar. 9, 1793; Cheval-Blanc. H. Baumont, "La Société populaire de Lunéville," *Annales de l'est* (1889), p. 337.

[72] H. Poulet, "L'Esprit public à Thann pendant la Révolution," *Revue historique de la Révolution française* (1918), p. 243. E. Pionnier, *Essai sur l'histoire de la Révolution à Verdun* (Nancy, 1906), p. 316. AD, Gironde, 12 L 39. F. Martin, *Les Jacobins au village* (Clermont, 1902), p. 61. PV: Bourg, Mar. 8, 1793; Magnac-Laval, Apr. 11, 1793; Fécamp, May 23, 1793; Beaumont, Mar. 6, 1793; Montpellier, Mar. 22–24, 1793; Mayenne, Apr. 7, 1793.

[73] PV, Valence, Apr. 8, 1793.

[74] See the minutes of these societies.

[75] H. Denis, *Le Club des Jacobins de Toul, 1793–1795* (Nancy, 1895), pp. 9–10. PV, Aire. Dubail-Roy, "La Société populaire de Belfort," *Bulletin de la Société belfortaine d'émulation* (1906), pp. 61–68.

reformed on February 20 and met every day in April and May. Nearby Tartas reopened and admitted so many new members in March that it had to look for a new assembly hall. Eu, along the channel coast, engaged in few meaningful enterprises until February–March 1793, when it became involved in sundry war-related activities. Practically defunct clubs like Monpazier, Montbard, and Beaumont revived and threw themselves into patriotic endeavors. In general, the rebellions in the Vendée also stimulated increased activity. For societies in the immediate region, however, they were disastrous. Chinon and Loudun shut down when these places were attacked by the rebels. Auray's sessions were interrupted for five months when Vendée-like insurrections occurred in the Morbihan.[76]

Without question, the most important cause of the "boom" of 1793 was the National Convention's decision, on March 9, to send eighty-two of its members into the departments as representatives-on-mission. Armed with extraordinary powers, these "proconsuls" reshaped political institutions and attitudes in *province*, and revitalized the clubs. The arrival of representatives-on-mission at Vire prompted the society there to convene for the first time since November 4. The deputies, Mazade and Ysabeau, breathed new life into Orthez. Lourdes assembled for the first time in nearly two years (May 8), after representatives-on-mission accorded it a new meeting place. St.-Dizier was resurrected by the deputies, Roux and Perrin, Salins by Leonard Bourdin, Guéret by Marc-Antoine Huguet.[77]

Instructed by the Committee of Public Safety to found new societies, the representatives-on-mission complied with gusto. The deputy, Chasles, boasted that he created twelve clubs in the Eure. His colleagues, Servières and Gleizal, instituted societies in "several communes" of the Lozère and Ardèche. Collot d'Herbois and Laplanche started a society at Moulins-Engilbert. Borie urged Limoges to repopulate the Haute-Vienne with societies. The society of Nevers was carrying out the wishes of represent-

[76] PV: Pau, Tartas, Monpazier, Beaumont, Eu, and Auray. A. Aulard, *Recueil des Actes du Comité de salut public* (Paris, 1899–1933), IV, 152.

[77] PV: Orthez, Apr. 10–12, 1793; Lourdes, May 6, 1793; St.-Dizier, Apr. 18, May 9, 1793. Chervy, *Guéret*, p. 436. *JD*, May 12, 1793.

atives-on-mission when some of its members formed clubs at Clamecy and Varzy.[78]

Some societies veered to the Left in 1793, and back to the side of the Paris Jacobins. The network remained pitifully mangled, however, the head disconnected in places from the torso. Its resources strained, the "mother society" ratified a project of its treasurer, Annibal Ferrières, on March 1 and shortly afterward mailed printed copies to the clubs. Ferrières perorated on all that the Paris society had done "to dissipate the dark night of ignorance"; then he warned of the dangers if it had to suspend its labors because of insufficient funds. Since the network constituted a "single family," he argued, all its units should shoulder a part of the financial burden. His plan called for each member of an associated society to pay the "tiny sum" of 3 sous 6 deniers per quarter into the coffers of the Paris club. In return, the societies were promised free correspondence with Paris; engraved cards for their members guaranteeing entry into every club of the network; a newspaper that printed, word-for-word, the debates of the Jacobins; a periodical entitled *Le Mensonge et la vérité*; and copies of truly "patriotic speeches."[79]

Seventy societies are known to have adhered to the plan, thus demonstrating their allegiance to the Paris Jacobins. The number of negative responses is more difficult to assess, since the *Journal des Jacobins* failed to print them. It is clear from an examination of surviving minutes, however, that a great many clubs tabled the proposal or refused outright to associate themselves with the Montagnard-led central society.[80] The persistent factionalism virtually guaranteed that the revival of the spring of 1793 would

---

[78] G. Vannereau, *Le District de Moulins-Engilbert pendant la Révolution* (1962), pp. 245–250. *JD*, June 7, 1793. Aulard, *Comité*, II, 560. AN, C II, 67. R. Baron, "La Société populaire de Varzy," *Annales de Bourgogne* (1968), pp. 162–163. PV: Lectoure, Apr. 30, May 15, June 1, 1793; Limoges, Apr. 2, 1793.

[79] *BN*, Lb⁴⁰ 2304.

[80] *JD*, Mar. 31–May 8, 1793. Aulard, *Jacobins*, V, 130. Martin, *Village*, p. 61. Labroue, *Bergerac*, p. 236. PV: Montbard, Mar. 24, 1793; Limoges, Mar. 20, 31, 1793; Bourbonne, Mar. 22–Apr. 3, 1793; Honfleur, Mar. 23, 30, 1793; Tonneins, Mar. 28, 1793; Le Havre, Apr. 7, 11, 1793; Ingouville, June 6, 1793; Nuits, March 28, Apr. 5, 8, 1793; St.-Hippolyte, Apr. 25, 1793; Châteauroux, Mar. 25, 1793. L. Lacrocq, "Notes sur les sociétés populaires de la Creuse," *Mémoires de la Société . . . de la Creuse* (1902), pp. 379–386. Poulet, *Thann*, pp. 374–375. C. Constant, *Histoire d'un club Jacobin en province pendant la Révolution* (Paris, 1905), p. 43.

be short-lived. In the southeast, on the eve of the Federalist rebellions, there was an epidemic of closures.[81] Clubs in other areas
experienced problems, too. Unfortunately, it is not always possible to determine whether politics or spring planting was responsible for the shutdowns and poor attendance.[82]

[81] H. Labroue, "La Société populaire de La Garde Freinet," *RF* (1908), p. 44.
PV: St.-Julien-de-Peyrolas, May 19, 1793; Vitrolles, May 13, 1793; Tulette, May
19, 1793; Malemort-du-Comtat, May 26, 1793; Violès, May 19, 1793; Jonquières,
May 26, 1793; St.-Hippolyte, May 19, 1793.

[82] PV: St.-Cyprien, Pithiviers, Boiscommun, Honfleur, Ars-en-Ré.

II

General Trends in
Personnel

AT THE moment of conception the average club of the Constituent Assembly was a diminutive organism of thirty members or less. To borrow a botanical phrase, growth was indeterminate. Typically, however, numbers had multiplied manyfold by September 1791. After this date, as a general rule, entry rates slowed. Grignols and Tain admitted no one, Villandraut but two. Colmar, which had 617 members in November 1791, added only 7 in 1792. Nine-tenths of those in the Montauban society were "on the books" by the end of 1791, and enrollment ceased totally in March 1792. Roughly 60 percent of all those who joined the Tulle club had done so by April 1791.[1] A look at known admissions in other societies in "phases one and two" reveals similar imbalances. (See appendix B.)

The relative decline in admissions in the "old" societies was attributable to several factors, including more selectivity, the exhaustion of available pools of revolutionaries, and especially, the on again off again existence of many clubs. Infusions of new blood often came in sudden spurts, during periods of peak network activity and when clubs were refounded after dormant spells. Predictably, some societies did not conform to the national norm. Toulouse invariably enrolled about twenty members per month from October 1791 to November 1792. Entries at La Réole ascended in a gradual curve from forty-one (1791), to fifty-five (1792), to sixty-five (1793). Nuits doubled in size in the first months of the Legislative Assembly, when the network was

---

[1] F. Galabert, "Le Club Jacobin de Montauban," *Revue d'histoire moderne* (1899), pp. 140–144. D. Ligou, *Montauban à la fin de l'ancien régime et aux débuts de la Révolution* (1958), pp. 310–313. Leuilliot, *Colmar*, pp. 454–478. Forot, *Tulle*, pp. 569–585. AD, Gironde, 12 L 38, 40.

in the doldrums. But Nuits was founded late in the Constituent and was thus almost a "new" society.[2]

In the new clubs (those formed after September 1791) there were sometimes goodly numbers of experienced Jacobins. Ninety of the charter members of the Vuillafans society, for instance, had formerly belonged to the club of Ornans.[3] Most of those who enrolled in the new organizations, however, were first-timers. Collectively, they account for much of the numerical increase in personnel in the middle years.

A correlation existed between the size of newborn clubs and the degree of outside involvement in the birthing process. Those sired by agents of the central government or other societies tended to be more fully developed (and more variegated socially). St.-Zacharie and Kielstredt, for example, began with roughly two hundred members each, Moulins-Engilbert with perhaps five hundred.[4] In contrast, when founders were locals, opening counts usually ranged from ten to fifty.[5] The small fry, like their predecessors in the Constituent, often matured rapidly. Varzy went from thirteen on May 1, 1793, to fifty by May 31. Villecroze doubled its initial enrollment in two months (54 to 108). Joinville's effectives jumped from 50 on January 15, 1793, to 101 by January 31, to 177 by April.[6]

The longer a club operated, the more likely it was for admissions to be wholly or partly offset by losses of personnel. Inevitably, some attrition resulted from deaths, illnesses, and changes of residence. Much more serious was the depletion caused by wartime mobilization. In all of the great levies it will be seen that clubbists gave generously of themselves.

Numbers in the societies were also depleted by "exclusions," "purifications," and mass resignations. Exclusions (temporary or

---

[2] PV, Nuits, Toulouse. AD, Gironde, 12 L 39.

[3] PV, Ornans. *JC*, Sept. 22, 1792.

[4] COR, St.-Zacharie. Vannereau, *Moulins-Engilbert*, pp. 245–250. *CD*, June 2, 1792.

[5] The following are representative totals: Varzy, 13; St.-Cyprien, 21; Beauzac, 60; Lioux, 77; Manciet, 12; Orthez, 49; Gondrin, 11; Joinville, 50; Pithiviers, 10; Malemort-du-Comtat, 13; St.-Amande-Tallende, 50; Sauxillages, 20; Viverols, 15; and Boiscommun, 45.

[6] AD, Haute-Marne, L 2017. Poupé, "Villecroze," pp. 132–135. Baron, "Varzy," pp. 192–193.

permanent suspensions) were common, random incidents involving a single member or a tiny group. They might be imposed for mere rules violations: failure to pay dues, dress code infractions, drunkenness, drawing a sword on a fellow member . . . trivial stuff! In contrast, schisms and purifications (wholesale purges) were normally triggered by political or ideological conflicts. Two procedures were employed in purifications. In one, all members voted on each other, using black and white balls. Those blackballed by a certain percentage were expelled. A variant technique was to set up a committee of stalwarts to weed out undesirables. The committee met in secret, a source of much anxiety for those under scrutiny; and admissions were suspended until its report was prepared, a process that might take weeks. In some cases the committee decision was irreversible; in others, the full assembly had the right of review.

Since the clubs were such unstable organisms, all statements about size are relative to chronology. The figures given in appendix C indicate *maximum* strength, and (for population and enrollment alike) they are often mere estimates. Determining the size of a club is not easy. Galabert and Ligou, two good historians, used precisely the same sources in analyzing the personnel of the Montauban club in 1792 and came up with totals of 1,396 and 1,749![7]

The largest clubs, obviously, were in the great urban centers, the smallest in communes of less than three thousand. However, the population of a town was not always a good measure of the size of the society. Witness the fact that prior to 1793 Lille had fewer members than Tonneins. As a rule, the percentage of citizen involvement was highest in the small towns of the Midi. This statistic is hard to calculate because of fluctuating population figures and the common practice of admitting nonresidents as members. Pithiviers enrolled citizens from twenty-four surrounding hamlets and had a town/country ratio of 3:2. Montauban and Vire had ratios of 3:1; at Saverne in May 1792 only one-third of the clubbists were town-dwellers.[8] A guess would place citizen involvement in the average club at between 2 and 3 percent.

Of course, the number of "militants," those who habitually at-

---

[7] Galabert, "Montauban," pp. 140–144. Ligou, *Montauban*, pp. 310–313.

[8] Galabert, "Montauban," pp. 140–144. Ligou, *Montauban*, pp 310–313. PV, Pithiviers. Nicolle, *Vire*, p. 78. Fischer, "Saverne," pp. 33–34.

tended the meetings and staffed the offices, was far less than 2.5 percent. Montauban's average attendance was about one hundred, Vitteaux's fifteen. Ars-en-Ré had thirty on good days; Boulogne set its quorum at fifteen. Blaye (18,000 population) had forty to fifty regulars; Sète (6,500) mustered forty to seventy-five; Le Puy (15,000) could count on fifty. Pithiviers, with a paper enrollment of 123, had a median attendance of thirty in late 1792 and less than twenty in the following spring. Boiscommun enrolled one hundred but normally assembled only twenty-five to thirty.[9]

During the Constituent Assembly the leaders of the clubs came almost exclusively from the middle and upper strata of the bourgeoisie. The rank-and-file was also overwhelmingly middle class. Two factors combined to insure bourgeois dominance. First, most clubs rigidly interpreted the Municipalities Act of December 1789, which denied the right of assembly to three million lower class males, or "passive citizens." The fee structure also constituted a barrier to lower class enrollment. Entry charges normally ranged from three to twelve livres. Annual dues were usually twelve to twenty-four livres, and occasionally as high as thirty-six. Such premiums were well beyond the means of urban wage earners and peasants.

The prospect of competition from "popular" societies and a rise in democratic sentiment caused a few clubs, in the late Constituent, to relax discriminatory policies.[10] During the Legislative Assembly the gradual lowering of standards continued. Montauban, which was far in advance of its sisters, admitted so many workers and landless peasants that collectively, they represented 23 percent of its membership. Annonay, which was quite conservative, nonetheless, decided to waive entry fees for twenty *ouvriers chamoiseurs* employed at the mill of a member. Sète resolved to accept anyone who was not "dishonest or a bad citizen." A number of societies experimented with sliding fee scales. Montreuil allowed members to pay six, ten, or fifteen sous per month, according to their abilities. Châteauroux considered the following gradations: two livres, ten sous per annum for the "less

[9] PV: Blaye, Sète, Pithiviers, Vitteaux, Boiscommun, Ars-en-Ré, Honfleur, Le Puy, Lille. Ligou, *Montauban*, p. 309.
[10] Kennedy, *Jacobins*, pp. 78–79.

well-to-do"; five livres, ten sous for the "well-to-do"; ten livres for the rich.[11]

After the fall of the monarchy, the legal distinction between active and passive citizens was swept away, and much lip-service was given in the clubs to egalitarianism. Secretaries hailed the beginning of a new era by dating minutes in the "fourth year of liberty and the first of equality." Many societies required the use of "Citoyen" and "Citoyenne" rather than the traditional "Monsieur" and "Madame." There was also a movement to substitute "tu" and "toi" in the second person for the more formal "vous." Most of the clubs decided, however, that in France one should be allowed to speak French, that to "thee" and "thou" someone was not necessarily to demean him.[12]

As noted, the majority of clubs at this time changed their titles to "Societies of Friends of Liberty and Equality." Some also dissolved temporarily, forced old members to reapply, and relaxed entry standards. Montpellier, for example, vowed to admit all "good citizens" and adopted a fee scale ranging from one to twenty livres annually. Auray set its fees at five sous per quarter. Several of the new clubs of the Vaucluse charged only three sous per month. Alas, it is also clear that many societies remained very exclusive. As late as December 1792, St.-Julien (Gard) boasted that it consisted wholly of "active citizens." Nice, founded in October, had a colossal entry fee of twelve livres and monthly dues of one livre, ten sous.[13]

In trying to gauge how far the process of democratization had gone by 1793, it would be helpful if we had good sources of data. Unfortunately, almost all of the extant lists (*tableaux*) of members were drawn up after October 16, 1794. They have dates of admission, full names, professions before and after 1789, ages, resi-

[11] PV: Châteauroux, June 2, 1792, Montrueil, Jan. 26, 1792, and Sète, Jan. 26, 1792. Testut, *Beaumont*, pp. 765–766. Rostaing, *Annonay*, p. 171.

[12] A. Aubert, *Un club en 1792* (Digne, 1887), pp. 1–20. Butet-Hamel, "Vire," p. 303. *JC*, Oct. 18, Nov. 5, 1792. Henriot, *Semur*, p. 160. Guillemaut, *Louhans*, II, 46. Fochier, *Bourgoin*, pp. 454–455. *AP*, Jan. 6, 1793. PV: Blaye, Oct. 17, 1792; Pithiviers, Sept. 16, 1792; Toulouse, Oct. 8, 1792; Orthez, Dec. 18–20, 1792; Périgueux, Oct. 22–24, 1792; Antipolitiques of Aix, Aug. 21, 1792.

[13] Holuigue, *Boulogne*, pp. 285–296. *JC*, Sept. 20, 1792. PV: Aire, Oct. 11, 1792; Montpellier, Sept. 7–13, 1792; Auray, Sept. 20, 1792; Lioux, Sept. 20, 1792; St.-Julien, Dec. 12, 1792. J. Combet, "La Société populaire de Nice," *Annales, Sociéte . . . des Alpes-Maritimes* (1909), pp. 378–384.

dences, and birthplaces. Precious details, one cannot deny! Yet, they tell us nothing about members who had resigned or been purged, and thus, they often give a distorted image of the clubs of earlier times. Minutes of meetings can sometimes be used as alternative or supplementary sources. Often, however, the minutes supply only last names, making positive identification difficult.

Gérard Maintenant is trying at present to compile a list of fifteen thousand Jacobins, with information on their ages, professions, and socioeconomic status before and after the Revolution. When he finally finishes his thesis (which is being directed by Michel Vovelle), it may greatly increase our knowledge about the clubbists. The table printed in appendix D is the result of my own analyses of the lists and/or minutes of thirty-two clubs.[14] Seven were founded after September 1791; seven others left records only for the period of the Constituent Assembly. Dispersed geographically, and located in both urban and rural areas, they represent a cross section of the Jacobin network. Collectively, they had a membership of perhaps 10,000 in 1789–91, 12,000 in 1792–93; but we know the professions of only 5,974 and 6,491. The large number of unknowns probably means that the figures for the "haute bourgeoisie" are too low. (Secretaries did not bother to give the vocations of prominent citizens.) Conversely, the inability to identify all of the master craftsmen and shopowners has almost certainly caused the category "artisans" to be inflated. Two classifications (servicemen and government officials) are unquestionably undervalued. Still, this table is fairly accurate in its representation of general trends.

The largest increase was registered by farmers; however, it did not take place across the board. Some clubs (Beauzac, Canville, Marcillac, Bruguières, St.-Amand-Tallende, and Mirande, for example) boasted of being "almost entirely composed of cultivators,"[15] and others had large contingents. But the majority of

[14] Aix (Friends of the Constitution), Béziers, Boiscommun, Boulogne, Bourbonne-les-Bains, Bourbourg, Breteuil, Foix, Gray, Grenoble, Huningue, La Réole, Le Havre, Lille, Marseille, Montauban, Neuville, Nuits, Pithiviers, St.-Dizier, Sauveterre, Semur, Strasbourg, Thann, Thonon, Toul, Toulouse, Tulle, Valence, Vauvert, Villeneuve-le-Roy, and Vitteaux.

[15] *ArchP*, Mar. 7, 1793. *JC*, May 31, Oct. 29, 1792. PV, Toulouse, Oct. 4, 1792. H. Soanen, "Les sociétés populaires du Puy-de-Dôme," *AHRF* (1927), p. 585.

societies enrolled few agriculturalists or none at all. Farmers who were admitted were more likely to be men "living from their rents" or prosperous smallholders than share-croppers, tenants, or simple laborers.

The percentage of shopkeepers (*marchands*) remained stable. But a strong, broadly based gain was posted by artisans and petty tradesmen (carpenters, barbers, shoemakers, and the like), and the percentage of urban wage earners rose. Even with the increases, however, less than one-half of the members of the *average* society of 1792–93 were artisans, small shopkeepers, and wage earners. And this bloc continued to provide few leaders. A good illustration of the last point is provided by the club of Ingouville, which had very low dues and attracted its members from an inferior social stratum. The chief of the Ingouville society was L.-M. Delapagne. Delapagne had a real sympathy for the poor and downtrodden, derived from having spent twenty-two years in prison. Yet, he was by no means a sansculotte. He was highly educated and at the time of his arrest had been employed in a mercantile house.[16]

Occasionally, through sheer force of personality, a man like the *perruquier* Pierre Boyer would surge to the forefront of a society. Boyer's ardor, truculence, and public-spiritedness earned him election repeatedly as secretary, vice-president, and president of the Bergerac club. Yet, this "Figaro bergeraçois" was no more a plebeian than Delapagne. He had sufficient income to qualify as an elector in 1791.[17]

The figures for servicemen are deceptively low, for whenever the civil status of national volunteers was known, it was given preference in the analysis of professions. In any event, the percentage of military personnel on membership rolls was not an accurate measurement of their degree of participation in the clubs. As spectators and guests, they packed meeting halls and reading rooms. Maubeuge claimed in August 1792 that three thousand soldiers and volunteers came to its meeting place daily to listen to the reading of newspapers.[18]

[16] G. Le Marchand, "Jacobinisme et violence révolutionnaire au Havre de 1791 à septembre 1793," *Cahiers Léopold Delisle* (1966), pp. 90–92.

[17] Labroue, *Bergerac*, pp. 18–19.

[18] *JC*, Sept. 1, 1792.

Enrollments of servicemen were highest in naval ports, garrison towns, and occupied cities. At La Teste, in the spring of 1793, virtually all of the members were sailors or marines; Landau, at the same date, consisted almost entirely of soldiers. Nice was so top-heavy with military personnel that it adopted a rule that at least 50 percent of those on its committees had to be Niçois.[19]

The "moyenne" and "haute bourgeoisie," by which we mean doctors, lawyers, teachers, priests, wholesale merchants, investors, government officials, and the like, declined in percentage after September 1791. Even with this slippage, however, they provided the clubs with *at least* two-fifths of their membership. Some societies, as late as the spring of 1793, were almost totally bourgeois in makeup. Of Guingamp's 199 members, 44 were lawyers or professionals, 20 were curates, the majority were wholesale or retail merchants, only one was an artisan.[20]

More importantly, the bourgeois primordial nucleus often continued to hold the reins of power. Three of the four men who had created the Lille society in 1789 were still influential on the eve of the June coup. The presidents and secretaries at St.-Affrique rotated seats as in a game of musical chairs. Every person elected to office at Toul after it resumed meeting in January 1793 was a founder. Similar conditions prevailed at Bourbonne, Bourgoin, Thann, Pau, Tartas, Lectoure, Lourdes, and Bourg-en-Bresse. New societies were also likely to be dominated by the bourgeoisie. Among the twenty-one patriarchs of the St.-Cyprien club was one artisan, no workers or peasants. The progenitors of the Manciet and Garlin societies were all bourgeois notables.[21]

The percentage of clergymen dipped to about four. Men of the cloth were under close scrutiny and were a little more likely to be denounced and expelled. The main reason for the decrease, however, was that there were few "patriotic" clergymen left to induct. The societies of the Constituent had, as a matter of course,

[19] *ArchP*, May 5, 1793. Combet, "Nice," pp. 377–381. AD, Gironde, 12L 39.
[20] Dobet, "Guingamp," pp. 78–82.
[21] Poulet, "Thann," pp. 411–415. Forot, *Tulle*, pp. 569–570. Denis, *Toul*, pp. 125–128. AD, Gers, L 698, PV, Manciet. PV: St.-Affrique, Pau, Tartas, Lectoure, St.-Cyprien, Lourdes, Bourbonne. See also G. Maintenant and H. Troisgro, *La Révolution à Bourbonne-les-Bains* (1979), pp. 28–29.

tried to enroll all of the constitutional priests in their vicinity. Only in regions where this process had not occurred by October 1791 was the entry rate likely to be high. Louhans, for example, admitted curés from a host of villages. At Pithiviers, a new society, twelve of the forty-one country residents were priests.[22]

In terms of influence ecclesiastics yielded to no vocational group. The constitutional bishops, Massieu and Gay-Vernon, for example, helped to guide the destinies of the clubs of Beauvais and Limoges. The episcopal vicar, Sirey, sat on the inner circle of the Périgueux society. Two of Tulle's seven known presidents were episcopal vicars. Strasbourg had a gaggle of diocesenal officials in its service. The most notorious were Philibert Simond, a deputy to the Convention, and the German expatriate Euloge Schneider.

The soul of a small society was likely to be the curé. The Abbé Delpit was elected as president of the Beaumont society on four occasions; Monsieur Raoul was three times president of Montbron. At Malemort-du-Comtat the curé Mistarlet was chief officer from the club's inaugural session on September 24, 1792 to March 3, 1793 (when he was replaced by another priest). Herblay, Steenbecque, and Polignac (among others) were founded by priests. Blanc curé was the initial president of the new society at Violès, Clément curé at St-Dizier, Restouil curé at Lioux, and so on. Priests also presided over the destinies of Eymoutiers, Aignay-le-Duc, Guebwiller, Donzenac, and Aigre. At Montauban, which had at least 460 Protestant members, the premier clubbist until his election to the Convention was the pastor Jeanbon St.-André.[23]

The teaching profession, which consisted in large part of ecclesiastics, was also a font of club leaders. Holding front rank because of their erudition, prestige, and forensic skills were the professors in the six-hundred-odd colleges of France. The historian Maintenant refers to the early Legislative Assembly as the "era of

[22] PV, Pithiviers. Guillemaut, *Louhans*, II, 37.

[23] E. Granier, "Un Club limousin: la Société . . . à Eymoutiers," *Annales révolutionnaires* (1923), pp. 299–300. AN, D XL 8, F¹ C III (Charente). *JC*, Oct. 18, 1792. Testut, *Beaumont*, p. 771. Ulry, "Donzenac," pp. 159–160. Gautheron, "Le Puy," p. 92. L. Levy-Schneider, *Le Conventionnel Jeanbon St.-André* (Paris, 1901). PV, Aire, June 13, 1792. See also PV, Lioux, St.-Dizier, Violès, and Malemort-du-Comtat.

professors" at Alençon because the club there was so absolutely dominated by college teachers. Ligny, like many other clubs, met in a college hall. In the Besançon society the best-known member was the brilliant young professor (and journalist) P.-J. Briot. P. Buchot was the leading light at Lons-le-Saunier, Le Mithois at Coutances, P.-A. Barquet at Bourg-en-Bresse.[24]

Of the teaching orders the Oratorians provided by far the most clubbists. At Saumur the two most conspicuous sociétaires, Pinvert and Villier, were Oratorians. Benaben was ofttimes president of the "Eastern Society" of Angers. His colleague, Mévolhon, a collaborator on the *Affiches* of Angers, was a "passionate friend of liberty." F. Isoard was the most infamous of the extremists who dominated the Marseille club in 1793. The celebrated and sinister Fouché was a leader of a club in Nantes. The Conventionnel Yzabeau did his political apprenticeship in the society of Tours.[25]

One of the preeminent revolutionaries at Bordeaux was a lay schoolmaster, J.-B.-M. Lacombe. At first active in the Récollets Society, Lacombe transferred his allegiance to the Club National during the Convention. Another colorful club leader was the *maître de pension*, Jouan le jeune of Tonneins. Jouan thought only of the Revolution. He corresponded with Carra, named his son Pétion after the great Parisian Jacobin, and passed his nights at the club where he delighted the audience with his pungent remarks about political figures, living and dead. Jouan's mastery of the Tonneins society helps to explain why it was one of the most radical in all of France.[26]

Teachers, along with lawyers and doctors, were placed in the category of "liberal professions." Percentage-wise the number of professionals in the clubs dropped. As was the case with ecclesiastics, however, this may have been due to the tapping of available reservoirs. Where clubs existed, most patriotic professionals

[24] G. Maintenant, "Les Jacobins d'Alençon," *Société historique . . . de l'Orne* (1976), p. 115. Brelot, *Besançon*, pp. 86–91. L. Braye, "Le Club de Ligny, 1791–1794," in AD, Meuse, AA 467. *JC*, Feb. 25, 1792. E. Sarot, *Les sociétés populaires et en particulier celles de Coutances* (Coutances, 1880), p. 41.

[25] Kennedy, *Marseille*, pp. 20–21. B. Bois, *La Vie scolaire . . . en Anjou pendant la Révolution* (Paris, 1929), pp. 108, 123.

[26] P. Bécamps, *La Révolution à Bordeaux . . . J.-B-M. Lacombe* (Bordeaux, 1953). PV, Tonneins. Caubet, "Jouan," pp. 165–200.

had rallied to them by the end of the Constituent. Among the old clubs Toulouse was unusual in that 21 percent of its known entrants after September 1791 were professionals, but Toulouse was an intellectual and legal center. New societies were likely to have higher ratios. Five of the fifteen known founders of St.-Jean-de-Maurienne were notaries or lawyers. Ten of the nineteen "fathers" of the Thonon society were learned professionals.[27]

Along with priests and intellectuals, lawyers were most likely to be the axis around which clubs revolved. Besançon had swelled to three hundred members by the summer of 1792, but the physiognomy of its central *bureau*, which consisted mainly of lawyers, had not changed much since 1790. Four of the seven presidents at Tulle were attorneys or judges. La Rochelle repeatedly chose Crassous de Medeuil, a public prosecutor, to be its chief officer.[28] Many of the doctors and lawyers, like Bentabole of Saverne, Bailleul of Le Havre, Boileau of Avallon, Lanot of Tulle, Birotteau of Perpignan, Duhem of Lille, Philippeaux of Le Mans, and Barbaroux of Marseille, to name only a few, sat in the Convention.

That these men were counted as lawyers in the statistical analysis of vocations explains the relatively low percentage of government officials. In actuality the number of clubbists holding public office had grown to an all-time high by the spring of 1793. Indeed, by that date, the clubs themselves had moved well along the road to becoming government agencies. Some clubs were founded by public functionaries. The originators of the Boiscommun society, for example, were principally district judges and administrators. The "general staff" of the Guéret club, which was refounded in March 1793, consisted of the district prosecutor, two justices, a municipal officer, and the city prosecutor.[29]

The haute bourgeoisie, by which is meant wholesale merchants (*négociants*), men living off their investments (*rentiers*), and manufacturers, was still the largest single bloc in the societies of

[27] F. Mugnier, *La Société populaire de Thonon* (Paris, 1898), pp. 7–8, 50–60. PV, Toulouse. A. Gros, *La Maurienne pendant la Révolution* (Chambéry, 1914), pp. 582–585.
[28] P. David, *Un Port . . . pendant la Révolution. La Rochelle* (La Rochelle, 1938), pp. 49, 56. Brelot, *Besançon*, pp. 86–91. Forot, *Tulle*, pp. 569–570.
[29] Lacrocq, "Creuse," p. 380. PV, Boiscommun.

a few mercantile centers. And it also provided some club leaders. P. Azema, J.-F. Ducos, J.-B. Boyer-Fonfrède, and P. Sers of the Récollets Society of Bordeaux may be cited as examples. Yet, relatively few affluent businessmen were admitted to the clubs after 1791, and this group experienced the largest percentage drop in members. This strongly suggests that power in the clubs was shifting to a lower bourgeois stratum.

Even in cities like Bordeaux, the richest men usually shunned politics, preferring instead to build up their fortunes. Their unwillingness to involve themselves in the Revolution made them vulnerable to criticism from the clubs. Antirich pronouncements were rare in 1790–91, but they became more common in 1792. Dislike of the rich was fueled by the belief that they were profiting from the economic crisis and from public misery. Another widely held feeling was that the ultra-affluent were not contributing their fair share to national defense.

By early 1793 the murmurings had risen to a concert pitch. Bergerac, for example, asked the Conventionnel Pinet: "Why have the benefits of the Revolution fallen up to the present only on the rich property owners and merchants? . . . The poor man, the artisan is burdened down by the excessive price of commodities." Infuriated by the speculation on assignats, Montauban stated in a published address that "a man who seeks to distinguish himself by great wealth detests liberty and equality as much as someone who covets titles of nobility." In another address Metz declaimed: "The rich have taken the place of nobles and priests. By means of their fortunes, they are trying to make sure that . . . they will not have to serve the fatherland." At Tonneins a clubbist shrieked that "the rich are always pitiless, as hard as steel"; and the redoubtable Jouan reprimanded the affluent for "deserting the society," saying that, in general, they were "bad men."[30]

THIS analysis of club personnel cannot be concluded without adding another element to the equation, one of which the importance is difficult to calculate—the role of spectators. The first societies were private institutions. Members huddled behind closed

---

[30] Labroue, *Bergerac*, p. 217. Levy-Schneider, *St.-André*, p. 124. COR, Poitiers, S 34. PV, Tonneins, Jan. 29, Mar. 3, 1793.

doors and took vows of secrecy. During 1790–91, however, many began to hold "public sessions" on Sundays and holidays to which all citizens were invited. With the encouragement of the "mother society," this practice expanded in the Legislative Assembly. By 1792–93 most of the leading clubs had open sessions on certain days, and some admitted the public to all of their meetings. No attendance records were kept. Many times, doubtlessly, audiences consisted merely of wives and children. Sometimes, however, we hear of huge throngs. Marseille met in an indoor tennis court which, according to one source, could hold four thousand; but the curious flocked to its sessions in such great numbers in early 1792 that it petitioned for a new assembly hall. At Libourne, on one occasion, a gallery collapsed under the weight of spectators. Those who fell let out "piercing screams" but, fortunately, were not seriously injured.[31]

Public sessions were originally intended to be "schools of patriotism" where the clubbists would explain constitutional decrees and read to the untutored masses from patriotic newspapers. Spectators were required to sit in special areas and were not permitted to speak. Discussion of sensitive issues was reserved for the private meetings. Many societies, as late as 1793, still pursued these policies; in some, however, the people in the *tribunes* (galleries) turned from onlookers to gamesters. They commented on speeches, made proposals, questioned members, and occasionally imposed their will. Their presence changed the character of the meetings. Debates became less academic and more raucous. Projectiles were launched at orators. Cutpurses came through the open doors along with good citizens. At Toulouse, in the public meetings, someone cried out every half-hour: "Citizens! Guard your wallets!"[32]

The issue on which the tribunes spoke out most consistently was the high cost of bread and consumer goods. Several incidents occurred at Le Mans in early 1792. On one occasion the president begged those in the galleries not to jeer and threaten speakers. During a debate on "subsistances" at Honfleur on September 30, members could not "express their opinions without fear of being

---

[31] AM, Marseille, I 2, carton 1792. Besson, *Libourne*, p. 143.
[32] PV, Toulouse, Dec. 2, 1792.

booed or spat upon"; and the next day, the club decided that all topics discussed in public sessions must be previously screened. Toulouse, which had experimented with having all of its meetings open to the public, concluded in December that it was "dangerous to speak of *subsistances* before citizens who reason not." A meeting at Mayenne on May 5, 1793, was interrupted by "tumultuous cries" from the galleries. The citizen who caused the troubles, on being questioned, said that the society should "concern itself more with *subsistances*"; and the club meekly sent addresses to the Convention and to local authorities asking that something be done to alleviate the crisis. Thus, at Mayenne, the "people" did have a voice, and the clubbists heeded it.[33]

[33] PV: Le Mans, May 27, 1792; Honfleur, Oct. 1, 1792; Toulouse, Dec. 6–15, 1792; Mayenne, May 5, 1793.

III

Popular Societies and Schisms

So BOUNTIFUL was the harvest of clubs from 1789 to June 1793 that at least 193 communes produced two or more. And this count does not include fundamentally counterrevolutionary groups like the Societies of Friends of Peace and the Societies of Friends of the Monarchical Constitution. If factionalism was not always the cause of the appearance of multiple clubs, sooner or later it was usually the result. All too often the source of contention was the clash of personalities. That curés were the foci of many disputes is evidence of the powerful emotions aroused by religion. Some rivalries were carryovers of feuds predating the Revolution. Two clubbists from Marseille found just how obscure and enduring village squabbles could be, when they journeyed to Méounes in August 1792 to mediate a schism. In a scene filled with high altercation, one of the factionalists, a "swarthy, emaciated, ghastly apparition," accused the curé of trying to break up his marriage. When the Marseillais asked the man how long ago this had happened, his reply was *twenty years!*[1]

Class consciousness also caused schisms and led to the formation of secondary and tertiary societies. A number of large, lower class associations were formed in the major towns and cities because high dues and the requirement of active citizenship restricted membership in the regular clubs to the bourgeoisie. In small towns rival clubs often corresponded to the social groupings, "bourgeoisie" and "people." At any rate, one society usually claimed to draw its members from "the class of artisans and peasants" and said that the other was a clavern of "bourgeois aristocrats." I have neither space, nor time, nor the inclination to dilate upon all of these incidents. In the following pages the most

[1] *JDM*, pp. 308–310.

important and interesting cases will be examined region by region.

THE most populous provincial city, Lyon, had two moderate, elitist clubs during the Constituent: the Society of Friends of the Revolution, which was founded in 1789 and last heard from in 1791; and the Society of Friends of the Constitution (Concert Society), which dated from early 1790 and was the official Jacobin affiliate. Because these two societies "excluded the poor," Roland, Lanthenas, and their circle of friends founded a Popular Society of Friends of the Constitution on September 10, 1790. Its purpose was to "instruct the people," and dues were set quite low. By 1791 it had three thousand members and branches in all twenty-eight sections and three outlying quarters. Each section sent representatives to a Central Club which met once a week. The Central Club received and initiated motions and canvassed the sectional societies for their opinions.[2]

Although there was tension between the Popular and Concert societies from the beginning, a breach did not occur until the Feuillant schism. At that time, the Concert Club broke with the Paris Jacobins; and the Popular Society, which was pro-Jacobin, was rewarded with affiliateship. Thereafter, the two organizations quarreled repeatedly. In February 1792, for example, the Popular Society accused the "rich" men at the Concert of "threatening the laboring classes of which our membership consist with the loss of their jobs if they do not leave us." When the Concert Society carried out a purification in May 1792 and abjectly begged for reaffiliation with the Paris Jacobins, the Popular Society foiled its plans by saying that it was still a haven for Feuillants, that only "the fiercest counterrevolutionaries" had been purged.[3]

The Concert Club disintegrated after August 10, but the Popular Society continued to face unremitting hostility from bour-

---

[2] PV: Bellecordière (Lyon), Aug. 31, 1791–May 16, 1793; Croix-Rousse (Lyon), Jan. 23, 1791–May 12, 1793. M. Wahl, *Les premières années de la Révolution à Lyon* (Lyon, 1894), p. 115. C. Riffaterre, *Le Mouvement anti-jacobin . . . à Lyon* (Lyon, 1912–28), I, 39–50.

[3] *JC*, Feb. 14, May 21, June 4, 1792.

geois moderates in Lyon. Under the leadership of Joseph Chalier, it was one of the most rabidly pro-Montagnard of all the provincial societies during the Convention. Chalier, who was the scion of a middle-class family of Briançon and a fairly successful merchant at Lyon before 1789, nonetheless became a tribune for the people. By August 1792 police informants were accusing him of calling for the "plundering of the rich who have manifested opinions contrary to liberty." Among the workers of Lyon he had a cult following. One laboring woman who frequented the Central Club called him the "holy Chalier, friend of the poor." He was apparently an emotional orator who rolled his eyes, waved his arms, and sobbed great tears. Unfortunately, we have only fragments of his addresses.[4]

In the winter of 1790–91, the founders of the Popular Society set up a clamor for the formation of "people's clubs" everywhere. "Clubs should be centers of instruction for the poor," said the *Journal de la Société populaire*, "let it not be the golden key which opens them." Simultaneously, in articles published by the *Patriote français*, Lanthenas skewered the Societies of Friends of the Constitution for their exclusiveness. Although it is not possible to establish a cause-and-effect relationship, a great many popular and fraternal societies came into being at this time.[5]

The closest facsimile of the Lyon Popular Society was that created at nearby St.-Etienne. It consisted of five sectional societies and a central committee composed of six representatives from each section. The St.-Etienne Popular Society finally gained affiliation in November 1792 and, thereafter, marched with the "party of the Mountain." The "Chalier stéphanois" was J.-B. Johannot, a fifty-year-old *fabricant de papiers*. Although a small shopowner, Johannot may have been a primitive communist. According to depositions made during the Federalist Rebellion, he was guilty of effusions such as: "The rich will always be enemies of the poor. . . . There will come a time when those who live by the sweat of their brows take the places of the rich. . . .

[4] Riffaterre, *Lyon*, I, 6–8, Wahl, *Lyon*, pp. 578–579. M. Wahl, "Joseph Chalier," *Revue historique* 34, 1–30.

[5] *Journal de la Société populaire*, Jan. 16, 1791. *PF*, Dec. 24, 1790, Feb. 14, 28, 1791. *Journal des amis de la Constitution*, Feb. 1, 1791.

Those who have two suits of clothes should be made to give one to those who have none."[6]

Dijon, by January 1791, had four sectional societies which assembled together periodically. Whether this was a "popular society" modelled on Lyon is unclear. Certainly, the Dijon club was very large and energetic. Even in late 1791, with the "thermometer of public spirit standing at thirty-two," its galleries were "always filled." In April 1792 it claimed to have eight hundred members. During the Convention it was exceedingly vocal in its advocacy of economic legislation favoring the poor.[7]

At Lons-le-Saunier the pattern was different. Both clubs of the Constituent called themselves Societies of Friends of the Constitution, and the original (founded about June 1790) was more democratic. The second, formed in early 1791, included most of the district and departmental administrators. In a kind of *coup de main*, it persuaded the Paris Jacobins to grant it affiliation instead of its rival. This touched off a controversy into which the Parisian press and provincial societies were drawn. Although the two groups merged in May 1791, dissension persisted, and the leaders of the second society were eventually pushed from the nest. Twice in 1792, Lons-le-Saunier reported to the Paris Jacobins that it had purified itself of "bad citizens." By late 1792 it supposedly had "six hundred members of whom most were unlettered proletarians." During the Convention, after an initial period of uncertainty, it was resolutely Montagnard.[8]

Strasbourg, the principal city of the northeast, had a single club during the Constituent, comprised chiefly of *négociants*, administrators, and army officers. Signs of discord did not surface until late 1791, when political neophytes and men of lesser standing in the community, like the journalist Laveaux and the German intellectual Schneider, began to challenge for power. After several

---

[6] J.-B. Galley, *St. Etienne . . . pendant la Révolution* (St.-Etienne, 1904), pp. 190–191, 485–486. *JD*, Nov. 9, 1792. There was also a popular society at St.-Chamond in 1791. It too was strongly pro-Montagnard in 1792–93.

[7] Hugueney, *Dijon*, p. 88. *JD*, No. 121. *JC*, May 5, 1792.

[8] A. Sommier, *Histoire de la Révolution dans le Jura* (Paris, 1850), pp. 96–97. *PF*, Feb. 2, 5, 8, 12, 25, Mar. 13, 31, May 20, 1791. *CD*, Feb. 3, 7, 10, 23, 1791. *Révolutions de France et de Brabant*, nos. 68, 78. *Journal des amis de la constitution*, Feb. 22, Mar. 1, 15, 22, Apr. 12, May 10, 1791. *Mercure universel*, May 10, 1791. PV, Lille, Feb. 22, Apr. 10, May 21, 1791.

furiously abusive exchanges, a concerned member cried out on December 31: "Messieurs! If we want to be respected, we must respect each other."[9] Alas! No one seemed to pay him any heed.

A gaping fissure opened when the mayor, Dietrich, attempted to impose martial law upon the city. Laveaux and Schneider claimed that this was a prelude to a military dictatorship and persuaded the majority in the club to protest to the Legislative Assembly. Whereupon, on February 7, 1792, 137 members, including Dietrich, withdrew and formed a new Society of Friends of the Constitution (popularly called the Auditoire Society). The old club (Miroir Society) was 286 strong. A propaganda war commenced between Laveaux's *Courrier de Strasbourg* and the *Feuille de Strasbourg*, the organ of Auditoire Society. And both bodies appealed for support from affiliates.[10] The Paris club, after two discussions, adopted a resolution of Robespierre praising the Miroir Society. Most of the provincial clubs took similar stands. The leftist Parisian press also screeched objurgations at Dietrich's group.[11] Notices of a reunion were circulated in April, but the accord soon broke down. When Laveaux was arrested on charges of sedition, there was a new explosion of fury from the network. The Auditoire Society, which was "outside the pale," died in the summer of 1792.[12]

During the Convention the Miroir club repaid Robespierre for his support with fierce loyalty to the Montagnards. It also held advanced social views, and by 1793 it referred to its members as sansculottes. Unfortunately, we do not have a full list of its members; its leaders were middling bourgeoisie on a lower social plane than those of the Auditoire. One of them, Philibert Simond, made the following statement in September 1792 on the eve of municipal elections. "Neither the best-educated nor the rich should be chosen, but instead the poorest citizens. We have

[9] Heitz, *Strasbourg*, p. 169.

[10] Ibid., pp. 178–185. *Courrier de Strasbourg*, Jan. 26, Mar. 9, 1792. *JC*, Feb. 16, 22, 1792. COR: Reims; Niort, 3003; Poitiers, S 26.

[11] *JD*, Nos. 144, 148. *AP*, Mar. 6, 1792. *CD*, Feb. 16–26, 1792. *JC*, Mar. 1, 10, 22, 29, 1792. COR, Colmar, Reims. Forot, *Tulle*, p. 173. PV: Toulouse, Feb. 20, 1792; Versailles, Feb. 20, 1792; Béziers, Mar. 6, 1792.

[12] Heitz, *Strasbourg*, p. 202. *M*, Apr. 9, 12, 1792. *JC*, Apr. 12, 1792. PV: Ornans, Apr. 30, 1792; Toulouse, Apr. 9, 1792; Le Mans, Apr. 12, 1792. COR, Poitiers, S 26.

seen the evils committed by the rich and educated in the administration of Dietrich."[13]

The same blaze of publicity does not illuminate the schisms in the Paris region and northwest. In early 1793, apparently, a splinter group of Jacobins formed a popular society at St.-Denis. The old society described the members of this group as "bloodthirsty men who have called for the assassination of the deputies in the Legislative Assembly and Convention who voted for the free circulation of grains." At Amiens, by April 1793, a pro-Montagnard "Société populaire" has also risen up in opposition to the Girondist, regular society. It became the official affiliate after the June coup.[14]

The history of the popular society of Caen is equally murky. Until the end of 1792, in this Norman city, we hear only of the affiliated Society of Friends of the Constitution which, in truth, was very active. In January 1793, however, it denounced the Paris Jacobins, broke off relations, and atrophied. From its shadow emerged the Carabots Club, an obscure fraternity of artisans and shopkeepers until its formal organization on February 10, 1793. Paul Hanson believes that it was a client group of the departmental administration and merchant elite. Among the popular societies it seems to have been unique in that it was pro-Federalist in May–June 1793. But earlier, in an address to the Convention after the execution of the king, it had lavished praise on "the brave and generous Mountain" for opposing those who had favored a nationwide referendum on his fate.[15]

At Le Mans, a Société fraternelle d'Outrepont, which admitted passive citizens, was founded in early 1791. After protracted negotiations, it amalgamated in February 1792 with the bourgeois Society of Friends of the Constitution. The Fraternal Society furnished almost 80 percent of the members of the united association; however, the leaders were former Friends of the Constitution like Levasseur and Philippeaux. The merger brought new

---

[13] Heitz, *Strasbourg*, pp. 238–239.

[14] AM, Amiens, 2 I 4–5. *ArchP*, Feb. 3, June 14, 1793. BN, Lb 40/760. *JD*, June 16, 25, 1793.

[15] AN, C 250. P. Hanson, "The Federalist Revolt of 1793. A Comparative Study of Caen and Limoges" (Ph.D. dissertation, Arizona State University), pp. 67–70.

life to the Jacobin movement in Le Mans without demonstrably radicalizing it.[16]

Both clubs of Angers dated from 1790 and were named Societies of Friends of the Constitution. The "Eastern Club" had 450 members, was the Jacobin affiliate, and was dowered with the "most learned, honest, and civilized men of Angers." The 350 members of the "Western Society" were mainly workers and passive citizens. Despite their social dissemblance, the two organizations lived in concord until the Convention. Early in the autumn of 1792, however, the Eastern Society condemned the leaders of the Paris club and threatened to break off relations. And some of its luminaries, including the Oratorian Benaben, defected to the Western Society. In early 1793, the Western Club appealed for affiliation from Paris, referring to itself as the "Société des Sans-Culottes, ou des Bonnets." The Montagnard deputy, Choudieu, advised the Paris Jacobins to comply with this request, saying that the Bonnets Club was the "true patriotic society of Angers."[17]

Nantes, a great port of more than sixty thousand, had three Societies of Friends of the Constitution in 1791, with a reputed collective enrollment of twelve hundred; but only two functioned in 1792–93. The official affiliate was at first called the Club des Capuchins and later the Club Mirabeau. According to Lallié, the historian of the Nantes clubs, it was made up of all the "enlightened men" of the city and had the ear of local authorities. Five of its members were elected as deputies to the Convention. The second society, called the Club des Cordeliers in 1791 and the Club St.-Vincent by 1793, consisted of men with "no personal situation and no reputation" who would have played second fiddle in the affiliated club. Its best-known leader, Pierre Chaux, was a merchant who had twice declared bankruptcy before 1789.[18]

In March 1791 the two clubs of Nantes agreed to try to forge a common set of rules, to concert with each other on important is-

---

[16] PV, Le Mans, Nov. 13, 1791–Feb. 2, 1792. A. Bouton, *Les franc-maçons manceaux et la Révolution française* (Le Mans, 1958), pp. 208–213.

[17] C. Uzureau, "Les Sociétés à Angers," *Andegaviana* (1912), pp. 377–382. A. Meynier, *Un représentant de la bourgeoisie angevine* (Paris, 1905), pp. 235–243. Bois, *Anjou*, pp. 167–175.

[18] Lallié, *Nantes*, pp. 14–103.

sues, and to grant joint voting privileges to members. This arrangement worked well. As late as January 1793 they collaborated in demanding the death penalty for the king, and in the spring of 1793 they worked together to halt the spread of the Vendéen rebellion. In early May 1793, however, the Club St.-Vincent lodged a protest against an anti-Parisian, anti-Jacobin address of the Mirabeau Society and the authorities of Nantes. After the Federalist Rebellion the Mirabeau Society was suppressed, leaving only the club of "Vincent-la-Montagne."[19]

Rennes had only one society during the Constituent. No list of its 740 members exists; but the names of many officers are known, and all were *bourgeoise de robins* (men of the long robe), the dominant class. Pro-Revolutionary but centrist, they admitted to their ranks the former deputy, Le Chapelier, who had sought membership on October 18, 1791, after his return from Paris. Now, Le Chapelier was one of authors of the controversial anti-Jacobin Law of September 29, 1791; and not a week after his admission Rennes received an address from the Club National of Bordeaux in which the latter vowed to cease corresponding with any society granting him entry. This address had been printed and distributed by the Paris Jacobins. Nonetheless, Rennes, on November 2, 1791, issued a circular defending Le Chapelier, denouncing the Club National for "blasphemies" against the Constitution, and declaring the Law of September 29 to be "wise and necessary." By so doing, Rennes became, overnight, a kind of pariah. The Paris Jacobins suspended correspondence until Le Chapelier was expelled. And, in a babel of voices, various affiliates also expressed their disapproval.[20]

This criticism caused a major rupture in the Rennes club. One of its members, the future Conventionnel and Montagnard Joseph Sevestre, published a letter in which he attributed Le Cha-

---

[19] Ibid. *Journal de la société populaire de Lyon*, No. 22.
[20] CD, Nov. 7, Dec. 17, 22, 1791. *JD*, No. 90. AP, Dec. 9, 1791. *Révolutions de Paris*, Nov. 12–19, 1791. COR: Reims; Montpellier, L 5547; Niort, 3001; Bordeaux, 12 L 31, 33. PV: Lorient, Oct. 20, 24, 27, Nov. 7, 9, 1791; Périgueux, Oct. 24, 1791; Toulouse, Oct. 14, Nov. 12, 30, 1791; Sète, Oct. 18, Nov. 1, Dec. 1, 1791; Versailles, Oct. 21, 26, Nov. 7, 9, 21, Dec. 5, 1791; Bergerac, Nov. 14, 1791; Libourne, Nov. 13, 1791; Tonneins, Nov. 15, 1791; Niort, Nov. 20, Dec. 4, 1791; Le Havre, Nov. 20, 1791; Montpellier, Nov. 25, 1791; Montauban, Dec. 1, 1791.

pelier's acceptance to an "odious minority." Unable to obtain the ouster of Le Chapelier, he and about 125 dissidents withdrew and formed a second Society of Friends of the Constitution in early December. Those who remained behind were led by Defermon and Lanjuinais, two future Girondist deputies to the Convention. Thus, the schism of 1791 mirrored that which developed in 1792–93. There is also a tantalizing hint of class conflict. The historian R. Dupuy has identified seventeen of the secessionists. They were mainly petty bourgeoisie, salaried employees, and artisans, not "men of the long robe."[21]

The Paris Jacobins immediately granted affiliation to the new club, as did most of the provincial societies. Completely ostracized by its sisters, the will of the original society finally broke. It ousted Le Chapelier in March 1792 and sought a reunion with its rival. By a narrow margin, the latter acceded to its request. Thereafter, a tenuous balance of power existed in the Rennes club. Interestingly, it was one of the few in Britanny that did not declare for the Girondins in late 1792. Until the spring of 1793, when it supported the Federalist movement, it urged party unity.[22]

Factionalism also took a heavy toll in the central departments and, in some cases, may have been class-related. At Clermont-Ferrand in late 1790 a schism occurred, and a "popular society" was established in emulation of that at Lyon. Carrier, the notorious Montagnard, helped to found a Surveillance Society at Aurillac on February 7, 1791, just about the same time that clubs of the same name were being formed at Valence and Bordeaux. In both Aurillac and Clermont-Ferrand, however, unity had been restored by the summer of 1791.[23]

At Châteauroux and Riom troubles began during the Feuillant schism, led to the bifurcation of the original societies, and eventually (April–May 1792) to the establishment and affiliation of

---

[21] B.-A. Pocquet du Haut-Jusse, *Terreur et terroristes à Rennes* (Mayenne, 1974), pp. 21–23. R. Dupuy, "Aux origines du fédéralisme breton," *Annales de Bretagne* (1975), pp. 344–345.

[22] Labroue, *Bergerac*, pp. 193–194. *JD*, No. 111. *AP*, Dec. 20, 23, 1791. *CD*, Mar. 23, 1792. *JC*, Nos. 1, 4, 6, 14, 18. COR: Niort, 3005; Poitiers, S 26. PV: Toulouse, Dec. 22, 1791; Tulle, Dec. 26, 1791; Lorient, Dec. 15, 1791.

[23] A.-G. Manry, *Histoire d'Auvergne* (Clermont-Ferrand, n.d.), p. 241. Soanen, "Puy-de-Dôme," pp. 581–582.

new ones. The club that emerged triumphant at Riom called itself the Society of Friends of the Constitution and Rural Economy but belied its title by enrolling very few peasants. The society founded at Châteauroux on April 9, 1792, seems to have been more "popular" in makeup, and, incidentally, remained faithful to the "mother society" throughout the Convention.[24]

On the conflict that occurred at Levroux only a few, chance remarks are vouchsafed us. In October 1792 a Society of True Friends of the Republic announced its formation and alleged that the affiliated club was composed of a "handful of individuals rendered insolent by their wealth." Craponne, in the same month, told the "mother society" that it had "narrowly missed annihilation" at the hands of a "bourgeois antipopular club." The Paris Jacobins tried to force two rival clubs at Mauriac to unite in the spring of 1791. If a reunion was achieved, it was fleeting, for there were more schisms in 1792. By August 1792 a "Society of Sansculottes" had been formed. It praised the Legislative Assembly for abolishing the distinction between active and passive citizens. "How inconsistent we were to have excluded the poor man from our assemblies. Did the bourgeois aristocracy, in doing this, wish to put itself in the place of the nobility?"[25]

From the small towns of the southwest come similar mutterings. At Fleurance the sequence of events followed almost exactly the same course as in Mauriac. There were two rival clubs by the spring of 1791, and the Paris Jacobins refused to recognize either as the affiliate until peace was restored. Commissioners from Lectoure who investigated the situation at Fleurance wrote to Paris to say that the disagreement was at an end. But by the following summer two societies were again in existence, and one complained to the "mother society" about the other, saying that an "aristocracy of riches was trying to erect itself on the ruins of the old."[26]

Factionalism also reared its hydra's head at Foix. The affiliated

[24] E. Roux, *Riom pendant la Révolution* (Riom, 1902), vol. I. Soanen, "Puy-de-Dôme," pp. 584–585. *JC*, Apr. 30, May 17, 1792. Jouet, "Châteauroux," p. 35. PV, Châteauroux, Aug. 11, 1792.

[25] *JC*, Sept. 13, 15, Oct. 29, Nov. 21, 1792.

[26] *JC*, June 29, 1792. PV, Lectoure, June 24, 1791. N. Cadeot, *La Société montagnarde de Fleurance* (Auch, 1914).

society here evolved from a reading circle of the Old Regime and was exceptionally elitist, admitting a number of nobles and all local government officials without vote. In early 1792, at the insistence of the clubs of St.-Girons and Pamiers, the Paris Jacobins revoked its affiliation and may have accorded it instead to a "Société dite Rivale" made up of "artisans." After the fall of the monarchy, "democrats" finally seized control of the original society, expelled the "Feuillants," and forged a union with the popular society. At their request, Paris renewed affiliation. [27]

The great metropolis of the southwest, Bordeaux, had at least five clubs in 1791–92. One citation in the February 19, 1792, issue of the *Courrier de la Gironde* is all that is known of the Society of Friends of the People. The Patriotic Society of la Merci was a neighborhood group that was absorbed by the Récollets Society in 1792. The Society of Surveillants was a little more significant. It had 250 members, mostly artisans and petty shopkeepers, and met from March 7, 1791 to December 1793. [28]

Towering above these in importance was the Récollets Society (Society of Friends of the Constitution), the official Jacobin affiliate. Its membership stood at 1,533 in December 1791 and may have topped 2,000 in the previous summer. Alan Forrest has called it "the unsullied preserve of the rich and powerful." Its sons, including many wealthy businessmen, successful lawyers, and intellectuals, dominated the delegations of the Gironde to the Legislative Assembly and Convention and held most of the local political offices. Although bourgeois, its members were not mean-spirited. They gave unstintingly of their time and money to patriotic and benevolent causes. One of the tragedies of the Revolution was that men such as these were proscribed during the Terror. [29]

The dean of the Bordeaux societies, the Club National, was formed in July 1789. It enjoyed a certain notoriety in the network and was granted "correspondent" status by the Paris Jacobins;

[27] PV, Foix. *JC*, Oct. 8, 1792. C. Anel, "Les rapports de la Société des Jacobins de Paris avec le club de Foix," *Revue des études historiques* (1926), pp. 47–64.

[28] P. Bécamps, "La Société patriotique de Bordeaux," *Actes, Congrès national des sociétés savantes* (1956), pp. 255–281. See also the book-length series of articles by R. Dubos on the Surveillant Society in *Revue historique de Bordeaux* (1933–1936).

[29] Flottes, "Bordeaux," pp. 337–362. A. Forrest, *Society and Politics in Revolutionary Bordeaux* (Oxford, 1975), pp. 65–72.

yet, prior to the Convention, it was a second-rate entity. In local politics it was an onlooker rather than a mover; it had only one hundred members in 1792, and in the summer of that year almost died for lack of attendance. During the Constituent its entrance fee was twelve livres and dues were twenty-four sous per month. Thus, it was not a popular society. Yet, its leaders came from a lower social echelon than those of the Récollets Society and seem to have had more contact with the people. François Desfieux was a modest merchant. The Sala brothers ran a cafe. Pierre Charles was employed at a printing house.[30]

In the early Convention, after two years of amicable relations, the Club National and the Récollets Society became estranged. The latter was militantly pro-Girondist and broke off relations with the Paris Jacobins. The Club National, which referred to its rival as the "Society of the Rich," was equally ardent in its support for the Mountain and was named the official affiliate in early 1793. Although the Club National was closed by local authorities on March 8, it was reopened after the Federalist Rebellion. At the height of the Terror, it was the lone club of Bordeaux.

Libourne, which is quite near Bordeaux, originally had three Societies of Friends of the Constitution. Locals referred to them as numbers "one," "two," and "three," after the sections in which they met. Number three was short-lived. Number two was the Libournais equivalent of the Récollets Society. It was quite active and large (468 members voted at a session in January 1793); its leaders were "excellent bourgeois" types; and it renounced its affiliateship in January 1793. Club number one was the "Club national" of Libourne. It had roughly twenty active members in 1793. They were property owners and taxpayers, but on a smaller scale than the men of number two. Some brazenly referred to themselves as "Maratists" and "Robespierrists."[31]

To all appearances, the "Friends of the Constitution" and the "Defenders of Liberty" of Cahors got along reasonably well until the early Convention. At that time, the "Defenders" wrote to the Paris Jacobins to ask for affiliateship. They claimed to have six

[30] Forrest, *Bordeaux*, pp. 63–65. PV, Club National (Bordeaux). J. Melchior, "Histoire du Club National," Thèse (U. of Bordeaux, 1951).
[31] Besson, *Libourne*, pp. 219–237.

hundred members and said that the "Friends" had been reduced by defections to about fifty. The two groups were contrasted thusly: "They are rich and occupy all of the offices. We are poor and without ambition."[32]

The "Friends" society (now called the Friends of Liberty and Equality) published an address denying these allegations, and yet, showing that up to that date it had indeed been elitist: "They (the Defenders) have claimed that our doors are always open to the rich and closed to the poor. Closed to the poor! Citizens, which of you has wanted to visit us and not been welcomed? Name someone who has wished to read our newspapers, and been refused. Our enemies are making these accusations in order to get the people to hate us. People! We will always be your friends."[33]

After this exchange the waters become muddy. On November 11, 1792, the two societies notified affiliates that they had united. It would seem from the papers of the Montauban club, however, that the divisions persisted, and that one society was pro-Montagnard, the other pro-Girondin. All we know definitely is that a Cahors club was on good terms with the Paris Jacobins in the spring of 1793.[34]

Club wars raged in numerous communes of the Gard. Alès had three societies in 1791–92. Beaucaire, by the spring of 1793, had bred six, including a pro-Montagnard "society of sansculottes."[35] Nîmes was the capital and largest city of the department. Its Society of Friends of the Constitution was a carbon copy of the rich, affiliated societies at Bordeaux, Angers, Nantes, and Libourne. It had five hundred members, many of whom held positions in local government. Beside this citadel of wealth and power, the Popular Society of Nîmes came into being on November 13, 1791. Its dues were low, and its thirty founders were middling and petite bourgeoisie, and artisans.[36]

One of the initial acts of the Popular Society was to seek affiliation with the "mother society of Nîmes." The latter at first de-

---

[32] *JC*, No. 2; see also the issues of Mar. 5, Apr. 21, Nov. 5, 1792.
[33] *JC*, Nov. 8, 1792.
[34] Levy-Schneider, *St.-André*, p. 188. COR, Bordeaux, 12 L 30. *JC*, Nov. 24, 1792.
[35] AD, Gard, L 2121–2122, 2129. *ArchP*, July 6, 1793.
[36] Rouvière, *Gard*, II, 68–73.

murred, but finally consented. The speech given on this occasion (December 1791) by the president of the Friends of the Constitution tells much about the character of the two organizations. He beseeched the Popular Society not to believe those who said that his club was possessed of a "spirit of domination" and was ruled over by an "aristocracy of riches." "Here, the glitter of wealth and the luster of holding public office are effaced before the noble title of citizen."[37]

The underlying animosity burst into full view in the spring of 1792. On March 23 the Popular Society denounced a leader of the other body. Then on April 9, the departmental Directory, which was composed largely of Friends of the Constitution, accused the Popular Society of working with the club of Marseille to foment disorders in the southeast. The Popular Society responded with a manifesto praising Marseille and deprecating the department. Marseille, incidently, had long called for a merger of the two clubs of Nîmes. In April, however, it affiliated the Popular Society after a member pointed out: "Union is impractical because one group is poor, and the other is rich. One has good principles, the other bad; one is Jacobin, the other Feuillant."[38]

The feud between the two clubs of Nîmes worsened in the summer of 1792. With the dissolution of the departmental Directory after August 10, the Popular Society momentarily gained the upper hand. It gloated to the Paris Jacobins in September that its rival was in its "last extremities" and virtually commanded the "Friends" to draw up a list of members who wished to abjure past errors and apply for admittance. Not surprisingly, this ultimatum was rejected. The conflict took another turn when three commissioners of the Convention arrived in Nîmes in early November and tried, in a heavy-handed way, to end the factionalism. The "Friends" seized on this opportunity, fusing their organization with a small Society of Friends of the Rights of Man to form the Republican Society of Nîmes. However, the Popular Society refused to adhere to any plan of union that did not also include a purification. In a circular of November 2 it denounced the commissioners for trying to arrange an "unholy marriage"

---

[37] Ibid., 74–79.
[38] *JDM*, p. 63. Cf. also PV, Toulouse, Feb. 15, Apr. 19, 1792.

and declared that the Republican Society contained "all of the rich and Feuillants of Nîmes."[39]

From November onward this struggle became part of the larger conflict between Girondins and Montagnards. The Republican Society aligned itself with the Girondins; the Popular Society was pro-Montagnard. The attitude of other clubs toward the schism in Nîmes often coincided with their opinions of the factions in Paris. The Récollets of Bordeaux had warm relations with the Republican Society. Marseille and its satellites in Provence loathed the men of the Republican Society. Thus spake Avignon in a circular to affiliates: "Born in that class called the *haut tiers*, they fought against aristocracy not to procure general equality, but to insure their own supremacy. They were supportive of the constitution before August 10 because it favored the rich."[40]

Provence itself was rife with schisms. At Toulon, the oldest organization and the Jacobin affiliate, the Patriotic Society of Friends of the Constitution (Club St.-Jean), was the most advanced politically. Its antagonist, the Society of Friends and Defenders of the Constitution (Club St.-Pierre), was aligned with the department. Tension between the two groups culminated in a street battle in August 1791. After that date the Club St.-Jean dominated the city. It seems to have been a coalition of popular and middle-class elements. Led principally by priests and lawyers, it had a sizable enrollment which, during the Convention, consisted "in large part of workers from the arsenal."[41]

Aix also had two clubs in the Constituent. The Society of Friends of the Constitution (Club Bourbon) had six hundred members and dominated local government. Its high dues made it the preserve of the "haute and moyenne bourgeoisie," and it long disdained to admit the "people," even as spectators. Consequently, the petty merchants, artisans, and small farmers of Aix, headed by the Abbé Rive, created their own association in No-

[39] Rouvière, *Gard*, III, 26–39. *JC*, Sept. 6, 20, Oct. 1, 29, Nov. 24, 1792. Poitiers Correspondence (S 26).

[40] Cf. Rouvière, *Gard*, III, 200–214. COR, Bordeaux, 12 L 29. PV: Malemort-du-Comtat, Dec. 23, 1792; St. Hippolyte, Jan. 13, March 30, May 10, 12, 19, 1793.

[41] H. Labroue, *Le Club Jacobin de Toulon* (Paris, 1907), pp. 1–37.

vember 1790. Although it had a bizarre name, "Antipolitiques," it was in essence a popular society. Dues were set at six sous per month, and later at only three, and it was so poor that it could not afford benches, tables, heat, or lighting.[42]

Until the spring of 1791 the two clubs at Aix had friendly relations. At this point, however, animosity surfaced. Marseille threw its support to the Antipolitiques, retracting its affiliation from the Club Bourbon and advising the other clubs of the Midi to do likewise. This insured the eventual demise of the Club Bourbon. In 1792 its remnants were absorbed by the Antipolitiques. The latter, with 1,000 to 1,200 members by early 1793, was one of the largest clubs in France. Politically, however, it was a junior partner of Marseille.[43]

Unlike Aix and Toulon, Marseille had only one club throughout the Revolution, but it was wracked by a number of crises that greatly affected its composition and outlook. The first came in August 1790, when an ambitious local politician, J.-F. Lieutaud, attempted unsuccessfully to dissolve it. The bitter feelings engendered by this failed coup led to an exodus of some leading citizens and haute bourgeoisie. Thereafter, the balance of power in the club gradually shifted to men of a lower station. This process culminated in the winter of 1792–93, just at the time that Marseille declared for the Montagnards. Four hundred members were purged. Others ceased to attend, and there were mass enrollments of "sansculottes." The radicals who directed the Marseille club in 1792–93 were much like those at Strasbourg. They were quintessential lesser men of the moyenne bourgeoisie. Envy of the rich may have motivated some of their policies.[44]

By 1792 the club of Marseille had gained an ascendancy over its region that was unparalleled in France. From its rural affiliates came a torrent of letters and delegations, vowing allegiance and seeking counsel, aid, and advice. In almost every town, so it seems, there were rival "bourgeois" and "popular" societies. As at Aix, they often called themselves Friends of the Constitution and Antipolitiques. Marseille meddled regularly in these dis-

---

[42] Bibliothèque Méjanes (Aix), mss. 872–873, PV, Aix (Friends of the Constitution). PV, Antipolitiques (Aix).

[43] Kennedy, *Jacobins*, pp. 27–28.

[44] Kennedy, *Marseille*, pp. 184–191.

putes, taking the side of the "popular" faction. Indeed, its "commissaires" waged a kind of class war against the bourgeoisie of
rural Provence.[45]

The initial skirmishes occurred in early 1792. In January, two
commissars from Marseille, accompanied by national guardsmen
brandishing sabers and muskets, broke up a gathering of "bourgeois-aristocrats" at Aubagne. On May 19, the ex-Oratorian
Isoard, with an "army" estimated at two thousand men, marched
into Sisteron, forced "bourgeois-aristocrats" to resign from office, and established a club. At Cotignac (Var) in June some commissioners from Marseille dissolved a club that was "especially
composed of bourgeoisie" and created one that was drawn "from
the ranks of the people." About the same date Marseille came to
the defense of a club in Le Val that "trembled under the yoke not
of a titled aristocracy, but even worse, one of riches." In July,
Marseille accused a faction at Istres of seeking to substitute an
"aristocracy of riches for one of titles and privileges."

The increasingly hard line taken by the Marseillais can be
traced in a series of letters that Isoard and a fellow clubbist, Tourneau, wrote to the members of a society at Manosque. Much of
the correspondence concerned the treatment that the "cultivators" of Manosque should give to the bourgeoisie. At first they
were advised simply to beware of the bourgeoisie and not to admit them as members. By 1793, however, the letters were quite
violent in tone. On January 30 Tourneau wrote: "The bourgeoisie are rogues, always trying to victimize patriots. Emulate the
farmers of Aubagne, even up to putting your bourgeoisie to
death, because they are the enemies of the Republic."

But these were mere words! More terrifying to the propertied
classes were the deeds of the Marseillais. In a number of communes where they intervened, they extracted reparations from
the "bourgeois-aristocrats." During a series of missions to Berre
(September 1792 to March 1793) agents of the club and department levied an indemnity of 8,800 livres on a "fatal league of aristocrats." At Auriol, in the autumn of 1792, seven commissioners
imposed a 40,000-livre tax upon the village elite. In January 1793,
two commissars tried to impose a 9,400-livre indemnity on the

---

[45] For what follows see Kennedy, *Marseille*, pp. 192–216.

"oppressive bourgeoisie" of Salernes, accusing them of holding the peasants in a kind of debt slavery. "They (the bourgeoisie of Salernes) force unfortunates to sell their crops at vile prices in good times, and in hard times refuse to lower bread prices or to give credit. If the poor man has no money, he is allowed to die of hunger."

The most sensational affair occurred at Salon. Here, in early 1793, some "commissaires" from Marseille imposed a veritable reign of Terror. A priest and three bourgeoisie were murdered. Imprisonments occurred; domiciles were ransacked; forced loans levied. Three of the commissars were later executed by the Federalists. At their trial a doctor claimed that they planned to extort 250,000 livres from the inhabitants of Salon, and that he paid 20,000 "to save his life." According to other testimony, they "preached unceasingly against the rich and the bourgeoisie." "We must destroy them," one of the Marseillais allegedly said, "we must not leave one of these bourgeoisie alive."

Part Two

Economics and Society

IV

Scarcity and Inflation:
The Problem of
Subsistances

SUBSISTANCES is roughly equivalent in English to provisions or supplies. Revolutionaries used it chiefly to refer to foodstuffs, and especially to grain. As everyone knows, bread was the staple of the French diet, and the common man was inordinately concerned that it should be available at an affordable price. Grain shortages and inflated bread prices were the yeast that almost always produced popular fermentation.

During the Legislative Assembly and early Convention, the problem of subsistances, that is, scarcities and rising prices, was a major topic of discussion in the clubs. The clubbists did not evince great concern about their own ability to procure the necessities of life, but they were disturbed by the plight of the "common people." To their credit, many seem to have had an altruistic interest in the welfare of "this precious class." Certain clubs relied upon the political backing of the sansculottes. Finally, there was a pervasive fear of popular revolt, a realization that "the people must be able to eat if they are to love the Revolution."

The clubbists subscribed to what might be called the "devil theory of economics." Almost all believed that traitors and enemy agents wanted to provoke famine in order to destroy the nation from within. They repeatedly accused merchants, farmers, bakers, butchers, and millers of greedy profiteering. The canker of suspicion gnawed incessantly.

A vast tome could be written on the efforts of clubs to alleviate popular suffering. Members pledged to let the poor sup at their tables. Plans were concocted for nonprofit bakeries. Committees were set up to procure food, fuel, and other commodities in short supply. Countless fund-raising drives were initiated. The club-bists of Marseille, on one occasion, contributed over 30,000 livres for the purchase of meat. Little Ars-en-Ré raised 13,400 livres to buy wheat, barley, and legumes.[1]

Many were the appeals to citizens to reduce voluntarily their consumption of basic commodities. Such a crusade was started by the Paris Jacobins in early 1792 after the cost of coffee and sugar soared to astronomical levels. All present at the "mother society" on January 30 took an oath not to use these two sub-stances until they fell to a certain price. Printed copies of this ses-sion were sent to affiliates with invitations to do the same. The "Amis" and "Amies" of the Constitution of Dijon adhered to the Jacobin resolution immediately. What is more, they published with all speed a circular of their own. The result was that club-bists all across the country raised their hands aloft and vowed to use coffee and sugar only in case of illness (the sick had been ex-empted by the Parisians and Dijonais). Some societies added amendments reflecting special concerns. Rodez also renounced the use of "foreign spirits." Avallon wanted the French to give up sugar entirely as long as it was produced by slave labor.[2]

The subject of pets came up occasionally in club meetings, without much being done. Villeneuve-l'Archévêque, for exam-ple, petitioned in April 1792 for the total eradication of dogs. This was an "infallible means," it said, to provide for the nourishment of 1,200,000 people. It is not clear, however, whether Villeneuve intended for people to eat the dogs or the food they had con-sumed. Since beer, hair powder, and starch were manufactured from grains, motions were also made to restrict their usage. Metz, in early 1793, called for a nationwide ban on the produc-tion of these "luxuries," reasoning that the "welfare of the poor should take precedence over the sensual comforts of the rich." However, various objections were raised to this proposal. Aire-sur-Adour, for instance, was quite ready to forgo starch and powder, but not beer. Referring to the Metz circular, one of its

[1] *JDM*, pp. 83–88. Richemond, "Ars-en-Ré," pp. 58–93.
[2] *JD*, Nos. 133, 136. *JC*, Mar. 15, 1793. *AP*, Feb. 25, 1793. Hugueney, *Dijon*, pp. 145–146. Aubert, "Douai," p. 236. PV: Le Mans, Mar. 4, 1792; Perpignan, Mar. 4, 1792; Versailles, Feb. 29, Mar. 7, 1792; Nuits, Feb. 29, 1792; Avallon, Feb. 12, 1792; Croix-Rousse, Feb. 12, 1792; Lille, Mar. 11, 1792.

members observed caustically: "Denying oneself beer is easy in a region which, like theirs, has wine, but impossible where beer is the only drink. Water . . . is unsuitable for the sustenance of citizens fatigued by their labors."[3]

Club nutritionists came up with sundry recipes for healthful breads with low wheat content.[4] More interesting were suggestions aimed at altering dietary habits. Much ado was made about the introduction of potatoes, which were then rarely raised or consumed. The Dijon society seems to have been the first to take up the cause of the lowly spud. It circulated printed extracts of its session of February 26, 1792, in which an Englishman named Pigott deplored the excessive consumption of wheat in France and advocated the substitution of potatoes, maize, and other crops. Pigott was seconded by a professor of medicine at Dijon who attributed a variety of ailments to the eating of bread. A year later several Parisian newspapers published articles claiming that France's enemies were exploiting its dependence on wheat, urging farmers to grow potatoes, and describing the proper methods of planting.[5]

The newspaper articles, in particular, generated much discussion. After listening to the reading of one, the indefatigable schoolmaster of Tonneins, Jouan le jeune, gave an impromptu lecture on potatoes to fellow clubbists. Tartas and Limoges decided to distribute printed matter on potato growing to the farmers of their regions. Pau demanded that the Convention promote potato cultivation. Alas, disturbances occurred in the galleries at Rouen when a member advocated the substitution of potatoes for bread. Some people, "not yet enlightened on their true interests," apparently found this idea repugnant.[6]

IMBUED with the liberal economic philosophy of Adam Smith and the Physiocrats, the deputies of the Constituent approved a

[3] *JC*, May 5, 1792. *JD*, Feb. 28, 1793. *ArchP*, Mar. 12, 1793. COR, Reims; Montpellier, L 5544. Libois, *Lons-le-Saunier*, p. 123. Holuigue, *Boulogne*, pp. 209–210. PV: Pau, May 17, 1793; Honfleur, Nov. 2, 1792; Aire, Feb. 25, 1793; Toulouse, Mar. 28, 1793.

[4] Cf. Besson, *Libourne*, p. 215. *JDM*, pp. 209, 451.

[5] Hugueney, *Dijon*, pp. 146–147. *PF*, Apr. 3, 4, 16, 1793. *AP*, Apr. 4, 1793.

[6] PV: Pau, Mar. 16, May 19, 1793; Tartas, Mar. 22, 1793; Limoges, Feb. 9, 1793; Tonneins, Mar. 3, 1793. Chardon, *Rouen*, p. 122.

series of acts deregulating the grain trade. Initially, the clubs were ardent apologists of this legislation.[7] The first glimmerings of a revival of regulationist spirit did not show up until late 1790 and early 1791 when rumors surfaced that speculators and counter-revolutionaries, under pretext of shipping grain to the southern departments by sea, were actually sending it to foreign countries. These stories were patently absurd since grain sold at a higher price in France than in surrounding countries. Nonetheless, many in the clubs believed them. Toulouse appealed to all the societies on the frontiers to be on guard. Lille demanded legislation requiring that domestic granaries be filled before any exports were permitted.[8]

After the relatively poor harvest of 1791, the alleged "sortie" of grains became a much more volatile issue. The central and southern departments, where the dearth was greatest, were forced to make purchases in the north where yields had been more satisfactory. Unfortunately, people in the better-off areas were fearful that their stockpiles would be depleted and that foreigners would be the beneficiaries. Grain barges and carts were stopped and pillaged by mobs, making farmers and merchants reluctant to send their crops to market, and, therefore, compounding the problem of scarcities.

The rumors and disturbances of late 1791 and early 1792 sparked much correspondence between the clubs and revealed differences of opinion. Libourne, Versailles, and Rennes wrote to affiliates in maritime centers urging them to see to it that the circulation of grains remained unfettered. Similarly, the grain merchants in the Bourbourg society seem to have been more concerned about profits than about the egress of cereals. Le Mans, however, wanted the "criminal" exports stopped and beseeched the clubs of Laval, Angers, and Nantes to survey traffic on the Mayenne and Loire. Le Mans was clearly feeling popular pressure. Its minutes of March 4 state that the "people" in the galleries were upset by the exit of grains, and that several members tried to calm them. A little later it reported to the Paris Jacobins

---

[7] Kennedy, *Jacobins*, p. 124.
[8] *Journal des amis de la constitution*, Jan. 18, 1791. COR, Lille.

that "counterrevolutionaries" were trying to persuade the "people" that it was to blame for the bread shortages.[9]

Lille was also quite alarmed about popular discontent and used its network ties to try to police commerce. Of the clubs in Marseille, Bordeaux, and La Rochelle, it asked how much grain the Midi needed; to Watten and Dunkirk it wrote to determine the amounts then being shipped from the Nord. It requested Bergues to keep a record of every vessel that passed through its port, the owner's name, number of crewmen, type and quantity of cargo, and ports of call.[10]

More importantly, several clubs petitioned for laws that would have limited free circulation to a greater or lesser degree. Yvetot wanted the Legislative Assembly to put guard posts and patrol boats on the Seine to stop the passage of contraband grain. Sète and Perpignan, concerned about meat shortages, demanded a prohibition on the export of livestock to Spain, saying that it was "contrary to the general interest." Dijon grumbled that the legislation granting freedom to the grain trade was being abused. "One part of the kingdom should not be reduced to starvation under the guise of supplying another." Béthune also made an impassioned appeal for the reimplementation of some regulations:

> The *law*, the *law*, obedience to the *law*, is our cry; but soon, *bread*, *bread*, give us *bread*, will be the reply. All of our grain is being taken, by whom we know not. . . . If these thefts continue, the people will rise up, and we may be forced to use our arms against them. We do not wish to interfere with the free circulation of grains. We merely solicit a decree which assures that no department lacks bread. Do other departments wish us to starve?[11]

Another sign of the gradual resurgence of protectionist sentiment was the demand for *greniers d'abondance*. In the early Legislative Assembly a number of clubs asked their municipal govern-

[9] G. Lefebvre, *La Société populaire de Bourbourg* (1913), pp. 23–25. PV: Le Mans, Feb. 23, Mar. 4, 1792; St.-Malo, Dec. 1, 1791; Lorient, Dec. 12, 1791; Libourne, Oct.6–Nov. 3, 1791; Sète, Nov. 22, 1791; Versailles, Nov. 25, 1791.

[10] PV and COR, Lille, Oct. 31–Nov. 10, 1791.

[11] *JC*, Mar. 17, Apr. 5, 1792. *CD*, Oct. 31, 1791. Hugueney, *Dijon*, pp. 148–149. *AP*, Apr. 13, 1792. PV: Perpignan, Feb. 16, 1792; Fécamp, Jan. 12, 1792; Sète, Jan. 5, 1792.

· ments to create them, or (less commonly) devised plans to set up
their own.[12] The basic premise behind such schemes was that
each year, after the harvest, grain was to be purchased and stored.
Some plans called for the municipalities to fix prices for the upcoming year. In good times the grain would be set a little above
cost so that it could be sold for less in bad years. Bakers would
purchase their supplies from the municipal granaries and be assured modest profits.

As early as December 4, 1791, Douai contemplated asking the
Legislative Assembly to establish a nationwide system of greniers
d'abondance. Arcis-sur-Aube, Guingamp, and Le Mans actually
sent such petitions to the Legislators in early 1792.[13] This drive
was stalled by the Paris Jacobins. In reply to the petition of Le
Mans, the correspondence committee of the "mother society"
wrote:

> Your energetic picture of the plight of France, of the
> hoarding of grain, has created a sensation here. Like you we
> execrate the vampires who prey on public misery, but we re-
> gard your remedies as being more harmful than efficacious.
> Trust, brothers and friends, in the riches of our soil. Brush
> aside the fears that sham famines have caused in some de-
> partments. Permit a public consensus to form on the free cir-
> culation of grains. Rely on a free market always alive to its
> own interests to bring aid to departments which have grain
> deficiencies.[14]

That most of the clubs still shared these sentiments was illustrated by their reaction to a tragic, much-publicized incident
which occurred at Etampes in March 1792. Finding no grain in
the market place, a mob shot to death the mayor, H. Simonneau,
who had stubbornly refused to fix prices. Simonneau may have
gotten his just desserts. The curé, Pierre Dolivier, in the name of
forty citizens of the environs of Etampes, accused him of collu-

[12] Galabert, "Montauban," p. 304. Dubos, "Surveillants," pp. 116–129. Hugueney, *Dijon*, p. 147. PV: Toulouse, Oct. 22, 1791; Sète, Dec. 20, 1791, Jan. 5,
1792; Lectoure, Dec. 27, 1791, Feb. 13, Apr. 26, 1792; Nuits, Sept. 20, 1792.
    [13] Aubert, "Douai," p. 235. Dobet, "Guingamp," p. 40. *JC*, Mar. 1, May 31,
1792. PV, Le Mans, Apr. 29, May 22, 1792.
    [14] COR, Le Mans.

sion with grain merchants and hoarders.[15] But the provincial clubs, with rare unanimity, followed the course marked out by the Legislative Assembly and the Paris Jacobins and hailed the fallen magistrate as a hero and martyr. They went into mourning, decked their halls with black bunting, sent touching messages to Simonneau's widow, named streets in his honor, and held funeral services.[16]

Many of the eulogies were printed and tell us much about the economic views of the clubbists in the spring of 1792. To the people they pointed out that everyone's interest demanded submission to the laws. Simonneau was glorified for not giving in to mob intimidation and for not imposing price controls. Finally, attempts were made to demonstrate the wisdom of the laws establishing the free circulation of grains. "If you want to cause famine in a country," opined a clubbist at St.-Etienne, "then arbitrarily tax foodstuffs. Suppliers will flee and go elsewhere in the hope of gain." "Our well-being," declaimed the society of Cognac, "rests on the legislation of the National Assembly. One law in particular is vital, that relative to the free movement of grains. Do not violate this wise decree! You in the countryside whose granaries are full, open them! Your property will be secure."[17]

The outbreak of war and the political agitation leading up to the fall of the monarchy in mid-1792 momentarily thrust the subsistances problem into the background. In the late summer and autumn, however, it reared up again, larger than before. The cause was not the harvest, which had been generally decent, but the unwillingness of farmers, from fear or greed, to bring their crops to market. Panic spread throughout much of the nation. With Apt leading the way, a host of southeastern societies petitioned the Convention to send emergency aid. At Lyon there

[15] *M*, Mar. 8–9, 1792. *ArchP*, May 1, 1792. A. Mathiez, *La Vie chère et le mouvement social sous la Terreur* (Paris, 1927), pp. 70–74.

[16] *JC*, Apr. 18–May 24, 1792. *M*, Mar. 16–May 1, 1792. *CD*, Mar. 20–May 6, 1792. *PF*, May 1–June 20, 1792. *AP*, Apr. 2, 1792. Dubois, *Ain*, II, 312–313. Flottes, "Bordeaux," p. 353. Constant, *Fontainebleau*, pp. 80–81. Bellanger, *Provins*, p. 42. Forot, *Tulle*, p. 176. Aubert, "Douai," pp. 236–237. PV: Montpellier, Apr. 22, 1792; St.-Affrique, Apr. 13–23, 1792; Montreuil, Apr. 25, 1792; Chalon, Mar. 22, 1792; Lorient, Mar. 26–Apr. 13, 1792; Toulouse, Apr. 16–17, 1792; Honfleur, May 17–22, 1792.

[17] Aubert, "Douai," pp. 236–237. Constant, *Fontainebleau*, pp. 80–81. Galley, *St.-Etienne*, I, 328. COR: Reims, Bordeaux, Poitiers, Niort.

were riots, and leaders of the Popular Society demanded that the guillotine be put on display as a warning to hoarders and speculators. The club of St.-Affrique thought the situation "menacing." St.-Cyprien was heart-sick when the people there found no bread in the market place on Christmas day, and trudged home with "tears in their eyes and money still clutched in their fists." The citizens in the galleries at Rouen would not let it forget that supplies of flour were dwindling. Another Norman club, Honfleur, discussed subsistances and little else for several weeks. Disturbances occurred throughout the Beauce. Burgundy was likewise hard hit. Pontaillier-sur-Seine, drawing from the darkest basements of human memory, said that conditions were the worst since 1709. At Chalon-sur-Saône the price of grain was twice as high as in 1788, and a pound of bread nearly three times as dear.[18]

Bordeaux was in such dire straits that the Récollets Society, for once, became the mendicant and prayed to nearby clubs to send grain. The response from the societies of the Lot-et-Garonne was heartwarming. Villeneuve, Tonneins, and Clairac pledged all possible help. Agen, which was still a believer in economic liberalism, stated that "grain is the property of the nation and belongs exclusively to no district." Marmande also declared that it was ready to do anything to preserve the free circulation of subsistances.[19]

For the most part, however, a philosophy of everyone for oneself prevailed. Each region jealously held on to its own produce, and movements of grain almost ceased. As a result, support for regulatory legislation began to rise in the clubs. Cries went up for total bans on exports, the surveillance of bakers, millers, waterways, and ports, and the death penalty for hoarders. The Bellecordière sectional society of Lyon demanded that the rich be

[18] *JC*, Sept. 20, 22, 1792. *ArchP*, Sept. 20, Nov. 28, 1792, Mar. 19, 22, 1793. AN, C 247. Mathiez, *Vie chère*, pp. 95–102. R. Carraz, "Girondins et Montagnards: Le cas chalonais," in *Actes du Colloque Girondins et Montagnards* (Paris, 1980), p. 176. COR, Lauris, Nov. 14, 1792. PV: Apt, Sept. 9, 1792; St.-Cyprien, Dec. 25, 1792; St.-Affrique, Sept. 11, 29, 1792; Honfleur, Nov. 11, 1792–Jan. 2, 1793; Rouen, Aug. 28–Nov. 2, 1792.

[19] Aulard, *Comité*, I, 150. COR, Bordeaux, 12 L 29. PV, Bordeaux, Oct. 18–Nov. 1, 1792.

taxed to buy bread for the poor.[20] Toulon and Agde circulated memoranda on the "circumstances of the times and the free circulation of grains." At Dijon, a clubbist said forthrightly on September 30: "Free circulation of grains has been a trap. Grain is moving badly or not at all. Those who compared the movement of grains to the circulation of blood, forgot that blood circulates only because of the regulatory movements of the heart."[21]

Agitation also began for the imposition of price controls. On August 27–28, the Rouen club debated the wisdom of such a policy, but no action was taken. At Lyon, in the same month, the La Juiverie sectional society, obviously inspired by the acts of the Paris Commune, resolved that grains should be requisitioned and sold at a Parisian price. The Popular Society of Nîmes, in early September, challenged the newly elected deputies of the Gard to enact legislation in the Convention raising the salaries of workers. When a deputation of coopers asked the Récollets Society to assist them in getting wage increases, however, they were chastised and retired in discomfiture.[22]

Already an interesting pattern was emerging. Pro-Montagnard societies were more likely to favor controls on prices and wages; pro-Girondist clubs were usually opposed. Now, according to the Mathiez-Soboul school of Revolutionary historiography, the Girondist deputies in the Convention were totally united on this issue. They obstinately defended economic liberalism and opposed the imposition of restraints. The Montagnards, so this theory goes, depended on the support of the Parisian masses, were more attentive to their demands, and eventually became willing to limit free trade. "This," states Roland Carraz, "is the great tactical difference which separates them from the Girondins."[23]

The studies of the Convention done by M. Sydenham and

[20] Gautheron, "Le Puy," p. 92. *ArchP*, Oct. 27, 1792. PV: Périgueux, Oct. 30, Nov. 3, 1792; Bellecordière, Oct. 14, 1792.

[21] Hugueney, *Dijon*, p. 150. PV: Toulouse, Aug. 22, 1792; Perpignan, Sept. 15, 1792.

[22] C. Mazauric, "A propos la manifestation Rougemaure . . . ," *Cahiers Léopold Delisle* (1966), pp. 68–69. Wahl, *Lyon*, pp. 578–579. Rouvière, *Gard*, II, 449–450. PV, Bordeaux, Oct. 10, 1792.

[23] Cf. M. Dorigny, "Les idées économiques des Girondins," and Carraz, "Chalonais," in *Actes du Colloque Girondins et Montagnards* (1980), pp. 81, 178.

A. Patrick have cast some doubts on this interpretation. Sydenham, for example, stresses that the Montagnards, like the majority of deputies, were long antithetical to calls from the Paris sections for the *maximum* (price controls on grains). He further argues that they finally adopted the *maximum* in April 1793 only because they "realized that the Revolution was in such dire peril that popular discontent could no longer be ignored." The threat of foreign invasion "made an appeal to popular enthusiasm seem essential." Even Sydenham admits, however, that by at last giving the *maximum* support, the Montagnards became "the acknowledged leaders of the people." Moreover, it cannot be gainsaid that a number of prominent Girondists fought price controls to the bitter end.[24]

Whatever position one takes on this historical debate, it seems clear that a desire for price controls could not have been *at first* a primary reason why some clubs threw in their lot with the Montagnards. Nor did these same clubs seek a return to regulation because the Montagnards had instructed them to do so. The explanation for the conduct of clubs like Lyon and Nîmes may lie in their internal composition, and in local political and economic conditions. They were "popular societies" in close contact with the suffering masses and locked in mortal struggles with moderate and Rightist groups.

SLOWLY, in October and November 1792, momentum built in the societies for national legislation. Toulouse (which was soon to reaffirm its loyalty to the Paris Jacobins) voted to ask the Convention to fix prices on grains. Châteauroux (another pro-Montagnard club) pushed for a requirement that municipalities in areas of oversupply routinely buy up surplus crops for resale to deficient regions.[25] On November 20–21 two important circulars appeared. In the first, Dijon (for union of the factions in Paris) sued for price controls on "all primary necessities." In the other, La Rochelle (pro-Montagnard by 1793) declared grain to be "national property" and called for an end to its export, its equitable

---

[24] M. Sydenham, *The Girondins* (London, 1961), pp. 167–169.
[25] PV: Toulouse, Oct. 20, 1792; Châteauroux, Oct. 30–Nov. 23, 1792.

distribution in the departments, fixed prices on bread, and death to hoarders.[26]

The circulars of Dijon and La Rochelle precipitated more petitions to the Convention in December. Nuits would not go as far as Dijon, but nonetheless pressed for a decree that would have forced farmers to obtain licenses in order to sell their crops. St.-Hippolyte voted to seek price controls on "certain basic necessities." St.-Dié-sur-Loir was for a *maximum* on grain as long as it guaranteed modest profits for merchants and farmers. Castres circulated a petition, to which Tonneins adhered, calling for a *maximum* of two sols six deniers on a pound of bread, to be underwritten by taxes on citizens with annual revenues in excess of five hundred livres.[27]

In November and early December there was a protracted debate in the Convention on economic policy. Ultimately, on December 8, the deputies approved a decree forbidding the export of grains, but otherwise totally reconfirming free trade. Indeed, they annulled an emergency war measure of September 16 commanding all departments to carry out an inventory of grains. And they proscribed penalties ranging from death to one year in irons for those involved in riots and demonstrations that hindered the free circulation of cereals. The passage of this legislation was due, in no small measure, to the orthodox economic arguments of Girondins like Barbaroux, Serre, and Creuzé-Latouche. However, the Montagnard deputies did little more than defend the law of September 16. Not a single one spoke out in favor of price controls. The Paris club, too, kept a discreet distance between itself and the exponents of price fixing. On November 29 it declined even to comment on a petition of the Commune and sections.

Thus, at this stage, the Paris sections and a few of the provincial clubs held more advanced economic views than the Montagnards in the "mother society." Probably, however, the majority of clubs opposed price controls, and many were against any sort of regulations. The Récollets Society would not even discuss

[26] COR: Poitiers, S 1; Limoges, L 826; Niort, 3005; Reims. *JC*, Dec. 1, 1792. Forot, *Tulle*, p. 241. Hugueney, *Dijon*, p. 150.

[27] *JC*, Dec. 8, 1792. COR, Bordeaux, 12 L 30. PV: Tonneins, Dec. 23, 1792; Lons-le-Saunier, Dec. 6, 1792; Nuits, Dec. 7–15, 1792; St.-Hippolyte, Dec. 16, 1792.

the circulars of Dijon and La Rochelle. Moulins treated the circular of Castres similarly, and Périgueux thought that Castres' proposals were "absurd." When a member at Lorient presented a plan to stop the hoarding of grains, another "wisely observed that the word 'hoarding' was often confused with the most honest speculation." Lorient voted to read the decree of December 8 in full and to adhere to its provisions.[28]

The law of December 8 merely slowed the drive for regulations. The "Enragés," extreme radicals in Paris, continued to fan the flames of popular discontent. And in early 1793 the Parisian sections produced manifestos condemning the trading aristocracy, monopolists, and the deputies who favored free circulation. On February 12, delegates of the forty-eight sections, claiming to represent France, marched to the Convention to demand a *maximum* on grains. Again the deputies, including the Montagnards, refused. Even Marat opposed the petition, categorizing it as subversive.

Although the Mountain had not yet been won over, the sections continued to be seconded by some provincial clubs. The Popular Society of Lyon was in close contact with radicals in Paris, and between January 1 and 13 it put together a thirteen-point program on subsistances. Carried by special emissaries to the capital, it commenced with these words: "The welfare of the Republic depends on the regulation of the grain trade." At St.-Denis the leaders of a popular society were accused of calling for the murder of the deputies who had voted for the free circulation of grains. Even in the usually undemonstrative St.-Cyprien club, there was strong sentiment for price fixing.[29]

Dijon was the most persistent proponent of regulatory legislation. Twice, in January and early February, it sent petitions to the Convention. In the first it renewed its call for a *maximum* on all commodities. The second, which was printed and distributed nationwide, commenced with this quotation from the preamble

---

[28] PV: Lorient, Dec. 24, 1792; Bordeaux, Nov. 28, Dec. 10, 1792; Moulins, Dec. 30, 1792; Périgueux, Jan. 30, 1793.

[29] AN, DXL 23, and F 1, C III (Rhône). *ArchP*, Feb. 3, 1793. COR, Poitiers, S 33. PV: Bellecordière, Jan. 1, 10, 1793; Croix-Rousse, Jan. 9, 1793; St.-Cyprien, Jan. 11, 1793.

of the law of September 16: "When all citizens are sacrificing for the fatherland, speculation on commodities is a crime . . . , and all owners of granaries should be regarded as simple trustees." After lamenting that these words had been forgotten on December 8, Dijon put forward a five-point program: an end to free circulation until the peace; revocation of the law of December 8; the selling of grain in only specified markets; no purchases by outsiders until satisfaction of the needs of locals; and the death penalty for hoarding and speculation.[30]

In response to these calls, echoes came bouncing back from the clubs. Périgueux, which was beginning to waver in its devotion to economic liberalism, discussed Dijon's circular at length and ended by entreating departmental officials to force farmers to sell their produce in specified markets. Lure adopted certain parts of Dijon's program. Lons-le-Saunier, Marseille, Lille, and Pontaillier-sur-Seine adhered totally. Pontaillier wailed that Frenchmen were starving in the midst of plenty and likened them to Tantalus, the mythological figure who was condemned by Zeus to hang above a pool of water just beyond his parched lips.[31]

Chalon-sur-Saône and Beaune were prompted by Dijon's action to publish circulars of their own. Chalon printed one thousand copies of a February 19 petition to the Convention demanding a *maximum* on all commodities, the death penalty for hoarders, and bounties for information leading to their successful prosecution. Beaune's petition of the same date attested that the grain laws of the Constituent had demonstrably failed and called for new legislation aimed at assuring the availability of foodstuffs at moderate prices. Beaune asked affiliates to send analogous petitions to the Convention by March 10.[32]

The Beaune and Chalon circulars often reached affiliates in the same week and were discussed jointly. Across the country the order of the day became the *taxe du pain*.[33] Nuits, Vaison, Tonneins,

[30] COR, Limoges, L 826. *JD*, Feb. 3, 1793.

[31] AN, C 247. Libois, *Lons-le-Saunier*, pp. 118–121. *JDM*, p. 611. PV: Lille, Feb. 21, 1793; Périgueux, Feb. 12–19, 1793; Chalon, Feb. 8, 1793.

[32] *JD*, Feb. 28, 1793. Carraz, "Chalonais," pp. 176–178. COR: Reims; Poitiers, S 33; Limoges, L 826.

[33] PV: Honfleur, Feb. 28, Mar. 2, 1793; Largentière, Mar. 27, 1793; Blaye, Mar. 3, 1793; Périgueux, Feb. 27–Mar. 7, 1793.

Toulouse, Toulon, Orange, and Arles sent petitions to the Convention demanding price fixing. Other societies appealed to the deputies to reimpose regulations on trade. Quoth Auxonne: "Those who voted for the free circulation of grains doubtless did not foresee that a menagerie of ferocious beasts would take advantage of this law to prey upon the people."[34]

By March 1793, therefore, many clubs had come to the conclusion that economic liberalism had not worked. Indeed, it seems that, at long last, proponents of regulation were a majority. There were, however, some societies that had scarcely budged on this issue. Bourbonne debated the Beaune and Chalon circulars but did no more than ask the Convention to take up the matter of subsistances. Boiscommun decided that it was not in the same "position" as Chalon and refused to adhere to its program. The clubbists at Pithiviers concluded that their brothers at Chalon were "unenlightened." Créon printed a rebuttal in which it stated that the free circulation of grains alone would provision the country and establish a "general equilibrium" of prices.[35]

In March and April the British blockade and the insurrection in the Vendée immeasurably worsened shortages. Disturbances occurred almost daily in the capital, and leaders of the sections appeared with menacing repetitiveness before the Convention. On April 5 the Quatre-Nations section called for an inventory of grains and taxes on the rich to provide for the poor. That night, the deputies voted in principle that bread prices should be stabilized at a level relative to workers' salaries, and that the costs of this arrangement should be borne by the well-to-do. This resolution was negated, however, by a proviso that no harm should come to commerce. On April 18 the Commune and Department of Paris presented a new petition demanding a *maximum* on grains and laws to compel merchants and farmers to open up their granaries. The Convention could not ignore it. By this date the Montagnards had accepted the need for such legislation and championed it. The opposition was led by Girondins like Barbaroux and Ducos, who argued that price controls would worsen scarcities,

[34] Carraz, "Chalonais," pp. 176–178; AN, C 247; PV: Nuits, Feb. 15–Mar. 4, 1793; Vaison, Mar. 10, 1793; Toulouse, Feb. 28, Mar. 5, 1793.
[35] COR, Bordeaux, 12 L 38. PV: Bourbonne, Feb. 27, Mar. 6, 1793; Boiscommun, Feb. 27, 1793; Pithiviers, Feb. 27, 1793.

weigh heavily upon farmers, and be impossible to enforce. Exasperated by delays, eight thousand sansculottes surrounded the Convention on May 1 and threatened an insurrection if their demands were not met. The next day the deputies decreed a *maximum* on wheat, which, however, was to be determined by each department.

During the debates that preceded the enactment of the *maximum*, a number of clubs aligned themselves with the sections. Ever vocal on the topic of subsistances, Dijon declared publicly that the April 5 resolution of the Convention was insufficient, and that the only remedy for the crisis was a nationwide tariff on grains. Blois, Nuits, and Tulle queued up behind Dijon. Ingouville and Le Havre called jointly for a *maximum* on wheat. Thann and Rouen solicited price controls on all basic commodities. Valence enthusiastically adhered to the April 18 petition of the Commune of Paris.[36]

While many societies deplored the tactics of the sections and their threats against the Girondist deputies, none, to my knowledge, protested against the *maximum* after its passage. On the contrary, it was generally hailed as a "wise and beneficent measure," and departmental officials were prodded to implement it immediately. Some clubs, particularly but not strictly the stalwarts of the Left, wanted the Convention to go further. Moulins sought a *maximum* on barley, hay, and straw, and requisitions from wealthy landowners. Toulouse called for a uniform price on all grains throughout the nation. Montauban campaigned for a *maximum* on all commodities. Yvetot, Magnac-Laval, and Tartas approved analogous resolutions. Even Lourdes, which was pro-Girondin, wished to expand price controls.[37] A remarkable *volte-face* had occurred since the murder of Simonneau in 1792. It was now clear to all but the most rigid ideologues of the Right that deregulation had not worked.

---

[36] COR, Poitiers, S 33. Forot, *Tulle*, p. 253. PV: Nuits, Apr. 28, 1793; Rouen, Apr. 28, 1793; Ingouville, Apr. 16, 1793; Le Havre, Apr. 15, 1793; Thann, Apr. 28, 1793; Valence, May 5, 1793.

[37] COR: Reims; Poitiers, S 33–34. PV: Toulouse, May 14, 26, 29, 1793; Tartas, June 9, 1793; Pau, May 9–10, 17, June 1–2, 1793; Magnac-Laval, June 2, 1793; Eymoutiers, June 6–8, 1793; Bourbonne, May 19–22, 1793; Laval, May 9, 1793; Lourdes, June 4, 1793; Mayenne, May 11, 1793.

V

The Monetary Crisis

Prior to the Revolution, France suffered from a chronic shortage of specie (*numéraire*). After 1789, gold and silver coins almost vanished from circulation. The dearth of capital caused the Constituent, in 1790, to approve the issuance of 1,200,000,000 livres of paper notes, the famous assignats. Public reluctance to accept paper money meant that from the first, the assignats were worth less than specie. Moreover, they were printed in large denominations of fifty livres or more and, therefore, did little to relieve the shortage of coin. Consequently, the Constituent was compelled to consider a new emission of assignats in smaller denominations.[1]

Many deputies were hesitant to take this step, arguing that it would cause the brunt of the effects of depreciation to fall on the working class; in addition, they predicted that base coins (*monnaie de billon*), with which workers were paid, would disappear. However, proponents of a new emission countered that the plight of laborers was already bleak. Trade was declining, said they; and employers were laying off workers. Ultimately, in May 1791, the Constituent approved an emission of five-livre assignats. It also asked royal mints to coin enough *billon* to meet the needs of the country and facilitate the exchange of the five-livre bills.

Unhappily, months passed, and few of the five-livre notes reached the departments. The large assignats in circulation, which had fallen only 7 to 10 percent in value in most areas up to June 1791, began to depreciate more rapidly. To make matters worse, the monnaie de billon promised by the deputies failed to materialize. On the contrary, it became scarce. On the eve of the

---

[1] Most of the general information in this chapter is taken from S. E. Harris, *The Assignats* (Cambridge, 1930), and the previously cited classic of A. Mathiez, *La Vie chère*.

Legislative Assembly, France was in the throes of a veritable monetary crisis.

There were practical reasons for the delays and shortages. Mints, for example, were too few in number and did not have sufficient quantities of copper. But the clubs glibly laid the blame for the crisis on hoarding, speculation, and exports of bullion by émigrés. Toulouse, in a published circular, railed at the "boundless greed of capitalists." Bar-sur-Aube caused a primal shudder to go through the network when it announced the discovery, in late September, of two chests filled with hoarded five-livre notes.[2]

In August–September 1791, the clubs launched a campaign for the minting of more billon and an additional emission of petite assignats. The lobbying effort commenced when Thionville and Chalon-sur-Saône distributed printed copies of petitions that they had sent to Paris. Only bits and pieces of Thionville's circular have come down to us. Chalon's, which was dated August 24, demanded that all assignats over three hundred livres be withdrawn from circulation and replaced with notes of twelve to thirty-six livres, or ten to thirty livres. It began thusly:

> The creation of assignats is one of the most glorious operations of the National Assembly. They have saved France. That today, however, they are falling greatly in value is a truth that even good citizens cannot deny. And the dearth of money is such that the exchange of paper against specie is becoming impossible. It is the poorest citizens, and consequently the most precious, who are suffering because of the truly perverse men who are hoarding or exporting their riches.[3]

By the end of November 1791, more than thirty clubs had approved petitions of the same type. Poitiers, Valenciennes, and Bédarieux published and circulated theirs. All of the societies concurred on the need for more base coins and the conversion of large assignats into petty ones, but they differed greatly on the

[2] COR, Montpellier, L 5549. *CD*, Oct. 3, 1791.
[3] R. Carraz, "A propos de l'émission de billets de confiance à Chalon-sur-Saône," *Revue d'histoire économique et sociale* (1975), pp. 37–51. COR, Bordeaux, 12 L 30. PV, Toulouse, Sept. 3–5, 1791.

values that should be assigned to the new notes. Some left the details up to the legislators. Others, like Chalon, favored units
ranging from ten to thirty-six. A great many advocated more
five-livre coupons, and a few wanted units as low as fifty sous
(two-and-one-half livres).[4]

On December 17, after considerable debate, the Legislative Assembly authorized an emission of 300,000,000 livres worth of assignats of ten, fifteen, and twenty-five livres. A week later, after
additional wrangling, it approved the issuance of a quantity of assignats of ten, fifteen, twenty-five and fifty sous. Neither action
did much to relieve the monetary crisis because it took an uncon-
scionable length of time to design and print the new bills. On
April 3, a spokesman for the Committee on Assignats reported
that the twenty-five livre denominations were only then being
circulated; those under fifty sous were not expected to be ready
until June.

In early 1792 the five-livre assignats approved the previous
May finally reached the departments in significant numbers. Paradoxically, their appearance merely aggravated monetary woes.
Because of the persistent shortage of small coins, employers had
to use the assignats to pay salaries. Since five livres was more than
the worker needed for food and daily necessities, he had to break
it down into smaller quantities, to trade the paper notes for scarce
coins. In the process, he paid dearly. Many merchants and farmers refused to accept assignats at all. Those that did often charged
two prices, one for paper and one for coin.

S. E. Harris has calculated that in most regions, by the opening
of 1792, the assignat had plunged to about 60 to 75 percent of its
face value. And these figures jibe closely with comments made by
the clubs. Roubaix, for example, reported that in exchanging
five-livre assignats for coins, its citizens were losing thirty to
forty sous. Annonay lamented: "Copper coins are so rare that
one cannot change them for assignats unless he is willing to part

[4] AN, D VI, DVII 2. *JD*, Nos. 76, 104, 111. Forot, *Tulle*, p. 154. *Journal patriotique de Grenoble*, Sept. 24, 1791. *ArchP*, Oct. 20, 23, 1791. Carraz, "Billets," pp.
37–51. Aubert, "Douai," pp. 232–233. PV: Bar-le-Duc, Sept. 3, 19, 24, 1791. PV:
Montpellier, Sept. 26–30, Nov. 8, 1791; Versailles, Oct. 21, 28, 1791; Tonneins,
Oct. 23, 1791; Niort, Oct. 26, Dec. 9, 1791; Sète, Oct. 15, 1791; Toulouse, Sept.
3–5, Oct. 19–26, 1791; Lorient, Oct. 6, 1791; St.-Malo, Sept. 9, 1791; Chalon,
Nov. 3, 1791. COR: Reims; Poitiers, S 19.

with twenty sous." Le Mans grumbled: "Capitalists here do not blush at demanding twenty-four to thirty sous in exchanging an assignat of five livres." Ornans claimed that forty to fifty sous was the going rate there, and whimpered: "The rich and selfish are profiting. Citizens with middling fortunes are being ruined. The poor are reduced to misery."[5]

The worsening conditions gave rise to a new spate of demands from the clubs for legislative action. The deputies were cajoled to speed up the issuance of the small assignats approved in December. New emissions were called for in denominations below ten sous. Some societies pressed for the establishment of mints in each department. Others lobbied for the total suspension of the manufacture of gold and silver coins. A few advocated the use of metal from church bells, which, they said, "serve only to deafen the living under pretext of honoring the dead."[6]

Much emphasis was placed on legislation designed to stop hoarding and speculation. Boulogne, Béthune, Ornans, and others wanted official bureaus in every major city and district, where citizens could get coin for their paper notes without fear of loss. A multitude of societies sought fines or prison sentences for those who profiteered from the exchange of assignats. Many also pled for criminal penalties for exporters of specie and merchants who put two prices on their wares.[7] The implementation of such legislation would have marked a retreat from the laissez-faire economic system instituted by the Constituent, as the clubs were well aware. Indeed, in a petition of January 23, which was printed and circulated to affiliates, Lorient called specifically for the revocation of a resolution of May 17, 1791, which declared that the money trade was free like all other forms of commerce. Following Lorient's lead, at least eleven other clubs (Poitiers, Bergerac, Toulouse, Lectoure, Marseille, Aix-en-Provence, Le Havre,

[5] COR: Poitiers, S 26; Colmar, B 34; Niort, L2ᵉ Supp 2. *JC*, Feb. 22, 1792. *CD*, Feb. 20, Mar. 1, 1792. Rostaing, *Annonay*, p. 175.
[6] AN, D VI, D VII 2. *ArchP*, Feb. 22, 1792. *JC*, Feb. 22, Mar. 8, 19, 31, Apr. 5, 12, May 26, 1792. *CD*, Feb. 20, 1792. COR, Niort, L2ᵉ Supp 2. PV: Niort, Jan. 11, 1792; Lille, Jan. 17, 1792; Perpignan, Feb. 4, 1792.
[7] AN, D VI, D VII 2. Rostaing, *Annonay*, p. 175. *JD*, Jan. 4, 1792. *JC*, Feb. 27, Mar. 15, Apr. 20, 1792. *CD*, Feb. 20, 1792. *AP*, Feb. 12, 1792. Forot, *Tulle*, p. 167. Holuigue, *Boulogne*, pp. 240–241. COR, Lille, Jan. 31, 1792. PV: Lorient, Jan. 16, 1792; Montpellier, Feb. 5, 1792; Lille, Jan. 29, 1792.

Auxerre, Toulon, St.-Maximin, and Pertuis) also demanded the repeal of this resolution.[8]

By far the most radical cure for the monetary crisis was suggested by Granville on January 11, 1792. It urged Frenchmen, whenever possible, to pay in kind for goods and services, and touted the virtues of a barter economy: "In lands where money is rarest, the people live in plenty. In those where gold and silver circulate, one sees only two conditions: misery and opulence. Twenty *écus* of our money would have made the fortune of a Roman senator in the time when that infant republic was laying the foundations of a universal empire."[9]

From the clubs came a bevy of addresses in early 1792 designed to instill confidence in the assignats. Citizens who were willing to accept paper notes in trade or pay were praised to the skies. Wishing to be models for others, the clubbists took vows to do nothing to discredit the nation's currency. Lorient's oath of January 9, which it printed and circulated, was couched in the following terms: "I vow never to sell or buy French money or assignats with the intent of profiting from their resell. I vow never to profit from the exchange of small assignats for large ones, a commerce which is as shameful as it is harmful to the welfare of my country. I pledge . . . never to assign to the same object separate prices for silver and assignats."[10]

THE inability of the Legislative Assembly to provide abundant supplies of money led, in early 1792, to a resurgence of interest in *billets de confiance*. They were, in essence, local paper notes intended to replace specie. Employers paid them to their workers; workers used them to buy food; merchants redeemed them at special banks called *caisses patriotiques*. They had first appeared in 1790, and by 1791 they were circulating in numerous towns. The Constituent Assembly, unable to stop their spread, officially rec-

---

[8] *JC*, Feb. 27, Mar. 1, 5, June 14, 1792. *JDM*, p. 209. Labroue, *Bergerac*, p. 202. COR, Lorient, Jan. 25, 1792. PV: Lectoure, Mar. 14, 1792; Le Mans, Feb. 16, 1792; Le Havre, Jan. 29, 1792; Niort, Feb. 5, 1792; Toulouse, Feb. 6, 1792.

[9] *JC*, Jan. 24, 1792.

[10] *JC*, Feb. 27, Mar. 10, 1792. *CD*, Mar. 1, 1792. Labroue, *Bergerac*, p. 198. COR, Poitiers, S 26; Niort, 3003. PV: Lorient, Jan. 9–10, 1792; Le Mans, Feb. 26, 1792; Le Havre, Jan. 29, 1792; Niort, Jan. 25, 1792; Montreuil, Feb. 7, 1792.

ognized their existence on May 20, 1791, putting them under the purview of municipal authorities.

Initially, the clubs were all abubble with enthusiasm for the billets. In many instances, they conceived the idea for their issuance, drew up the plans, and provided the initial investment of money and assignats. By the end of the Constituent, however, misgivings had begun to develop. For unspecified reasons, Chalon-sur-Saône, after persuading its commune to emit forty thousand livres of billets de confiance, suddenly demanded on September 10, 1791, that their issuance be postponed indefinitely. At Paimboeuf, on the other hand, there was clearly popular resistance to the billets. Maritime operations in this small city were at a standstill because of the disappearance of specie. To remedy matters, the club had decided in July 1791 to establish its own caisse, which would emit coupons of ten sous. On August 2, however, this scheme was abruptly abandoned when a member warned that "it could not be implemented without causing the most lively fermentation among the workers." The coupons that had already been printed at Nantes were put in storage and later burned.[11]

A similar sequence of events unfolded at Boulogne. Here too, commerce was in decline and jobs were being lost. And the society, in August 1791, decided to try to stimulate the economy by issuing over forty thousand livres in billets de confiance. Alas, the local workers preferred to be paid in specie and assignats. They first petitioned the club to reverse its decision and then coerced it into doing so. On September 30 there was a surpassingly ugly scene. Wage-earning coopers and carpenters, who had come to the session en masse and packed the galleries, threatened members by name and went "beyond the limits of civility and decency." Thoroughly cowed, the clubbists promised to burn the billets and never to speak of them again.[12]

By early 1792, however, the monetary situation had become so bleak that billets de confiance returned to favor. The clubs, as in the previous year, led the charge. As "the only means to put an end to the distress of workers," Douai voted on January 1 to ask

[11] Kennedy, *Jacobins*, pp. 134–137. PV, Paimbeouf, July 5–Sept. 5, 1791.
[12] Holuigue, *Boulogne*, pp. 258–264.

its Commune to create coupons of five, ten, and twenty sous. At Bourbourg, on January 1, the club denounced city fathers for denying a similar request. A project for printing billets was discussed at Honfleur on January 8–10 and approved on the 17th. Aiguesvives, about the same date, adopted a plan to fabricate paper notes ranging from one to fifty sous. In a speech of January 23, the president of the Montreuil club said that the issuance of billets of five to twenty-five sous was the "only antidote for the disappearance of specie, the ruinous speculation on five-livre assignats, and the losses suffered by workers in exchanging them." Three weeks later the Municipality of Montreuil agreed to manufacture some. The "total disappearance" of numéraire and the "ruinous losses" that citizens were incurring in making small purchases with five-livre assignats also caused Chatillon-sur-Chalaronne to petition its Commune to print billets de confiance.[13]

This agitation continued right up to the Declaration of War in April.[14] The reader has surely noted how often the clubs claimed to be acting in the interest of poor workers. To doubt the sincerity of these pronouncements would be unduly cynical; but one also detects, occasionally, a note of self-interest, a fear of social revolution. Lorient and Crémieux, in February, admitted that they were afraid of "insurrections" because of the rarity of specie and the depreciation of five-livre assignats. Le Mans, in the same month, asked the Department of the Sarthe to issue billets, and in an aside said that the people were blaming it for the shortage of numéraire.[15]

Under such circumstances even the clubs that had backed away from emissions in August and September were ready to try again. On February 22 Chalon petitioned its municipality to issue billets.[16] Boulogne was also compelled to reevaluate its position. It must have spoken of its past troubles in a letter to Lille in which

[13] Lefebvre, *Bourbourg*, p. 25. Rouvière, *Gard*, II, 30–31. Aubert, "Douai," p. 233. PV: Montreuil, Jan. 23, 1792; Chatillon-sur-Chalaronne, Jan. 22, Feb. 19, 1792; Honfleur, Jan. 8–19, 1792.

[14] Guillemaut, *Louhans*, I, 486–489. PV: St.-Affrique, Apr. 8, 1792; Nuits, Apr. 15, 1792; Tonneins, Mar. 16–19, 1792.

[15] *JC*, Feb. 27, Mar. 26, 31, 1792. PV: Le Mans, Feb. 12, 19, 1792; Lorient, Feb. 23, 1792.

[16] Carraz, "Billets," pp. 50–51.

it sought help in obtaining *monnaie de billon*. For Lille, on February 4, 1792, sent this reply: "The veritable remedy for this evil, and the only one which has had success is, as you know, the emission of *billets de confiance*. It is true that the people, like bad children, at first balk at taking this medicine. But good patriots have to try to persuade them of its worth."[17]

It was not the advice of Lille, however, but the voice of the people that caused Boulogne finally to act. The situation of the workers became so desperate that even they were ready for the introduction of billets. On April 20, a delegation representing "the seamen and the majority of inhabitants of Boulogne" appeared before the club and demanded the creation of local paper notes of five, ten, and fifteen sous. The club carried this request to the municipality, which agreed a week later.[18]

While some workers had become reconciled to the billets de confiance, it is clear from club minutes that formidable opposition was still encountered from other quarters. At Tonneins, in March, several members objected to their issuance on the grounds that they were too easily counterfeited and would exacerbate the shortage of specie. Before the Louhans club could get them introduced, it had to allay fears that farmers would take their crops elsewhere.[19] In truth, peasants were likely to sell their crops in cities that did not have the billets. Merchants also put up a stubborn resistance to the paper coupons.[20]

The proliferation of local paper notes in 1792 caused tremendous problems, as even the clubs came to realize. Valenciennes became so concerned about the excessive numbers and types that it asked the Legislative Assembly in June to establish special "banks" in departmental cities, where they could be redeemed and exchanged. Rodez, in December 1792, sent to the Montpellier society a package containing billets from 105 communes and at least 8 departments of the Midi. Nearly all, it said, belonged to workers and indigents of Rodez, and it begged for help in trying

[17] COR, Lille.

[18] Holuigue, *Boulogne*, pp. 267–268.

[19] Guillemaut, *Louhans*, I, 486–489. PV, Tonneins, Mar. 16–19, 1792.

[20] Aubert, "Douai," p. 234. PV: Vannes, May 17, 1792; Lorient, Dec. 29, 1791; Toulouse, Feb. 3, 1792.

to negotiate them. "They [the coupons] will die in the hands of the poor if you do nothing."[21]

AFTER April 20, 1792, for a span of about four months, club minutes and correspondence speak less of monetary matters. The war and the death rattles of the monarchy transfixed all France. Besides, there is evidence that the monetary crisis eased somewhat. At any rate, the slippage of the assignats was checked, and they actually gained some ground. In the fourth quarter of 1792, however, depreciation recommenced. By the spring of 1793, assignats were worth only 30 to 50 percent of their face value. The result, in the clubs, was a renewal of concern about monetary questions.

That the clubs, in late 1792 and 1793, were greatly troubled by the monetary crisis is evidenced by the number of times that they petitioned the Convention on this and related matters. Calls for the death penalty for anyone who trafficked in assignats or refused to accept them at face value, became increasingly common.[22] The decree of May 17, 1791, recognizing freedom of commerce in gold and silver, once again became a major issue. In early October, Condom called for the repeal of this measure. The Récollets Society approved a similar petition on October 24–26 and sent copies to affiliates with appeals for adhesion. Many clubs did adhere. Another petition drive, linking the repeal of the May 17, 1791, resolution with a ban on the possession of gold and silver coins, started in 1793. Interestingly, some of the petitions of 1793 contained violent attacks upon the rich. The club of Machecoul hammered at the "newly arisen, pecuniary aristocracy . . . engaged in the shameful traffic in money." Aix-en-Provence also thundered against the "cupidity" of plutocrats.[23]

The Convention long resisted such demands, just as it did calls for the regulation of the grain trade. On April 11, 1793, however, it yielded to the outcries of the clubs and the Paris sections and

---

[21] *JC*, June 29, 1792. *ArchP*, July 10, 1792. COR, Montpellier, L 5547.

[22] *JC*, Sept. 24, 1792. AN, C 247. Forot, *Tulle*, p. 236. PV: Ornans, Sept. 15, 1792; Toulouse, Oct. 10, 1792.

[23] *ArchP*, Oct. 16, 1792; Feb. 7, 25, 1793. Poulet, "Thann," p. 377. COR, Bordeaux, 12 L 29. PV: Bordeaux, Oct. 24–26, 1792; Valence, Feb. 10, 1793; Aix, Feb. 1–14, 1793; Toulouse, Feb. 26, 1793.

decreed that all commercial transactions should be in assignats alone. The clubs were jubilant. Sarrebourg, on learning of the passage of this law, insisted that local authorities promulgate it before assemblies of the people. Epinal published an extract of its session of May 19 in which those in attendance vowed to uphold this act. Tartas suggested that a one-hundred-livre bounty be given to anyone who denounced a violator. [24]

On the eve of June 2, in spite of the depreciation of the assignats, most of the clubs still had faith in them. Indeed, even at this date, some called for new emissions of small notes. It is true that Caen circulated a petition in March and April asking affiliates if it "would not be expedient to annihilate the great mass of assignats." And Toulon, Dijon, and Toulouse answered this query affirmatively. Apparently, however, Caen was referring to the large denominations, not the smaller ones. [25]

[24] A. Troux, *La Vie politique dans le département de la Meurthe* (Nancy, 1936), I, 328–329. AN, C 255. PV, Tartas, May 20, 1793.

[25] Chardon, *Rouen*, p. 27. *ArchP*, Apr. 15, 1793. PV: Toulouse, Feb. 26, Apr. 11, 1793; Pau, June 4, 1793; Marseille, Mar. 11, 1793.

VI

Land Reform and Emigré Properties

THOSE WHO championed liberal economics in the Convention contended that price controls on commodities were an infringement of property rights, a step toward an agrarian law. The *loi agraire!*" Today these words would likely evoke puzzlement rather than apprehension; but in French Revolutionary times, they were a phantom that haunted property owners. Educated Frenchmen had a keen knowledge of Roman history and were likely to think immediately of the Licinian Rogations which restricted the amount of land that any citizen could hold, or of the efforts of Tiberius and Gaius Gracchus to limit the size of estates and divide the surplus among the poor.

Time and again, the clubs expressed repugnance for such legislation. Replying to allegations made against the Paris Jacobins, Robespierre stated that the agrarian law was "an absurd scarecrow set up for the stupid by the depraved, as if the defenders of liberty were madmen capable of conceiving such a project." The societies of Orthez and Thann reassured farm owners in their districts that the Convention would never countenance a measure that "violated the sanctity of persons and properties." Montargis rejected a motion to restrict the amount of lands that an individual could lease or hold, on the grounds that it was "impossible to limit the distribution of properties in a free country." The Popular Society of Nîmes grumbled to the Convention about the "dangerous sect which is charging us with preaching the division of lands, we who regard the preservation of persons and properties as one of our sacred responsibilities." Nîmes went on to demand the execution of those who called for a redistribution of property as well as those who falsely accused others of this. Even Marseille renounced the agrarian law. One of its members printed this admonition to peasants in the summer of 1792:

"Equality of fortunes can no more exist than equality of bodily strength and height. . . . Every time someone says to you: THE PROPERTY OF YOUR NEIGHBOR IS MORE EXTENSIVE THAN YOURS. YOU SHOULD HAVE HALF OF IT. Shun that man. He is a veritable enemy of the constitution." Later in that year Marseille published a circular on the same subject, inviting affiliates to propagate its principles in the countryside "where there are many less enlightened men easily induced into the error that property should be shared equally."[1]

The sanctity of property! No agrarian law! These then were the professed credos of the clubs in the Legislative Assembly and early Convention. Yet, the societies prided themselves on being "guardians of the poor and oppressed." As quickly as an indigent was brought to their attention, an impromptu collection was held on his behalf. Receptacles were placed in assembly halls for the reception of alms. A perennial topic of discussion was: How can poverty be abolished? From such debates came a plethora of plans for public workshops and charitable institutions. Versailles, in late 1791, even broached a proposal for a national welfare system.[2]

This concern about poverty was not just a manifestation of a Christian upbringing, or a crass, politically inspired move to win over the masses. It was an extension of the most advanced social thinking of the Enlightenment, of the belief that extremes of opulence and indigence were detrimental to the good health of society. Club orators stressed that the poor needed the economic means to insure the full exercise of their political rights, and they fully concurred with Rousseau's dictum that "in a free country there must not be extreme inequality of wealth." The problem, as the society of Périgueux saw it, was: "What are the means to prevent an excessive increase in personal fortunes, which might one day be injurious to liberty . . . , while at the same time respecting justice and property?"[3]

[1] A. Mathiez, *The French Revolution* (New York, 1929), p. 211. *JDM*, Oct. 20–25, 1792. AD, Bouches-du-Rhône, L 2038. Rouvière, *Gard*, III, 195–196. PV, Orthez, Nov. 22, 1792. Poulet, "Thann," p. 376. PV, Montargis, May 24, 1793.

[2] Cf. *AP*, Oct. 23, 1791. AD, Saône-et-Loire, 4 L 1. PV: Versailles, Sept. 31–Oct. 19, 1791; Condrieu, Oct. 2, 1791; Le Mans, Oct. 16, 1791; Chalon, June 1–4, 1792.

[3] *JC*, Aug. 16, 1792. PV, Périgueux, Mar. 12, 1793.

One possible solution to this conundrum was the modification of inheritance laws. Revision of statutes and customs relating to succession commenced in the Constituent Assembly. On March 15, 1790, the rule of primogeniture was abolished for noble property. Then, in April 1791, equality of succession was decreed in all cases in which the deceased left no will. At the time of the passage of the first of these measures, few clubs existed. During the debates that preceded the second act (October 1790–April 1791) more than thirty societies sent petitions to the Constituent demanding specific reforms.[4] No significant laws were enacted in the Legislative Assembly, and there was little comment from the clubs. The Convention renewed the assault upon old customs, however, and the societies once more interjected their opinions. On October 27–28, 1792, entailments were suppressed. Then, on March 7, 1793, the Convention approved the principle of *égalité des partages*, that is, the equal rights of all legitimate children to the estates of their parents.

On the subject of inheritance, club opinion was almost fully formed in 1790–91 and evolved little thereafter. Primogeniture was regarded as "an odious vestige of feudalism," a "slow-acting poison" that had resulted in extreme inequality in France. The clubs also endorsed the legislation regarding intestate properties. Only on égalité des partages did differences arise. Some tiptoed around the issue, saying that it was a "delicate matter that warranted close scrutiny." Others would have accorded to the head of the household the prerogative of disposing of from one-tenth to one-half of his estate, with the rest divided equally among his direct descendants. A few flatly opposed égalité des partages; and one, Le Beausset, lobbied for the repeal of the March 7, 1793, law. Le Beausset argued that it would weaken parental authority

---

[4] AN, D IV 64, 67, C 125. *CD*, Nov. 17, 1790, Jan. 13, 1791. Combes de Patris, *Rodez*, pp. 51–54. Holuigue, *Boulogne*, pp. 245–246. *Journal des amis de la constitution*, Dec. 7, 1790–June 7, 1791. Galland, "Cherbourg," p. 335. Aulard, *Jacobins*, II, 195–202, 272. *Journal de la Société populaire de Lyon*, Nos. 3, 4. Bellanger, *Provins*, p. 15. *Mercure Universel*, Mar. 20–May 17, 1791. COR: Reims; Poitiers, S 1, 19; Bordeaux, 12 L 30. AD, Drôme, F 207, PV, Valence (Friends of the Constitution), Sept. 21, 1790. PV: Versailles, Oct. 12, 1790; Toulouse, Nov. 11–28, 1790; Reims, Dec. 16, 1790; Rouen, Dec. 17–28, 1790; Poitiers, Jan. 10, 1791; Perpignan, May 30, 1791.

and that it was inherently unfair to put prodigal and disrespectful children on a par with loyal and caring ones. Sound arguments! Yet, the club of Aire censured Le Beausset on the grounds that its views were "contrary to equality and tended to revive hideous feudalism."[5]

The majority of societies, like Aire, endorsed the principle of égalité des partages. They insisted that this was not an infringement of property rights because the *père de famille* was merely the trustee of the family fortune. They likewise pointed to the "monstrous abuses" of parental authority that had occurred during the Old Regime. Then, following a Rousseauistic line of reasoning, they asserted that inequality of bequests was contrary to the "general will," that laws should not favor the few at the expense of the many. Lastly, they declared that Frenchmen would never be equal in rights as long as they had customs that led to inequality of fortunes. To favor one offspring over another violated natural law. Besides, it defiled God's law, causing obdurateness in fathers and dissension among siblings. In the land of the Declaration of the Rights of Man, Jacob and Esau had to be equal.

The benefits to agriculture and to commerce were also touted. "This is a truth too palpable to need elucidation," said one club. "Properties accumulated by the few will be badly tended, sterile. The more landowners in a state, the better the land will be worked and the more goods will be produced." Endless division and redivision of land would not leave France a country of "miserable peasants, bereft of commerce and arts." On the contrary, history proved that "commerce, arts, and sciences flourish in countries where honorable mediocrity is the rule."

THERE was a far quicker means to broaden property ownership than to wait for égalité des partages to take effect. This was to insure an equitable division of national properties. One of the most fateful actions of the Constituent had been to confiscate and sell the holdings of the Church. Unfortunately, only a tiny percentage fell into the hands of land-hungry peasants and sansculottes.

---

[5] Labroue, "Garde-Freinet," p. 57. Levy-Schneider, *St.-André*, pp. 224–229. PV: Aire, May 19, 1793; Bourbonne, May 19, 1793; Blaye, May 25, 1793; Pau, May 28, 1793; Reims, May 12, 1793; Lons-le-Saunier, May 22, 1793.

If this troubled the clubs at that time, they did not show it. To my knowledge, only two, Lille and Béthune, asked the Constituent to implement regulations favoring small buyers. One possible reason for club silence was that the conditions under which the auctions took place—in large tracts at the district seats—favored their membership.[6]

By the end of the Constituent the bulk of the Church lands had been sold. The great issue of the Legislative Assembly was to be the fate of émigré properties. The clubs had long bellowed for the punishment of the exiles and, by October 1791, were drawing up projects of decrees regarding their properties. Douai, for example, called for the seizure of the possessions of the rebels until they returned or renounced their counterrevolutionary activities. Metz stipulated that if they engaged in actual hostilities against France, their properties should be confiscated.[7]

The decree of November 9, 1791, commanding the émigrés to return by January 1 or face criminal prosecution and the loss of their possessions ended the first phase of this agitation. After the king vetoed this decree, there was another round of speechifying and petitions in December–January. In the din of indignant, uplifted voices was a concerted chorus of demands for the sequestering of émigré properties and the use of the revenues therefrom for defense expenditures.[8] When the Legislative Assembly ordered the sequestration of émigré properties on February 9, 1792, Blois lauded the deputies for freeing themselves from "the shackles of the royal veto." Perpignan warned the king: "If you veto this act, the nation will rise up and snatch the veto from your 'patricide' hands."[9]

In the weeks following the sequestration decree, demands for its implementation descended in a remorseless rain on local authorities. Haste in implementing it brought commendations. Dijon, for example, published a circular boasting of the measures

[6] Kennedy, *Jacobins*, p. 142.

[7] Aubert, "Douai," p. 229. *M*, Oct. 23, 1791.

[8] Labroue, *Bergerac*, pp. 199–202. Rouvière, *Gard*, II, 83–84. *ArchP*, Feb. 5, 1792.

[9] PV: Blois, Feb. 27, 1792; Gaillac, Mar. 25, 1792. *JC*, Mar. 19, 1792. *AP*, Mar. 1, 1792.

taken by the Department of the Côte-d'Or and citing them as a model to others. On the obverse side of the coin, failure to execute the provisions quickly elicited criticism. At Lons-le-Saunier, a vituperative exchange occurred between the club and department. The latter procrastinated, pleading uncertainty about the whereabouts of absent citizens. The club accused departmental officials of being paid agents of the royal ministers, and said that the burden should be on the accused to prove his place of residence.[10]

In point of fact, the objections of the Department of the Jura had some merit. It was often difficult to determine who was truly an émigré. Recognizing this problem, the clubs undertook a variety of actions to lessen it. Marseille, Limoges, and Chalon-sur-Saône compiled lists of émigrés and their holdings and invited citizens to make corrections and additions. Semur wrote to all of the clubs of its district for similar information. Since émigrés sometimes owned property in several departments, Vannes suggested that the Legislative Assembly collect and publish lists prepared by the societies.[11]

With the coming of war, a campaign was mounted for measures in addition to sequestration. Vannes (May 8, 1792) voted to ask the Legislative Assembly for the sale of the movable property of exiles and the use of the revenues for military purposes. On June 3, a congress of clubs of the Côte-d'Or, at Dijon, published and circulated a petition (to which several societies adhered) demanding that real property be sold as well. The Antipolitiques of Salon made an analogous proposal on July 20, but gave it a novel twist. They urged that a portion of the proceeds of the auctions be given to the families of volunteers fighting on the frontiers. Influenced perhaps by Salon, Manosque and St.-Maixent drew up almost identical petitions in August and September.[12]

Salon's proposal had radical social implications, for most of the

[10] *JC*, Mar. 10, 15, May 3, 1792. Sommier, *Jura*, pp. 96–97. *JDM*, May 3, 1792. COR, Poitiers, S 26. PV: Versailles, Mar. 9, 1792; Chalon, Mar. 8, 1792.

[11] Henriot, *Semur*, pp. 129–130. *JDM*, Mar. 26, 1792. *AP*, May 12, 1792. PV: Limoges, May 13, 1792; Vannes, Apr. 5, 17, 1792.

[12] COR, Poitiers, S 26. *JC*, Aug. 30, 1792. *ArchP*, Aug. 15, 1792. PV: Vannes, May 8, 1792; Toulouse, June 8, 1792.

volunteers of 1792 came from peasant and working-class origins. The club of Allauch, another small town in the Bouches-du-Rhône, was to push this idea further in a petition of August. Quoth Allauch:

> The excessively great landowners, the citizens who amass gold, could, if they wanted to be just, give their surplus to these defenders of property (the volunteers); but do not expect such sublime patriotism from them. Characteristically, riches stifle virtue; gold and humanity do not mix. . . . One thing can be done, legislators. Decree that the property of rebels to the fatherland should belong to its defenders. In the place of a few hundred renegades . . . , you will have gained a million loyal citizens, and the constitution will be assured a firmer base. You well know, legislators, that presently property is unevenly distributed.[13]

On July 27, 1792, two weeks after declaring the fatherland to be in danger, the Legislative Assembly voted unanimously to confiscate and sell all of the property of the émigrés. No provisions were made for the families of volunteers; but after the fall of the monarchy, the rump that had remained in session decided in principle to auction off the land in small blocks and to permit extended periods of payment. This was clearly a sop to the people. So too was the decision, on August 14, to divide common lands.

Procedures for the disposal of the personal property and household goods of émigrés were spelled out on September 2, and auctions got underway shortly afterward. Almost immediately, the clubs received reports of irregularities and peculation. Lorient complained to the interior minister that administrative negligence and the intrigues of a "cabal" had caused some precious items to be sold for less than half their real value. It urged a modification in rules so that the auctions would take place in cities rather than in isolated locales. The Récollets Society, which was also alarmed over "dilapidations," formed a special committee to oversee all matters relating to émigré property. In a circular of

[13] *JC*, Aug. 30, 1792.

November 24, it asked affiliates to emulate its action, and many did so.[14]

Of greater concern were the depradations taking place in what had been common lands and forests. In certain areas the people had not waited for authorization, but had simply seized common lands or begun to fell trees and carry off timber. Several clubs implored the Convention to do something.[15] It responded, on October 11, with exhortations and warnings to miscreants, but unfortunately, it did nothing to implement the division of the common lands. As a result, from October onward, the clubs dispatched great numbers of petitions to Paris demanding that the partitions of the common lands be carried out promptly. Most advocated that allotments be made equally and by head.[16]

The motivation behind some of these petitions was probably the fear of social revolution and further infringements on property rights. But most dwelt with seeming sincerity on the poverty of the common people and the good that could derive from more widespread ownership of property. Kindred sentiments were expressed in petitions and addresses regarding the disposal of the lands of émigrés, which had also been delayed. In April 1793, Montpellier and Marseille proclaimed that these lands ought to be sold in smaller portions "so that less affluent citizens can participate in greater numbers and experience the joy of owning property."[17]

Calls for the simple division of the holdings of the émigrés among the poor also became more common, although they were not always well received. On January 8, 1793, Montauban branded as extravagant a suggestion of the wandering actor Dorfeuille to give émigré lands to the poor. Likewise, Tulle rejected, on February 6, a member's motion to distribute one-half of the properties of émigrés to "defenders of the fatherland." But on the same date Laval decided to ask the Convention to grant

[14] COR, Lorient, Dec. 12, 1792; Poitiers, S 26. PV: Bordeaux, Oct. 9, Nov. 7, 1792; Vannes, Dec. 15, 1792. Forot, *Tulle*, p. 245.

[15] Rouvière, *Gard*, III, 80–81. ArchP, Aug. 28, 1792. JC, Nov. 12, 1792. PV: Boiscommun, Dec. 19, 1792; Blaye, Aug. 25, 1792; Largentière, Mar. 14, 1793; Lourdes, June 2, 1793; Honfleur, Mar. 28, 1793.

[16] Cf. Guillemaut, *Louhannais*, II, 46. ArchP, Oct. 25, Nov. 11, 1792, Mar. 23, 1793. JD, Mar. 22, 1793. PV, Tulette, Feb. 13, 1793.

[17] *JDM*, p. 647. PV, Montpellier, Apr. 28, 1793.

volunteers an unspecified portion of émigré estates. And in May, Moulins published a circular that suggested that one-quarter of émigré lands be accorded to needy volunteers.[18] Laval and Moulins would not have admitted it, but what they advocated amounted to no more nor less than a *loi agraire*.

[18] Ligou, *Montauban*, p. 263. Forot, *Tulle*, p. 248. COR, Niort, 3003. PV, Laval, Feb. 6, 1793.

VII

Defense of Local Interests and Public Education

THE CLUBS performed countless good works. They rendered aid to victims of illness, accidents, fires, and natural disasters. Stranded travellers (and captives of Barbary pirates) were the beneficiaries of their largesse. So, too, were foundlings and homeless waifs. Much concern was expressed in the sessions about jail conditions and the maltreatment of prisoners. Then there were the causes that can be placed under the heading of local improvements: procuring fire pumps, installing street lamps and public fountains, removing obscene grafitti from walls, putting gates on cemeteries, and so forth.

Add to the above the farsighted proposals to improve the quality of life in France. Valognes, for example, petitioned for the installation of "asylums" for the sick and elderly in each parish so that "invalids would not be deprived of consoling visits from relatives, the elderly would not be removed entirely from their children or the former companions of their labors." Also praiseworthy was the opposition of many clubs to the proposed alienation of former royal forestland. "If our national forests are sold," cried Epinal, "only rich capitalists and speculators will profit. . . . Wood will gradually become more scarce and expensive. . . . After a few generations all of our forests will be gone."[1]

On the other hand, the societies were sometimes guilty of crass local boosterism, of me-first, neighbor-be-damned attitudes. Those of the Constituent Assembly had affinities with present-day civic groups like the Jaycees. They had correspondents in the

---

[1] BN, Lb 39/ 10521, "Ne vendez pas nos forêts." Cf. E. Chardon, *La Société populaire de Rouen* (Rouen, 1909), p. 68. *JC*, Jan. 24, June 2, 1792. PV, Versailles, Feb. 25, 1792.

capital with whom they worked to secure the enactment of pork-barrel legislation, and they labored diligently to protect local economic interests. This sort of activity did taper off in the second half of 1792 and in early 1793. One reason was the prodigal expenditure of energy on war-related projects. Another may have been that the personnel of the societies was changing, that they were becoming less bourgeois. Nonetheless, defense of local interests remained a facet of club behavior right up to the Terror.

The minutes of societies of maritime centers abound with projects for the repair and expansion of port facilities. At Boulogne, for example, a plan for port improvements was read on September 24, 1791, and for ten months thereafter the club lobbied for the money and authorization needed to implement it. Above and beyond the benefits to commerce that would accrue from this project, Boulogne accentuated the need to provide jobs for starving, unemployed workmen. Whether this was truly a prime concern, or so much rhetorical pap, cannot now be determined. For better or worse, on July 6, 1792, the Legislative Assembly awarded the city a grant of 120,000 livres.[2]

Alas, in their mad pursuit of government funding, clubs of coastal towns often clashed with each other. The dust of these battles is preserved in network correspondence and in the papers of the Comité de la marine and the Comité du commerce et de l'agriculture in Paris. Cherbourg, which wished to improve its port facilities, argued that it ought to be favored over Le Havre. Dunkerque was the target of many jealous attacks. Calais said spitefully that Dunkerque's merchants were front-men of the English and bore responsibility for flooding the country with cheap British wares.[3]

Clubs of the interior looked benignly upon ideas designed to nurture internal trade and commerce. Poitiers and Niort continued to discuss a proposed water route from La Rochelle to Châtellerault. Périgueux backed a scheme to make the Isle navigable. A new canal was one of the main planks in a "Program to Stimulate the Commerce of the Southern Departments," published

[2] Holuigue, *Boulogne*, pp. 268–272. Cf. Honfleur Minutes.
[3] *JC*, Apr. 7, May 3, 1792. *ArchP*, May 2, 1792. Galland, "Cherbourg," p. 382.

and circulated by Toulouse. Bergerac longed for the rebuilding of a bridge over the Dordogne. Diverse demands were made for construction of highways, repair of secondary routes, pruning of trees along country lanes, and installation of signposts.[4]

An anxious watch was kept on legislation affecting local industries. On February 24, 1792, for example, with war close at hand, the Legislative Assembly voted to ban the export of certain raw materials, including hemp. Now, every year the citizens of the Bischwiller area sold thousands of tons of hemp at the Frankfurt fair. Consequently, the club of Bischwiller protested this law, sending addresses to the Assembly, to the Paris Jacobins, and to affiliates throughout the country. Not only did Bischwiller predict economic ruin for its people, but it suggested that the measure might be part of a "treasonable plan" to detach good citizens from the Revolution.[5]

During the vast reorganization of France in 1789–91 there was a wild scramble for judicial tribunals, departmental and district administrations, bishoprics, and the like. Municipal competition was intense, and the clubs were often thrust into conflict. Ill will persisted into the Legislative Assembly. Winners feared the possibility of revisions; losers felt cheated and looked for a chance to despoil their neighbors. Thus, the society of Peynier schemed to rob Trets of the *chef-lieu* of the canton. Bayonne, Huningue, and Beaumont-de-Lomagne tried to pluck district seats from Ustaritz, Altkirch, and Grenade. Gray had not given up hope of bagging a Tribunal de Commerce. Marvéjols claimed that Mende was a haven of counterrevolutionaries and did not deserve to be the administrative and ecclesiatical center of the Lozère. When Caen sought to have the episcopal residence transferred there, Bayeux begged the Paris Jacobins to intervene on its behalf, saying: "We cherish the constitution too much to complain of all the sacrifices that we have made for it. But we also think that it would be sovereignly unjust to take away the only advantage that

---

[4] COR, Poitiers, S 26–27. *ArchP*, Feb. 6, 1793. Labroue, *Bergerac*, pp. 47–48, 185. PV: Périgueux, Nov. 30, Dec. 4, 1791; Sète, Dec. 27, 1791; Toulouse, Mar. 26–29, May 23, 1792; Marseille, Apr. 4, 1793.

[5] *JC*, Mar. 24, June 7, 1792. COR: Niort, 3001; Bordeaux, 12 L 30. PV: Chalon, Mar. 26, 1792; Lille, Mar. 25, 1792.

it accords to us, to deprive us of a resource that we have always possessed only to enrich a city which has a flourishing commerce and all of the great public offices."[6]

Marseille had long resented the decision to make Aix the administrative center of the Bouches-du-Rhône, and after the fall of the monarchy it used naked force to rectify this "wrong." A band of eight hundred Marseillais kidnapped the departmental directors. Emboldened by this piece of banditry, Pertuis appealed to the Marseille club to make it the capital of Apt's district. Apparently Lambesc had designs on the district administration at Aix, for the Antipolitiques of Aix beseeched Marseille to take their side. The club of Albi petitioned the Convention to designate it as the seat of the Tarn instead of its rival, Castres. Tartas still aspired to be the capital of the Landes in May 1793.[7]

WIDESPREAD competition took place in 1792 over the placement of proposed new educational institutions. The Revolution had dealt education a grievous blow. By the end of 1791 colleges in many communes had become practically defunct. Primary schools were also hard hit. The clubs were in part responsible for this deplorable state of affairs. They had called for the ouster of professors who had not sworn allegiance to the Civil Constitution of the Clergy, and they had repeatedly denounced suspect teaching orders. Yet, to be fair, it should also be noted that the societies petitioned city fathers to fill professorships vacated by resignations, and initiated searches for replacements.[8]

The clubs had a deep interest in education. Not only did they value learning for its own sake, but they realized that the reforms of the Revolution would not endure if the next generation was not indoctrinated in the principles of liberty and equality. For too long tyranny had battened on ignorance. The best laws were use-

[6] *JDM*, p. 87. *ArchP*, Oct. 31, 1791, Jan. 14, 15, 1792. *JC*, Feb. 13, Mar. 24, Sept. 20, 1792. PV: Honfleur, Dec. 3, 1791; Toulouse, Mar. 10–21, 1792; St.-Affrique, Apr. 2, 1792.

[7] F. Ponteil, "La Société populaire des Antipolitiques," *Revue historique de la Révolution française* (1918), pp. 456–457. *JDM*, p. 352. PV: Lauris, Sept. 8, 1792; Tartas, May 1, 5, 1793; Castres, Nov. 26, 1792.

[8] PV: Lauris, Nov. 6, 1791; Eymoutiers, June 9, 1793; Beauvais, June 24, 1792. COR, Poitiers, S 26.

less if men did not learn to cherish them. "It is vital," said a club-bist at Auray, "to deliver infants from the hands of men who would impregnate their tender minds with vile prejudices. It is essential at an early hour to mold their malleable hearts with love of the fatherland and profound hatred of tyrants. Hannibal vowed at the age of seven to exterminate a tyrannical people, and he came within inches of causing their ruin."[9]

Believing as they did, they printed instructional manuals for youths, such as the *Alphabet constitutionnel* of a certain Venault of Tours. It blended the study of the alphabet and the Declaration of the Rights of Man. In addition, they gave their stamp of approval to short courses and seminars. One at Honfleur covered the following topics:

Sunday—Duties of a Republican
Monday—Agriculture, commerce, and industry
Tuesday—Philanthropy, public works, community interests
Wednesday—The laws, especially those on the grain trade
Thursday—Taxes: Their usefulness and type
Friday—Courts and the Rights of Man
Saturday—Readings from the best passages of ancient and
modern history, especially the crimes of French kings.[10]

The societies also backed members who established "progressive" schools. In late 1791, for example, the Paris Jacobins notified affiliates that Leonard Bourdon would soon found a Société des jeunes français which would be "the model for all genres of public instruction." A little afterward, J.-B.-M. Lacombe and another clubbist of Bordeaux announced plans to form a "national school" and asked departmental officials to let them use a former church. When the department responded that it was prohibited from doing so by law, the Récollets Society asked affiliates to petition the Legislative Assembly to grant the two educators a special dispensation. Most of the pupils in this school, which even-

---

[9] PV, Auray, Sept. 23, 1792.
[10] PV, Honfleur, Oct. 23, 1792. See also *JC*, Dec. 6, 1792. COR, Poitiers, S 26. PV, Châtillon-sur-Chalaronne, Mar. 11, 1792.

tually got underway in June 1792, were children of members of the Récollets Society.[11]

Local initiatives could go only so far. Realizing this, the clubbists, from 1789 to 1791, published a number of proposals for a national public school system. Hope ran high for a time that the Constituent Assembly would create such a system. Indeed, in September 1791, Talleyrand read a lengthy *Report on Public Education* in the name of the Constitution Committee and presented a project of a decree. However, the deputies merely printed copies of Talleyrand's report and opted to leave the resolution of this issue to the Legislative Assembly.

The Legislative Assembly gave this assignment to its Committee on Public Instruction founded on October 14, 1791. Meanwhile, that autumn, the clubs hotly debated Talleyrand's report. Bar-le-Duc, Strasbourg, Lyon, and Bischwiller put forward their own plans for teacher training institutions, and for primary and secondary schools. Most clubs contented themselves, however, with calls for legislative action. The Société des éleves de la constitution of Saintes maintained that public schools were "all that were needed for the constitution to be perfect." Vire reminded the deputies that "each moment which passes is precious, for the first impressions are the most lasting."[12] The lone dissenting voice came from the club of Ecully-les-Lyon, which seemed to be in favor of the pedagogical approach outlined in Rousseau's *Emile*: "It was in Geneva, from his father and from Plutarch, that Rousseau escaped prejudices. . . . Impose on youth only the obligation of knowing the laws. . . . Do not demand more; self-interest and nature will do the rest. . . . Require each municipality to hire one or more people to teach students the constitution, and how to read and write. Any other type of school is just a snare."[13]

For a short time, in early 1792, legislation seemed imminent.

[11] *JD*, No. 104. *JC*, Apr. 21, 1792. Bécamps, *Lacombe*, p. 69. PV: Tulle, Jan. 1, 1792; Périgueux, Apr. 16, 1792.

[12] AN F^{17} 1309, D XL 1. *Procès-verbaux du Comité d'instruction publique* (hereafter *CIP*), ed. J. Guillaume (Paris, 1889), pp. xvii, 148–151, 409–411, 416–417, 432–434. COR: Reims, Niort, Poitiers. Heitz, *Strasbourg*, pp. 168–171. *JC*, Mar. 3, 10, 1792. *AP*, Feb. 6, 1792. PV: Lille, Oct. 27, 1791, Jan. 15, 1792; Versailles, Dec. 7, 9, 1791; Le Havre, Oct. 6, 13, 1791; Le Mans, Mar. 26, 1792; Perpignan, Mar. 29, 1792; Montpellier, Dec. 21, 1791; Beauvais, Dec. 21, 1791; Sète, Jan. 6, 1792.

[13] *JC*, Mar. 12, 1792.

On March 9 the Committee on Instruction made a preliminary decision to put lycées (roughly equivalent to universities) at Paris, Strasbourg, Montpellier, Rennes, Lyon, Bordeaux, and Douai. In the next six weeks it worked out the details of a proposal which was read before the Legislative Assembly on April 20–21 by the great Condorcet. It called for five levels of instruction: primary schools in each town with four hundred inhabitants; secondary schools in district seats and in cities of more than four thousand; 114 institutes (or colleges), including at least one in each department; 9 lycées (instead of the original 7); and at the apex, a National Society of Sciences and Arts.[14]

During the discussions that preceded and followed the reading of this plan, a kind of free-for-all took place. A host of cities sent letters and deputations to Paris demanding lycées and institutes for themselves. Not surprisingly, many clubs became involved. The society of Clermont-Ferrand helped to win a lycée for that city. In a petition to Paris it reminded the deputies that Clermont had been a center of learning since the time of Gregory of Tours and Gerbert of Aurillac. Caen also lobbied for a lycée and got its affiliates in the Calvados to send supportive letters to Paris. Billom, Chinon, and Boulogne printed memoirs stating why they should have institutes. Chabot, the future Conventionnel, worked with the commune and club of Rodez to have an institute placed there, and he boasted that he had extracted a commitment from the majority of the committee.[15]

The competition was cutthroat. Autun, for example, petitioned the Legislative Assembly for an institute in the event that only one was awarded to the Saône-et-Loire. In this petition it ticked off its own qualifications ("vast, commodious, new buildings," "well-disposed promenades suitable for all types of exercises") and beggared its potential rival Chalon-sur-Saône, which, it said, was "surrounded by swamps and lacking in resources." When the club of Chalon learned of these underhanded tactics, it immediately wrote a letter of warning to its deputy in Paris. Chalon was so mad that it resolved not to support Autun's claim

---

[14] *CIP*, pp. 188–246.
[15] AN, F^{17} 1643. Cf. also Combes de Patris, *Rodez*, pp. 167–168. PV, Honfleur, May 15, 1792.

even "if more than one institute was accorded to the department."[16]

Toulouse had begun to gird itself for battle in late 1791. On November 16 it voted to order copies of Talleyrand's plan. Then, in December it formed a special committee on public instruction and asked local officials to petition the Legislative Assembly for "l'établissement le plus complet d'instruction publique." By March 1792 the delegation of the Haute-Garonne and agents of the Commune of Toulouse were lobbying in Paris for a lycée, while the club joined with local authorities, the clergy, and the Academy of Sciences in sending petitions to the capital. It also sought the aid of the Paris Jacobins and regional affiliates. St.-Affrique and Beaumont are known to have dispatched letters to Paris on Toulouse's behalf. The sharpest competition came from Bordeaux, the original choice of the Committee on Instruction. Toulouse emphasized its ancient literary and educational heritage and depicted the Bordelais as crude merchants. For weeks the club waited anxiously for news. On March 12 and 21 correspondents in Paris gave hopeful reports. At last, on April 11, the committee fixed the site of the lycée of the southwest at Toulouse.[17]

There were clashes on two levels in the Corrèze. The club of Tulle was deeply troubled when it learned on May 16 from its deputy to the Legislative Assembly, Brival, that the lone institute might go to Brive. Since it regarded the presence of an institute as a matter of "prime importance" for Tulle, it called for an emergency meeting of the commune. It also commended Brival for his "courage and rectitude" and urged him to remain vigilant (the majority of the delegation of the Corrèze favored Brive). Meanwhile, the club of Bort was determined that it should have a secondary school. In a letter to the Legislative Assembly it maintained that Ussel (the district seat) was unworthy because of "the poor citizenship which reigns there."[18]

---

[16] AN, F[17] 1643. *CIP*, pp. 289, 297. *JC*, Mar. 23, 1792. PV, Chalon, May 2, 16, 1792.

[17] AN, F[17] 1643. PV: Toulouse, Nov. 16, 1791–Apr. 25, 1792; St.-Affrique, Apr. 6, 1792. Levy-Schneider, "Le Plan de Condorcet et les prétentions rivales de Montauban, Toulouse, Bordeaux et Cahors," *Revue des universités du Midi* (1896), pp. 83–93.

[18] *CIP*, pp. 272, 312, 327. *JC*, July 28, 1792. Forot, *Tulle*, pp. 178–188.

Strife also occurred in what was then the Lot department. The club of Montauban was keenly interested in the proposed educational reforms and in the welfare of its college which, since the Constituent, was staffed mainly by its members. In late 1791 it formed a committee to study ways to revitalize the college and drew up a "model plan" for public schools. Then, in March, it petitioned for the placement of a lycée in Montauban. This petition was carried to Paris by Jeanbon St-André, the leader of the club and an official lobbyist for the city. When it became clear to St.-André that Toulouse would get the lycée, he turned his considerable talents to trying to win an institute. Unfortunately, the legislative delegation of the Lot favored Cahors, and the Commune of Cahors had five lobbyists in the capital. The Cadurciens argued that they deserved compensation for the losses of their Cour des Aides and former university (merged with that of Toulouse in 1751) and sneered that the Montalbanais were business oriented and indifferent to culture. St.-André countered that Montauban had a rich educational lineage and that Cahors had already profited disproportionately from the Revolution. But the Committee on Instruction finally awarded the institute to Cahors.[19]

Ironically, all of this back-biting was wasted in the end. Action on Condorcet's report was adjourned and never implemented. The failure of the Legislative Assembly to enact meaningful educational reform was one of the reasons radicals used to justify its virtual overthrow on August 10. On the eve of August 10, the following remarks appeared in the *Manuel du laboureur et de l'artisan*, a periodical of the club of Marseille: "The Legislative Assembly has not only neglected to attend to the most urgent measures needed to assure public welfare, it has also disdained to take the time to organize a system of national education. Corrupt men! They have considered only their own self-interest."[20]

Throughout the early Convention the clubs continued to cry out for a national system of public education. Indeed, this was one of the major themes of the nonaligned societies, those who criticized both the Girondins and Montagnards and demanded

[19] Galabert, "Montauban," pp. 297–299. Ligou, *Montauban*, pp. 274–275. Levy-Schneider, "Condorcet," pp. 83–93. AN, F^{17} 1309.
[20] *Manuel du laboureur*, No. 10.

that they carry out the duties for which they had been elected. These indignant words came from little Gardanne. "Think about it citizens. If you delay in organizing public instruction, you will be guilty of the crime of *lèse humanité*. The corrupt Romans asked of their officials only bread and circuses. . . . We want only national schools."[21]

[21] *ArchP*, Mar. 11, 1793.

PART THREE

National Defense

VIII

The Army and Volunteers to
the Declaration of War

THE REVOLUTION wrought havoc in the line army. Enticed by the siren calls of liberty and equality, noncommissioned officers and soldiers formed barrack-room "committees" and talked mutinously of their "rights." The aristocratic officers, on the other hand, generally opposed the Revolution and took stern measures against subordinates who had been corrupted by its teachings. The results were spiraling tension between officers and soldiers, desertions, incidents of insubordination, and reprisals. For the clubs, who dreaded a military reaction, the turmoil in the army posed an opportunity and a challenge. It was a propitious moment to forge an alliance with the soldiers and destroy the power of the counterrevolutionary officers. And yet, fighting strength and military discipline somehow had to be maintained.

Step one, that of cementing a working partnership with the soldiers, was achieved by the end of the Constituent. From the outset, some clubs had admitted troops to their sessions and reading rooms and given them "lessons in citizenship." Garrison commandants, for their part, tried to prevent fraternization. A major controversy erupted in late 1790 and early 1791, when the war minister, Duportail, enjoined all servicemen from attending the clubs, citing a law of September 19, 1790, which prohibited "associations and corporations" from engaging in correspondence with army regiments. The clubs protested to the Constituent Assembly and, in the end, had their way. On April 29, 1791, the deputies decreed that off-duty soldiers had the right to participate in all societies that met peacefully and without arms.[1]

The decree of April 29 effectively removed the barriers placed between line troops and the societies. In May alone, Valence enrolled ninety-one soldiers and noncommissioned officers.

[1] Kennedy, *Jacobins*, pp. 183–186.

Chartres admitted fifty-five soldiers to membership. Nevers claimed on May 13 that the entire regiment of Royal-Piemont now attended its sessions. Clubs of other garrison towns also flung open their doors to their *frères d'armes*. At Boulogne, by late 1791, regulations had been relaxed to the point that the men of the Eighty-first Regiment were permitted to be late for bed checks on the evenings of sessions.[2]

The solidarity that reigned between the clubs and the bulk of the line troops was made manifest in late 1791 and early 1792 when many units were transferred to the frontiers. Some societies were so distraught about losing patriotic units that they protested the reassignments. Tearful farewells were bidden to the departing men. Clubs along their route of march accorded them special receptions. Alençon alone honored eleven passing regiments between July 1791 and August 1792. On reaching their destinations the soldiers went promptly to the local Jacobin "temple" to pay their respects, and the clubbists responded with invitations to attend their meetings.[3]

As a matter of course, individual soldiers traveling through France went to the societies for aid if they ran short of funds or were the victims of misadventure. Libourne, in September 1791, set up the following scale of payments for military men who showed up, begging, at its doors: for men on leave, six sous per league up to the next town on their route that had a club; for men returning because of illness, three sous per league; and a generous six sous per league for deserters rejoining their units. Alas, many soldiers abused the generosity of the clubs. And numerous societies, including Libourne, were swindled by flimflam men bearing false credentials.[4]

In early 1791, while they were still fighting for the right of soldiers to attend their sessions, the clubs launched a massive campaign to have the entire officer corps "licensed" (cashiered) and replaced by patriotic volunteers. The Constituent, however, would go no further than requiring all officers to take an oath to

[2] Ibid., pp. 82-83, 186. Holuigue, *Boulogne*, pp. 140-141.

[3] Kennedy, *Jacobins*, pp. 187–188. Maintenant, "Alençon," pp. 96–97, 145–147.

[4] Besson, *Libourne*, pp. 137–138.

To make matters worse, the fleeing troops murdered their own commander, General Dillon, who had tried to rally them.

The political consequences of the defeats will be looked at later. At this juncture it is only necessary to say that they caused suspicion to fall anew upon the army staff. The Valenciennes club, which first reported the shameful details of this incident to the network, accepted the tales of the fleeing soldiers and accused Dillon and Biron (the commander of the second column) of treason. Rochambeau, the commander-in-chief of the Armée du Nord, was denounced at the Paris Jacobins. Once again cries went up for the "licensing" of the officer corps. The Popular Society of Lyon, which had a "Samson in the Temple" mentality, demanded, in addition to licensing, amnesty for the soldiers involved in the Dillon affair; the immediate amalgamation of the line and volunteer armies; and the selection of Paoli, the Corsican patriot and future traitor, as commander-in-chief.[2]

To their credit, however, most societies perceived that in this particular affair, the burden of guilt fell upon the soldiers. Douai, after first suspecting Rochambeau, wrote to reassure him of its confidence. It also called upon affiliates to labor jointly to restore discipline. Calais, in a published letter, described Colonel Berthois, who had died alongside Dillon, as a "good patriot" and demanded the punishment of his killers. Loriol and Périers praised Dillon and denounced his "cowardly assassins." Boulogne, Lille, Nuits, and others held commemorative services for the dead officers.[3]

Club orators tried to put a gloss on the initial defeats, referring to them airily as "checks." Roubaix demanded another offensive, saying: "We know that the people in the low countries are awaiting our arrival." Tarbes and Marseille found it inconceivable that France was reduced to fighting a defensive war. Behind the bravado and the vows to throw the enemy back, however, lurked fear of an invasion. Rumor multiplied every Austrian and Prussian soldier into twenty. Enemy raiding parties were said to have "violated women, despoiled children, and pillaged all that they

[2] *JC*, May 5, June 7, 18, 1792.

[3] Aubert, "Douai," pp. 240–241. *M*, May 13, 1792. *PF*, May 20, 1792. Holuigue, *Boulogne*, p. 443. *JC*, May 19, 1792. PV, Nuits, June 21, 1792. E. Debièvre, *1792. La Guerre dans les environs de Lille* (Lille, 1892), p. 16.

the Constitution.[5] This objective (the purge of aristocratic officers) was to be won largely by default. After the flight to Varennes (June 20–21, 1791) officers began to desert and emigrate in droves. By the early Legislative Assembly emigration had reached monstrous levels. Between September 15 and December 1, 1791, alone, 2,160 officers left France. Every regiment was affected.[6]

Ironically, the same clubs that in early 1791 had clamored for the purge of the officers denounced those who emigrated later in the year. Brest, Poitiers, and Besançon circulated petitions calling for military and civil authorities to publish the names of the traitors. When action was slow in forthcoming, Besançon, Dunkerque, and Lille asked affiliates to compile their own lists and to send them to the Legislative Assembly to be collated and printed.[7]

All the while, known "aristocrats" who lingered at their posts were harassed. Intense scrutiny was given to the upper-echelon appointees of the new war minister, Narbonne. Grenoble, for example, wrote to the clubs of the southwest to warn them that the recently named head of the eleventh military district, M.-C. Duchilleau, was a "partisan of Leopold." Duchilleau was soon to emigrate. Similarly, Perpignan, Limoux, and Toulouse declared their opposition to the choice of C.-G. de Choisy as commander of the Armée du Midi. Choisy resigned for "reasons of health."[8]

The places vacated by the émigrés were filled by noncommissioned officers and volunteers, just what the clubs had sought during the "licensing" campaign. By early 1792 the line army was "on the way to recovery," and the relationship between clubs and officers was improved. Indeed, certain army chiefs began, for the first time, to cultivate the friendship of the societies.

[5] Kennedy, *Jacobins*, pp. 189–194.

[6] S. F. Scott, *The Response of the Royal Army to the French Revolution* (Oxford, 1978), pp. 106–111.

[7] *JC*, Feb. 11, May 26, 1792. *M*, Oct. 11, 1791; *AP*, Oct. 10, 1791, Feb. 29, Mar. 17, 1792. COR, Poitiers, S 19, 26; Colmar, B 34. PV: Lille, Mar. 1, 1792; Falaise, Oct. 27, 1791; Alençon, Feb. 13, 1792; Vannes, Nov. 3, 1791; Chalon, Oct. 23, 1791; Toulouse, Oct. 8, 1791.

[8] *CD*, Jan. 19, 1791. *JC*, Mar. 22, Apr. 21, 1792. PV, Perpignan, Feb. 27, Mar. 26, 1792.

Rochambeau *fils* befriended the club of Givet and frequently spoke in the sessions of Maubeuge. Luckner and Kellermann won the good will of Strasbourg and Landau.[9] Dumouriez, an adventurer who saw the Revolution as an opportunity for career advancement, took especially great pains to ingratiate himself with the clubs. He was elected president of the Niort society on December 30, 1791, and gave a patriotic discourse there on February 2, which was printed and circulated nationally. This speech greatly impressed the network, which rejoiced a short time later when Dumouriez was named war minister.[10]

ENEMIES of the clubs charged them with inciting insubordination and mutinies in the army. Under these dark coatings of Revolutionary malice, the truth is not always discernible. Several times, clubs averted military rebellions or intervened to restore order. And club orators repeatedly counselled soldiers to obey the laws. Yet, there can be no doubt that the societies undermined the authority of army chiefs, sided with servicemen who were "maltreated" by their superiors, and popularized the insidious doctrine that soldiers had "rights" like other Frenchmen.

The issue of discipline versus soldiers' rights was at the root of a controversy that occurred in the early Legislative Assembly. The clubs recognized the need for a new code of military justice. Indeed, a great many adhered to the draft of a code circulated by Besançon in October 1791.[11] But they became tremulous with indignation over projects emanating from the War Ministry and the Right in the Assembly. In December Lorient raised a cry of protest over a proposal to mete out the death penalty to subalterns who struck their officers or threatened them with physical violence. Lorient thought this an overly harsh punishment for what might be an impulsive action committed in a *moment électrique*. It also argued that justice, to be fair, must cut both ways. If soldiers

---

[9] Scott, *Army*, p. 161. *CD*, Dec. 24, 1791, May 9, 13–14, 1792. *PF*, Oct. 28, Dec. 4, 1791. *AP*, Oct. 30, 1791. Heitz, *Strasbourg*, p. 224. COR, Reims.

[10] PV, Niort, Dec. 30, 1791, Jan. 13, 1792. COR, Niort. *JC*, Feb. 28, 1792.

[11] Forot, *Tulle*, p. 171. PV: Le Mans, Oct. 9–16, 1791; Versailles, Oct. 7, 10, 1791; Sète, Oct. 15, 1791; Chalon, Oct. 21, 1791; Bar-le-Duc, Oct. 10, 1791.

were to be put to death, then "despotic" officers who hit or threatened their men ought to be executed too.[12]

New regulations issued by the war minister, Narbonne, on January 1 pleased neither the troops nor the clubs. When the Béthune society read them to some companies of the Forty-fifth Regiment, the men vowed not to obey. At Calais troops of the Eighty-first reacted similarly. The club of Calais, and several others, formally protested. Mâcon, for one, described the regulations as a "work of despotism . . . , too severe, too nit-picking, too German." Most thought that officers had been given too much latitude in disciplinary matters. And all argued that the rules were unconstitutional since they had not been sanctioned by the Legislative Assembly. The Assembly concurred, and on April 7 it ordered the war minister to prepare new regulations and submit them for approval.[13]

The most celebrated breach of discipline during the Constituent was a mutiny that occurred at Nancy. It was crushed by General Bouillé, an ardent royalist, at the cost of several hundred casualties; and terrible penalties were inflicted on the mutineers of the Swiss Regiment of Châteauvieux. One was broken at the wheel. Twenty-two were hung, and forty-one were sentenced to the galleys for thirty years.

At first, most of the clubs approved of the suppression of this mutiny, but by the end of the Constituent opinion had changed. Bouillé had emigrated and was despised as a traitor. The Nancy affair was commonly referred to as a "massacre," and there was much sympathy for the soldiers of the Châteauvieux Regiment who were still in the hulks at Brest. The most outspoken public advocate of these unfortunates was the club of Brest. In September 1791, it petitioned for their inclusion in an amnesty that had been declared in connection with the promulgation of the Constitution. It also announced by circular that it was collecting money to buy clothing and goods for the prisoners, and asked for donations. Collot-d'Herbois, who was a native of Brest, started a subscription drive at the Paris club and contributed 1,500 livres

[12] COR and PV, Lorient, Dec. 5–28, 1791.
[13] *JC*, Mar. 22, Apr. 9, 30, 1792. *ArchP*, Feb. 25, Mar. 5, 25, Apr. 7, 1792. PV: Perpignan, Mar. 26, 1792; Chalon, Mar. 20, 1792.

from the profits of the *Almanach du Père Gérard*. Although few provincial clubs responded with cash at this time, some did write to the Legislative Assembly to demand the release of the forty-one prisoners.[14]

At last, on December 31, 1791, the Legislative Assembly rendered a decree freeing the soldiers of the Châteauvieux. When the news reached Brest, citizens rushed to the prison to congratulate the Swiss, and there were many touching scenes. On January 6, the Brest club expressed its appreciation to Collot-d'Herbois, comparing his efforts to Voltaire's campaign to vindicate the name of the persecuted Protestant, Calas. Three days later, it reiterated its appeal to affiliates for cash contributions. This time the response was good. By February 7, twenty-eight clubs had sent 3,499 livres, and more was to come in. Brest itself raised 5,000 livres.[15]

To the great anger of the clubs, the king was dilatory about sanctioning the decree of December 31.[16] The chains of the prisoners were not broken until February 20. On that day bells began to peel at dawn in Brest. By 8:00 A.M. a throng estimated at ten thousand had gathered at the club. Singing and cheering, the crowd marched to the prison to see the Swiss freed and to be embraced by the soldiers of the garrison. After thanks were rendered to God, there were two hours of speeches at the city hall. Then each one of the ex-convicts was taken to a private home and treated to a feast.[17]

A few days afterward, the freed men set out for Paris, escorted by some clubbists of Brest. Guingamp, Alençon, and other societies on route gave splendid ceremonies in their honor. Clubs as far away as Bordeaux and Lyon also commemorated their release. Lille wrote to Brest to ask for some links of the chains so that they could be kept as relics. At Paris a magnificent fete was

[14] COR, Niort, 3002. *JD*, Oct. 31–Nov. 5, 1791. *Révolutions de Paris*, No. 130. PV: Le Mans, Oct. 2, 1791; Versailles, Oct. 3, 5, Nov. 4–7, 1791; Lorient, Nov. 3, 1791; Toulouse, Oct. 8, 1791; Niort, Oct. 5, 1791.

[15] *Révolutions de Paris*, No. 130. *CD*, Jan. 15–Mar. 22, 1792. COR, Poitiers, S 26. PV: Niort, Jan. 18, 1792; Sète, Jan. 22–24, 1792; Lorient, Jan. 19, 1792; Toulouse, Jan. 7, 1792; Lille, Jan. 17, Feb. 1, 24, Mar. 15, 1792.

[16] *JD*, Nos. 128, 143, 144. *CD*, Jan. 21, Feb. 28, 1792.

[17] COR, Poitiers, S 26. *CD*, Feb. 29, 1792.

held on April 15. The ex-prisoners wore the Phrygian bonnet, and in so doing helped to popularize it as the symbol of liberty.[18]

There was high irony in this outpouring of sympathy for the soldiers of the Châteauvieux. For most foreign regiments were suspect in the eyes of the clubs, and the Swiss were especially distrusted. Nowhere was animosity toward the Swiss keener than in Provence. After lengthy conflicts, eight hundred national guardsmen from Marseille marched on Aix on February 19, 1792, and forced the Regiment of Ernest to lay down its arms and quit that city. Informants of the interior minister claimed that this coup was engineered by the Marseille club. What is certain is that shortly afterward, on March 16, the club printed and circulated a petition to the Legislative Assembly demanding the "licensing" of all foreign regiments.[19]

Toulouse, Châtillon-sur-Chalaronne, Blaye, Périgueux, Montauban, and Libourne are known to have adhered to Marseille's proposal. Libourne told the Legislative Assembly that France's "precious liberty should not be confided to mercenaries commanded by titled slaves." Montauban published its own circular to which Montpellier and Tonneins adhered. Huningue was quite willing to send the Swiss packing but wanted German, Scottish, Irish, and Belgian contingents to be permitted to stay if they wished to do so. Bischwiller, which was concerned about the loss of fighting men, believed that the most prudent course would be to dismiss the officers of foreign regiments and integrate the troops into regular army units. None of this had a discernible effect upon the Assembly. Not until August 20, after the fall of the monarchy, were the Swiss regiments "licensed."[20]

Uppermost in the minds of the deputies was a desire to bolster French military strength. It seemed impolitic to "license" foreign regiments with war imminent and the line army sorely depleted in numbers. In an effort to replenish army ranks, on January 25,

[18] Dobet, "Guingamp," pp. 96–97. Maintenant, "Alençon," pp. 98–100. *PF*, Mar. 19, Apr. 23, 1792. PV and COR, Lille, Mar. 4, 8, 1792.

[19] Scott, *Army*, pp. 147–148. Kennedy, *Marseille*, p. 100.

[20] *JC*, Mar. 26, Apr. 28, 1792. *PF*, Jan. 24, 1792. PV: Le Mans, Mar. 22, 1792; Châtillon-sur-Chalaronne, Mar. 21, 1792; Libourne, Mar. 21, 1792; Montauban, Mar. 23, 1792; Blaye, Mar. 22–Apr. 1, 1792; Montpellier, Apr. 1, 1792; Tonneins, Apr. 12, 1792; Lille, Mar. 29, 1792; Toulouse, Mar. 19, 1792; Périgueux, Mar. 22–Apr. 17, 1792.

1792, the Legislative Assembly had authorized a levy of men. No quotas were set as in earlier or later levies. Enlistment bonuses were fixed at 80 livres for the infantry, and 120 livres for other branches. Age limits were sixteen to fifty; foot soldiers were required to be five feet four inches tall, cavalrymen had be five feet seven inches.

By word and deed, the clubs did much to encourage enlistment. Blois wrote to all of the societies of the Loir-et-Cher to urge them to do their part. Forty-six members of the Condom club enrolled before the decree was promulgated locally. Brive let the public know about an overaged patriot who promised to provide for the family of a young recruit. Libourne lauded an elderly man who offered his sixteen-year-old son and a gold louis to anyone who would serve alongside him. From many societies came reports of success. Semur boasted of three hundred enlistments, Bordeaux of fourteen hundred, Lubersac of fifteen hundred.[21]

All was not sugar and spice, however. Brest fumed about grafters who enrolled in several places for the bonus money, but who had no intention of joining the army. Verdun complained about a provision of the law that permitted the men to choose their regiments, saying that recruits, on finding certain units filled, were returning home. There was considerable muttering about the height requirements. Citizens who failed to meet them, according to the Récollets Society, were "inconsolable with grief." St.-Mihiel wanted special battalions for short men so that France could "utilize their courage."[22]

Most ominous of all were the scattered murmurings against the rich. A feeling developed that the wealthy were not contributing their fair share to national defense. A member at Marseille snarled: "Why is it that every time it is necessary to go to the aid of the fatherland, only the less well-to-do volunteer?" The Grenoble society scolded "opulent citizens" who had failed to contribute to a fund-raising drive. At Périgueux two clubbists were persuaded to reverse announced plans to volunteer for military service after the "people" pleaded with them to stay and continue

[21] PV, Blois, Jan. 25, 1792. *JC*, Mar. 17–25, 1792.
[22] *JC*, Mar. 17–31, 1792. *PF*, Mar. 9, 1792. *M*, Feb. 11, 1792.

to "protect the indigent classes against the oppression of the rich."[23]

ATTRITION in the line army had led the Constituent, in January 1791, to vote in principle to create auxiliary and reserve branches made up of national guardsmen from all of the departments. After the flight of the king, it decreed the immediate formation of an auxiliary force of 300,000 to 400,000. Then in July and August, it ordered 101,000 of these men to go to the front as soon as possible. Organized by departments into battalions, they were to render valiant service to France. Historians refer to them as the "volunteers of 1791."

The clubbists were strongly in favor of a volunteer force. They offered themselves and their children, urged citizens to enlist, raised funds for arms, equipment, and bonuses, and sometimes made long-term financial commitments. Lunel, for example, promised one hundred livres of extra pay annually to eighteen of its "sons." For the societies and the volunteers, the late summer of 1791 was the beginning of a long and fateful association.[24]

Most of the battalions did not actually leave for the fronts until after the opening of the Legislative Assembly. The clubs, typically, gave them stirring send-offs. There were public ceremonies, feasts, embraces, tears, gifts, and patriotic exhortations. The Libourne club surprised the First Battalion of the Gironde with 4,155 livres in spending money. At Cognac, a mother, in true Lacedaemonian style, said to her son: "If you have to fight, better to die than to fall back." A professor at Dijon lectured to the volunteers on the victory of Athenian democracy over Persian despotism at Marathon. At Ornans a clubbist discoursed on the invincibility of free men. Bishop Massieu, at Beauvais, emphasized the need for obedience and moral purity. The Abbé Barquet, of the Bourg society, reminded the men that the safety of the fatherland rested on their shoulders. A volunteer of Pont-de-Vaux, the future general B.-C. Joubert, reminded those who were staying behind that they too had responsibilities: to pay their taxes without murmur, to survey public officials, to foil

[23] *Courrier patriotique de Grenoble*, Apr. 13, 1792. *JDM*, p. 7. PV, Périgueux, June 15, 1792.
[24] Kennedy, *Jacobins*, pp. 194–198.

aristocratic intrigues, and so forth. What a blow to the club of Pont-de-Vaux to lose a man like Joubert, but what a gain for France![25]

Like doting parents, the clubs kept watchful eyes upon the volunteers after their departures. Many societies had correspondents within the battalions. In one case, we know of an enlistee who contracted to send regular reports in return for a monthly pension for his wife. Another means to send and acquire information was by way of the societies of garrison towns. Perpignan, for example, received numerous queries from Carcassonne regarding the battalions of the Aude.[26] The clubs were particularly anxious that correspondence flow freely between volunteers and their kin. As early as October 4, 1791, Niort urged affiliates to persuade fathers to send letters to their volunteer sons telling them to do their duty and to be courageous. According to Niort's plan, which won much network support, the clubs were to compose the letters for illiterates and provide for the postage. By 1792 it had become common practice for the societies to help wives and parents to contact their menfolk at the frontiers. And in 1793 Montauban started a campaign to abolish all charges on mail between volunteers and their families.[27]

News that the clubs received from the volunteers in late 1791 and early 1792 was often rather pitiful. Many of the cities where they were stationed had no barracks to lodge them, little bread for nourishment, and no money to exchange for assignats. The Strasbourg club got reports that the volunteers of the Bas-Rhin at Landau lacked shoes and shirts and had to sleep in vermin-infested quarters, two or three to a bed. Afraid that disease might break out, Strasbourg shipped "care packages" to Landau filled with an assortment of items donated by a wealthy Jew.[28]

[25] *AP*, Sept. 12, 1791. PV: Cognac, Sept. 26, Oct. 28, Nov. 18, 1791; Beauvais, Nov. 15, 1791. Besson, *Libourne*, pp. 166–168. Dubois, *Ain*, II, 429–430, 446–447.

[26] PV, Orthez, Aug. 28, 1792–Apr. 21, 1793; Perpignan (L 1449).

[27] *JD*, Oct. 14, 1791. COR, Montpellier, L 5544–5545. Hugueney, *Dijon*, p. 108. PV: Versailles, Oct. 14, 1791; Tonneins, Oct. 15, 1791; Niort, Oct. 19, 1791; Sète, Oct. 18, Nov. 1, 1791; Le Mans, Oct. 16, 1791; Poitiers, Oct. 10, 1791; Lille, Oct. 18, 1791; Toulouse, Oct. 14, 1791; Chalon, Oct. 16, 1791; Périgueux, Feb. 25, 1793.

[28] *CD*, Nov. 6, 1791.

The volunteers also complained repeatedly that they had no arms, or that those which they had been given were of poor quality. The rich Récollets Society decided to provide weapons for some of the battalions at its own expense. But most of the clubs reacted by demanding action from the Legislative Assembly. Blame for the shortages was placed upon aristocratic officers and the war minister, Duportail. There was a networkwide drive in October-November 1791 to have Duportail dismissed from office and prosecuted.[29]

The most distressing single incident was caused not by ministerial perfidy, but by human folly. In March 1792 sixty-nine volunteers from the Gard were drowned when their overcrowded boats capsized in the Rhône. The clubs of the Gard were staggered when news arrived of this tragedy. Most went into mourning and organized funeral ceremonies. Even the two rival clubs of Nîmes held a joint service and made a collection on behalf of the widows and orphans. Societies as far removed as Dijon sent their condolences.[30]

Idled by the lack of arms and equipment, the battalions were prone to mischief. Recent histories of the volunteers of 1791 have debunked older accounts that depicted them as "undisciplined marauders." Nonetheless, they were frequently involved in disorders, as the minutes of the clubs bear witness. The battalions of the Oise disturbed the peace on so many occasions that the club of Beauvais had to call them to order. Toulouse fretted that its volunteers were spending too much time with prostitutes and sinking into debauchery. The First Battalion of the Gironde, in training at Bordeaux, first broke regulations by seizing a convoy of arms and then "arrested" a number of nonjuring priests. At Mirepoix volunteers insulted "aristocrats" in streets and cabarets, threatened merchants who would not accept assignats, and sacked a church where nonjurors had gathered. In Honfleur there were fights between volunteers and sailors.[31]

---

[29] Cf. *ArchP*, Oct. 26–Dec. 7, 1791. *CD*, Oct. 18–Dec. 17, 1791. *AP*, Oct. 20–Nov. 25, 1791. PV, Blois, Oct. 6–Dec. 28, 1791.

[30] Rouvière, *Gard*, II, 182–183. PV: St.-Affrique, Apr. 27, 1792; Courthézon, Apr. 24, 1792; St.-Hippolyte, Mar. 28, 30, 1792.

[31] H. Baumont, "Le Département de l'Oise pendant la Revolution," *Bulletin, Société . . . de l'Oise* (1907), p. 63. Arnaud, *Ariège*, pp. 299–304. Besson, *Libourne*, pp. 166–168. PV: Honfleur, Mar. 6, 1792; Toulouse, May 5, 1792.

Sometimes the clubs themselves were victimized. The Carvin society, in late 1791, was taken over by a battalion from the Aube. Its civilian members "retired in disgust" while the Aube volunteers, whose spokesman was the quartermaster, Forgeot, bombarded the Parisian *journaux* and the Legislative Assembly with letters and manifestos. At the Toulouse club in 1792 there were several incidents involving volunteers. On one occasion an amorous band penetrated into the area reserved for females. Aire had much trouble with volunteers stealing newspapers. The St.-Affrique society was sacked by volunteers of the First Battalion of the Tarn.[32]

In most towns, however, the presence of volunteer battalions enhanced the power of societies. The Pamiers club, tormented by a *bande noire* of aristocrats, asked for a battalion to be stationed there. Saverdun felt endangered when it lost a battalion and entreated Toulouse, Pamiers, and Perpignan to aid it in getting another. The clubbists of Ste.-Croix-de-Vie admitted that it would have been "dangerous" to form their society had it not been for the nearness of the Ninth Battalion of the Gironde.[33] The participation of volunteers in club meetings was to have very important consequences; for often, they prodded otherwise moderate societies into taking radical actions.

[32] *JC*, Nov. 17, 25, Dec. 18, 1791; *ArchP*, Feb. 6, 1792. *JC*, Nov. 10, 1792. PV: Aire, Dec. 9, 19, 1792; Toulouse, Apr. 21, 1792; Honfleur, Mar. 6, 1792. St.-Affrique, Nov. 26–Dec. 18, 1792.

[33] Arnaud, *Ariège*, pp. 299–304. COR, Bordeaux, 12 L 31.

IX

Peace or War?

I N OCTOBER 1791, the Society of Friends of the Constitution of Aix circulated an "Adresse aux Nations" delivered by one of its members, Hyacinthe Morel. The gist of his oration was that the Abbé de St.-Pierre's *Project of Perpetual Peace* (1713) was no longer a chimera. "Today the torch of philosophy has lit up the world. . . . Nothing would be more worthy of France than to seize the initiative in this project, to invoke peace with the same ardor with which others seek war. Let us instruct peoples! . . . Appeal to them as brothers. . . . Let us renounce war!"[1]

Alas, this speech is merely a historical curio, one of the last of the bric-a-brac of peace proposals that originated in the clubs in 1790–91. At that very moment, as observant clubbists well knew, chances for a durable peace were rapidly fading. Almost to a man they placed the blame for this upon the emperor of Austria. Leopold II, who succeeded his brother in early 1790, was one of the ablest men ever to sit on a European throne. Yet, his very name made the men of the clubs palpitate with fury. They regarded him as a "crowned knave," a "perverted monster," who along with his sister, Marie Antoinette, was "plotting the ruin of the Revolution."

In the summer of 1791 Leopold and the king of Prussia had signed the preliminaries of an alliance. In addition, they had declared publicly that the position of Louis XVI was a cause of "common concern" and asked the Powers of Europe for their cooperation in restoring his authority. This declaration was merely a sop to the émigré princes and a crude attempt to bring the Revolutionaries to their senses by threats. Leopold was leary of war; but, ironically, his actions made war more likely. The clubbists were enraged. Amid a din of oaths and bellicose utterances, one voice of sanity is worth recording. At Avallon on October 9, a

[1] *PF*, Oct. 18, 1791. PV, Le Havre, Oct. 23, 1791.

member contended that "Leopold has no other interest than the good of his people. He proved this during his twenty-year reign in Tuscany." Nonetheless, even this citizen admitted that it would be wise for France to be alert.[2]

In the view of the clubbists, the archconfederates of Leopold were the émigrés. As we have seen, there was a great surge of emigration after the flight to Varennes. By the autumn of 1791, club correspondence was saturated with talk of this exodus. Guingamp, for example, reported that sixty-one wagons, loaded with families and their goods, had passed through there in a single night. Domfront claimed that nobles and priests were departing in droves and selling everything that was not portable, even at a loss.[3]

The exiles were also the subject of some of the first petitions of the clubs to the Legislative Assembly. Dijon demanded that warrants be issued for their arrest. Metz wanted the law of August 1, 1791 (subjecting the property of émigrés to a triple tax) to be put into effect.[4] Poitiers admonished affiliates to prepare for any acts that might be passed, by compiling lists of émigrés from their departments. When Strasbourg announced that "cowardly deserters" had manhandled two French businessmen in Germany, a score of clubs asked the king to proclaim that the next such act would be regarded as a *casus belli*.[5]

Inevitably, the mass flight generated wild rumors. Fears were fed by the publication of émigré correspondence that fell into club hands. Confolens came into the possession of the following note from an exile at Coblentz to a local aristocrat. "Decide promptly, I beg you. It is certain that foreign armies are on the march." Longwy found a letter from Coblentz containing this plea: "At last my dear knight, the happy day is nigh. Do not

[2] PV, Avallon.

[3] *AP*, Oct. 8, 16, 1791. *CD*, Oct. 8, 1791. Dobet, "Guingamp," pp. 45–46.

[4] *ArchP*, Oct. 23–Nov. 6, 1791. *M*, Oct. 23, 1791. *AP*, Nov. 9, 1791. Galland, "Cherbourg," pp. 339–340. Aubert, "Douai," p. 229. PV: Versailles, Oct. 21, 1791; Périgueux, Oct. 28, 1791; Nuits, Dec. 8, 1791; Toulouse, Oct. 14, 1791. Labroue, *Bergerac*, p. 191.

[5] AN, F⁷ 4397. COR: Reims; Poitiers, S 19. *Révolutions de Paris*, No. 121. PV: Niort, Nov. 4, 1791; Bar-le-Duc, Nov. 1, 1791; Lectoure, Oct. 18, 25, Nov. 18, 1791; Périgueux, Oct. 26, 27, 1791; Montpellier, Nov. 4, 1791; Toulouse, Oct. 29, 1791; Chalon, Nov. 1, 1791; Lorient, Nov. 7, 1791; Falaise, Nov. 2, 1791; Versailles, Oct. 28, 31, 1791.

tarry. Come and join us. Convince your comrades who are still wavering to do the same."[6]

Coblentz, of course, was the Rhineland city where the Count of Provence had established a small court, declared his brother (Louis XVI) to be a prisoner, and proclaimed himself the regent of France. Here, and at Mainz and Trier, émigré "armies" were assembling under the command of the Duke of Condé. Small matter that Provence was debt-ridden and that part of Condé's forces drilled with sticks and barrel staves, the clubs believed them to be a menace to France and a casus belli. Metz, in particular, sent a steady stream of warnings to Paris about the movements of the émigré regiments.

Gradually, the jingoistic press in Paris sugared and frosted all of the rumors into an outlandish confection, the "Conspiration d'outre Rhin." The bare outlines of this "Conspiracy" were as follows. Forty thousand émigrés were poised to invade France. They were to march directly on Paris, while the Austrians pillaged the countryside. In the initial stages of the invasion, aristocratic French army officers would desert, and fifth columnists would congregate at agreed-upon spots and massacre patriots left defenseless by the treason of the ministers.[7]

Brissot, in his maiden speech at the Legislative Assembly, suggested that the best defense against an émigré invasion was for France to attack them. This theme was soon taken up by orators at the Paris Jacobins. Roederer, an Alsatian, said that his contacts indicated that the people of the Rhineland would rise up and aid the French. The irrepressible journalist Carra declared: "For the French, the free French that is, the offensive system is best. Heaven is with us! We need only to attack to conquer."[8]

On November 27, the Diplomatic Committee of the Legislative Assembly recommended that the king be asked to issue an ultimatum to the electors of Mainz and Trier. They were to be given two weeks to disperse the exile bands, or France was to declare war. This motion was adopted on the twenty-ninth after the deputy, Isnard, gave a fiery, half-hour address on its behalf. Said he: "Every combattant who shows fear, merely heightens the

---

6 Babaud-Laribière, *Etudes*, I, 289. *AP*, Oct. 28, 1791. *JD*, Nos. 70–76.
7 Cf. *JD*, Nos. 55, 74. *AP*, Oct. 12, 13, 1791. *CD*, Oct. 14, 1791.
8 G. Walter, *Robespierre* (Paris, 1961), I, 238–241. *AP*, Dec. 13, 1791.

courage of his adversaries. Let us tell Europe that if the cabinets engage kings to wage a war against peoples, we will incite the people to combat kings."[9]

By early December, the majority of politicians in the capital favored war. Brissot, Isnard, and the Left in the Legislative Assembly strongly espoused it. The Right was bellicose too, and even the Court had concluded that hostilities were desirable. Victory, it reasoned, would unite the French people behind the throne. Defeat would lead to the suppression of the Revolution by foreign powers. The king himself was playing a dangerous double game. On December 14, he went in person to the Assembly to announce that the elector of Trier had been given one month to put an end to the hostile acts of the émigrés, or be regarded as an enemy of France. Secretly, however, Louis urged the elector not to comply with his demand.

Initially, everyone at the Paris Jacobins also seemed to be avid for war. Billaud-Varenne was the first to dissent. In an oration of December 5, he maintained that the army was unready and led by traitors. He raised doubts about the good faith of the king, and he argued that France should deal with domestic enemies before embarking on foreign adventures. The wisdom of these remarks should have been apparent to all, but they might have been drowned in a flood of warlike rhetoric had not the popular Robespierre taken the same line in a speech of December 11.[10]

The next few weeks were critical ones in the history of the Paris club. On December 16, with the assembly hall overflowing with spectators, Brissot showed up to justify his position and combat Robespierre's. Two days later, in an equally memorable session, Robespierre delivered a refutation. Brissot gave a rebuttal on December 30 to which Robespierre replied on January 2 and 11. By the latter date it was clear that the dispute was personal as well as philosophical. On January 20, at the invitation of a mediator, the two men embraced in the club; but this public reconciliation notwithstanding, they were henceforth to be rivals.

While Brissot and Robespierre were dueling forensically, others at the Paris club were speaking their minds. Carra, Roe-

[9] Walter, *Robespierre*, I, 244–245.
[10] Ibid., I, 245–251.

derer, Lasource, Réal, Louvet, and Sillery called for offensive war. Billaud-Varenne, Machenaud, Doppet, Desmoulins, and Danton opposed it. Historians have rightly viewed the great peace-war debate of the winter of 1791–92 as the origin of the schism between the Girondins and Montagnards. At this date, however, it was a fissure rather than a gulf. Both groups were so inchoate that it is premature to speak as though they already existed. Not until September 1792 were the battle lines rigidly drawn.

The assembly of the Paris club voted to print and circulate the speeches of both sides in the debate. But the Parisian press was loaded with prowar rubbish, and the correspondence committee of the "mother society" also presented a slanted view to affiliates. In the circular of January 17, the committee flatly stated that the majority in the society wanted an offensive war. Since conflict was "inevitable," it reasoned, France stood to gain by striking first. Frenchmen, it went on, were "anxious to fly to the aid of oppressed victims of despotism," and the patriots of Liège and Belgium were only "waiting for a signal" to throw off their chains. Besides, victory would restore order to the kingdom and confidence in its monetary system.[11]

As we have seen, Billaud-Varenne and Robespierre denounced this circular when they learned of its contents; and in future public pronouncements the committee was somewhat more circumspect. But in its private letters the committee continued to beat the war drums. To Le Mans it wrote on April 5: "It (offensive war) is now the wish of all patriots. France can no longer remain in a state of uncertainty."[12]

Debates on the question of peace or war had begun in the provincial clubs in November-December. As in the Paris society, there were a few "doves." On November 6, for example, a volunteer at Beauvais gave a stirring oration against wars of conquest. France, he stressed, should defend its frontiers and avoid perilous foreign ventures. At Douai, Merlin, the ex-Constituent, also declared that war was undesirable.[13] From the outset, however, a "hawkish" spirit prevailed. Isnard's warmongering ad-

[11] *JC*, Feb. 3, 1792.
[12] *JD*, Nos. 148–149. COR, Le Mans, L 1007.
[13] PV, Beauvais, Nov. 6, 1791. Aubert, "Douai," pp. 238–239.

dress of November 29 was read over and over again, each time to greater applause.[14] A number of societies thanked the king for his ultimatum of December 14.[15] Lorient (December 20) petitioned for "war to the death" against the émigrés. Lille (December 29) voted to demand war after reading Brissot's "eloquent" address at the Paris Jacobins. Vienne, Montpellier, Strasbourg, Dole, Thionville, and Versailles likewise signified their wish for an offensive war.[16]

Five clubs published circulars in early 1792 urging affiliates to shower the king and the Legislative Assembly with prowar petitions. Dijon (January 23) declaimed: "War! Such is our hope, such is our vow!"[17] The Ambulant Society of the Vendée (February 7) preached a crusade of "peoples against Kings."[18] Clermont-Ferrand (March 10) wanted war in the name of the "welfare of the people" and to "break the union of the king and foreign powers."[19] Caen (February 15) warned that "the Temple of Janus must be opened quickly or the one of Liberty will be closed forever."[20] Beaune (March 1) wailed: "The land of liberty is surrounded by vultures. . . . War alone can extract us from this labyrinth of perplexities."[21]

Beaune asked affiliates to assign two members to hand deliver their petitions to the capital by April 5. The Paris society, according to the plan, was to present them all at once to the Legislative Assembly. Le Mans, claiming to be acting in the name of all of

[14] Le Gallo, "Cognac," p. 244. PV: Honfleur, Dec. 4, 1791; Sète, Dec. 8, 1791; Chalon, Dec. 8, 1791; Tonneins, Dec. 29, 1791.

[15] Rossignol, *Gaillac*, p. 68. Aubert, "Douai," p. 238. Besson, *Libourne*, p. 147. PV: Le Havre, Dec. 18, 1791; St.-Hippolyte, Dec. 27, 1791. ArchP, Dec. 17, 1791.

[16] *JD*, No. 116. PV: Lorient, Dec. 15, 1791; Versailles, Dec. 24, 26, 1791; Montpellier, Dec. 21, 1791; Lille, Dec. 29, 1791. COR: Niort, 3005; Lorient, Dec. 20, 1791. *PF*, Dec. 23, 1791. *AP*, Jan. 13, 1792. *Courrier de Strasbourg*, Jan. 2, 1792.

[17] Cf. Henriot, *Semur*, p. 132. COR: Reims; Poitiers, S 26. *JC*, Feb. 16, 1792. PV: Le Mans, Feb. 12, 1792.

[18] Cf. Forot, *Tulle*, p. 177. PV: Perpignan, Mar. 26, 1792; Le Mans, Mar. 22, 1792; Versailles, Feb. 26, Mar. 9, 1792; Périgueux, Feb. 26, 1792. *JC*, Mar. 10, 22, 1792. Labroue, *Bergerac*, p. 204. COR: Le Mans, L 1007; Niort, 3005.

[19] *JC*, Mar. 29, 1792. Forot, *Tulle*, p. 177. PV: Le Mans, Mar. 22, 1792; Perpignan, Mar. 26, 1792. COR: Poitiers, S 26; Bordeaux, 12 L 30.

[20] PV: Versailles, Feb. 22, 1792; St.-Affrique, Feb. 4, 1792; Lille, Mar. 15, 1792. Forot, *Tulle*, p. 173. *CD*, Feb. 20, 1792. COR: Bordeaux, 12 L 30; Poitiers, S 26. *JC*, Feb. 27, 1792.

[21] *AP*, Apr. 2, 1792. COR: Reims; Poitiers, S 26.

the clubs of the Sarthe, conformed entirely to Beaune's wishes. Tulle's straitened finances did not permit it to send two members to Paris, but it did dispatch a petition by mail. Blaye and St.-Hippolyte were excited by Beaune's proposal and decided to write to the societies of Bordeaux and Montpellier to see what they planned to do. Tournus and Chalon-sur-Saône adhered in principle, but sought the opinion of the "mother society" before sending messengers. Chalon thought that it would be an "imposing spectacle for more than 1,200 men to converge on Paris bearing addresses with perhaps 1,000,000 signatures."[22]

Cosne, St.-Affrique, Villeneuve-le-Roy, Gaillac, and Lille debated Beaune's plan, but then tabled it after learning that Leopold had died suddenly on March 1. They figured that this might "change the European political situation" and make war "unnecessary." Overall, however, the emperor's demise seemed to make the clubs more hawkish. They looked upon this event as a sign that God was on the side of France and as a golden opportunity to implant the tricolor in the Austrian Netherlands and the Rhineland. Many societies had the bad taste to celebrate Leopold's passing. Jouan le jeune suggested that Tonneins warn the Devil of the coming of this archvillain, so that steps could be taken to safeguard hell.[23]

IN THE period from December 1, 1791, to April 20, 1792, 154 clubs are known to have articulated opinions on the peace-war debate. Of these, eight expressed uncertainty. Chantilly, for example, stated that it had been impressed by the arguments of Billaud-Varenne and Robespierre, but would await a "definitive statement" from the Paris club. Speaking of the orations of Brissot and Robespierre, Allevard said: "The magic eloquence of one is counterbalanced by the pressing logic of the other. We are apprehensive about war; yet, we desire it." Montech whimpered

[22] *JC*, Mar. 22, 29, Apr. 7, 23, 1792. PV: Blaye, Mar. 15, 25, Apr. 9, 1792; St.-Hippolyte, Mar. 14, 1792; Montpellier, Mar. 17, 1792; Le Mans, Mar. 15, 20, 1792; Chalon, Mar. 8, 11, 13, Apr. 3, 5, 1792. *AP*, Mar. 29, 1792. Henriot, *Semur*, p. 132. Forot, *Tulle*, p. 175. COR, Montpellier, L 5548. *M*, Apr. 6, 1792.

[23] *JC*, Mar. 31, Apr. 5, 7, 9, 1792. PV: St.-Affrique, Mar. 24, Apr. 6, 1792; Gaillac, Mar. 22, 1792; Tonneins, Mar. 16, 25, 1792; Le Mans, Mar. 15, 1792; Villeneuve, Mar. 13, 20, 1792; Montreuil, Mar. 12–19, 1792; Lille, Mar. 11, 15, 1792. *CD*, Mar. 22, 1792.

that the debate in the Paris club had "hollowed an abyss of doubt. . . . Time will tell, but perhaps too late, what is the wisest course."[24]

Three clubs sided with the peace "party" in the Paris Jacobins. After debating the issue in several public sessions, a small majority at Auxerre declared itself opposed to an "offensive war." Fécamp also wrote to the Paris society to say that France should restrict itself to the defense of its frontiers. Beaugency at first espoused war, but its "humanitarian sentiments" finally caused it to adopt the views of Robespierre, Billaud-Varenne, and Machenaud.[25]

Four others may be placed in a "doubtful" category. Gérard Maintenant states that Alençon was prowar as early as December, but in a letter of February 23, it apparently expressed reservations about an offensive strike, pointing out that the army was commanded by traitors and that many soldiers lacked arms. Vesoul at first declared that it was "impatiently waiting for the signal to attack," but later it urged the Legislative Assembly to resolve the internal problems of France before launching a war. A club at "Guitrès," which I have been unable to locate, allegedly decided that the "favorable moment for battle has not yet arrived." Besançon reprinted and circulated Robespierre's speeches, but this may not necessarily reflect its views because some otherwise bellicose societies rendered justice to the "wise reflections" of Robespierre.[26]

All of the remaining clubs in our sample (141) demanded offensive war. Most did so insistently, echoing the warmongers in the capital and the correspondence committee. From the thickets of verbiage in club petitions, the following typical remarks have been thinned: "Since conflict is inevitable, it must not be delayed." "It is unseemly for a free people to wait for an attack." "France's warriors burn to be on the march." "War is absolutely necessary for the well-being of the fatherland. It will consolidate the Revolution . . . and restore confidence in our currency." "We

---

[24] *JC*, Mar. 10, 15, 22, 31, Apr. 21, 1792.

[25] *JC*, Feb. 13, Mar. 10, 1792. PV, Fécamp, Feb. 5, 9, 1792.

[26] *JC*, Feb. 13, Mar. 1, 3, 10, 24, Apr. 5, 1792. Maintenant, "Alençon," pp. 116–117.

agree with Roederer. To demand war is to want peace!" "War is better than the deceptive and perfidious peace in which we slumber." "The silence of the peace in which we vegetate is the tomb of liberty." "War alone can save us!" "Victory is assured!" "France is lost without an offensive war!" "Thousands will suffer, but millions will be saved!" "War brings only death; the murderous peace that we have, leads to slavery."

Since the avowed aims of the war were to punish the "traitors and despots beyond the Rhine" and to free "oppressed peoples," the clubs produced much propaganda in late 1791 and early 1792 directed at "brothers" in other lands. Toulon put copies of the Constitution on ships bound for foreign ports. To its neighbors across the Rhine, Strasbourg declared: "The moment is nigh when the tricolor will float over your soil. But we are not making war against peoples or for conquests. It will be waged solely to safeguard liberty." Clubbists in the Nord implored the Belgians and Germans not to assist the émigrés. "Do not help these enemies of mankind. Do not forget that each blow levelled against your French brothers will only rivet your own chains more tightly." Bourg addressed men of all "colors and climes," saying: "Peoples of the World! . . . Recognize that you, too, have rights which have long been defiled. Be assured also that the nightmare of despotism is at an end."[27]

In summation, although unanimity was not total, the clubs were overwhelmingly in favor of war. When they received the news of the April 20 declaration, there was carnival gaiety. Bonfires were lit. Te Deums were sung. Cheers of "Vive la guerre" rang out in the assembly halls. Oaths were taken. Letters of thanks to the Legislative Assembly spilled forth like a torrent. There was also much crowing by the warmongers. The correspondence committee of the Paris Jacobins wrote to Le Mans: "Your wishes are fulfilled. War is declared. The Society of Friends of the Constitution of Paris was divided in its opinion on this subject; but like you, nearly all of the societies of the kingdom have indicated their

[27] Dubois, *Ain*, II, 311. *AP*, Jan. 12, 1792. *JC*, Feb. 16, 1792. Heitz, *Strasbourg*, pp. 168–169.

wish for it." La Tremblade vaunted: "To whom do we owe this act of severity but of absolute necessity. We will not conceal it. It was the strongly expressed wishes of the patriotic societies, supported by a patriotic minister, which caused Louis XVI to assume the carriage of a constitutional king."[28]

[28] COR, Le Mans, L 1007. *JC*, May 14, 1792.

X

The War Effort to Valmy

GIFTS! GIFTS! GIFTS! Many a club meeting, in the weeks following April 20, may be summarized in these words. Just one speaker might say that more was needed than mere courage, that "money is the nerve of war." A single member might lay an offering at the podium, and seemingly everyone would be gripped by a patriotic fever. Men, women, and children would come forward in that session, or in succeeding ones, with offerings for the war. The gifts came in the form of assignats and specie, weapons (from pistols to inlaid swords), precious stones, and a full panoply of gold and silver objects: buckles, snuffboxes, spoons, earrings, rings, chains, buttons, bracelets, watches, medallions, crucifixes, and the like. Skilled craftsmen volunteered days of labor on military works. Actors performed plays and donated the proceeds.

Some of this treasure was disgorged on local projects such as the purchase of arms for national guardsmen or the repair of dilapidated fortifications. But a sizable portion was forwarded to the Legislative Assembly to be used for general expenditures. In May–June the Assembly received over 650,000 livres in contributions from at least 114 clubs. The largest single amount, 77,000 livres, came from the Récollets Society. Rouen, Brest, and Rennes each gave about 18,000; Montauban donated 11,650. Proportionately, some clubs of smaller places sent just as much or more.[1]

Early setbacks in the war added impetus to the gift giving. As the clubs had hoped, hostilities had opened on April 28–29 with a thrust into Belgium. Despite all of the talk about Gallic bravery and predictions of easy victory, however, two columns of the Armée du Nord were thrown back before Mons and Tournai and retreated in wild and humiliating panic back across the border.

---

[1] See especially AN, C 149–152.

could find." There was much whimpering about rundown defenses and a lack of arms. Calls went up for new levies of volunteers.[4] By July, in frontier clubs, the gloom was Cimmerian. Landau and Strasbourg published circulars in which they begged abjectly for assistance.[5]

On July 11, 1792, the Legislative Assembly declared the *patrie en danger*. In the following days it ordered new levies of forty-two battalions of volunteers and fifty thousand troops to complement the line army. These decrees caused a tautening of muscles in the clubs. Committees met round the clock. Emergency sessions were scheduled. Members took oaths to live free or to die. Inspirational addresses were printed and distributed. And in many cities, delegates from the clubs sat with local elected officials on "committees of national defense."

As in earlier mobilizations the clubs were transformed overnight into recruitment bureaus. No sooner did the Récollets Society receive news of the levies than it dispatched into each district of the Gironde four recruiters armed with authority to promise fifty livres to each enlistee. Inspired by a circular from Bordeaux reporting these actions, Libourne also sent out recruiters. One returned with eight volunteers in tow. Commissars from Marseille traversed a vast area from the Isère to the Tarn encouraging enlistment. Perpignan persuaded its Commune (July 25–27) to sign up and arm volunteers; by early September, eighty men were ready for action. Cherbourg helped to raise three companies in a two-week period. Senlis promised one hundred livres to the first four enlistees. Semur assembled three battalions of national guardsmen and lectured to them on the perils of the fatherland. When the speeches were over, a great number of guardsmen rushed forward to enroll.[6]

Many of the recruits were club members. Ste.-Foy boasted of having provided twenty-five; Lorgues claimed to have given forty. Boulogne said that it had furnished "nearly all" of the sev-

[4] Cf. *JC*, May 14–June 7, 1792. *JDM*, p. 134. PV, Lille, June 8, 1792.
[5] Heitz, *Strasbourg*, p. 232. COR: Reims; Poitiers, S 26–27.
[6] *JC*, Aug. 4, 1792. *ArchP*, Aug. 1, 1792. Heitz, *Strasbourg*, pp. 234–235. COR, Poitiers, S 26. Besson, *Libourne*, p. 183. PV: Senlis, Aug. 1–8, 1792; Perpignan, July 25–27, 1792. Henriot, *Semur*, p. 133. *JDM*, p. 336. Galland, "Cherbourg," p. 342.

enty-two cannoneers recruited there, and that they longed "to blaze a road to Brussels and transform all of the forests in Germany into trees of liberty." Enlistees who were not already clubbists were often inducted into membership and given rousing send-offs. Thirty-one volunteers were invited to the September 23 session of Ars-en-Ré and presented with 1,141 livres for travel expenses. Le Havre had a mass said for those about to leave. At Rouen women gave the Fourth Battalion of the Seine-Inférieure a flag on which was the devise, "Guerre aux châteaux, paix aux chaumières." The president amplified on these words, telling the men to show no mercy to tyrants, but to spare women and children and "those beings who are merely ignorant or blind instruments of despotism."[7]

By and large, the volunteers of 1792 came from lower socio-economic strata than those of 1791. Most were poor peasants. This had important consequences. To paraphrase J. Bertaut, it grafted a layer of sansculottes onto the regular army. In addition, it fueled class antagonism in the clubs. Strasbourg prepared a list of "plutocrats" who had done nothing to support mobilization. Lure lamented to the Paris Jacobins that it was becoming more difficult to recruit men for the armies. The peasants, it said, had already made many sacrifices and "the young well-to-do citizens of the class of 'honest people' do not come forward." St.-Rémy summed up the growing resentment when it wrote on August 1: "Emigrés and refractory priests are not the only enemies of the Republic. Add to them the bourgeoisie, that class of citizens which has benefitted most from the Revolution and contributed least."[8]

The poverty of many recruits also explains why the clubs took such a keen interest in the welfare of their families. As early as July 28, Perpignan published a circular in which it announced its intention of providing assistance to the dependents and relatives of poor volunteers. Three members of its central committee were assigned the task of identifying needy relatives. Money was given to the relatives in the form of annual pensions, disbursed in quarterly installments. At first the pensions were generous, ranging

---

[7] Richemond, "Ars-en-Ré," pp. 38–44. *ArchP*, Sept. 1, 1792. PV, Rouen, Sept. 10, 1792.

[8] *JC*, Aug. 16, 1792. Heitz, *Strasbourg*, pp. 238–239.

from 100 to 250 livres. By October, however, Perpignan had made so many commitments that almost all of the grants were provisional, and in amounts of 10 to 15 livres.[9]

Elsewhere one finds the same spirit of generosity. Like Perpignan, Beaune notified affiliates that it had opened a collection for the parents, spouses, widows, and children of volunteers and had established a special committee to watch over their interests. The Antipolitiques of Aix and Récollets of Bordeaux pledged such colossal sums for relief that each, by 1793, claimed to be doling out over 1,500 livres per month. At St.-Hippolyte a teacher offered free schooling to the children of volunteers. Aid was also given in the form of food supplements, jobs, and housing.[10]

The German powers delayed their attack until harvest time. Not until August 19 did the Prussians cross the frontier. They moved slowly but inexorably at first. Longwy fell on August 23, Verdun on September 2. Simultaneously, an Austrian army marched into France and invested Lille and Thionville. For a time hysteria gripped the capital and the country. On September 20, however, forces under Dumouriez halted the Prussian advance in a day-long battle at Valmy. Ravaged by dysentery and short of supplies, the Prussians fell back upon Luxembourg. After a savage bombardment that lasted from September 24 to October 8, the Austrians lifted the siege of Lille. On all of the major fronts, French armies went on the offensive.

Each report of the marvels performed by French arms exhilarated the clubs. Nothing could match the excitement and euphoria of that autumn. Burgeoning with new-found confidence, Bordeaux and Cherbourg purchased maps of the principal theaters of operations, with overlays so that modifications could be made with each French advance.[11] Several clubs drew up wildly optimistic plans for the spring campaigns. Potentially dangerous in its consequences was the hero worship of the victorious generals. Montesquiou, the conqueror of Savoy, was attributed "the courage of Mars and the modesty of Minerva." Custine, the vic-

<hr />

[9] PV, Perpignan, Aug. 15–Oct. 17, 1792.

[10] *ArchP*, Mar. 26, 1793. Ponteil, "Antipolitiques," p. 268. Forot, *Tulle*, p. 234. PV: Bordeaux, Sept. 11, 1792; Montpellier, Oct. 14, 1792; St.-Hippolyte, Aug. 20, 1792.

[11] PV, Bordeaux, Oct. 23, 1792. Galland, "Cherbourg," p. 384.

tor in the Rhineland, was saluted as a "new Achilles." Nice wanted to give D'Anselme, its liberator, a marshal's baton. Soaring above all in popularity was Dumouriez. The hero of Valmy was hailed as "the savior of the fatherland."

Encomiums were also accorded to the citizens and soldiers of Lille and Thionville.[12] And aid was rendered to the hundreds of "brave Lillois" who had been injured or left homeless by the bombardment. Blaye gave 300 livres, Lorient 308, the Republican Society of Nîmes 1,070, Nancy 1,553, St.-Quentin 1,706, Brest 1,898, and La Rochelle 2,722. Other benefactors included Condrieu, Vernon, Mulhausen, Laon, Beauvais, Rouen, Agen, Toulouse, Troyes, Lyon, and the Récollets Society of Bordeaux. Some of these sums were sent in care of the club of Lille. Unfortunately, those whom Lille assigned to handle the money were guilty of unpardonable negligence and let it sit idle for months.[13]

On September 28 the Convention decreed that civic festivals be held in honor of the recent triumphs. Scores took place in the ensuing weeks. The clubs planned a great many and participated in almost all.[14] Collectively, they have been referred to as the *fête savoisienne* to distinguish them from earlier and later revolutionary fetes. But they were intended to celebrate all of the victories and the proclamation of the Republic, not just the conquest of Savoy. They were a collective exclamation of relief after the traverse of the perilous months of August and September. The Popular Society of Nîmes, which announced its decision to hold a fete in a circular of November 11, bespoke the feeling of the whole nation when it said that a "brilliant dawn" had succeeded a long night of "tempest, desolation, and sadness."[15]

The centerpiece of the Nîmes fete was a banquet which "citizens of every condition and state" could attend as long as they

[12] Debièvre, *Lille*, pp. 224ff. *Journal de Nancy*, Oct. 18, 1792. COR, Lorient. *JDM*, pp. 404–405. PV: Aire, Nov. 1, 1792; Lille, Nov. 8–30, 1792, Mar. 24, 1793; Nuits, Oct. 28, 1792.

[13] See especially PV, Lille, Nov. 8, 1792–Feb. 3, 1793, and Registre des délibérations de la municipalité de Lille, Jan. 3–Feb. 26, 1793.

[14] Cf. Forot, *Tulle*, p. 227. PV: Bordeaux, Oct. 4, 1792; Boiscommun, Oct. 21, 1792; Courthézon, Nov. 8, 1792; Orthez, Nov. 4–16, 1792; Honfleur, Nov. 5–8, 1792; Cognac, Nov. 18, 1792; Limoges, Oct. 20, 1792.

[15] Rouvière, *Gard*, III, 4.

brought a dish. The Nuits club also had a "pot-luck" dinner and tried to keep it a simple affair, the reverse of the royal pageants of old which were characterized by "luxury and insolent profusion." Tables were placed near the tree of liberty. No one was given a place of distinction except for the president. Burghers offered countryfolk places to sleep.[16]

Most of the fetes, however, were elaborate, carefully orchestrated affairs. Religion, as yet, had not been banished from revolutionary spectacles. Prayers were said. Te Deums were sung. Thanks were rendered to the Supreme Being for delivering France from its enemies. Portions of the ceremonies took place in churches. At Troyes a confrontation occurred when the Municipality refused the club's request to use the cathedral. However, a compromise was reached that permitted the club to erect an altar before the cathedral.[17]

Usually, the *procès-verbaux* mention the presence of *citoyennes*. At Annonay a number of young women of good family were theatrically costumed. One, with a "nymphean figure" and long tresses that fell in ringlets to the ground, represented liberty and rode aloft on a parade float. At her feet were boys and girls strewing flowers. Following her were three maidens carrying the flags of France, Britain, and the United States, the "nations which had cast off the yoke of tyranny." Then four girls, with mournful faces and lowered eyes, and wearing black crepe and chains, brought up the rear. They represented the enslaved peoples of Europe.[18]

Lavish use was made of visual effects. Marchers in processions wore bonnets of liberty and tricolor sashes and carried pikes. Mannequins emblematic of royalty were solemnly interred. Symbols of tyranny were burned on funeral pyres. Fireworks were shot off. Streets were illuminated. Dancing and music were likewise common. The fêtes savoisiennes were the first of their kind in which the strains of the "Marseillaise" rang out. But many songs were composed especially for the occasion. At Nancy and Toul clubbists made up nasty ditties about the Prus-

[16] PV, Nuits, Oct. 25–27, 1792.
[17] A. Babeau, *Histoire de Troyes pendant la Révolution* (Paris, 1873), II, 5–6.
[18] Rostaing, *Annonay*, pp. 183–188.

sians, who had thought to conquer France and instead got only dysentery.[19]

Bread and wine were distributed to indigents, and money was given to the widows of fallen soldiers. Posthumous praise was bestowed on heroes like Beaurepaire, the commandant at Verdun who had committed suicide rather than surrender it to the enemy. The soldiers themselves were not forgotten. The Récollets Society bought and shipped barrels of wine to the volunteers of the Gironde so that they too could "drink to the health of the nation."[20]

Above all, the fetes were an occasion for effusive rhetoric. The clubbists were careful to distinguish France from conquering states of the past. Yet, they chattered like popinjays about the successes of French arms and the glittering prospects for future triumphs. From St.-Quentin came these frothings: "Soon, it can no longer be doubted, the enemies of the human race and all the partisans of tyranny will be defeated." A speaker at Annonay contended that the French should not lay down their arms "until they have effaced from the globe all traces of its former servitude. Then we will enjoy the rights of man in peace. Then all peoples will adopt our laws. We will be as one family. . . . Citizens! That is the happy future that the Revolution prepares for us. And its end is not far away."[21] Regrettably, this glorious apocalypse was not to be.

[19] Troux, *Meurthe*, p. 122.

[20] Ibid., p. 123. *JC*, Nov. 1, 1792. PV: Bordeaux, Nov. 28, 1792; Nuits, Dec. 12, 1792.

[21] *JC*, Oct. 25, 1792. Rostaing, *Annonay*, pp. 367–369.

XI

The Occupied Lands

FROM ABOUT 1770 onward, Europe was rocked by a series of rebellions against the old, aristocratic order. These movements intensified in scope and number after 1789 as the ideals of liberty and equality washed across French borders. "Patriots,," or revolutionary sympathizers, agitated for reforms in almost every European country; and many made hejiras to France where they flocked to the clubs or formed associations of their own. The goals of exiles were twofold: to diffuse revolutionary propaganda in their native lands, and to return as conquerors.[1]

The political stirrings near its frontiers and the activities of the exiles placed Revolutionary France in a dilemma. Its desire to render assistance to "enslaved" peoples clashed with its own pacifistic protestations. On May 22, 1790, the Constituent Assembly had solemnly renounced wars of conquest. And this resolution was reaffirmed in the Constitution of September 1791 and again in the Declaration of War of April 20, 1792. In the end, however, missionary and acquisitive instincts won out. Abetted by a small minority of foreigners and a few "foreign" clubs, France, by 1793, had annexed all of the lands on its periphery up to the "natural frontiers" of the Rhine and Alps.

The first area to be absorbed was Avignon and the County Venaissin. French speaking and entirely surrounded by French territory, it was particularly susceptible to revolutionary impulses. On June 14, 1790, radicals in Avignon rebelled against papal rule and solicited union with France. But the County Venaissin remained wedded to the popish cause, and a bloody civil war ensued. For a time France refrained from sticking its nose into this trough of troubles. The Constituent did not wish to alienate the papacy or to violate the May 22 resolution renouncing conquests. But there was much sympathy for the rebels, and the

---

[1] Cf. R. R. Palmer, *The Age of Democratic Revolution* (Princeton, 1959), I.

clubs loosed countless petitions calling for union. Ultimately, in May 1791, the Constituent decided to occupy the enclave and to determine "the wishes of the population." On September 14, 1791, it was annexed to France.[2]

The tumult over Avignon was just a prelude to what was to come after the great victories of the autumn of 1792. The first conquests occurred in the southeast, at the expense of the Pied-montese. On September 21–22 an army under Montesquiou invaded Savoy, and by early October, in what amounted to a triumphal march, it had occupied this whole region. The planting of the tricolor was followed shortly by the germination of clubs. Most, it seems, sprang up at the coaxing of commissioners of the Convention and returning exiles such as François-Amédée Doppet and Philibert Simond. Both had been forced to flee in 1790. Simond, whom we have met before, took refuge in Strasbourg where he was active in the club and then elected to the Convention. Doppet, who was a colorful character, went first to Grenoble and thence to Paris where he was a mainstay of the Jacobins and the director of the Société des Allobroges, a group of Piedmontese refugees. From Paris he maintained contact with a "secret society" formed in Chambéry.[3]

As chief of the Legion des Allobroges, Doppet accompanied Montesquiou into Chambéry and presided over the opening session of its club on September 26, 1792. The Chambéry club circulated printed accounts of its inaugural along with requests for affiliation. Favorable responses came from such far-flung places as Paris, Limoges, Lorient, Grenoble, Bordeaux, Toulouse, St.-Hippolyte, and Cognac. The other clubs of Savoy (Annecy, Le Carouge, Rumilly, Sallanches, Thonon, and St.-Jean-de-Maurienne) also won prompt acceptance from the network. Indeed, the Paris Jacobins accorded special authority to Simond, who was being sent there, to grant affiliation to them on the spot.[4]

---

[2] Kennedy, *Jacobins*, pp. 225–228.

[3] Cf. F.-A. Doppet, *Mémoires politiques et littéraires* (Paris, 1824).

[4] *AP*, Oct. 15, 1792. *CD*, Oct. 15–16, 1792. *ArchP*, Oct. 6, 1792. *JC*, Oct. 25, Dec. 6, 1792. Gros, *La Maurienne*, pp. 42–43. *M*, Oct. 17–19, 1792. Mugnier, *Thonon*, pp. 7–8, 23–24. *JD*, Sept. 30, Dec. 4, 1792. E. Le Gallo, "Les Jacobins de Cognac," *RF* (1904), p. 409. PV: Toulouse, Oct. 31, Nov. 3, 1792; Bordeaux, Oct. 7, 1792; St.-Hippolyte, Nov. 25, 1792; Limoges, Oct. 14, 1792. COR: Reims, Lorient, Poitiers.

The clubs of Savoy, in contrast to those in most of the other occupied lands, appear to have been composed mainly of local citizens. The largest and most vigorous was Chambéry. On October 12 someone claimed that it had 1,200 members. And a little later, officials from Paris described it as being very "numerous and patriotic." Most of its known officers were bourgeois professionals; of the rank and file, little can be said. The smaller societies, like Thonon and St.-Jean-de-Maurienne, were largely middle class, with just a sprinkling of artisans. There were almost no peasants.[5]

On October 6, Montesquiou and the commissioners of the Convention ordered each commune of Savoy to elect representatives to a General Assembly in which there would be a referendum on the type of government to be installed. In the absence of any regular authorities, the Chambéry club, which had already declared for union with France, sent out agents to organize the local electoral assemblies. Under the circumstances, it was a foregone conclusion that the General Assembly, which met on October 22, would proclaim an end to the rule of Piedmont and vote to seek incorporation into France.[6]

The Convention was at first hesitant to accede to Savoy's request. Some of the deputies were still opposed in principle to conquests. Others hoped to use the occupied territories as bargaining chips in peace negotiations with Austria and Prussia. As the club of Avignon had done in 1790, Chambéry and Annecy appealed for assistance from the network. Annecy circulated an address that argued that the Savoisiens were French in language and customs, and should be in law as well. The covering letter asked for affiliates to persuade their deputies to vote for annexation. "Help us!" supplicated Annecy. "We want to be French." If the departmental societies had any scruples about annexing occupied territories, this circular removed them. Many decided to write to Paris; and others were preparing to do so when they learned of

[5] Gros, *La Maurienne*, pp. 583–585. Mugnier, *Thonon*, pp. 23–24. *ArchP*, Oct. 20, Dec. 24, 1792. *JC*, Oct. 25, 1792. *PF*, Oct. 19, 1792.

[6] Gros, *La Maurienne*, pp. 46–47. *ArchP*, Oct. 20, Nov. 26, 1792. *JC*, Nov. 26, 1792. Libois, *Lons-le-Saunier*, pp. 77–78. Forot, *Tulle*, p. 240. COR, Poitiers, S 26. PV, Lille, Nov. 30, 1792.

the decree of November 27, making Savoy the eighty-fourth French department.[7]

While Montesquiou was conquering Savoy, his subordinate, D'Anselme, took the County of Nice. It too had belonged to Piedmont, but its official language was Italian and most of the population spoke a dialect called Nissard. The first club to be formed here was Nice itself. It was brought to life on October 2, 1792, by commissioners of the Convention and a delegation from the society of Grasse. A little later, elements of the French army and local patriots instituted a club at Sospel. By December clubs were in operation at Contes, L'Escarene, Roquesteron, Menton, St.-Martin-du-Var, and Monaco.[8]

Nice's initial actions were to seek affiliation from the Paris Jacobins and to adopt a resolution stating that the county belonged to France by right of conquest, the will of its citizens, and treaty provisions dating back to the time of the Kingdom of Arles. Thereafter, the club was to be actively involved in the campaign for union and called upon the network for backing. When news arrived on February 7, 1793, of the decree declaring the county to be the eighty-fifth department, it held a Te Deum and sent its thanks to the Convention by special messenger.[9]

In contrast to Savoy, the campaign for unity in Nice has all the earmarks of a put-up job by the French. One has only to look at the composition of the Nice club for this to become evident. Its enrollment was about 350 to 400, rather low for a city of 24,000 souls. Moreover, it was originally dominated by outsiders. The first president was a clubbist from Grasse, and most of its members were French soldiers. The few residents came mainly from the Marseille merchant colony. Native Niçois apparently feared that the French occupation would not be permanent. Only gradually did their numbers grow.[10]

On April 28–29, 1792, as a defensive move, General Custine had seized the so-called Bishopric of Basel, a strategic area of northwest Switzerland. The prince-bishop fled; however, a re-

[7] COR: Reims; Poitiers, S 26.
[8] *M*, Oct. 17, 23, 1792. *ArchP*, Oct. 22, 1792. *JC*, Oct. 27, Nov. 21, 1792. Combet, "Nice," pp. 377–378, 416–417. *JDM*, p. 417. Aulard, *Jacobins*, V, 18.
[9] Combet, "Nice," pp. 401–404.
[10] Ibid., pp. 384–387. *M*, Oct. 27, 1792.

gency was set up, and there were at first no substantive political changes. This policy did not please nearby French clubs or pro-Revolutionary exiles like Joseph-Antoine Rengguer. Twice in May, Rengguer attempted coups. And throughout the summer the societies of Belfort, Delle, and Besançon summoned the Legislative Assembly to impose direct French rule. The *Vedette*, the organ of the Besançon club, urged the Bisontins to do as the Marseillais would do, and "march to the passes at their own expense." Ultimately, in October 1792, partisans of Rengguer, backed by the French commissioner, Gobel (Rengguer's uncle), and the commandant, Demars, assumed control. A "national assembly" met from December 17 to January 8 and proclaimed the establishment of the "Republic of la Rauracie." The Republic lasted until April 23, 1793, when it was formally annexed to France and became the department of Mont-Terrible.[11]

As early as 1791, Rengguer and Gobel had formed in Paris an exile society under the title of "Suisses de la Porte." But there were no clubs in the "Bishopric" until the overthrow of the regency. Porrentruy appeared first, on October 21, 1792. Delémont, Ste.-Ursanne, Laufen, and Seignelégier tagged along after. At the moment of birth, the Porrentruy club claimed to speak for the whole region and allegedly had two hundred members. Alas, its bright promise was soon dimmed by schism. Two rival societies existed there by early 1793. The representative-on-mission J.-F. Ritter said that one was composed of supporters and ex-officials of the prince-bishop; the other consisted mainly of French soldiers. It was the second club, apparently, that sent deputies to the Paris Jacobins in March, and a circular to affiliates in April, demanding unification with France.[12]

Some of the most spectacular conquests came along the middle Rhine. Here, from September 25 to October 21, an army commanded by General Custine took the storied German cities of Spires, Worms, Mainz, and Frankfurt. At that point, however, the advance stalled; and by December ground was being lost.

[11] G. Gautherot, *La Révolution française dans l'ancien évêché de Bâle* (Paris, 1908), I, 1–269. Aulard, *Comité*, II, 93–101. *JC*, June 9, 11, 1792.
[12] Gautherot, *Bâle*, pp. 178–181. *JD*, Nov. 11, 1792, Mar. 26, 1793. Aulard, *Comité*, II, 66, 93–101, 176–177. *ArchP*, Jan. 26–27, 1793. Heitz, *Strasbourg*, p. 242. COR, Bordeaux, 12 L 32.

General Bournonville was forced to lift the siege of Trier. And the citizenry of Frankfurt rose up, opened the gates to the Hessians, and massacred the French garrison. After reenforcements were hastily dispatched, the front was momentarily stabilized. In March, however, the Prussians launched a major offensive, and by summer they had liberated the whole region.

During the brief occupation, clubs were set up at Mainz, Worms, Aachen, and Spires. Mainz held its opening meeting on October 23 in the château of the elector. Those in attendance included G.-W. Böhmer, secretary to Custine and an ex-professor at a Lutheran school in Worms, and Georg Forster, the librarian of the University of Mainz. The Worms society was instituted by Böhmer and A.-J. Dorsch, a cleric who had taught logic at the University of Mainz before fleeing to Strasbourg in 1790. Dorsch and Böhmer also assisted in the foundation of the society of Spires. All four clubs secured affiliation with the Paris Jacobins.[13]

The Worms club was small and dominated by orators from Mainz and Strasbourg. Citizen involvement at Aachen was also low. Out of 23,000 inhabitants, only 26 joined the society. At Mainz (a city of 28,000), however, enrollment swelled in the first weeks of the occupation from 20 to 454. Of these, 132 were artisans; the remainder were intellectuals, lawyers, merchants, and the like. Most of the leaders were attached to the university. The Mainz club was by far the most active. Its members published numerous propaganda tracts, raised war materiel for the French armies, and lobbied for unification with France. In the minds of the Mainz burghers, however, always lurked the fear of being abandoned by France. By March 1793, public confidence in the club had eroded to the point that French officials purified it, saying that it was "worth nothing." After the beginning of the Prussian counteroffensive, most of its leaders dispersed.[14]

[13] *AP*, Nov. 5, 27, 1792. J. Hansen, *Quellen zur Geschichte des Rheinlandes im Zeitalter der französischen Revolution* (Bonn, 1933), II, 695, 743ff. R. Dufraisse, "Tendances girondines et tendances montagnardes chez les Jacobins de la rive gauche du Rhin, 1792–1795," *Actes du Colloque Girondins et Montagnards* (1980), p. 220.

[14] K. Bockenheimer, *Die Mainzer Klubisten der Jahren 1792–1793* (Mainz, 1896). J. Godechot, *La Grande Nation* (Paris, 1956), I, 260–261. *JC*, Nov. 24, 1792. Dufraisse, "Tendances," pp. 219–246. A. Chuquet, *Les guerres de la Révolution: May-*

Today, Landau is a German city too, but in 1792 it lay within the boundaries of France. It had a very active club, which dated from December 1790; but like Nice, its members were mostly soldiers or volunteers. The Landau club helped to precipitate one of the major foreign policy decisions of the Revolution by encouraging the inhabitants of the Duchy of Zweibrucken to rebel and to seek union with France. When the Convention learned on November 19, 1792, that the duke was using troops to suppress the movement, it approved a resolution stating that France would "grant aid and fraternity to all peoples who wish to recover their liberty." This resolution, usually called the First Propagandist Decree, was a watershed in the history of the Revolution. France, which had once renounced wars of conquest, had now proclaimed its willingness to come to the aid of revolutionaries throughout the world.[15]

The last lands to be conquered in 1792 were the Austrian Netherlands and the Archbishopric of Liège, which collectively were equivalent to modern-day Belgium. Both regions had been wracked by revolutions in 1789–90. And after these movements were ground into rubble by the Austrians, a swarm of refugees had descended upon France. Some gathered in Paris where they formed a Comité des Belges et Liègeois unis. Others settled in the Nord, where they were alternately befriended and watched suspiciously by the clubs. The problem was that there were two factions of exiles: "Vonckists," who were democratic and pro-French; and "Statists," moderates who wanted to preserve Belgium's ancient liberties and the privileges of the upper classes and the Church.[16]

This was the situation until October 27, 1792, when French forces headed by Dumouriez and bolstered by some 2,500 exiles went on the offensive. At Jemappes (near Mons) they won a memorable victory. Austrian resistance crumbled, and by early December all of Belgium was under the French boot. The day after Jemappes (November 7), a club was started at Mons by a

---

ence (Paris, 1892), VII, 1–45. H. Scheel, "Der Jakobiner Club zu Worms, 1792–1793," *Jahrbuch für Geschichte* (1977), pp. 321–400.

[15] Mathiez, *French Revolution*, p. 284.

[16] Kennedy, *Jacobins*, p. 229. PV, Lille, Dec. 27, 1791, Jan. 15, 1792. *AP*, Dec. 7, 1791.

member of the Comité des Belges et Liègeois unis and by French army officers. Dumouriez was present and gave a speech. In the next few weeks clubs appeared in at least twenty-seven Belgian towns.[17] Many were fathered by French military men, commissars from Paris, and former refugees. But some were set up by local patriots or were the offspring of other societies. Agents from the Brussels club founded Malines and Louvain. Bruges instituted clubs at Dudzeele and Oedelem. Missionaries from Liège set up clubs at Verviers, Jongres, Huy, and probably Herve and Spa.[18]

Most of the Belgian clubs called themselves "Societies of Friends of Liberty and Equality." And their sessions and internal practices were almost identical to those of the societies in France. Brussels, for instance, modelled its regulations on those of Valenciennes; Bruges and Tournai aped Lille. The Belgian clubs wasted no time in seeking affiliation, often sending plenipotentiaries to Paris. The "mother society" is known to have granted thirteen such requests, waiving the usual application rules. Belgian clubs likewise established contacts with departmental societies. Lille corresponded with its "daughter" at Tournai. Ath announced its existence in a circular that reached such places as Marseille, Lorient, and Bordeaux. Brussels exchanged letters with Bordeaux and Auch. Antwerp sent a manuscript letter to the Récollets Society in which it applauded the execution of the king and expressed its desire for union with France.[19]

Alas, the number of native Belgians in the clubs was never great and had fallen drastically by 1793. Mons was an exception in being vigorous and well-attended until the final days of the oc-

[17] Mons, Tournai, Ghent, Namur, Ypres, Bruges, Louvain, Malines, Dudzeele, Oedelem, Liège, Dinant, Tubize, Genappes, Gembloux, Soignies, Brussels, Antwerp, Courtrai, Herve, Verviers, Tongres, Huys, Ath, Spa, Philippeville, Rocroi.

[18] Most of what follows comes from the fine works of S. Tassier, "Les Sociétés des amis de la liberté et de l'égalité en Belgique en 1792–1793," *AHRF* (1933), pp. 307–316, and *Histoire de la Belgique sous l'occupation française en 1792 et 1793* (Brussels, 1934), pp. 212–240, 339–342. For summaries of Tassier's research see Godechot, *Grande Nation*, I, 318–323, and Palmer, *Democratic Revolution*, II, 74.

[19] *JD*, Nov. 14, 1792–Mar. 21, 1793. PV: Lille, Nov. 30, Dec. 7, 1792; Bordeaux, Dec. 4, 1792. COR: Bordeaux, Poitiers, Niort. *AP*, Mar. 21, 1793. G. Hubrecht, "La Société . . . d'Anvers et les Jacobins de Bordeaux," *AHRF* (1933), p. 537.

cupation. Elsewhere, the story was grim. At Liège the strength of the Jacobin movement was undermined by the rivalry of two clubs. French soldiers in the garrison alternately sided with one and then the other. Courtrai perished after a few meetings. Although Antwerp was still functioning in March, most of the locals withdrew in December. Louvain had 250 people at its first session, but by February it had shrunk to a small nucleus of "French warriors." The membership of Malines, on January 4, consisted of ninety-four Frenchmen, ten Malinois. At Bruges, which was quite active in November–December, only a "few patriots" still attended in February. Brussels, which attracted crowds of five hundred to some of its early meetings, averaged only fifty by February.

Like the Niçois and the Rhenish Germans, ordinary Belgians fretted that their old rulers would return and figured that they would be compromised if they joined the clubs. The Statists withdrew from the societies in protest over the policies of the Vonckists. Goaded by French volunteers, the Vonckists were militantly anticlerical. They also wanted to reduce the privileges of guilds and other special economic interests, and they demanded the execution of the Second Propagandist Decree of December 15. This famous law, which displeased the vast majority of Belgians, required the occupied lands to pay for the costs of their "liberation." It also confiscated the property of former rulers and religious communities and provided for the introduction of the despised assignats.

Given the makeup of their personnel, it is scarcely astonishing that the Belgian clubs were eager for union with France. To forcefeed revolutionary doctrines to the populace, they formed "corps of sansculottes" which were precursors of the "Armées révolutionnaires" of the Terror. They also endeavored to influence the electoral assemblies that the Convention, on January 31, called to decide the fate of Belgium. Great was their rejoicing when Belgium was annexed in March. By this date, however, the clubs had become islands in a hostile sea. The clubbists who remained behind after the French evacuation in March were apprehended and punished by the Austrians and the civilian population.

XII

England: Friend or Foe?

ENGLAND was the nemesis and arch-rival of eighteenth-century France. Yet paradoxically, a broad and deep-running current of Anglophilism coursed through the earliest clubs. The clubbists admired English political institutions and attributed to them England's military and economic triumphs. They were also bedazzled by English scientific and cultural achievements. Club orators habitually referred to the island kingdom as the "cradle of liberty," "the mother of Locke and Newton."

At first, the love affair seemed mutual. English residents in France sought and obtained admission into the clubs, and political associations in Britain extended the hand of friendship. A very cordial relationship developed between the French clubs and the London Revolution Society, which was headed by Francophiles such as Charles Stanhope and Richard Price. Contacts commenced in November 1789 after the Revolution Society congratulated the Constituent Assembly for "vanquishing aristocracy and despotism." By the end of the Constituent about fifty clubs had entered into correspondence with the Revolution Society.[1]

It was the Revolution Society that first advanced the idea of a Franco-British alliance, possibly including Holland and the United States. At a gala fete held on July 14, 1790, to commemorate the fall of the Bastille, Price declaimed that such a pact would guarantee world peace. Intoxicated by Price's noble vision, the Limoges club, on October 13, published a circular letter in which it suggested that the French societies send representatives to London to concert with the Revolution Society in bringing about an alliance of the "first two nations of Europe." Twenty-seven clubs are known to have adhered to Limoges' plan; others supported it with minor amendments; only a few disapproved.[2]

[1] Kennedy, *Jacobins*, pp. 233–241.
[2] Ibid., pp. 236–239.

Ironically, Price's speech was also a major factor in causing Edmund Burke, on November 1, 1790, to publish his celebrated *Reflections on the Revolution in France and on the Proceedings in Certain Societies in London Relative to that Event*. Although radicals like the chemist Joseph Priestley and the irrepressible Tom Paine published refutations to Burke, his counterrevolutionary opus had an immense impact on British public opinion. In July 1791, an anti-French mob broke into Priestley's home near Birmingham, destroying his books, papers, and scientific apparatus. This incident was a straw in the wind, evidence of deteriorating Franco-British relations. The French clubs exploded with fury, offered Priestley asylum, and wrote to the Revolution Society to denounce Burke and the Pitt cabinet. Yet, as the Constituent drew to a close, they continued to profess good will toward the English people and to believe in the chimera of an Anglo-French entente.[3]

Shortly after the opening of the Legislative Assembly, the Jacobin luminary Jérome Pétion paid a visit to London. There he saw Stanhope, Paine, Priestley, and other Francophiles and was guest of honor at a November 4 meeting of the Revolution Society. Exactly two weeks later, in his new guise as mayor of Paris, Pétion reported on his journey at the Paris club. When the Jacobins heard that the French and English flags were draped together in the Revolution Society, they resolved to do the same in their assembly hall, and to hang the American flag as well. The formal installation of the flags of the "three free peoples of the universe" took place on December 18 before a huge throng, including a "Constitutional Whig" from London.[4]

News of the Jacobin resolution was flashed to the nation in late November by Parisian journalists. Whereupon, it became de rigueur for the provincial clubs to have fetes commemorating the "union of all free peoples." As was its wont, the Récollets Society led the way, holding a civic banquet on December 8, in which it solemnly installed the French, English, American, and Polish flags. An account of this affair, which preceded that of the Paris Jacobins by ten days, was printed and distributed. A month later (January 13) a much larger ceremony took place in Bordeaux in

---

[3] Ibid., p. 241. C. B. Cone, *The English Jacobins* (New York, 1968), pp. 91–95.

[4] M. Reinhard, "Le Voyage de Pétion à Londres," *Revue d'histoire diplomatique* (1960), pp. 1–60. *AP*, Nov. 27, 1791. *JD*, Nos. 97, 113.

which representatives of all the clubs, male and female, were involved. No expense was spared.[5]

On December 18, the clubs of Bergerac and Marseille also "inaugurated" the flags of the "free nations." At Bergerac the four pennants were paraded through the streets. Then a festive banquet took place. For the Marseillais, it was one of those elect, long-remembered moments. All the English in the city were invited to the spectacle which supposedly attracted eight thousand spectators. Someone gave an elegy to Captain Cook. Poets, or rather rhymers, read an "Ode on the Alliance of the Constitutional Flags of France and England" and "Couplets on the Union of French and English Patriots." English and French embraced. Women shed "tears of happiness" and tossed bouquets of flowers into the air.[6]

Between January 1 and July 14, 1792, flag fetes were organized by the clubs of at least twenty-three other French cities.[7] Much planning went into these local productions, and they were a great success. At Libourne citizens feasted and danced into the morning's wee hours. In Niort the fete took place under a clear blue sky, making revelers feel that they had the blessing of heaven. There was much eloquent rhetoric. A speaker at Rouen paraphrased Louis XIV's famous words delivered on the eve of the War of Spanish Succession, saying: "Il n'y plus d'Océan."[8]

The historian Claude Mazauric, who has looked at the fete of Rouen through the peephole of Marxist dogma, says that in these ceremonies "class interests dominated every other consideration," that the merchants of the great ports dreamed of a vast, Anglo-French "thalassocracy" from which they would profit. Some port clubs did, indeed, think that a Franco-British entente

---

[5] *JC*, No. 1. *AP*, Feb. 7, 1792. Ligou, *Montauban*, p. 269. COR, Poitiers, S 21. PV: Libourne, Dec. 11, 1791; Toulouse, Dec. 1, 1791.

[6] *CD*, Jan. 6, 1792. *AP*, Feb. 7, 1792. AM, Marseille, 1 D 9. BM, Marseille, 4717. COR, Poitiers, S 22. Labroue, *Bergerac*, p. 192. *JD*, No. 122.

[7] Brest, Calais, Sète, Rouen, Orléans, Chalon-sur-Saône, Aix-en-Provence, Lorient, Poitiers, Libourne, Montpellier, Angers, Cognac, Niort, Périgueux, Limoges, Tulle, Valognes, Aurillac, Clermont-Ferrand, Blaye, Toulouse, and Tonneins.

[8] PV, Niort, Mar. 25, 1792. Chardon, *Rouen*, p. 58. Besson, *Libourne*, pp. 151–152.

would be "good for commerce," but it is hard to believe that this was the major cause of the festivals. The professions of fraternity have a ring of sincerity. Besides, many of the installation celebrations did not take place in big ports at all, but in towns of the interior where the participants had little to gain economically from a Franco-British alliance.[9]

That the clubs were driven by nobler motives than economics is evident from their decision to honor the Polish flag. They had watched Polish efforts at reform with fascination and had hailed the famous, abortive Constitution of May 3, 1791, as one of the greatest achievements of the Age of Reason. Many tried to establish correspondence with a "Society of Friends of the Constitution" reported to have been founded in Warsaw. Enthusiasm for Poland ran strong until mid-1792 when King Stanislas-Auguste Poniatowski stated his opposition to democracy and Jacobinism and dissolved some political groups. At that time the Récollets Society considered the possibility of stenciling these words on the Polish flag in its hall: "Poland! Its liberties suspended by the treason of its king!" Someone at Montpellier demanded that the flag be taken down because the "Poles have not been able to keep their liberties." Périgueux did remove it "until the time when Poland regains its liberty."[10]

Added incentive was provided for the flag installations of late 1791 and early 1792 by the reading in the Legislative Assembly on December 6 of a letter from the London Society of Constitutional Whigs. The Whigs acclaimed the French constitution to be a work of "wisdom and integrity" and vowed to aid France if she was attacked by "one of the several despotic powers." Thus cheered, many French clubs sent letters of thanks to London. Montpellier expounded on the "glories" of Franco-British friendship. Lorient hailed the Whigs for letting themselves be "guided by reason rather than national biases." Brest waxed eloquent on the "worthy descendants of those intrepid Whigs of the seventeenth century who had defended the rights of man and to

---

[9] C. Mazauric, *Sur la Révolution française* (Paris, 1970), pp. 163–179.

[10] Palmer, *Democratic Revolution*, I, 430. COR, Colmar, B 34. *JC*, Nov. 9, 1791. PV: Montpellier, Oct. 19, 1792; Périgueux, Mar. 3, 1793; Tain, June 5, 1791; Croix-Rousse, June 2, 1791; Toulouse, June 6, 1791.

whom the English of today owe their economic prosperity and political stability." The Revolution Society responded: "Soon our two nations will renounce forever their absurd, ambitious, and destructive policies of the past."[11]

The Whig address brought renewed cries for a Franco-British diplomatic alliance. Motions to this effect were presented at Toulouse on December 5 and Lille on January 15. "England is powerful and free like us. Our cause ought to be hers," said Vendôme on January 17 to the Paris club. Montauban, in a circular of January 24, called for a "sacred alliance" of Britain and France as a "prelude to the confederation of the human race" and urged the "mother society" to arrange a meeting between club representatives and the Whigs. At least seven French societies notified the Paris Jacobins of their support for Montauban's plan. Dieppe wanted an alliance with America too. Périgueux envisioned a four-power coalition including Poland. The Paris club replied that it too was anxious "to federate with the London Whigs and other societies of England which are very numerous and which, for the most part, love our revolution," but it would await the results of a diplomatic mission of Talleyrand to Britain.[12]

That there were still prorevolutionary groups in Great Britain in 1792 was manifestly apparent. On April 13, James Watt, Jr., and Thomas Cooper showed up at the Paris Jacobins to seek affiliation for the Manchester Society for Constitutional Information. When the Jacobins granted this request, the London Society for Constitutional Information sent a note of thanks. On April 30, Toulouse received a letter from an organization in York, effusively praising the French Revolution. In September, a certain John Bell of the London Society of Constitutional Whigs showed up at Rouen, sang a patriotic hymn, and left behind two copies of Paine's *Rights of Man*. The next month another Constitutional

[11] *ArchP*, Dec. 6, 1791. *CD*, Dec. 28, 1791, Jan. 8, Mar. 9, 1792. *PF*, Dec. 27, 1791. Ligou, *Montauban*, p. 269. PV: Montauban, Dec. 24, 1791; Auray, Jan. 22, 1792; St.-Hippolyte, Dec. 25, 1791; Fécamp, Dec. 8, 1791; Versailles, Feb. 13, 15, 1792; Honfleur, Dec. 20, 1791, Jan. 15, 1792.

[12] *JC*, No. 9. *CD*, Feb. 3, 1792. *AP*, Feb. 7, Mar. 17, 1792. Forot, *Tulle*, pp. 169–171. COR: Reims, Niort, Montpellier, Poitiers, Bordeaux. PV: Toulouse, Dec. 3, 1791; Lille, Jan. 15, 1792; Lorient, Feb. 20, 1792; Chalon, Feb. 5, 14, 1792; Périgueux, Feb. 15, 19, 1792; Niort, Feb. 12, 1792; Rouen, Feb. 26, 1792.

Whig was received at Cherbourg as though he were an ambassador of the British government.[13]

After the outbreak of war with Austria and Prussia, societies of Britain and Ireland sent gifts and well-wishes to the Legislative Assembly. The Toulouse club was so moved that it resolved to establish ties with the "Irish patriots." Britishers in France also made showy displays of support. At Cherbourg, an Englishman named "Carteroit" (Cartwright?) demonstrated a rapid-firing cannon. The club was so impressed that it accorded him honorary membership and wrote to the Paris Jacobins about his invention. Cherbourg likewise honored an English sea captain who donated a conventional cannon to a battalion of volunteers.[14]

Because of its proximity to Britain, Cherbourg was especially anxious lest the island power become a military adversary. In July 1792, in an address to the English people, it cried out: "English! We hear constantly that you are arming against us. We cannot believe it. A free and magnanimous nation would never exterminate us because we wish to be free like her!" In another address it pleaded: "Six nations are attacking us. Rise up, generous English, be our auxiliaries!" A response from the London Society of Constitutional Whigs, which Cherbourg printed, reassured France that the "wise part of the English nation" supported its "courageous fight against despots."[15]

Up to the overthrow of the monarchy, the Pitt government pursued a policy of strict neutrality. After August 10, however, the British ambassador was recalled from Paris, and the French ambassador in London was placed in an unofficial "quarantine." The September Massacres, meanwhile, heightened Francophobia among the English public. The chilling of relations caused the club of Vannes to urge the Convention to issue a proclamation of friendship for the English nation. Langon, in early October, implored the Récollets Society and the Paris club to maintain close correspondence with the "good citizens" of England and to con-

[13] *AP*, May 3, June 22, 1792. PV: Le Mans, June 10, 1792; Toulouse, Apr. 30, 1792. Galland, "Cherbourg," p. 384. Chardon, *Rouen*, pp. 27–28.
[14] *ArchP*, July 11, Aug. 18, 1792. Galland, "Cherbourg," p. 341. PV, Toulouse, Aug. 11, 1792.
[15] *JC*, Aug. 18, 1792. *CD*, Aug. 30, 1792. COR, Poitiers, S 26. PV: Bordeaux, Nov. 6, 1792; Honfleur, Nov. 21, 1792.

vince them of the good intentions of the French Republic. "This nation which was once our model . . . will become our enemy if we are not careful."[16]

The Paris Jacobins anticipated Langon's request, publishing in early October an address to the "Popular Societies of England, Scotland, and Ireland." It denounced British newspapers for printing twisted accounts of the September Massacres and proffered its own version which tended to condone the deeds of the Parisians. The Jacobins claimed that the victims of the Massacres had intended to force their way out of prison and murder the womenfolk of absent volunteers. "You can understand that when this horrible plot was discovered the people wreaked a terrible vengeance."[17]

The Massacres notwithstanding, France still had a noisy minority of sympathizers in England. In the autumn of 1792 at least ten British societies wrote to the Convention to gush over French military successes and to castigate the policies of Pitt.[18] These letters excited the clubs and perpetuated false impressions that most Englishmen were pro-French. The Récollets Society was moved to hold a fete on December 8 on the first anniversary of the installation of the four flags. The keynote speaker, J.-H. Duvigneau, renewed the call for a Franco-British alliance. "Our two peoples, so redoubtable in enlightenment and in arms, will guide the rest of Europe."[19]

Unfortunately, Franco-British relations continued to worsen. The aggressive policy of conquest followed by the Republic caused England in November and December to begin to arm and to pursue negotiations with the Germanic Powers. By December 31 the situation had become so bleak that the French naval minister, Gaspard Monge, wrote to the clubs of maritime centers to say that the English king and Parliament wanted war even if "free Englishmen" did not. Then he proclaimed: "We will fly to their aid. We will make a descent on this island and plant the tree of

[16] *JD*, Oct. 16, 1792. *JC*, Oct. 15, 18, 1792. PV, Bordeaux, Oct. 9, 1792.
[17] *JC*, Oct. 8, 1792.
[18] *ArchP*, Nov. 7–Dec. 1, 1792. *M*, Nov. 8–30, 1792. Cone, *English*, p. 125.
[19] *JC*, Nov. 17, 1792. Libois, *Lons-le-Saunier*, p. 94. COR, Poitiers, S 26. PV: Bordeaux, Nov. 6, Dec. 2, 1792; Lorient, Nov. 8, 1792; Aire, Nov. 9, 1792; Toulouse, Nov. 5, 1792.

liberty there. War with the King of England will purify English liberties!"[20]

Monge asked the societies to provide him with information on the whereabouts of old cannon and war materiel, and to encourage seamen to enroll for military service. The clubs responded with alacrity, appointing commissions to procure the data Monge had requested, transmitting his letter to curés to read to their parishioners, and placarding copies in taverns and public squares. The always civic-minded Récollets Society circulated an "Adresse aux Marins," replete with such "beautiful sentiments of patriotism" that many societies voted to reprint it. Toulon and Cherbourg produced similar addresses. Cherbourg's appealed to self-interest as well as to patriotism, stressing that in this war talents and bravery counted for more than birth. Anyone could rise through the ranks and become a new "Duquesne" or "Jean-Bart."[21]

To the very end, however, Cherbourg tried to stave off hostilities. Convinced that the English people did not want war, it invited all French clubs, in a circular of late December, to write to the popular societies of England and beckon them to do something to avert a rupture. Libourne was inspired to send the following message to the London Society for Constitutional Information: "Do not let guilty men turn us against each other. We have confidence in the English people. But be warned! France will never bow down before another European Power." For its part, the Constitutional Information Society, on January 25, adopted a resolution stating that war with France would be a "calamity for the human race."[22]

After the execution of Louis XVI the English court went into mourning, and Pitt expelled the French ambassador. It was France, however, that actually declared war on February 1. When the news reached the clubs, some acted as if they were delighted and flippantly predicted victory. The Récollets Society exclaimed

[20] David, *La Rochelle*, p. 77. *PF*, Jan. 17, 1793.

[21] *ArchP*, Jan. 18, 1793. *CD*, Feb. 5, 1793. *PF*, Feb. 8, 1793. *AP*, Jan. 19, Feb. 5, 1793. PV: Honfleur, Jan. 3–10, 1793; Toulouse, Jan. 17, 1793; Lille, Feb. 21, 1793; Lorient, Jan. 7, 17, 1793; Le Havre, Jan. 4, 1793.

[22] *PF*, Jan. 4, 1793. *AP*, Jan. 5, 1793. *M*, Feb. 11, 1793. Galland, "Cherbourg," p. 341.

that the "only thing which had been lacking to the glory of the French name was to have freed the seas." Cherbourg, now bellicose, described the war as a "glorious" one and appointed a committee to draw up plans for *an invasion of England*! Lorient called the seamen of the Morbihan to arms. At Aire, a member sang a nasty ditty about George III, and the president led those in attendance as they chanted: "Death to tyrants! Death to the despot of England!" La Tremblade fulminated: "Under despotism, war was a calamity. Under liberty it is a necessity." Orthez urged war on Spain as well, and was to get its wish on March 7.[23]

Once belligerency was declared, the maritime societies became beehives of activity. Many, in early February, received a letter from Monge, announcing the armament of some fifty ships of the line and soliciting the names of mariners who, by virtue of their "talents" and "patriotism," merited commands. This assignment was fulfilled with much care. Committees compiled lists of candidates; these lists were discussed and voted on in full assembly; and the names of the most worthy were sent to Paris. La Rochelle boasted to Monge that its picks were veritable "seawolves."[24]

Monge appealed to the clubs of the interior to do their part by promoting the cultivation of hemp. Tartas, Boiscommun, and Pithiviers promptly drew up addresses to local farmers, entreating them to produce hemp. Bourbonne proposed to its municipality that the gardens of a former convent be used for this purpose. Guéret urged its department to print and distribute Monge's epistle. Le Mans offered a civic crown to anyone who had useful ideas on this subject.[25]

The societies also took to heart a resolution of the Convention adjuring maritime cities to arm corsaires. The Récollets Society secured pledges of 300,000 livres in one session and boasted in a

[23] AN, DXL 19. *CD*, Feb. 5, 1793. *ArchP*, Feb. 24, 1793. PV: Aire, Feb. 13, 1793; Orthez, Feb. 17–28, 1793; Lorient, Feb. 24, 1793. Galland, "Cherbourg," p. 385.

[24] COR, Marseille, L 2076. *CD*, Mar. 7, 1793. *JDM*, pp. 611–621. PV: Lorient, Feb. 14–28, 1793; Marseille, Mar. 4, 1793; Le Havre, Feb. 14–15, 1793.

[25] BN, Lb 41/2792. PV: Bourbonne, Mar. 22, 1793; Pithiviers, Mar. 17, 1793; Boiscommun, Mar. 20, 1793; Tartas, Mar. 22, 1793; Guéret, Mar. 24, 1793; Le Mans, Mar. 17, 1793.

February 10 circular that it would outfit three ships within a month. Libourne, the dutiful disciple of Bordeaux, decided to build two corsaires and opened a register for contributions. Only 1,000 livres was given by club members, however, and an appeal for donations had to be made to outsiders. In a verbal sleight of hand, Libourne said that it would not "insult" citizens by reminding them that "enormous profits could be derived from sharing out prizes."[26]

The sessions of Marseille were often interrupted by crews of corsaires coming to say their *adieux*. And one of its members armed a vessel which he called the *Club de Marseille*. Toulon outfitted a corsaire at its expense and vaunted that five-sixths of the crew were its members. Little Eu raised 1,300 livres for the same purpose. Cherbourg armed a cutter called the *Club de Cherbourg*. In addition, it conceived the grandiose idea of organizing a joint-stock company for the armament of corsaires. It informed affiliates, by circular, that each share would cost five hundred livres.[27] Even societies of the interior like Lyon became involved in shipbuilding and outfitting. And Strasbourg asked all the clubs of France to contribute money for the construction of a man-of-war to be called *The Jacobin*. Beaune, Tonneins, and Rouen are known to have done so.[28]

By February 1793 the presence of the English flag in club assembly halls had become a source of embarrassment. Some removed it as soon as war was declared. A few debated whether to burn it, and at Tonneins a member suggested that it be torn into small pieces and used as wadding for cartridges. Most left the Union Jack temporarily in their meeting places, albeit folded up, turned upside down, or lettered in some fashion. Libourne's read: "English! Out of respect for the rights of man, your flag will remain folded up in our hall until the time when your actions show

[26] PV, Bordeaux, Feb. 5–10, 1793. Besson, *Libourne*, pp. 212–214. *PF*, Feb. 16, 1793.

[27] *JDM*, pp. 608–613. Galland, "Cherbourg," pp. 384–385. Aulard, *Comité*, II, 78. AN, C II, 62. COR, Bordeaux, 12 L 30. PV: Marseille, Feb.–Mar. 1793; Lorient, Mar. 4, 1793; Montpellier, Mar. 5, 1793; Eu, Feb. 14, 1793.

[28] Riffaterre, *Lyon*, I, 40, 43. *JD*, Mar. 3, Apr. 5, 1793. COR, Limoges, L 829. Aulard, *Jacobins*, V, 228. PV: Bourbonne, Mar. 22, 1793; Tonneins, Mar. 28, 1793; Rouen, Mar. 24, 1793.

that it again warrants placement next to ours. If you prove, after all, to be slaves of royalism, we will deliver it to the flames."[29]

At Marseille, where hopes of a reconciliation continued to flicker, the clubs long refused to remove the British flag from its place of honor. The Marseillais also encouraged privateers to treat captured English seamen humanely. Their purpose was "to prove invincibly that the French have declared war only on tyrants and their satellites, and will always fraternize with peoples." As late as March 25, 1793, when a troupe of captives was paraded into the hall, the president of the club pointed to their flag and exclaimed: "This shows that King George alone is our enemy, that all Englishmen are our brothers and will always be treated as such."[30]

At this date (March 1793), Englishmen were still highly visible in the French clubs. It was not long, however, before all were to be suspect, before the "cradle of liberty" had become the "new Carthage" against which total war had to be waged. Anglo-French fraternity was a parenthesis that had closed before the eyes of the clubbists.

[29] Besson, *Libourne*, pp. 211–212. Combet, "Nice," p. 420. *JDM*, p. 600. David, *La Rochelle*, p. 79. *PF*, Feb. 16, 1793. PV: Tonneins, Feb. 10, 1793; Montpellier, Feb. 7, 1793; Rouen, Mar. 11, 1793; Bordeaux, Feb. 9, 1793.

[30] *JDM*, pp. 612, 648. PV, Marseille, Mar. 9, 25, 1793.

XIII

New Defeats, Treason,
and Terror

HAVING tasted the first, exhilarating draughts of military victory, the French were to have the cup dashed from their lips. Hints of an impending crisis came in November–December 1792, when the clubs received reports that the troops were ill-clothed and unprepared for the rigors of the upcoming season. Strasbourg, as early as November 14, appealed to citizens to come forward with wearing apparel for the volunteers of the Bas-Rhin. Nuits (December 7–10) became so distraught on hearing of the "urgent needs" of the men of the Armée du Nord that it asked the Convention to send them blankets and bedding from the property of émigrés. By January several clubs had demanded an investigation of the shortages and the prosecution of those who were responsible.[1]

The most notable action was taken by Sedan. On December 18 it published the following entreaty to all the societies of the Republic: "Brothers! Our brave warriors lack everything, but especially clothes. Winter is coming, and they will be susceptible to colds, lung inflamations, pleurisy, and fever. . . . Start collections. Give them clothes, not money. They need shoes, hose, warm vests, uniforms, greatcoats, . . . Keep in mind the women of antiquity who gave their dearest possessions, even their long hair for the rigging of vessels to repulse the enemy."[2]

By the end of December a number of societies had published circulars in which they seconded Sedan's plea. Dijon exhorted the clubs of the Côte-d'Or "to provide for the needs of the army."

[1] Heitz, *Strasbourg*, p. 243. PV, Nuits, Dec. 7, 10, 1792. *JC*, Dec. 20, 1792. Labroue, *Bergerac*, p. 217. *ArchP*, Feb. 7, 1793.

[2] COR: Poitiers, S 26; Limoges, L 825. *PF*, Jan. 5, 1793. *AP*, Jan. 8, 1793. *JD*, Dec. 30, 1792.

Villeneuve (Lot-et-Garonne) announced that it had collected large quantities of woolen hose. Nevers sniffled that French troops were "naked and suffering." The Récollets Society printed an account of a session in which scores of people donated clothes after an orator reproached them for "slumbering in peace while our brave heroes fight in snows up to their waists."[3] In addition, on January 4, the minister Roland circulated thousands of copies of an address in which the club of Cherbourg challenged all communes of the Republic to furnish one greatcoat and two pairs of shoes for "our brave volunteers."[4]

This publicity caused hundreds of clubs to start clothes procurement drives. By March, in an extraordinary display of patriotism, they had raised at least 400,000 pairs of shoes, 250,000 pairs of hose, 150,000 chemises, and lesser quantities of gaiters, vests, trousers, culottes, knapsacks, greatcoats, hats, mittens, gloves, and blankets.[5] Some of these items were probably castoffs; but others were specially made by craftsmen or women. We can get some idea of the cash value of these goods by noting that at Provins in early 1793 the going prices were nine livres for shoes, five livres for hose, eight livres for chemises.

Procuring the clothing was easier than getting it to the troops. All too often it did not reach its destination until the winter was over. Some societies shipped their offerings directly to departmental battalions. Others, believing that "all soldiers of the Republic should be equal," sent their consignments to generals, the War Ministry, or the Convention, to be distributed as the latter saw fit. On March 9 Bergerac was rebuked for doing this by a lieutenant of the Second Battalion of the Dordogne. Why, he asked, didn't the clubbists give the clothes to their friends and relatives? He added that the 218 shoes and other items were probably moldering away, unused in some military depot. Duly penitent, the Bergerac society promised the lieutenant that next time it would follow his suggestions.[6]

[3] PV: Nuits, Jan. 11, 1793; Montbard, Jan. 20, 1793. COR: Poitiers, S 26; Limoges, L 828. *CD*, Jan. 4, 15, 1793. *PF*, Jan. 17, 1793.

[4] Cf. AD, Tarn, L 1515/2, COR, Albi. PV: Vaison, Feb. 22, 1793; Malemort, Feb. 21, 1793; Montpellier, Jan. 24, 1793; Béziers, Feb. 1, 1793; Tartas, Jan. 28, 1793; Bourbonne, Jan. 13, 1793; Vannes, Jan. 20, 1793.

[5] See especially AN, C 246–252.

[6] Labroue, *Bergerac*, pp. 218–238.

The shortages of clothing exacerbated another problem—attrition. At the end of 1792 the French army seemed to melt away. Tens of thousands of fighting men, mainly volunteers, abandoned their units and returned home. Technically, what they did was not unlawful. They had enrolled for one year's service, and these terms expired on December 1. Nonetheless, their actions put France in grave jeopardy.

Anxiety over the "desertions" first surfaced in the clubs in October. On learning that most of the volunteers of the Indre were planning to quit their battalions, Châteauroux begged them to remain at their posts. Lons-le-Saunier drew up an address praising the accomplishments of the volunteers of the Jura, but telling them that more needed to be done. Castres resolved not to readmit those who returned. In November, December, and January, apprehension mounted. Lectoure implored local officials to do something. Toulouse, Baume-le-Jura, and Chef-Boutonne penned letters urging volunteers to stay in service. Trying to shame the quitters, Poitiers published a speech of a wounded man who was headed back to the front. Largentière suggested the revival of a practice of the old regime, the issuance of yellow cartridges as a sign of infamy. St.-Hippolyte approved of a suggestion of the journalist Carra, urging patriotic females to have nothing to do with the returnees.[7]

By February the number of soldiers under arms had fallen from 400,000 to 228,000, and France faced an enemy coalition that had 340,000 troops poised on the five major fronts. Strong action was required, and the Convention took it on February 24, ordering a levy of 300,000 men. All widowers without children and unmarried men between the ages of eighteen and forty were made liable for military service. Departments were given just twenty-four hours to set quotas for districts. Districts, in turn, fixed them for communes. Communal quotas not met in three days by voluntary inscriptions were to be filled by a method agreed upon by local voters.

Fundamentally, the clubs approved of the levy and made haste

---

[7] PV Châteauroux, Oct. 14, Nov. 18, 1792; Castres, Oct. 29, Nov. 30, 1792; Toulouse, Dec. 20, 1792; Lectoure, Dec. 9, 1792; Poitiers, Dec. 23, 1792; Largentière, Mar. 22, 1793; St.-Hippolyte, Feb. 18, 1793. *JC*, Nov. 8, 1792. *AP*, Jan. 18, Feb. 21, 1793. *CD*, Feb. 11, 1793.

to implement it. A clubbist of Lectoure cried out: "We must contact the priests, engage all affiliates in our district to act energetically. A grand movement is needed to exterminate the crowned despots." Toulouse, Bordeaux, and Strasbourg threatened members between eighteen and forty with expulsion if they did not enroll immediately or justify why they could not. Périgueux exhorted the clubs of the Dordogne to "employ all means of persuasion to secure defenders for the fatherland"; St.-Cyprien responded by sending twelve recruiters out into the countryside.[8]

A great many societies, including the Paris Jacobins, published calls to arms. In some instances, special pleas were made to the rich. "Rich people! Give!" exclaimed Montpellier. "It is to safeguard *your* property that the young and unmarried are going to fight."[9] As in past levies, the clubs bestowed money, arms, and equipment upon the volunteers. The Récollets Society disbursed 100,000 livres. Arbois gathered 5,000 for its volunteers and promised to cultivate their lands. Foix gave 2,000 livres as well as an assortment of clothing. When volunteers of Nîmes said that they would not march one foot without a bonus, the Republican Society charged them with "vile, sordid self-interest" and "trafficking in their own blood." Yet, having delivered this rebuke, it raised 200 livres for each of the 520 men, and pledged to care for their families.[10]

There were many acts of patriotic self-abnegation. Vierzon related the tale of a man who had volunteered so that one of three conscripted brothers could stay behind and care for his father, a seventy-year-old vine-dresser. At the Provins club, a certain Droux announced that though married and a father, he was enlisting. A veteran who had already lost one hand joined up at Libourne. A mother at Toulouse had but to say that two of her boys were already in service and that the third, who wished to go, lacked only equipment, and instantly, the clubbists gave the lad a sword, gun, clothes, and money.[11]

[8] PV: Lectoure, Mar. 6, 1793; St.-Cyprien, Mar. 5, 16, 1793; Heitz, *Strasbourg*, p. 257. *ArchP*, Mar. 26, 1793. *PF*, Apr. 2, 1793.

[9] Aulard, *Jacobins*, V, 83–84. Gautheron, "Le Puy," p. 24. AN, C 252. J. Duval-Jouve, *Montpellier pendant la Révolution* (Montpellier, 1879), II, 42–43.

[10] Rouvière, *Gard*, III, 139. *ArchP*, Mar. 20, 26–27, 1793. AN, C 249, 252, 258. Arnaud, *Ariège*, pp. 386–391. BN, Lb 40 1044.

[11] Besson, *Libourne*, pp. 220–222. *Bulletin de la Convention*, Mar. 28, 1793. Bel-

Much publicity was accorded to recruiting triumphs. Arbois and Mirande asserted that they had exceeded their quotas by 33 and 44 respectively. Die said that 16, 3 above the required number, had enrolled and that all were club members. Aire boasted that most of its 130 volunteers were clubbists. Toulouse claimed that 400 of its members were already at the front and that more were on the way. Orange and Clairac stated that their quotas were filled within moments and that no coercion was needed. Fleurance, Fontainebleau, Auxerre, Nay, Aurignac, Argentat, and Chalons-sur-Marne also reported good recruiting.[12]

Despite such announcements, the levy of February 24, 1793, was not nearly as successful as those of 1791 or 1792. Tucked away in the correspondence and minutes of the clubs are many references to opposition that it incurred. Angry mobs threatened to uproot trees of liberty at Castres and Evreux. At Toulouse, one night, malcontents put up posters encouraging resistance. St.-Quentin and Grenoble denounced "traitors" who were urging noncompliance. Bergerac initiated a search for draft evaders who had gone to ground in the teeming warrens of Bordeaux. Young men of Pau took jobs as mule-drivers to get out of front-line service. Orthez and the Popular Society of Nîmes expelled members who had refused to serve. Obstinate peasants of the Quartier des Roves replied to entreaties and threats from commissars of the club of Marignane by saying that they were "free men" and would not go to the wars.[13]

One matter of dispute, even in the clubs, was the method by which deficiencies in quotas were to be made up. There were two alternatives, balloting by citizens or drawing lots. Tartas favored a lottery. Pau preferred elections and drew up its own list of fifty good men. St.-Jean-D'Angely concurred with Pau, contending that random name-drawing was "a coercive system transmitted to us by despots" and that "soldiers inducted by constraint or by chance will serve the fatherland badly."[14]

---

langer, *Provins*, p. 54. M. Albert, *Le Féderalisme dans la Haute-Garonne* (Paris, 1931), p. 29.

[12] AN, C 249–252, 258. *AP*, Mar. 31, Apr. 24, 1793.

[13] AN, C 252. Labroue, *Bergerac*, p. 226. *JD*, Apr. 5, 1793. *ArchP*, Apr. 6, 1793. PV: Toulouse, Mar. 16, 1793; Orthez, June 9, 1793. COR, Marseille, L 2072. Rouvière, *Gard*, III, 139, 225.

[14] AN, C 252. PV: Pau, Mar. 20, 22, 1793; Tartas, Mar. 6–7, 1793.

Another bone of contention was the provision that allowed draftees to hire substitutes. Several clubs adhered to a petition that Nevers circulated in mid-March. It demanded an end to substitutions on the grounds that they were an affront to equality and favored the rich. "The rich," said Nevers, "are typically enemies of popular government . . . and accustomed to profit from the misery of the people. Why should they be exempted? . . . Put packs on the backs of these vile and evil men and force them to leave. Place them under the command of sansculottes."[15]

During the levies of 1792, as has been seen, clubbists muttered about the rich taking from the Revolution and returning little. By February 1793, there was talk of forcing the wealthy to give their fair share. A Jacobin at Lyon declared that the poor would leave for the frontiers only "when bloated landlords and capitalists promise to provide for their wives and children." At Aire, someone growled: "The rich ought to provide for the poor or march themselves." An Antipolitique of Aix declaimed: "Imperious circumstance demands that all rich capitalists and bourgeoisie, . . . all those who up to now have been content to pay their taxes and give modestly for clothing and equipment, . . . be invited to give their surplus possessions to the commune."[16]

In early March a campaign began for a war tax on the surplus revenues of the rich, the proceeds of which were to be expended on volunteers and their dependents. The Club National of Bordeaux seems to have been the first provincial society to make such a demand. But Vannes, Toulouse, Nevers, and Metz were not far behind. Metz, in its petition, grieved that only sansculottes were enrolling for service and stormed against the developing aristocracy of affluence.[17]

Some of the proposals were quite detailed. Sens, which emphasized that it was only denouncing "the evil rich," nonetheless suggested that all bachelors with annual revenues over 5,000 livres be taxed 500 livres or required to clothe and equip one vol-

[15] *JD*, Mar. 22, 1793. COR, Poitiers, S 34. Chardon, *Rouen*, p. 113. PV, Saverne, Apr. 21, 1793.

[16] Heitz, *Strasbourg*, p. 257. PV, Aire, Feb. 27, 1793. Ponteil, "Antipolitiques," pp. 581–582.

[17] *JD*, Mar. 31, 1793. PV, Vannes, Mar. 24, 1793. *ArchP*, Mar. 12, 1793. COR, Poitiers, S 33.

unteer. Tartas called for the very rich to be taxed one-fourth of their incomes, for all childless men with revenues in excess of 2,000 livres to equip one volunteer, and for those with incomes above 3,000 to equip two.[18] Chaumont moved that 150 livres be assessed on every citizen with a male servant under forty-five. Nevers, in addition to demanding that "surplus revenues be requisitioned," wanted a prohibition on male servants and the conscription of all idle young men.[19] Reacting to popular pressure, and to the disasters in the Vendée and Belgium, the Convention, between March 18 and 21, approved in principle a progressive tax on the rich.

OPPOSITION to the new conscription law led, on March 11–13, to the outbreak of a great rebellion in western France. It is usually called "La Vendée," although it erupted almost simultaneously in several departments. Clubs on the periphery of the insurrection helped to mobilize armed forces to stamp it out.[20] Unfortunately, at the moment of combat with the "brigands," the hastily recruited warriors often turned tail. The 1,200-man force, which the club of La Rochelle had provided with shoes, used them for flight when ambushed by rebels near St.-Herman on March 19. It was characteristic of the times that La Rochelle placed blame for this setback on the commander, Marcé, rather than the "green" troops. In a letter to the Paris club it said that its men were "filled with invincible ardor. . . . With a general worthy of them they would have annihilated the rebellion."[21]

While the Vendeé was boiling over, events of transcendant importance were taking place in the north. On March 18 Dumouriez was defeated at Neerwinden, and on the twenty-first he abandoned Louvain. Insane with anger and fearful of possible arrest, he entered into secret negotiations with the enemy, agreeing to evacuate the Low Countries, march on Paris, dissolve the Jacobin club, and restore the monarchy. On March 29 he arrested four

[18] *ArchP*, Mar. 18, 1793. PV, Tartas, Mar. 29–Apr. 1, 1793.
[19] COR, Poitiers, S 34. PV: Toulouse, Mar. 27, 1793. *ArchP*, Apr. 11, 1793.
[20] *CD*, May 11, 1793. Chardon, *Rouen*, p. 124. Richemond, "Ars-en-Ré," pp. 58–70. PV: Limoges, Apr. 6, 1793; Lorient, Mar. 21, 1793; Rouen, May 12, 16, 1793.
[21] David, *La Rochelle*, pp. 87–95. COR, Niort, 3005.

deputies sent by the Convention and turned them over to the Austrians; but he was unable to persuade his soldiers to follow him to Paris, and on April 5 he fled across the border.

The Convention outlawed Dumouriez and placed a bounty on his head. For many of the societies, the head of this fallen idol was not enough. Troyes suggested that all his properties be razed, and that on the sites pyramids be erected bearing these words: "Here was a house of the traitor, Dumouriez." Toul wanted Dumouriez's childhood home preserved as a "monument to infamy." Cambrai, which shuddered at having been the birthplace of such a criminal, proposed that a defamatory inscription be placed on columns near its gates. At other places mannequins of the general were burned, hung, or dismembered.[22]

La Vendée and the treachery of Dumouriez caused fear of treason to become obsessive. Strangers, former priests and monks, aristocrats, and the relatives and servants of émigrés came automatically under suspicion. So too did citizens who dropped a chance remark against the Revolution or who had done nothing to further it. In a petition to the Convention the club of Rennes offered as a model "the laws of Solon which meted out death to all citizens who, in troubled times, were indifferent or declared their neutrality."[23]

Secret committees (variously styled *comités de surveillance, comités de sûreté publique*, and *comités centraux*) were founded by a host of clubs.[24] The most elaborate security net was set up in the southeast. Its nerve center was the twelve-member central committee founded on February 12, 1793, by the society of Marseille. This committee met daily and corresponded with the central committees of at least thirty-three societies of Provence.[25]

On March 21 the Convention ordered that all communes were to have an official surveillance committee to keep tabs on stran-

---

[22] AN, C 252, DXL 18–23. *ArchP*, Apr. 23–May 24, 1793. *AP*, Apr. 28, 1793. COR, Poitiers, S 33. PV: Pau, Apr. 8, 1793; Montreuil, May 7, 1793.
[23] *ArchP*, May 6, 1793.
[24] Dobet, "Guingamp," p. 98. *JD*, Apr. 7, 1793. Troux, *Meurthe*, pp. 280–281. Heitz, *Strasbourg*, p. 258. Rostaing, *Annonay*, p. 204. PV: Le Havre, Apr. 6, 1793; Béziers, Apr. 8, 1793; Largentière, Apr. 9, 1793; Tartas, Apr. 10, 1793; Lourdes, May 9, 1793; Beaumont, Mar. 20, 1793; Nuits, Jan. 25, 1793; St.-Malo, Feb. 18, 1793.
[25] Kennedy, *Marseille*, p. 121.

gers. The societies hailed the passage of this law and were quick to demand its execution. Frequently, the representatives-on-mission gave them the right to designate a certain number of members of these committees (usually two of six).[26] Title two of the law of March 21 included a requirement for which many clubs had been lobbying.[27] Henceforth, every citizen over eighteen had to have a *certificat de civisme* showing his place of birth and profession, and attesting to his performance of civic duties. Quite often, the clubs were assigned the responsibility of investigating public officials and recommending to the surveillance committees whether they were worthy of receiving these certificates. At Bourbonne and St.-Dizier, virtually every session in May was taken up by inquests of this nature.[28]

At Marseille rigorous surveillance soon ripened into outright Terror. On March 14, a deputation from the central committee of the club presented to the municipality a plan for the disarmament of "suspects." Either at this meeting or at a later one, the committee also called for the arrest of the "suspects" and the establishment of a revolutionary tribunal. The municipality managed to turn aside the demand for arrests but allowed disarmaments to take place on March 19.[29]

Similar tales come from other cities in mid-March. Fearful of the Vendéen rebels, the clubs of Nantes united to demand disarmaments, arrests, and the establishment of a revolutionary court. Bourges appealed to the representatives-on-mission in the Cher to disarm and jail "suspects" and marked down two individuals for immediate incarceration. Vannes demanded the razing of châteaux and the confinement of suspects on twenty sous per day. After receiving a petition from the club of Arras, the municipality cordoned off the city and sent commissioners into each quarter to search for strangers. When a visitor at Libourne expressed sur-

[26] G. Moreau, *Tonnerre pendant la Révolution* (Tonnerre, 1890), p. 129. Rossignol, *Gaillac*, pp. 272–273. Bled, *St.-Omer*, p. 34. Cadéot, *Fleurance*, pp. 10–11. Troux, *Meurthe*, pp. 280–283. Denis, *Toul*, p. 20. Albert, *Haute-Garonne*, pp. 30–31. PV: Mayenne, May 19, 1793; Magnac-Laval, Apr. 11, 1793; Lectoure, Apr. 9, 1793; Toulouse, Mar. 27, 1793.

[27] Besançon called for such a law in a circular of Mar. 14. Several clubs adhered to this circular.

[28] PV: Bourbonne, St.-Dizier.

[29] PV, Marseille. AD, Bouches-du-Rhône, L 3037, 3104.

prise that no arrests had yet occurred there, the club agreed that the time for half-measures was over. A committee was assigned to meet all of the next day to receive denunciations of suspects and to transmit the names to district authorities.[30]

The Convention approved an act on March 26 ordering the disarmament of suspects. On learning of its passage, the clubs clamored for its immediate execution. More often than not they also demanded arrests.[31] As it turned out, responsibility for the implementation of this legislation often devolved upon them. On their own initiative, and at the behest of representatives-on-mission and local administrators, they compiled lists of suspects. So many arrests followed that by May, prisons in some locales had become overcrowded.[32]

To the credit of the societies, it should be noted that they were often the first to complain when injustices were committed. Verdun tried to obtain the release of some citizens whom it believed to have been arrested arbitrarily by an agent of the Department of the Meuse. Bourges, which had been responsible for the imprisonment of a certain aristocrat, had second thoughts when it learned that he was to be sent before the Revolutionary Tribunal in Paris. Too late, a group of its members, calling themselves "enemies of aristocracy" but "friends of humanity," composed a letter stating that the prisoner was not "truly dangerous."[33]

In early April, for the first time, the expression *armée révolutionnaire* began to be used in club circles. The idea may have originated with Robespierre. On April 3 at the Paris Jacobins he spoke of the need for a force of sansculottes drawn from the sections of the capital. Within the week the society of Lyon was petitioning local authorities to levy an armée révolutionnaire, which would "strike terror into the souls of the enemies of liberty." On April 14 Châteauroux received a letter from the club of Argenton ad-

[30] E. Lecesne, *Arras sous la Révolution* (Arras, 1882), I, 348–349. T. Lemas, *Etudes sur le Cher pendant la Révolution* (Bourges, 1887), pp. 214–221. Besson, *Libourne*, pp. 222–224. Lallié, *Nantes*, pp. 108–110. PV, Vannes, Mar. 22–26, 1793.

[31] Cf. Rossignol, *Gaillac*, p. 90. Babeau, *Troyes*, II, 46. Dobet, "Guingamp," p. 44. PV: Mayenne, Apr. 15, 1793; Gray, Apr. 14, 1793.

[32] Poulet, "Thann," p. 376. Gautheron, "Le Puy," p. 26. Rossignol, *Gaillac*, p. 91. PV: Valence, May 20–21, 1793; Gray, May 12, 1793.

[33] A.N. C 252. Pionnier, *Verdun*, pp. 317-325. Lemas, *Cher*, pp. 218-219.

vocating a revolutionary force in each department that would be prepared to act against internal and external enemies.[34]

The most important proposal came from the society of Montpellier. On April 10, Montpellier voted to petition for the formation of a departmental armed force powerful enough to defend liberty wherever it was threatened. In a circular of April 12, it urged affiliates throughout the nation to do the same. Montpellier's petition caused the Department of the Hérault to adopt a plan for a departmental army of five thousand men, composed of the "purest patriots" and paid for by special impositions on the rich. Delegates from the Hérault went to the Convention and got its approval, and the Committee of Public Safety on April 27 instructed the representatives-on-mission to recommend the Hérault plan to other departments.[35]

The Hérault plan was discussed widely. On April 30, the Châteauroux club decided to petition its department to create a salaried armed force of six hundred men to be supported by a "progressive tax on the rich." Citing the example of the Hérault, Lyon browbeat the Department of the Rhône-et-Loire into decreeing the formation of an armée révolutionnaire on May 3. It too was to be maintained by taxes on the rich. The Department of the Corrèze summoned club representatives to a meeting at Tulle on May 11 to consider the wisdom of establishing a departmental legion. The Conventionnel Levasseur urged Le Mans in a letter of May 15 to implement the Hérault plan. "Poor citizens," he said, "should no longer waste their time guarding the properties of the rich." Pau (May 20) determined that the measures taken in the Hérault ought to be adopted in the Basses-Pyrénées. At the club of Laval on May 19–20, opponents of the Hérault plan maintained that it was unjust to impose forced contributions on the rich. But proponents argued that it was unfair for patriots to fight and die for the fatherland while aristocrats and the selfish rich did nothing.[36]

[34] R. Cobb, *Les armées révolutionnaires* (Paris, 1961), I, 34–38. Riffaterre, *Lyon*, I, 16–22, 29–33. PV, Châteauroux, Apr. 14, 1793.

[35] PV, Montpellier, Apr. 10–12, 1793.

[36] Riffaterre, *Lyon*, I, 16–22, 29–33. Ulry, "Donzenac," pp. 161–163. PV: Châteauroux, Apr. 30, 1793; Pau, May 20, 1793; Laval, May 19–20, 1793. COR, Le Mans, 1005.

PART FOUR

Faith and Thought

XIV

The Press

CLUB SESSIONS were timed to coincide with postal deliveries. Societies that lay off the beaten track made arrangements to pick up their mail at the nearest waystops or lobbied for the extension of postal routes through their towns.[1] The failure of the *courrier* to arrive on schedule was frustrating in normal times and positively unnerving in periods of crisis. Numbed by such an occurrence in April 1793, the clubbists of Ars-en-Ré sent four of their number to the postmaster's residence to demand an explanation. Finding that he had retired to bed, they pounded on his door and filled the night air with halloos and curses. Alas, he was fast asleep and could not be awakened.[2]

Rare indeed was the postmaster who was not denounced for negligence or treason. Montauban, which feuded incessantly with its *contrôleur des postes*, believed that postal officials were "detestable without exception." Figeac groused that "nearly all were mortal enemies of the Revolution." Several clubs petitioned the Legislative Assembly to overhaul the postal system. Chalon-sur-Saône proposed the creation of a corps of postal inspectors. Nérac, Montauban, Toulouse, and Villeneuve (Haute-Garonne) demanded that all postal officials be elected by the people, reasoning that they were "entrusted with the secrets and fortunes of citizens" and that "every proprietor has the incontestable right to have his affairs managed by agents of his choosing."[3]

The most precious items in the mail coach were the newspapers to which the clubs subscribed. Almost every society subscribed to at least one paper, and some took more than twenty. Meetings in smaller bodies often consisted entirely of the reading

[1] Cf. PV: St.-Hippolyte, Sept. 15, 1792; Pau, May 24, 1793; Orthez, July 8, 22, 29, 31, Aug. 5, 7, Oct. 4, 1792.

[2] Richemond, "Ars-en-Ré," p. 69.

[3] *JC*, Jan. 30, Mar. 15, May 3, 5, 14, June 7, 9, 1792. Ligou, *Montaugan*, p. 279. Toulouse Minutes, May 28, 1792. *ArchP*, Oct. 27, 1791.

of periodicals. In large clubs, conscientious Jacobins grumbled about "frères" who rushed home immediately after the parts of the session devoted to the "papiers publics." Members had the right of access, at specified hours of the day, to rooms where periodicals were stored. In addition, at the public sessions non-members could listen to the clubbists read the "meilleurs journaux" and explain passages that were "beyond the grasp of unlettered citizens."

Since the clubs were so instrumental in purveying news and shaping public opinion, it is critically important to determine what they regarded as the "meilleurs journaux." The loss of most of the account books of publishers makes this a difficult assignment. Analyses of letters to the editor in individual periodicals provide some information on this topic, and a few surveys have been done on the local level.[4] But the only national study, based on the records of the clubs themselves, is that which I have done on the period of the Constituent.[5] This chapter extends that study up to June 1793.

Less than 10 percent of the societies of "phase two" have left behind appreciable records. Usually, only the bound registers of minutes survive, and they do not always identify the newspapers to which the clubs subscribed. Nonetheless, I have managed to compile partial or complete subscription lists for ninety-five societies.[6] From this sample, I have prepared a ranking of the top

---

[4] Cf. M. Fajn, "La Diffusion de la presse révolutionnaire dans le Lot, le Tarn et l'Aveyron," *Annales du Midi* (1971), pp. 299–314. A. Quesnot, "Les Dieppois et la presse périodique à la fin du XVIII siècle," *AHRF* (1935), pp. 54–66. M. Dommanget, "Le Symbolisme et le prosélytisme révolutionnaire à Beauvais et dans l'Oise," *AHRF* (1930), pp. 41–53.

[5] Kennedy, *Jacobins*, pp. 53–72, 365–370.

[6] Aiguesvives, Aire-sur-la-Lys, Aix-en-Provence, Alençon, Ars-en-Ré, Artonne, Avallon, Bar-le-Duc, Beauvais, Bergerac, Blaye, Blois, Boiscommun, Bordeaux (Récollets), Bordeaux (Surveillants), Bordeaux (Patriotic Society), Boulogne-sur-Mer, Bourbonne-les-Bains, Bourbourg, Cahuzac, Callas, Castres, Chalon-sur-Saône, Châtellerault, Châtillon-sur-Chalaronne, Cognac, Condrieu, Courthézon, Douai, Eu, Eymoutiers, Falaise, Gaillac, Grambois, Gray, Guéret, Guingamp, Honfleur, Jonquières, Lectoure, Le Havre, Le Mans, Libourne, Ligny, Lille, Limoges, Lioux, Lons-le-Saunier, Lorient, Lunéville, Lyon (Croix-Rousse Society), Malemort-du-Comtat, Marseille, Marsillargues, Mayenne, Méthamis, Montauban, Montbard, Montpazier, Montpellier, Montreuil-sur-Mer, Neuville, Niort, Nuits, Orthez, Paimboeuf, Pau, Pellagrue, Perpignan, Pithiviers, Poitiers, Riez, Rouen, St.-Affrique, St.-Cyprien, St.-Hippolyte, St.-Malo, St.-Roman-de-Malegarde, St.-Servan, St.-Zacharie, Semur, Sète, Sierck,

twenty-eight periodicals. (See appendix E.[7]) Twenty-four were published in Paris, four in the departments. The majority were dailies or quasi-dailies. The most common formats were four pages in-quarto or eight pages in-octavo; but two were mere placards, and two were more akin to magazines than to newspapers.

Parisian publications on this list may be clustered according to their political views. The extreme Right was not represented; however, a few clubs subscribed to counterrevolutionary sheets for surveillance purposes, and many, to their consternation, received copies gratis in their mail.[8]

Two publications of the moderate Right, the *Journal de Paris* and the *Gazette universelle*, are charted, but strictly because of residual popularity. The prestige and generally pro-Revolutionary views of the *Journal de Paris* (the first French daily) had made it the seventh most subscribed to paper of the Constituent Assembly. In October 1791, however, André Chénier joined its board of editors, and it became rabidly anti-Jacobin. Chénier's editorial foamings brought a brutal response from the societies. Bordeaux and Nantes dismissed him as a "slave of the court" and announced in November that they were terminating their subscriptions. Maubeuge, Brest, Beauvais, and Uzés cancelled their orders in December, and Montpellier burned the *Journal* because of its "ministerial principles." Within a few months nearly all of the clubs had cleared it from their reading rooms.[9]

The *Gazette universelle* was the sixth-ranked newspaper of 1789–91 and one of the best published in the capital. After July 1791, however, it became the principal voice of the Feuillants, the moderates who had seceded from the Paris society; and its edi-

---

Tartas, Tonneins, Toul, Toulouse, Tulette, Vaison, Vannes, Versailles, Verteuil, Villecroze, Villeneuve-le-Roi, Violès.

[7] The figures for 1789–September 1791 in this appendix are based upon a sample of eighty clubs. Sixty-five are cited in Kennedy, *Jacobin Clubs*, pp. 365–370. Since the publication of that book, I have uncovered subscription lists for fifteen others: Moulins, Mas-d'Azil, Villeneuve-le-Roi, Montbard, Nuits, Tartas, Alençon, Pellagrue, Courthézon, Libourne, Chalon-sur-Saône, Bourbonne, Honfleur, Mayenne, and Lourdes.

[8] Cf. PV, Toulouse, Dec. 27, 1791.

[9] *Journal de Paris*, Feb. 26, 1792. *M*, May 10, June 19, 1792. PV: Montpellier, Dec. 5, 1791; Honfleur, Jan. 1, 1792. *JC*, Apr. 30, 1792. *CD*, Nov. 26, Dec. 1, 13, 1791. *AP*, Dec. 1, 1791, Jan. 2, 4, 1792.

tors, Boyer and Cerisier, engaged in a mud-slinging contest with Jacobin journalists. The result was an erosion of support in the clubs. Chalon-sur-Saône, on October 21, appointed a committee to determine if the *Gazette* was still suitable for reading. The Récollets Society annulled its subscription in November because of some "indecent" remarks about the Jacobin deputies in the Legislative Assembly. By early 1792 the clubs of Nîmes, Le Havre, Mâcon, Chalon-sur-Saône, and La Rochelle had cancelled their orders. Lisieux, Brienne, Cherbourg, Bayeux, Bourg, Castres, Orléans, Le Mans, Dunkerque, Agde, St.-Venant, and Avesnes burned the *Gazette* and sent the ashes to Paris. Nantes threatened to sue the editors for libel. The society of Châtillon-sur-Chalaronne, Cerisier's birthplace, delivered the most cutting blow, excising his name from its roll of honorary members. It should be noted, however, that a few clubs bucked the trend. Lectoure, for some unknown reason, subscribed to the *Gazette* quite late (May 15, 1792). The conservative clubbists of Neuville (Rhône) persisted in reading the *Gazette* until they ceased to meet in late June 1792.[10]

Up to the outbreak of war, the clubbists had, by and large, championed the principle of press freedom. Afterward, calls for censorship came with much greater frequency. In June 1792, for example, Langres proposed that all "authors of incendiary papers and placards" should be put to death. In addition, it demanded that the Legislative Assembly publish a national journal, "written in a vigorous but simple style, which would impose a uniform opinion on all of the empire." By early August the clubs had mounted a local campaign to eradicate right-wing publications. Montpellier and Le Faouet announced that the administrators of their departments had finally listened to public outcries and had ordered the seizure of "poisonous sheets." Lille and Toulouse called for similar measures in the Nord and Haute-Garonne. After the fall of the monarchy the Paris Commune suppressed

[10] PV: Chalon, Oct. 21, Nov. 29, 1791, Feb. 19–21, 1792; Le Havre, Feb. 3, 9, 1792; Lectoure, May 15, 1792; Neuville, Oct. 15, 1791–June 20, 1792. *CD*, Dec. 1, 13, 1792, Feb. 6, 15, Mar. 5, 24, Apr. 28, May 6, 22, 25, 1792. *AP*, Dec. 1, 1791, Feb. 17, Mar. 1, 10, 24, Apr. 2, 9, 13, 14, May 17, June 12, 15, 1792. *PF*, Feb. 21, Mar. 4, 28, May 5, 1792. E. Dubois, "La Société populaire de Châtillon-sur-Chalaronne," *Société des naturalistes de l'Ain* (1932), pp. 190–194. *JC*, Mar. 3, Apr. 30, May 7, June 18, 1792.

most of the royalist *journaux* printed in the capital. The clubs roundly applauded this action.[11]

IF one excludes the weekly illustrated *Révolutions de Paris*, which is difficult to classify and which elicited few comments from the clubs, the most subscribed to journal of the far Left in "the middle years" was the *Ami des citoyens*. But its success was only ephemeral. Tallien's *Ami des citoyens* was a placard, and essentially a work of propaganda. It was founded with great fanfare in October 1791, long before the Left began to fragment into "Girondins" and "Montagnards." The Paris society sent sample copies to affiliates, explaining that it was intended to counteract the effect of an aristocratic placard, the *Chant du coq*. Gorsas and Brissot even advertised it. In consequence, there was a rush of orders.[12] That the clubs soon lost interest in it, however, is evident from efforts of the Paris Jacobins in the spring of 1792 to increase its circulation. Tallien sided with the Montagnards in the party strife of the Convention and changed the name of his paper to the *Ami des sans-culottes*. His partisanship cost him more subscribers, for the vast majority of societies, initially, were either pro-Girondist or nonaligned. Falaise, for one, informed Tallien that it no longer cared to read his sheet.[13]

The other Montagnard periodicals fared no better. Save for Limoges, the clubs almost totally ignored the *Journal universel* of Audouin. Historians have perhaps overemphasized the "great influence" of Robespierre's *Défenseur de la Constitution*, for it languished in a tie for last place in the rankings.[14] The *Républicain, ou Journal des hommes libres de tous les pays* was not founded until the end of 1792, and it did not really begin to capture the fancy of the societies until April–May 1793.[15] The *Père Duchesne* was often

[11] PV: Lille, Aug. 2, 1792; Toulouse, Aug. 17, 1792. *JC*, July 2, Aug. 18, 23, 25, 1792.

[12] PV: Versailles, Oct. 14, Nov. 2, 1791; Lorient, Oct. 9, Nov. 17, 1791; Sète, Dec. 12, 1791; Tonneins, Oct. 14, 1791; Falaise, Feb. 9, 1792. *PF*, Oct. 26, 1791. Labroue, *Bergerac*, p. 183.

[13] PV, Falaise, Jan. 9, 1793.

[14] J. Godechot, *Histoire générale de la presse en France* (Paris, 1969), I, 459–461.

[15] Max Fajn, *The Journal des hommes libres de tous les pays* (Paris-La Haye, 1975). Lacrocq, "Creuse," p. 386. PV: Mayenne, Apr. 21, 1793; Lille, May 26, 1793; Monpazier, May 21, 1793.

read in the clubs, for the vulgar-minded loved its earthy style. But references to it are often so vague that one cannot tell if the clubbists were reading the *Père Duchesne* of Hébert, the *Pére Duchêne* of Lemaire, or imitations. That Lemaire was well liked is attested by the fact that several societies subscribed to the *Courrier de l'égalité* which he launched on August 19, 1792.[16]

The most celebrated of the journalists of the extreme Left, Marat, continued to be regarded as the devil incarnate by most of the clubs. Indeed, abhorrence of Marat helps to explain why so many societies declared for the Girondins in the early days of the Convention. When he issued the prospectus and initial numbers of a new paper in October 1792, Cherbourg and Lesparre burned them to rid their meeting places of the stench that had been introduced. Morlaix described them as a "tissue of deceptions and calumnies." The Récollets Society engaged all citizens of the Republic *not* to subscribe. Langon, Bazas, Libourne, Castres, Autun, Annonay, Perpignan, and Lisieux are also known to have reacted in horror.[17]

Antipathy to Marat was never universal, however. At Tonneins, the *Ami du peuple* was read on February 19, 1792, and the minutes state that it "merited reflection." Perhaps the same number impressed Chalon-sur-Saône, for two days later, a member proposed, unsuccessfully, that the club should subscribe. Blois was the first society known to have ordered the *Ami du peuple*, on April 16, 1792, but no explanation was given for its decision. By 1793 Marat's disciples had become a little more numerous and vocal. At Condrieu, in February, a motion to censure him was defeated, and in April someone proposed that his paper be substituted for Brissot's. Chalon-sur-Saône completed a shift from the Girondist to the Montagnard camp in early May by deciding to order his paper. Marseille voted to subscribe in April, justifying this action on the grounds that "time, which is the father of truth, demonstrates more and more that the sanguinary reputa-

---

[16] PV: Châtellerault, Sept. 8, 1791, Aug. 11, 1792; Boiscommun, Dec. 23, 1792, May 26, 1793; Tonneins, Mar. 18, 1792. Maintenant, "Alençon," pp. 102–103.

[17] COR: Bordeaux, 12 L 29–33, 38–40; Poitiers, S 26. PV, Libourne, Nov. 7, 1792. Rostaing, *Annonay*, p. 182. *JC*, Nov. 21, 1792. *ArchP*, Nov. 8, 1792. *AP*, Nov. 1, 17, 1792. *PF*, Nov. 2, 7, 13, 1792. *CD*, Nov. 1, 2, 1792.

tion of Marat was more the result of calumny and intrigue, than the manifestation of his own opinions."[18]

During the Constituent Assembly the Paris club had two semi-official voices. The popular *Journal des amis de la constitution* printed its correspondence with affiliates; the *Journal des débats de la Société des . . . Jacobins* published accounts of its sessions. The death of the former in the Feuillant schism meant that for four months, no record of Jacobin correspondence was made. Belatedly, in late December 1791, the Paris club authorized A.-C. Deflers, the editor of the *Journal des débats*, to form a paper modelled on the *Journal des amis de la constitution*. On January 11, 1792, a *Journal de la correspondance de la Société des . . . Jacobins* began to appear three times weekly in conjunction with the *Débats*.[19]

The *Journal des débats/correspondance* is an important historical source and was well liked by the provincial clubs. Unfortunately, it fell victim to the factionalism that poisoned French politics in the Convention. On October 31, 1792, one of the Paris Jacobins accused Deflers of distorting what was said in the meetings. Then on December 21 he was expelled from the society. In place of Deflers, the Paris Jacobins designated Milscent le Creole as their journalist. None of the departmental clubs seem to have been interested in the *Creole patriote*, however, and it died in February 1793.[20] Acutely in need of a voice and faced with budgetary woes, the "mother society," as has been seen, called upon affiliates in March to help defray its expenses. In return it promised two newspapers: *Le Mensonge et la vérité* and a "journal logotachygraphique" of the debates of the "mother society." Some of the societies that responded affirmatively began to receive the *Mensonge et la vérité* in May. But the "journal logotachygraphique" never saw the light of day. Not until the founding of the *Journal de la Montagne* on June 1, 1793, did the Paris society again have an official chronicle of its debates.[21]

Scarcely a meeting of the Paris society passed in late 1792 with-

---

[18] PV: Tonneins, Feb. 19, 1792; Chalon, Feb. 21, 1792, May 8, 1793; Condrieu, Feb. 10, Apr. 21, 1793. PV, Blois, Apr. 16, 1792. *JDM*, Apr. 9, 1793.

[19] *JD*, Dec. 8, 26, 1791.

[20] *JD*, Nov. 1, 1792–Jan. 4, 1793. Aulard, *Jacobins*, IV, 372–514.

[21] Cf. H. Gough, "Les Jacobins et la presse: Le 'Journal de la Montagne,' " *Actes du Colloque: Girondins et Montagnards* (Paris, 1980), pp. 272–273.

out references to the "corruption of opinion" in the departments. Critical letters from affiliated clubs vastly outnumbered laudatory ones. A major reason for this disparity was that the Girondist press was much more widely read. Of the eleven "principal Girondist papers,"[22] only four, the *Thermomètre, Journal de Paris national, Bulletin des amis de la vérité,* and *Journal des amis,* failed to make the top twenty-five. And not one of these four was totally without influence. The *Thermomètre,* for example, was standard reading material of the societies of Bordeaux and Clermont-Ferrand.[23] Clermont subscribed because the editor, Dulaure, was a deputy of the Puy-de-Dôme in the Convention. Similarly, the *Journal des amis* of their deputy and bishop, Fauchet, was long Holy Writ for the clubs of the Calvados. In 1793, however, Fauchet fell from grace at Honfleur, Falaise, and St.-Pierre-sur-Dives because of some religious pronouncements and his criticism of the "majority" in the Convention.[24]

With the fifteenth-ranked *Journal de Perlet,* the clubs had a love-hate affair. Some swore by it; others complained about its uncritical reporting and "irregular" delivery.[25] The *Chronique de Paris* and *Chronique du mois* had slightly more subscribers. The former was so akin to Brissot's *Patriote français* in content and philosophy, however, that it was dropped by some budget-minded clubs. The latter was a monthly magazine made up of in-depth essays on various topics. It is probable that the clubs ordered it in deference to its distinguished cast of editors, which included Condorcet, Clavière, and Lanthenas. Rouen, for one, eventually cancelled its subscription because "no one read it," and because the Girondist minister, Roland, often distributed free copies of its articles.[26]

The *Sentinelle* of Louvet was originally a large-character, three-columned poster. (Many readers preferred columns, believing that "long lines tire the eyes.") During the Convention it was one of the most polemical Girondist sheets, but in the Legislative

---

[22] Godechot, *Presse,* I, 504.

[23] PV, Bordeaux, Aug. 30, 1792–Jan. 1, 1793. M. Boudet, *Les Conventionnels d'Auvergne: Dulaure* (Paris-Clermont, 1874), pp. 130, 187.

[24] *Journal des Amis,* Jan. 26, 1793. PV, Honfleur, Jan. 3–Feb. 28, 1793. J. Charrier, *Claude Fauchet* (Paris, 1909), pp. 194–272.

[25] PV: St.-Cyprien, Feb. 3, 1793; Montreuil, Dec. 21, 1791.

[26] PV, Rouen, Dec. 20, 1792.

Assembly it drew plaudits from all segments of the Left. Roland clandestinely subsidized it. Jeanbon St.-André recommended it to the society in Montauban. The deputy Ingrand, like St.-André a Terrorist-to-be, forwarded numbers to the club of Châtellerault. And the Paris society asked its affiliates to circulate it.[27]

With such broad backing, the *Sentinelle* was an instantaneous hit. After its initial reading, the Jacobins of Limoges, Valence, and Lorient gave it thunderous applause. Montauban organized public sessions to impart its message to the "people." Two members at Périgueux donated money to purchase fifty copies of each issue. The recorder of the minutes at Tonneins marvelled at its "influence . . . on all attentive minds." Châtellerault read the *Sentinelle* conscientiously from June to September. Perpignan sent copies to soldiers in a nearby garrison. Tulle, on August 27, 1792, charged some members to carry the text of one of Louvet's editorials to the departmental electoral assembly, which was meeting at Brive, and to engage the electors to adopt its recommendations. By November 1792, however, the *Sentinelle*'s star was waning. Perhaps Louvet's vicious attacks alienated the clubs that were trying to reunite the two factions.[28]

The *Patriote français* of Brissot and the *Courrier des 83 départements* of Gorsas were the fourth and sixth most subscribed to journaux. During the Legislative Assembly both men had the status of minor prophets. Shortly after the opening of the Convention, however, the Paris Jacobins notified affiliates of the expulsion of Brissot; and the *Patriote français*, under the direction of Brissot's friend, Girey-Dupré, incited the clubs to break off relations with Paris. The *Courrier* also endeavored to discredit the leaders of the "mother society." Thereafter, with those clubs that were pro-Montagnard or leaning in that direction, the standing of the two papers began to slip. Tulle substituted the *Annales patriotiques* for the *Patriote* when its deputy in the Convention, Lanot, wrote that Brissot "seemed suspect to him." In Novem-

---

[27] E. Hatin, *Bibliographie historique et critique de la presse périodique française* (Paris, 1866), pp. 236–237. Levy-Schneider, *St.-André*, p. 240. PV: Courthézon, May 27, 1792; Châtellerault, June 17, 1792.

[28] PV: Le Havre, May 24, 29, Aug. 19, 1792; Valence, May 24, 1792; Limoges, May 22, 1792; Tonneins, June 27, 1792; Périgueux, May 27–Aug. 22, 1792; Lorient, June 7, 1792; Toulouse, May 28, 1792; Le Mans, July 23, 1792; Montauban, June 6, 1792; Châtellerault, June–Sept. 1792; Perpignan, July 28, 1792.

ber–December, the club of Limoges, Gorsas's hometown, dropped the *Courrier* for the *Républicain*. At Le Havre, on December 31, there was a motion to cancel the *Courrier*. Marseille, in January, accused Gorsas of preaching federalism and royalism. Versailles and Blois also decided that the *Courrier* was "dangerous to the Republic."[29]

By the spring of 1793 the *Courrier* and *Patriote* were under siege from the Left. In the Indre-et-Loire, Tallien, who was a representative-on-mission, banned their circulation along with fourteen other papers. Nîmes, Orange, and Joinville clamored for similar measures in their departments. Toulouse declared Gorsas's paper to be unsuitable for reading. Pau, Fontenay, and Strasbourg incinerated copies of the *Patriote*. So many clubs burned the *Courrier* that Gorsas cracked acidly: "Vesuvius has never disgorged so much lava and ash." It should be emphasized, however, that right up to the June coup, Gorsas and Brissot still had many admirers in the clubs.[30]

The *Annales patriotiques et littéraires* had the same price as the *Patriote français* and a similar format, but it was far more popular in the clubs. Its principal editor, J.-L. Carra, boasted in 1793 that it was read daily by twelve hundred societies and reached a total audience of one million; and this might not be an exaggeration. Carra was probably the best-known journalist in France in 1792. The clubbists called him the "patriotic," "incorruptible," "generous," "celebrated," and "sublime Carra," "the sentinel of the nation," and the "apostle of liberty." Eight departments elected him to the Convention, a total nearly twice that of any other man.[31]

Carra paid court to the departmental clubs by printing laudatory accounts of their activities. Moreover, unlike Brissot and Gorsas, he was extremely active in the Paris society until his election to the Convention. Not only did he appear at the evening sessions with the punctuality of a mechanical clock figure, but

---

[29] Fray-Fournier, *Le Club des Jacobins de Limoges* (Limoges, 1903), p. xxi. Libois, *Lons-le-Saunier*, p. 32. Forot, *Tulle*, pp. 225, 233. *JDM*, Jan. 5, 1793. *CD*, Feb. 5, 1793. PV: Falaise, Nov.13–Dec. 2, 1792; Le Havre, Dec. 31, 1792.

[30] Rouvière, *Gard*, III, 224–225. PV: Toulouse, Mar. 2, 1793; Marseille, Mar. 16, 1793; Pau, Apr. 9, 1793. *CD*, Apr. 9, 1793. *ArchP*, Apr. 29, 1793.

[31] Cf. M. Kennedy, "L'Oracle des Jacobins des départements," *Actes du Colloque: Girondins et Montagnards* (Paris, 1980), pp. 247–268.

from July 16, 1791, to April 1, 1792, he was a secretary of the correspondence committee. Circulars and letters to affiliates bore his signature. The *Annales'* immense appeal was also due to Carra's sense of the theatrical. His columns had an Arabian Nights quality: they were a mixture of fact and fancy, alternately daring, amusing, extravagant, and bizarre.

Historians have usually cast Carra as an auxiliary of Brissot and his *Annales* as a Girondist publication. But these stereotypes are subject to question. That he was Marat's enemy cannot be doubted, and he was beheaded on October 31, 1793 with the Girondins. But he voted with the Montagnards in the trial of the king. And he remained a member of the Paris club until June 1793, eight months after the expulsion of Brissot. Another complicating factor is that Carra spent about five months in late 1792 and early 1793 on mission in the departments. During his absence the chief editor of the *Annales* was J.-B. Salaville, a stubbornly independent republican. Salaville was highly critical of the feuding deputies and demanded that they do their duty and write France a constitution. His editorials, and the vacillations of Carra, caused the *Annales* to be denounced by both parties in Paris.

The reputation of the *Annales* with the departmental clubs long remained untarnished. Tulle, as noted, thought the *Patriote français* to be suspect in October 1792, but not the *Annales*. Périgueux and Orthez annulled their subscriptions in November because the *Annales* was suffering "extremely from the absence of Carra" and contained "morsels which only the Marats can savor." However, life without the *Annales* proved to be so dull that both clubs resubscribed in early 1793. Violès and Tartas put in their first orders in January 1793. In the same month, after acrimonious debates on the Girondin-Montagnard schism, the clubbists of Châtellerault decided to take the *Annales*, apparently because it divided them least. Someone at St.-Cyprien, on February 20, proposed that two journaux be purchased so that "from their conflict the truth can be discerned." But the majority wanted only "Carra." Lectoure wavered between the *Républicain* and the *Annales* but eventually opted for the latter. Marseille, in early 1793, called repeatedly for the arrest of Gorsas, Brissot, and Louvet but displayed no animosity toward Carra. Lons-le-Saunier purged Brissot from its membership rolls in January but did not do the same to

Carra. Tonneins and Toulouse were also anti-Girondist in early 1793 but continued to subscribe to the *Annales*.[32]

Only on the eve of June 2 is a change in attitudes detectable. Bergerac and Orthez (April 6 and 8) displayed irritation over Salaville's criticism of the Convention. After the representative-on-mission, Duhem, maligned Carra's character on April 16, Lille replaced the *Annales* with the *Républicain* and the *Courrier de l'égalité*. Two days later, at Laval, someone charged that Carra, Gorsas, and Perlet were in league with the traitor, Dumouriez. Prodded by Tallien, the club of Blois inquired in May if Carra had changed his principles. Orthez finally cancelled its subscription on May 26, when the representative-on-mission, Yzabeau, warned it "to be on guard against the perfidious suggestions of journalists . . . who debase the Convention and deceive the people."[33]

SOME Parisian journaux were centrist or hard to classify. The *Journal général de l'Europe* and *Mercure universel*, which tied for twelfth in the rankings, fall into this category. The clubs of Aire and Villeneuve-le-Roy deemed the *Journal* to be among the "meilleures feuilles" of the times. The *Mercure* was an inferior imitation of the *Moniteur*; but it printed more club news, and some societies swore by it. Several papers appeared under the title *Journal du soir*; and one, edited by Sablier, was Montagnard. Unfortunately, it is not always possible to identify those to which the clubs subscribed. Lons-le-Saunier, which was pro-Montagnard in 1793, read Sablier religiously.[34]

The *Moniteur* was the quintessential middle-of-the-road journal and had no peers as far as quality was concerned. Its moderation and a lack of sensationalism partially explain why it finished a distant second to the *Annales* in popularity. The clubbists of Chalon-sur-Saône clearly did not think that the *Moniteur* was

[32] Planté, "Orthez," pp. 105, 178. Forot, *Tulle*, p. 233. *JDM*, Jan. 31, Feb. 16, Mar. 9, 1793. Libois, *Lons-le-Saunier*, pp. 99, 104–107, 193. PV: Périgueux, Nov. 5–6, 1792, Feb. 3, 1793; Châtellerault, Nov. 1792–Jan. 1793; St.-Cyprien, Feb. 20, 1793; Lectoure, Apr. 3, 1793; Violès, Jan. 6, 1793; Tartas, Jan. 20, 1793.

[33] Planté, "Orthez," p. 170. Labroue, *Bergerac*, pp. 239–240. PV: Lille, Apr. 16, 1793; Laval, Apr. 18, 1793.

[34] PV: Aire, July 1, 1792; Bar-le-Duc, Oct. 15, 1791. Prévost, "Villeneuve-le-Roy," July 2, 1791 session.

lively enough. They opened their sessions with readings from it because it had the "most authentic political news," but it interspersed them with "the most piquant morsels from the *Patriote français* or the *Annales patriotiques.*" Another reason why the *Moniteur* lost potential subscribers was its high price. Pithiviers and Neuville cancelled their orders because they could not afford it. Presumably, others did the same.[35]

In 1789–91 a host of newspapers specialized in reporting the proceedings of the Constituent Assembly. The number of publications of this type plummeted during the Legislative Assembly, and only two, the *Journal des débats et des décrets* and the *Logographe*, had a measurable effect on the clubs. The former gradually lost subscriptions to general newspapers like the *Moniteur*, which arrived earlier and carried good accounts of the debates. The *Logographe*, which some clubs believed to be superior to the *Moniteur*, closed after August 10 when evidence surfaced that its editors had accepted bribes from the court.[36]

The space left by the closure of the *Logographe* was filled by the creation of an official *Bulletin de la Convention nationale* in September 1792. The *Bulletin*, which was a large placard, became the subject of passionate interest in the clubs. Indeed, after October 1792 it was read with greater regularity than the *Annales patriotiques* or the *Moniteur*. Its name does not appear among the top twenty-five for the simple reason that it was free. At first the clubs obtained the *Bulletin* from deputies in the Convention with whom they corresponded, or by way of district administrators. On March 15, 1793, however, in response to numerous petitions, the Convention decreed that every society should have a copy. Shortly afterward, two governmental agencies appealed to the clubs to provide their names and addresses.[37]

A great many papers were founded in Revolutionary times for the purpose of instructing "the people"; but only one, the *Feuille villageoise*, was truly a success in the clubs. A sociétaire at Ton-

[35] PV: Chalon, May 20, 1792; Neuville, Sept. 25, 1791; Pithiviers, Dec. 23, 1792.

[36] PV: Rouen, Dec. 20, 1792; Versailles, Oct. 21, 1791; Lille, Oct. 4, 1791; Libourne, Nov. 22, 1791.

[37] COR, Joinville. *ArchP*, Dec. 9, 1792. Quesnot, "Dieppois," p. 62. PV: Magnac-Laval, Apr. 28, 1793; Boiscommun, Oct. 5–14, 1792; Pithiviers, Oct. 7–17, 1792; Mayenne, Apr. 21–June 2, 1793; Pau, June 3, 1793.

neins likened its editor, the Abbé Cerutti, to Rousseau, Mably, and Seneca. When Cerutti died in February 1792, many societies held memorial services. Perhaps his death diminished the *Feuille*'s appeal, for its name appears less frequently in Jacobin minutes of 1792–93. Still, it was the third most subscribed to newspaper and remained very influential. At Bergerac it had to be kept under lock and key to prevent thefts. Honfleur and L'Aigle called upon all "good" priests to read it to their parishioners.[38]

Similar to the *Feuille villageoise* in purpose was the *Almanach du Père Gérard* of Collot d'Herbois. Though not a newspaper, it created such a sensation in club circles that it merits attention. In September 1791 the Paris Jacobins offered a prize for an almanac designed for "countryfolk" and written in a simple style. Out of forty-two entries Collot's was adjudged the best and published in November. The "mother society" asked affiliates to make its contents known to the public, and the clubs complied. Annonay, Rodez, Gray, and Nancy reprinted the *Almanach*. Vannes and Dunkerque translated it into Breton and Flemish. Auray asked the government in Paris to provide every French commune with an edition. Toulouse and Fécamp admonished affiliates to purchase it. Vienne read extracts from the *Almanach* three times per week in its sessions. Provins and Meaux bought 108 and 200 copies respectively and distributed them to schoolmasters. Lorient ordered 300 *Almanachs* and considered giving rewards to people who memorized the contents. Few works of the Revolution were more widely disseminated.[39]

BY far the most successful provincial journal was the *Courrier de Strasbourg* of J.-C. Laveaux, a clubbist of that city and the future editor of the *Journal de la Montagne*. The society of Strasbourg forewarned the network of its publication in a circular of November 1791 and pledged that it would provide accurate news on

[38] M. E. Edelstein, *"La Feuille Villageoise"* (Paris, 1977). Labroue, *Bergerac*, pp. 181–182. *JC*, Mar. 22, Oct. 4, 1792. PV: Le Havre, Oct. 13, 16, 1791, Feb. 12, 15, 1792; Honfleur, Nov. 6–Dec. 4, 1791; Tonneins, Nov. 6, 1791.

[39] *M*, Nov. 20, 1791, Feb. 9, 1792. *JC*, Nos. 3, 15–17, 44. Lemaire, *Dunkerque*, p. 339. Bellanger, *Provins*, p. 30. PV: Fécamp, Jan 24, 1792; Honfleur, Dec. 26, 1791; Toulouse, Nov. 24, Dec. 19, 1791; Lorient, Nov. 29, 1791, Jan. 9, 1792; Niort, Dec. 25, 30, 1791; Auray, Sept. 5, 1792; Vannes, Nov. 17, 22, 1791; Gray, Jan. 1, 1792; Tonneins, Nov. 22, 1791.

the Germanies and the Rhine frontier. With war clouds building, a few clubs subscribed immediately. More did so when the Paris society, in two circulars of January 1792, announced that it had subscribed. The *Courrier* gained further notoriety in the spring when Laveaux was arrested by the Feuillantist mayor of Strasbourg. After his release he went to Paris. In his absence, some other members of the club of Strasbourg assumed responsibility for directing the *Courrier*.[40]

The *Argus du Nord* also owed its success to the war and to the endorsements it received. It was edited by a secretary of the club of Valenciennes, and its first number was preceded by a published advertisement from that body (March 29, 1792). Later, in May, the society of Lille advised clubs who wanted news of the fighting in the north to subscribe. Several did so. Unfortunately, some came to rue this decision. Aire received very poor service, and Rouen dropped the *Argus* because its news was "mostly false."[41]

The *Journal des ecclésiastiques constitutionnels*, edited by P. Capon and endorsed by the club of Orange, debuted in early January 1792. It was dedicated to countryfolk and filled with attacks on refractory priests. Although Tonneins ordered it, the *Journal* found few takers and by May had been superseded by the *Courrier du Midi*. The *Courrier* also remained virtually unknown until June 3, 1792, when the club of Marseille issued a manifesto blasting local officials for "persecuting" Capon. The Marseillais vowed not to allow Capon to be silenced and urged the clubs of the Midi to subscribe to his paper. So many societies responded to this plea that the *Courrier* is listed among the top twenty-five newspapers. However, one subscriber, Orthez, was disappointed with it because its news was "very old."[42]

Oddly enough, the *Courrier du Midi* had more known subscrib-

[40] Strasbourg, six times weekly, 4 p. in-4°, Dec. 1791–Apr. 1793. Cf. Heitz, *Strasbourg*, pp. vii–viii. Hatin, *Bibliographie*, p. 207. Labroue, *Bergerac*, p. 186. Aulard, *Jacobins*, III, 30–31. *JC*, No. 9. COR, Reims. PV: Niort, Nov. 4, 1791, Jan. 4, 1792; Toulouse, Nov. 10, 1791; Versailles, Nov. 4, 1791; Lorient, Nov. 7, 1791; Sète, Jan. 25, 1792; Vaison, May 28, 1792.

[41] Valenciennes, six times weekly, 8 p. in-8°, Apr. 1792–Feb. 1793. Cf. M. Martin, "Journaux d'armées aux temps de la Révolution," *AHRF* (1972), pp. 567–605. COR: Lille; Poitiers, S 26. PV: Aire, July, 1, 29, 1792; Rouen, Dec. 20, 1792; Toulouse, May 31, 1792; Chalon, Apr. 5, 1792. *JC*, Apr. 9, 1792.

[42] Orange-Avignon, six times weekly, 4 p. in-4°, Jan.–Dec. 1792. COR, Riez. PV: Vaison, July 19, 1792; Chalon, Apr. 25, 1792; Castellane, June 29, 1792.

ers than the *Journal des départements méridionaux*, the official voice of the club of Marseille. The latter, which was founded on March 6, 1792, published summaries of the meetings of the Marseille club and scores of letters from the societies of the southeast. In an advertisement of February 29, 1792, Marseille invited all branches of the network to subscribe. The only clubs known to have reacted positively were in the Midi, but the *Journal* was often quoted in Parisian papers. On April 9, 1793, Marseille voted to distribute it free of charge to affiliates. Whether it carried out this resolution is uncertain.[43]

PERHAPS forty other newspapers were published between October 1791 and June 1793 by Jacobin clubs or their members. Many were continuations of works founded in the Old Regime or the Constituent. Six of these, the *Journal du département de l'Oise*,[44] *Journal patriotique du Dordogne*,[45] *Journal patriotique du département de la Côte-d'Or*,[46] *Courrier de la Loire-Inférieure*,[47] *Journal patriotique du département de Lot-et-Garonne*,[48] and *Journal du département de Maine-et-Loire*,[49] suspended publication in the first months of the Legislative Assembly when the network was in a state of semi-paralysis. The last known issues of the *Journal patriotique du Jura* appeared in September 1791.[50] The *Correspondance générale de l'Europe*, which was originally endorsed by the club of Reims,

[43] Marseille, six times weekly, 4 p. in-4°, Mar. 1792–May 1793. M. Kennedy, "Some Journals of the Jacobin Club of Marseilles," *French Historical Studies* (1972), pp. 607–612.

[44] Beauvais, bi-weekly, 4 p. in-4°, Oct. 1790–Oct. 1791. Cf. Dommanget, "Symbolisme," pp. 41–43.

[45] Périgueux, weekly, 32 p. in-8°, Jan.-Dec. 1791. This paper, which was a continuation of the *Journal du Périgord*, was edited by the clubbist Pipaud-Desgranges.

[46] Dijon, weekly, 8 p. in-8°, May 1790–Dec. 1791. Hugueney, *Dijon*, p. 134.

[47] Nantes, 16 p. in-8°, Nov. 1790–Dec. 1791. Lallié, *Nantes*, p. 76.

[48] Agen, four times weekly, Jan. 1791–Feb. 1792. An outgrowth of the *Journal patriotique de l'Agenois* (founded in 1789), this paper was "dedicated to the friends of the constitution." In the last number the printer says that he has been "forced to suspend publication for an indefinite time because several of his workers have just enrolled for service in the line army."

[49] Angers, weekly, 24 p. in-8°, Jan. 1791–Jan. 1792. Cf. E. Quéreau-Lamerie, "Notice sur les journaux d'Angers pendant la Révolution," *Revue de l'Anjou* (1892), pp. 150–154.

[50] It first appeared about April 1790. Cf. M. Vosne, *La Presse périodique en Franche-Comté* (Besançon, 1978), p. 41, and Sommier, *Jura*, pp. 77–84.

faded away in December 1792.[51] "Public indifference" forced the *Nouvelles intéressantes* of Montauban to shut down in March 1793.[52] The *Journal de . . . Rennes* survived until October 1795, although its editor, R. Vatar, moved to Paris in August 1792. Vatar, incidentally, became an editor of the *Journal des hommes libres*.[53] The *Journal patriotique de Grenoble*[54] and *Journal des Deux-Sèvres*[55] appeared under various titles until 1796 and 1830 respectively. The former would have succumbed in 1792, however, without cash transfusions from the Grenoble club.

Another holdover from 1789–91, the *Journal de Rouen*,[56] cannot be called a "Jacobin" paper until 1792, when S.-B.-J. Noël became its editor. It was a sorely needed counterweight to the three royalist papers of Rouen, of which the most dangerous, in the view of the societies of the Seine-Maritime, was the *Chronique nationale*. In contrast to the *Journal de Rouen*, the *Journal de Lyon* was at first indubitably "Jacobin." Its editor in chief, a clubbist named Carrier, had to flee briefly to Paris in late 1791 to escape threatened prosecution by the Department of the Rhône-et-Loire, and the Paris Jacobins raised six hundred livres for his legal defense. During the Convention, however, Carrier accepted a stipend from Roland and became a violent critic of the Montagnards who directed the societies of Lyon and Paris.[57]

Until the Legislative Assembly the *Journal de Bordeaux et du département de la Gironde* was the semi-official organ of the great Récollets Society. In December 1791, however, the proprietors fired the editor, B.-G. Marandon, who, in turn, founded the *Courrier de la Gironde* on January 1, 1792. Henceforth, the *Courrier*

---

[51] Reims, tri-weekly, 8 p. in-8°, Dec. 1790–Dec. 1792. Cf. Reims Minutes, Dec. 12, 1790.

[52] Montauban, weekly, 8 p. in-8°, Nov. 1790–Mar. 1793.

[53] Rennes, five times weekly, 8 p. in-8°, July 1790–Oct. 1795.

[54] Grenoble, every other day, 4 p. in-4°, Feb. 1790–96. R. Tissot, *La Société populaire de Grenoble* (1910), pp. 33–35. H. Rousset, *La Presse à Grenoble* (Grenoble, 1900), pp. 2–10, 72–74.

[55] Niort, weekly, 4 to 6 p. in-8°, Jan. 1790–1830. The author printed numerous acts of the Niort club.

[56] Rouen, daily, 4 to 8 p. in-4°. Under the title cited in the text, this paper ran from May 1791 to 1799. However, it could trace its lineage back to 1762. Cf. Mazauric, "Rougemaure," pp. 54–61.

[57] Lyon, six times weekly, 4 p. in-4°, 1791–Aug. 1793. Cf. A. Vingtrinier, *Histoire des journaux de Lyon* (Lyon, 1852), pp. 13–89.

became the voice of the Bordeaux society and the chronicler of its sessions.[58]

The first Jacobin periodical founded in the Legislative Assembly was apparently the *Journal hebdomadaire pour le département de l'Hérault* directed by F. Vendryes, a member of the Montpellier club. On October 4, 1791, Montpellier circulated a memorandum recommending it to affiliates. Toulouse subscribed on October 29, Marsillargues on March 8, 1792. It probably died shortly after the last date.[59]

On October 15, 1791, by circular, the club of Besançon announced the formation of the *Vedette, ou Journal du département du Doubs*, offering to exchange it for newspapers published by affiliates. The *Vedette* mirrored the philosophy of the Besançon society and published extracts of its meetings. Two of its three editors were clubbists. Another Jacobin sheet, the *Feuille hebdomadaire*, was founded at Besançon in February 1793 and for a time competed with the Vedette. But the *Feuille* was accused of Girondism and closed by authorities in August 1793.[60]

After hanging its editor in effigy and burning copies in the streets, the clubbists of Le Mans finally succeeded in closing, in February 1792, the lone paper of that city, a conservative publication called the *Journal général . . . de la Sarthe*. Two gazettes produced by Jacobins appeared in its stead: the *Courrier patriote . . . de la Sarthe* and the *Défenseur de la vérité*. The former was apparently ephemeral; the latter, written by Philippeaux, subsisted until November 30, 1793. Thirty-two issues were printed at Le Mans. After Philippeaux took his seat in the Convention, it was published in Paris.[61]

Club documents of early 1792 abound with references to new

[58] Bordeaux, daily, 8 p. in-8°, Jan. 1792–May 1793. Cf. E. Labadie, *La Presse Bordelaise pendant la Révolution* (Bordeaux, 1910), pp. 66–93. PV, Blaye, Apr. 1, 1792.

[59] Montpellier, weekly, cahiers in-8°. The BM, Montpellier has some printed and manuscript copies of this paper. Cf. PV: Toulouse, Oct. 29, 1791; Marsillargues, Mar. 8, 1792.

[60] Cf. Godechot, *Presse*, I, 498–499. Brelot, *Besançon*, pp. 92–94. M. Dayet, *Un Révolutionnaire franc-comtois: Pierre-Joseph Briot* (Paris, 1960). AD, Hérault, L 5562. COR, Limoges, L 826. PV, Toulouse, July 9, 1792.

[61] *Défenseur de la vérité*, weekly, 16 p. in-8°, Feb. 1792–Nov. 1793. PV, Le Mans, Jan. 4, Feb. 26, 1792. P. Mautouchet, "Philippeaux journaliste," *RF* (1889), pp. 401–425.

periodicals. Some were never more than gleams in the eyes of would-be journalists. The society of Sables-d'Olonne announced prematurely that it was founding a gazette. Twice at Annonay, a Protestant pastor, J.-J.-H. Koenig, resolved to start a weekly called the *Babillard*. In a circular Annonay also called for subscriptions to a *Journal du citoyen* to be published bi-monthly by one of its members. Autun notified affiliates that it had charged M. Fairin, a cleric, to put out a bi-weekly called the *Ami des loix et de l'égalité, journal du département de Saône-et-Loire*. Chalon-sur-Saône ordered it, but it never came. The public library of Marseille conserves a prospectus of the *Mercure de Marseille*, which three clubbists pledged to publish.[62]

A *Journal du département de Loir-et-Cher* was launched about March 2 with the backing of the Blois society and apparently lasted a few weeks.[63] About the same date, three clubbists of Nantes established the *Courrier du département de la Loire-Inférieure* and put out at least seventeen numbers.[64] A short-lived *Journal des débats de la société patriotique de Caen* was started about April 1.[65] In circulars of April and June, Orléans begged affiliates to purchase the *Journal de la Haute Cour nationale*; but there was no market for this work, and it was soon interred in the newspaper graveyard.[66] On April 10 the club of Bourg announced the birth of the *Journal du département de l'Ain*. It clung to life about six months. Castres, on April 17, voted to print a weekly carrying its debates. The plan called for a rotating board of editors serving three-month terms; but the *Journal du Tarn*, as it was called, ran such a deficit that it was suppressed in the autumn of 1792.[67] A *Journal des séances des amis de la constitution de Montauban* was printed from May 13 to 19.[68]

The *Journal de Nancy et des frontières*, the organ of the Nancy

[62] BM, Marseille, 4717. Rostaing, *Annonay*, p. 175. *JC*, Feb. 18, Mar. 3, 1792. PV: Toulouse, Apr. 18, 1792; Chalon, Feb. 26, May 6, 1792.
[63] Blois, bi-weekly, 8 p. in-8°, Mar. 1792. PV, Blois, Mar. 2, 1792.
[64] Nantes, tri-weekly, 8–12 p. in-8°. Cf. Lallié, *Nantes*, p. 76.
[65] Caen, weekly, 8 p. in-8°, Apr.-May 1792.
[66] Orléans, weekly, 24–36 p. in-8°, Apr.–June 1792. This paper was published by Jacob l'aîné, a member of the Orléans club. COR, Poitiers, S 26. PV, Toulouse, Apr. 5, 1792.
[67] The Bourg paper was a weekly in-8° Cf. Dubois, *Ain*, II, 320–321. PV: Castres, Apr. 17–Sept. 23, 1792; Gaillac, June 8, 1792.
[68] Lévy-Schneider, *St.-André*, p. 148.

club, was exceptional in that it endured for one year, from June 10, 1792, to June 6, 1793. Its goal was to promote "advanced ideas," but it was fairly moderate in spirit.[69] The club of Apt sponsored a weekly *Courrier d'Apt*; the *Courrier* commenced about June 1792 and was apparently still being printed in February 1793.[70] The *Manuel du laboureur et de l'artisan*, written by a clubbist of Marseille, ran from June 6 to late August 1792, and was fundamentally a propaganda tract. In weekly "conversations" a fictional rustic sage, "Anselme," taught good citizenship to peasants. The club of Marseille advised affiliates to purchase the *Manuel* and to recommend it "to constitutional priests and to the new educators."[71]

After June 1792 new journaux continued to be proposed and founded, although in smaller numbers. At Perpignan on July 29, the central committee apparently did not like the looks of a projected paper called the *Journal des Pyrénées-Orientales*, for it asked a citizen, Le Grand, to draw up another prospectus. Toulouse, on August 26, assigned four "frères" to establish a gazette designed to instruct the "countryfolk."[72] At Montpellier on September 21, someone proposed to create a *Chronique générale des contrées méridionales de France*. Several numbers of this journal were printed.[73] The *Observateur du Midi*, fostered by the Carpentras club, appeared three times weekly from September 26, 1792, to April 13, 1793.[74] At Libourne, near the end of September, a local printer proposed to establish the *Sentinelle du district de Libourne*, a triweekly "dedicated . . . to the Societies of Friends of Liberty and Equality." It was scheduled to appear on October 15.[75]

The *Wochenblatt*, edited by members of the Colmar society from November 1, 1792, to October 24, 1793, was a German-language weekly. It featured a mythical wiseman, "Antoine,"

[69] Nancy, bi-weekly, 8 p. in-8°. Cf. Mansuy, "Nancy," p. 438.

[70] PV: Grambois, June 10, 1792; Lioux, Feb. 24, 1793. This paper was to be a weekly.

[71] Marseille, weekly, 8 p. in-4°, June–Aug. 1792. Cf. Kennedy, "Journals," pp. 607–612. Copies of this paper may be found at the AM, Toulon.

[72] PV: Perpignan, July 29, Aug. 1, 1792; Toulouse, May 3, Aug. 26–27, 1792.

[73] PV: Montpellier, Sept. 21, Oct. 27, 1792. BN, 4°, Lc^{11} 668.

[74] The Bibliothèque Inguimbertine (Carpentras) has a virtually complete run of this paper. Cf. PV: Méthamis, Nov. 11, 1792; Malemort, Sept. 24, 1792.

[75] Labadie, *Presse*, pp. 94–95.

who indoctrinated peasants in Jacobin ideals.[76] Comparable to the *Wochenblatt* in purpose was the *Entretiens patriotiques*, written by A. Jubé, a militant clubbist of Cherbourg. The only known copy is that of December 6, 1792.[77] A *Journal de la Société des amis de la liberté et de l'égalité de Bruxelles* ran from November 18, 1792, to March 1793 and provides interesting accounts of the debates of a club in an occupied land.[78] Over roughly the same period, members of the Mainz society published four periodicals.[79] On January 1, 1793, C. Payan, a Jacobin of Valence, launched the *Vérité au peuple, Journal . . . de la Drôme et de l'Ardèche.*[80] In the same month the future Terrorist, J.-J. Clément revived the *Journal du département de l'Oise*,[81] and someone tried to resurrect the *Journal patriotique du Dordogne.*[82] Lorient, on April 11, ordered an instructional periodical recommended by the society of Quimper.[83] Finally, the weekly *Sans-culotte du département de la Mayenne* was formed at Laval on April 6. It superseded a paper called the *Patriote de la Mayenne.*[84]

[76] Colmar, weekly, in-8°, Nov. 1792–Oct. 1793. Leuilliot, *Colmar*, pp. 43–45.

[77] No. 23, 8 p. in-8°

[78] Brussels, daily, 8 p. in-8°

[79] Chuquet, *Mayence*, VII, 36.

[80] Valence, tri-weekly, 4 p. in-4°, 1793–97. PV, Malemort, Jan. 10, 1793.

[81] Beauvais, bi-weekly, 4 p. in-4° Cf. Dommanget, "Symbolisme," pp. 43, 47–51. PV, Beauvais, Mar. 27, 1792.

[82] PV, St.-Cyprien, Jan. 1793.

[83] PV, Lorient, Apr. 11, 1793.

[84] Laval, 24 p. in-8° The BM, Laval, has a partial collection. For more details on newspapers published by the clubs see H. Gough's recent article, "The Provincial Jacobin Club Press During the French Revolution," *European History Quarterly* (1986), pp. 47–76.

XV

The Clergy

AT FIRST most of the French clergy were favorably disposed toward the Revolution. Only gradually did the realization dawn that the "faith was in peril." Tender consciences were shocked in November 1789 by the seizure of Church property to pay off the national debt. The suppression of monastic orders and the refusal of the Constituent to declare Catholicism the religion of state (February–April 1790) led to the first widespread protests. Then, in June 1790, the deputies approved a sweeping reorganization of the Church—the Civil Constitution of the Clergy. It provided, among other things, for the election of bishops and priests, and their payment by the state. Resistance to this act was so intense that the Constituent, in exasperation, voted on November 27, 1790, to require all clergy holding public office to take oaths to the Constitution. Nearly all of the bishops and about one-half of the lower clergy refused. The nonjurors, or *réfractaires*, were given pensions but forbidden to perform the sacraments. However, many continued to minister to the faithful. They received powerful reinforcement in March–April 1791, when the pope publicly condemned the Revolution and the Civil Constitution.

The religious schism caused passions to run white-hot in the clubs. It was the premier issue of the Constituent and continued to occupy center stage in the early Legislative Assembly. Club minutes, letters, pamphlets, and petitions abound with references to it; and it was the most alluded-to problem in the reports on the "state of the departments" that were prepared in response to the November 16, 1791, circular of the Paris Jacobins.

Contempt for the pope gradually increased. Smoke from the ceremonial burnings of papal encyclicals darkened the skies of France in the spring of 1791, and again in April–May 1792 after Pius VI circulated a missive asking jurors to retract their oaths. On the latter occasion, the clubbists of Rostrenen danced around the bonfire, singing "Ca Ira," to show that they were unafraid of papal "thunderbolts." And a number of clubs stated publicly that the papacy owed its existence to "ignorance" and "superstition."[1]

Ill will toward nonjuring priests and bishops likewise intensified. Mortain declared that in its region they had caused more havoc than the "locusts which ravaged Egypt." The clubs regarded them as France's "most dangerous internal enemies." The misdeeds for which they were denounced ran the gamut from illegally administering the sacraments to plotting counterrevolution and murder. A source of special concern to the clubbists was the influence that réfractaires had over females. In club minutes we read about women being goaded by their old curés to take part in riotous assemblages, of husbands enduring unspeakable agonies because new brides had been convinced that their marriages were invalid, and of mothers who had been persuaded not to take their babies to jurors to be baptized.

During the Constituent the clubs had lobbied for punitive laws against the réfractaires, and they resumed this agitation after the opening of the Legislative Assembly. Dax told the legislators that it feared "fanatics" more than the Prussians and Austrians. Montpellier complained that "hordes of hypocritical priests" had brought France to the brink of civil war.[2] Under pressure from the clubs and the Paris sections, the Assembly, on November 29, 1791, passed a bill that would have compelled all priests to take a civic oath. Those who refused were to be deprived of their pensions, and departments were empowered to move them from their ordinary places of residence.

The king refused to sanction this bill, but, egged on by the clubs, some local authorities emasculated the veto by taking unilateral measures against nonjurors. Many societies asked their departments to emulate a November 2 ordinance of the administrators of the Haut-Rhin that forced all réfractaires to reside at Colmar (the departmental seat). According to one account,

[1] Kennedy, *Jacobins*, pp. 172–174. *JC*, Apr. 28, May 29, 31, June 18, 1792. PV, Toulouse, May 14, June 6, 1792.

[2] *ArchP*, Oct. 24, 1791. *CD*, Oct. 19, 1791. Duval-Jouve, *Montpellier*, I, 189–190. PV: Vannes, Nov. 5, 1791; Lorient, Nov. 3, 1791; Toulouse, Oct. 10, 1791.

forty-two departments had done so by April 1792.[3] At the insistence of the two clubs of Nantes, the Department of the Loire-Inférieure ordered the imprisonment of nonjurors (March—June 1792). Like lemmings, St.-Malo, St.-Servan, St.-Léonard (Haute-Vienne), Lorient, and Vannes entreated their departments to do the same.[4]

Much to the fury of the clubs, many departments, districts, and communes refused to restrict the liberties of réfractaires. The indulgence of local officials, coupled with the king's veto, emboldened the dissidents and their partisans. In early 1792, religious troubles blazed up in all parts of the country. The Center and Midi seem to have been particularly hard hit. At Pamiers, there was a series of incidents, commencing with a public celebration in honor of the veto. A clerical-aristocratic faction took over Mende and forced the club to close. Fleurance claimed that in its district one constitutional priest had had his arm broken by a blow from a rifle butt, a second had been nearly killed by nephews of the old curé, a third had almost been hung, and a fourth had been murdered in his bed.[5]

The increasing audacity of "fanatics" in the Bouches-du-Rhône, and the complicity of local officials, provoked a brutal reaction from the club of Marseille. On February 26–28, eight hundred armed Marseillais, supported by thousands of volunteers from the small towns around, converged on Aix and purged the departmental directory. Then, in March, the club declared that it would "not allow anything impure to exist around it" and announced that an expeditionary force of five thousand Marseillais was marching on Arles to extirpate the "Chiffonistes," a clerical-aristocratic group that dominated that city. On March 30, the "Armée marseillaise" triumphantly entered Arles. In April, it occupied Avignon and freed a number of imprisoned "patriots."[6] Meanwhile, commissars from Marseille crisscrossed Provence,

[3] COR, Colmar, B 34. *JDM*, Apr. 3, 1792. Lallié, *Nantes*, p. 80. A. Aulard, *Christianity and the French Revolution* (New York, 1966), p. 86. P. De La Gorce, *Histoire religieuse de la Révolution française* (New York, 1969), II, 79.

[4] Lallié, *Nantes*, pp. 80–83. PV: St.-Malo, Mar. 24, 1792; Vannes, May 8, 12, 1792; Lorient, Apr. 26, 1792. COR, Limoges, L 823.

[5] See especially Arnaud, *Ariège*, pp. 270–276. *JC*, Mar. 12, 15, 19, 31, Apr. 5, Apr. 28, 1792. *ArchP*, May 8, 1792.

[6] Kennedy, *Marseilles*, pp. 98–103.

terrorizing "fanatics and aristocrats" in the small towns. Two Marseillais filed the following report from the Vaucluse in March: "Instructed that in several towns, seven- to eight-month-old children had not been baptized, we had recourse to a method which baptized an infinity. Preceded by numerous musicians, our caravan went to the houses which had been designated to us. We took the infants, and accompanied by patriotic godmothers, marched in pomp to the churches to have baptism administered by the constitutional priests."[7]

Marseille's actions dealt a stunning blow to "clerical fanaticism" in the southeast. Club after club wrote to the Paris Jacobins to gloat that réfractaires and "papists" had fled or gone into hiding.[8] It is also possible that Marseille's example inspired the use of force in other parts of France. After violent reprisals against "fanatics" had occurred in the Cantal, the society of Arpajon asserted that the people had "rid those parts of everything which is impure and were awaiting, like the Marseillais, the blessings of France." In April an "army" from Le Puy descended on Yssingeaux and killed about twenty members of a fanatical band that dominated that place.[9]

On April 23, 1792, the interior minister, Roland, presented a report to the Legislative Assembly in which he accused réfractaires of being the principal authors of the troubles in the kingdom and urged vigorous measures against them. Whereupon, the deputies Merlin de Thionville and Vergniaud demanded the banishment of nonjurors from the kingdom. The clubs agreed wholeheartedly with this idea. Several had already called for a law of deportation, and more were to do so in April–May. Gourdon proposed that réfractaires be sent as gifts to the pirates of Tunis and Algiers.[10]

On May 27, 1792, the Legislative Assembly passed a bill providing for the exile of nonjurors if they were denounced by twenty citizens. The king again exercised his right of veto; but after his dethronement, this bill became law along with the one

[7] *JDM*, pp. 45–46. See also *JC*, Apr. 23, 1792.
[8] *JC*, Apr. 7, 14, 23, May 3, 24, 1792.
[9] *JC*, Apr. 5–12, 21, 1792.
[10] Cf. *JC*, Apr. 28, May 11, 17, 19, 1792. *ArchP*, May 25, 1792. PV, Le Mans, Mar. 22–26, 1792. Rouvière, *Gard*, II, 461. La Gorce, *Histoire*, II, 145–156.

of November 29, 1791. On August 26, 1792, a tougher law was enacted, giving *all* nonjurors two weeks to leave the kingdom. Moreover, a number of "bad" priests were murdered during the so-called first Terror (July–September 1792). The problem of réfractaires was by no means solved, but after this date it was no longer quite such an obsession of the clubs.

The period following the fall of the monarchy also saw the resolution of the "monastic problem." Although the Constituent Assembly abolished all monastic orders under vows, it had permitted nuns to remain in their convents and monks to reside in specified monasteries. This state of affairs rankled the clubs because the monks and nuns let their houses become centers of counterrevolution. After months of sporadic complaints, the clubs launched a concerted campaign against the regular clergy in early February 1792.

Poitiers initiated this drive by printing and circulating a petition to the Legislative Assembly calling for the closure of the convents, "those asylums consecrated to piety, in the depths of which the fanatics sharpen their daggers." The nuns were dismissed as "ingrates" who had "proven themselves unworthy of the benefits bestowed upon them."[11] Niort and Auxerre immediately adhered to this circular. Rouen went farther, circulating a petition of February 11, demanding the suppression of *all* monastic houses. Le Mans, Le Havre, Marseille, Dijon, Périgueux, Cherbourg, and Chalon-sur-Saône are known to have adhered. Shortly after Chalon did so, a workman of that city discovered a manacled skeleton in a subterranean chamber. Since a community of monks had long existed on that spot, the club concluded that the deceased was a victim of "monastic despotism." It decided to put the chains on display as an example to "weak spirits" who believed that the closure of monasteries was an "attack upon religion."[12]

How much effect this petition drive had upon the deputies cannot be measured; but in the end, the clubs got what they wanted.

[11] COR, Niort, 3003.
[12] Galland, "Cherbourg," p. 339. PV: Le Havre, Mar. 11, 1792; Chalon, Mar. 6, 11, 1792; Le Mans, Feb. 12, Mar. 4, Apr. 15, 1792; Niort, Feb. 5, 1792; Périgueux, Mar. 6, 1792. *JC*, Mar. 15, 17, 1792. Forot, *Tulle*, p. 170. COR, Poitiers, S 26.

The Legislative Assembly first suppressed secular congregations (mainly teaching and charitable orders) of twenty members or less. Then, on August 11, 1792, it emptied all monasteries and convents and put them up for sale. Last, on August 15, it abolished the remaining secular congregations. In France, the regular clergy had officially ceased to exist.

WHILE the clubs waged a *guerre à outrance* against réfractaires, they were at first very supportive of the constitutional Church. In propaganda tracts of 1790, they stressed that the Civil Constitution impaired in no wise Catholic dogma or the spiritual authority of the hierarchy. Clerics were encouraged to take their oaths and beatified when they did so. Many club members were chosen as bishops or priests. And following their elections, the new Church dignitaries were given triumphal receptions by the societies.[13]

Up to the end of 1791 and early 1792, the clubs remained busily engaged in finding juring priests to fill vacant positions. Falaise (October) wrote to Argentan, Vire, and Coutances to inquire if they knew of unplaced priests. In the same month the Surveillants of Bordeaux urged the Bishop of the Gironde to do something about unstaffed parishes. Thrice, in December, Montgaugier penned letters to Poitiers begging for help in finding a priest. Rieumes sent three deputations to Toulouse in March on a similar quest. Auray (January) entreated its department to procure curés for the parishes of its environs. Versailles (November) proposed as a remedy to shortages the creation of a corps of itinerant priests to roam the countryside. Lille (October) petitioned for the naturalization and employment of foreign priests.[14]

Until 1792, the societies also continued to hold the constitutional clergy in high esteem. As has been seen, new priests were often abused by their erstwhile flocks, while local officials looked the other way. This helps to explain why constitutional priests were so active in the clubs. The club was a kind of castle to which they could repair when under attack, and from which sorties

[13] Kennedy, *Jacobins*, pp. 158–174.

[14] PV: Falaise, Oct. 5, 1791; Versailles, Nov. 12, 1791; Auray, Jan. 22, 1792; Toulouse, Mar. 7–19, 1792; Lille, Nov. 3, 1791. Dubos, "Surveillants" (1934), pp. 25–36. COR, Poitiers, S 19.

could be launched against their enemies. Bergerac went so far as to offer an armed bodyguard to a clergyman. And as late as February 1792, the Paris club counselled affiliates: "Constitutional priests are perhaps the only public functionaries who love the Revolution. . . . Sustain them!"[15]

During the spring of 1792, however, cracks began to appear in this solid wall of support. Some clergymen had taken their oaths in the hope of material gain. Once in office, they were just as acquisitive as any of their predecessors. Béziers, in April 1792, observed sorrowfully that priests were wheedling bequests from the dying, that "the grasping hands of ministers of a poor God are still extended toward earthly properties." It called for a law forbidding priests to inherit anything, save from relatives. In addition, a number of societies criticized curés for wrongfully collecting fees from their parishioners.[16]

One of the most notable complaints of this sort was made by the club of Ste.-Colombe in June 1792. It accused an "unworthy" curé of charging thirty sous in coin for giving first communion to children, and of refusing communion to the infants of parents who offered him assignats. Allegedly, he also weighed candles before and after burial services, and forced relatives of the dead to pay in specie for the wax that had been consumed. From this racket, said Ste.-Colombe, he had made such a tidy sum that other priests of the region had begun to follow his example. In addition, Ste.-Colombe charged several curés of its vicinity with perpetuating the "superstitious" custom of ringing bells and reading the "Passion" at the approach of storms. For these services, they extracted a "Passion tax" from farmers in the form of grain at harvest time.[17]

On April 6, 1792, the Legislative Assembly approved, in principle, a motion forbidding ecclesiastics to wear religious garb. Although this was an oblique blow at the privileged position of the constitutional clergy, only one club, Port Louis, is known to have protested; and it got no support from affiliates. Lorient replied thusly to Port-Louis' circular: "We differ totally from you on the decree regarding priestly 'masquerades.' . . . If they had

[15] Cf. Labroue, *Bergerac*, p. 186. Henriot, *Semur*, pp. 121–122.

[16] *JC*, May 3, 1792. Besson, *Libourne*, p. 156.

[17] *JC*, June 9, 1792.

been deprived of their ridiculous costumes a century ago, they would not be so egotistical today."[18]

Several societies wrote to congratulate the deputies on the April 6 resolution. In addition, they urged local authorities to enforce it as law and asked priests who were clubbists to set examples by not wearing religious regalia in the streets. Epinal published an address asserting that the first Christians had no cassocks, whimples, cowls, or colored robes. And it replied to those who said that the April 6 resolution was an attack upon religion, by asking if the faith was endangered when priests donned red vests to go hunting. "Priests," said Epinal, "are only men and should not have distinctive apparel."[19]

On August 18, 1792, the resolution was finally enacted into law. The failure of some priests to abide by it irked the clubs and provoked much discussion that autumn. A member at Toulouse wanted the Bishop of the Haute-Garonne to call a council on the subject. At St.-Affrique a clubbist demanded that the curé be censured for wearing religious costume. Thionville and Lectoure berated local officials for letting priests appear in the streets in their robes. "One class of citizens should not be distinguished from the rest."[20]

In addition to rising anticlericalism, one can dimly discern in early and mid-1792 the beginnings of an assault upon Catholicism itself. Dijon persuaded a few affiliates to adhere to an address demanding that the king renounce the title of "His Most Christian Majesty, Eldest Son of the Church." This salutation, it said, was "suitable only for a nation of monks, knaves, and fools." Moreover, several clubs were ready to despoil the Church of more wealth. Some recommended that the metal from surplus bells be used to alleviate the shortage of base coins; and Chalon-sur-Saône petitioned for the confiscation of "excess silver plate" for the minting of specie. The Legislative Assembly, after long debates, decided to allow individual communes to melt down

[18] *JC*, Apr. 26, 1792. COR, Lorient, Apr. 29, 1792.

[19] Besson, *Libourne*, p. 155. *JDM*, p. 324. PV: Beauvais, Apr. 9, 1792; Vannes, Apr. 12, 21, 1792; Lorient, May 29, 1792; Le Mans, Apr. 22, 1792. Philippe, *Epinal*, IV, 138.

[20] *JDM*, p. 324. PV: St.-Malo, Nov. 5, 1792; Toulouse, Oct. 15, 1792; St.-Affrique, Oct. 26, 28, 1792; Lectoure, Nov. 9, 1792; Thionville, Nov. 12, 1792.

bells in cases where the need was manifest. And just before it disbanded, it ordered that gold and silver objects in unused churches
be converted into ingots.[21]

It is impossible to determine if disbelief was common in the
clubs of the Legislative Assembly, for many had rules forbidding
theological discussions.[22] Evidence suggests that the vast majority of clubbists remained true to the faith. Speakers invoked
God's name and used Biblical texts to buttress their arguments.
Prayers were said for the success of French arms, and flags were
blessed by priests. Philosophy and religion were hailed as "sisters
given by God to console men on their misfortunes." Great store
was placed on the need for instruction in Christian ethics.[23] Indeed, there was a puritanical streak in Jacobinism. No off-color
jokes leavened the sessions. Swearing was taboo. Orators railed
against the sins of avarice, dishonesty, and prostitution. Officials
were hounded to close gaming houses. Billiard halls were regarded as dens of iniquity, and "aristocratic" to boot.[24]

There were freethinkers in the societies, however, and they became a little bolder in mid-1792. At Limoges, a member had to
be called to order for making sacrilegious remarks. From Tours,
a certain Veau whined to the Paris Jacobins that he was not free to
speak of religion at his club. He exulted at being a Deist, saying
that this was the faith of "Rousseau and Socrates"; and he dismissed Christianity as the "cult of the grand Lama." One also detects a relativist, anti-Catholic spirit in utterances made on the
subject of religious toleration. Lons-le-Saunier wanted a supplement to the *Almanach du Père Gérard* to be published, with an article on "Mohammed, Buddha, Moses, Socrates, and Confucius,
proving that there are just men who are not Christians."[25]

As they had done during the Constituent, the clubs staunchly

[21] PV: Le Mans, June 14, 17, 28, 1792; Tonneins, Mar. 4, 1792; Toulouse, June
8, 1792; Chalon, June 10, 1792. Hugueney, *Dijon*, p. 137. Galland, "Cherbourg,"
p. 339.

[22] Cf. PV: Valence, June 7, 1792; Le Mans, Dec. 8, 1791; St.-Affrique, Jan. 13,
1792. These rules were designed primarily to prevent dissension.

[23] Cf. Flottes, "Bordeaux," pp. 355–356. *JC*, May 10, 1792; PV, Auray, Sept.
23, 1792.

[24] Cf. *JC*, Mar. 10, 1792. Gautheron, "Le Puy," pp. 92–93. Caubet, "Jouan,"
pp. 166–167. PV: Courthézon, Dec. 25, 1791; Tonneins, Oct. 2, 1791; Aire, Sept.
20–21, 1792; Le Havre, Apr. 24, 1792.

[25] *JD*, Apr. 21, 28, 1792.

defended the newly won freedoms of Protestants. At Marseille and Clermont-Ferrand, members went en masse to attend the opening of Reformed churches. Lille asked local officials to give Protestants a Catholic church in which to worship, and space for a cemetery. Orthez campaigned successfully to get Protestants a burial area in the town cemetery, and then became enraged when it learned that the commune was planning to build a wall to segregate the dead by faiths. The Récollets Society moved to halt shameful practices of nuns at the Hôtel-Dieu. When a Protestant died, the sisters purportedly "dragged the cadaver from the bed, covered its face with slime, and put it in a latrine."[26]

For better or worse, liberty of conscience had not triumphed completely in the Constituent. Catholicism was still, in effect, the religion of state; and local ordinances forced citizens to observe its rites. Up to 1792, the clubs acquiesced in this. Indeed, in their zeal to sustain the constitutional Church, they were sometimes guilty of intolerance. Beaumont voted in September 1791 to expel members who did not attend the divine offices of the constitutional curé. The Surveillants of Bordeaux (January 1792) asked the commune to prohibit merchants from selling their wares during certain hours on Holy Days.[27]

By mid-1792, however, some clubs had begun to combat "blue laws" and to defend abstinence from cult-related rituals. When Orthez learned that a farmer had been forbidden by the commune to work on a Holy Day, a member voiced disbelief that it was "possible in a century in which liberty of religious opinions was a sacred right, that governing authorities were reviving prejudices contrary to humanity and to the Declaration of the Rights of Man." Orthez also protested in June 1792, when it heard that its commune had ordered citizens, under threat of fine, to observe traditional Corpus Christi Day customs such as hanging tapestries on their doors.[28]

Perhaps Orthez was inspired by the example of the Paris Commune, which had revoked police regulations obliging citizens to

---

[26] Planté, "Orthez," pp. 74, 103–104, 118–119. *CD*, Apr. 1, 1792. PV, Lille, Oct. 10, 16, 1791. COR, Lille. *PF*, Apr. 23, 1792. *JDM*, 81, 416, 432–433. *AP*, Apr. 26, 1792.
[27] Testut, *Beaumont*, p. 773–776. Dubos, "Surveillants" (1934), pp. 25–36.
[28] Planté, "Orthez," pp. 23–25, 109–113.

drape and decorate their doors and granted shopkeepers the right
to do business on Corpus Christi Day. When Périgueux read an
article in the *Annales patriotiques* reporting the policies of the Paris
Commune, the Vicar Sirey jumped to his feet and begged the
club in the name of "philosophy, liberty, and the religion of Jesus
Christ" to ask local officials *not* to force citizens to do homage to
the faith. This motion was defeated, largely due to the "intrigues" of two other priests. But three days later, the lawyer
Pipaud revived the motion, adding that the old laws discrimi-
nated against the poor. This time it passed unanimously.[29]

Closely tied to the issue of religious liberty was that of *état civil*.
The Constituent Assembly had approved this concept in principle, but left its implementation to the Legislative Assembly. For
the time being, constitutional priests (or their Protestant and Jew-
ish counterparts) continued to keep records of deaths, marriages,
and baptisms. At least one club, Strasbourg, declared itself in favor of Civil Status in August 1791, and some put the topic on
their agendas in the autumn. But it was only in the spring of 1792,
after the Assembly began to consider a plan to give municipalities
the responsibility of keeping vital statistics, that the societies took
up this matter in earnest.[30]

Most clubs seem to have approved of the proposed bill. At
Périgueux and Lille (March 1, 4) speakers "proved" that civil
marriage was not "contrary to religion" as critics charged, that
"those individuals who believe that marriage is a sacrament will
be free to go to their priest and have him administer it." On May
19, Angers circulated a petition (to which Toulouse and Tonneins
adhered) calling for vital statistics to be kept by public functionaries and enumerating the ways in which "Roman priests" had
abused this privilege. "Avid for riches, honors, and domination,
priests of all times and places have used this to enslave peoples.
Legislators! Free us from their yoke."[31]

---

[29] Aulard, *Christianity*, pp. 89–90. PV, Périgueux, June 7, 10, 1792.

[30] Heitz, *Strasbourg*, p. 163. PV, Versailles, Nov. 23, 1791. La Gorce, *Histoire*, III, 34.

[31] *JDM*, p. 362. PV: Toulouse, May 30, 1792; Vannes, May 28, 1792; Tonneins, May 31, 1792; Périgueux, Mar. 1, 1792; Lille, Mar. 4, 1792. *JC*, May 26, 1792. *ArchP*, July 18, 1792. COR: Niort, 3001; Bordeaux, 12 L 29.

On May 20, Epinal published an address on *état civil*. It, too, reassured the people that they would always be free to receive the sacraments. Then, it stated that this law was needed to bring uniformity to France, that Frenchmen must be citizens first, not Catholics or Protestants. Next, it argued that civil records were the safest means to safeguard the birthrights of children. Finally, tucked away near the end of this opus, was a plea for separation of Church and State. To justify this ideal, Epinal cited a passage from Paul's second epistle to Timothy: "Take your share of suffering as a good soldier of Christ Jesus. No soldier on service gets entangled in civilian pursuits, since his aim is to satisfy the one who enlisted him."[32]

While the legislation was still pending, a clubbist of Aire contracted his marriage before a justice of the peace. When the constitutional curé insisted in the club that the marriage was invalid, that the "old laws" were still in force, a divisive argument occurred. At last, on September 20, 1792, the Assembly approved a law requiring marriages, births, and deaths to be recorded by municipalities. The clubs applauded this decree, although one suggested slight modifications. St.-Martin-du-Touche complained to Toulouse that citizens of isolated hamlets were concerned about accidents that might occur to newborns who had to be transported long distances to communes. Toulouse agreed that this was a health hazard and petitioned for the creation of a corps of village record-keepers.[33]

On the same day that *état civil* was instituted (September 20), the Legislative Assembly legalized divorce. Much discussion of the pros and cons of divorce had taken place in the clubs in 1791–92, without a clear consensus being attained. After it became law, the clubs closed ranks behind the legislators, clashing in the process with constitutional priests. Rochefort, in April 1793, denounced a curé for refusing to marry divorced citizens (and for keeping records of marriages, baptisms, and deaths in defiance of the law). Brioude censured the Bishop of the Haute-Loire for denying the sacraments to a divorcee who had remarried. Indeed, it

---

[32] Philippe, *Epinal*, IV, 131–137.
[33] PV: Aire, June 15, 20, 22, 1792; Auray, Oct. 18, 1792; Toulouse, Nov. 19, 20, 1792. Guillemaut, *Louhans*, II, 46.

presumed to give the bishop a lesson in the scriptures, reminding him of the story of Elisha and Naaman.[34]

Another question in which the clubs were keenly interested was clerical marriage. Scattered comments were made about celibacy during the Constituent, and even then, it is clear, many clubbists looked upon this custom with repugnance. In September 1790, Vire suggested that priests be permitted to marry so that they could "truly become citizens." Two months later, the Paris Jacobins printed an address espousing clerical marriage. The curé of St.-Benoit-sur-Seine further developed this theme at Troyes in January 1791, and Dijon published a speech in August in which a member stated that "man is born and lives solely to procreate his species."[35]

During the Legislative Assembly it became fairly common for this subject to be placed on agendas.[36] Indeed, it ceased to be merely a theoretical exercise. Several Parisian newspapers printed accounts of the marriage of the Abbé Cournand in October 1791. The *Révolutions de Paris* urged "courageous" clerics to follow his example. In December, a curé of the Charente-Maritime asked the Legislative Assembly for authority to marry. And in January, an account of the nuptials of a cleric appeared in the popular *Feuille villageoise*.[37]

At Le Havre, on January 15, 1792, the future Conventionnel Bailleul read some passages from the article in the *Feuille villageoise* in the hope that priests would profit from this example. But another member said that public opinion was not "sufficiently enlightened" to accept clerical marriages, and a third advised his brothers not to become embroiled in religious controversies. The issue was discussed again on January 22 and February 2. On the former date, Bailleul gave a much applauded speech on the advantages of marriage over celibacy. Later (March 17), someone read a *Dialogue entre un père de famille et un vicaire qui lui demandait*

[34] PV: Le Puy, Feb. 21, 1793; Laval, Feb. 3, 1793; Versailles, Nov. 23, 1791. Bellanger, *Provins*, p. 49. Guillemaut, *Louhans*, II, 46. Lemonnier, *Rochefort*, pp. 61–62. *AP*, May 15, 1793.

[35] Kennedy, *Jacobins*, 176. Aulard, *Jacobins*, I, 382. Hugueney, *Dijon*, p. 115. La Gorce, *Histoire*, III, 42.

[36] Heitz, *Strasbourg*, p. 165. Holuigue, *Boulogne*, pp. 228–229. PV, Chalon, Nov. 6, 1791.

[37] La Gorce, *Histoire*, III, 45.

sa fille en marriage, which proved "irrefutably" that celibacy was contrary to "divine and human laws." These debates may have caused a curé of Le Havre to marry. The club announced his wedding in a letter of January 27, in which it also admitted that some of the populace was not pleased.[38]

When more clerical marriages occurred in early 1792, leaders of the constitutional Church and local officials attempted to stifle the burgeoning movement. In so doing, they drew fire from the clubs. Ampuis rebuked diocesan authorities for defrocking a curé of Montbrison who had taken a wife. St.-Pont (Hérault) complained when its municipality refused to recognize the marriage of a curé, opining that "wedlock is the first and most holy of nature's duties."[39] On April 27, at Le Mans, someone moved that Bishop Gratian of the Seine-Inférieure be censured for threatening to excommunicate priests who had the "courage to brave a prejudice which is destructive to society and to morals." Although one member vehemently opposed this motion, it was eloquently sustained by the future Conventionnel Levasseur, who based his arguments on "reason, the customs of the primitive Church, Holy Scripture, and the writings of Church fathers." The club not only censured the bishop, but asked the Legislative Assembly to allow married priests to keep their offices.[40]

On May 30, 1792, the club of Sommières proudly reported the marriage of a constitutional curé and an ex-nun and predicted that nine or ten clerics of its district would soon wed. A little afterward, Sommières printed an oration in defense of priestly marriages by J.-B. Loys. He charged that celibacy had been instituted by "wicked" Popes like Gregory VII, and he theorized that its abolition would cause priests to become more attached to the fatherland. "What could be more beautiful," he asked, "than for a priest to give his flock an example of marital bliss?" Throughout his address, Loys cited passages from Rousseau and the Bible. Alas, he knew more of Rousseau than the Good Book. He baldly declared that St.-Paul took his spouse with him on his missionary journeys![41]

[38] PV, Le Havre. *JC*, Feb. 13, 1792.
[39] *JC*, Mar. 15, Aug. 16, 1792. PV, Vannes, Apr. 12, 1792.
[40] PV, Le Mans.
[41] *JC*, June 9, 1792. COR, Montpellier, L5548.

The marriage of Lindet, Bishop of the Eure, set off a new round of debates in the early Convention. At the Récollets Society, speeches critical of celibacy were given on November 22–23. Vannes made this issue the order of the day on December 16. When the bishop and Conventionnel Fauchet issued a statement opposing clerical weddings, he was denounced by several clubs of the Calvados. Honfleur urged its commune to stop the circulation of Fauchet's paper, the *Journal des amis*.[42]

By 1793, the campaign against celibacy had taken on the character of a crusade. In February, Carra printed an account of the nuptials of a "virtuous curé" of Châtillon-sur-Chalaronne (sent to him by the club), as "proof of the progress of public spirit and the decay of antique prejudices." Pézenas, in April, boasted by circular that "fifty or sixty" priests of the Hérault had wed, or would soon do so. In the same month Poitiers announced that it had voted to give a civic crown to the first priest who entered into matrimony. Several clubs, including Limoges, followed Poitiers' example. No sooner had Limoges adopted this resolution than the newly wed curé of St.-Bonnet-la-Rivière came forward to claim his crown. It was presented to him in a solemn and widely publicized ceremony.[43]

ON November 13, 1792, the deputy Cambon announced to the Convention that the finance committee, of which he was a member, was formulating a bill to abolish the budget for public worship. He explained that this action would save the government 100,000,000 livres annually and guarantee that all faiths were treated equally. The Convention declined to approve this proposal. On the contrary, it twice affirmed that it did not intend to "deprive citizens of the ministrations of religion that the Civil Constitution of the Clergy had given them." Still, the very fact that such a suggestion was made provoked much comment from the clubs, and gives us some idea of the strength of anticlerical feeling at the end of 1792.[44]

[42] PV: Bordeaux, Nov. 22, 23, 1792; Vannes, Dec. 16, 1792; Honfleur, Dec.1792–Feb. 1793. Charrier, *Fauchet*, pp. 254–275.

[43] *AP*, Feb. 21, 1793. Chardon, *Rouen*, p. 27. PV: Perpignan, Apr. 24, 1793; Magnac-Laval, June 2, 1793; Limoges, Apr. 20–24, 1793; Périgueux, Apr. 6–7, 1793; Le Puy, Apr. 28, 1793; Montargis, May 17, 1793.

[44] Aulard, *Christianity*, p. 95. La Gorce, *Histoire*, III, 24.

Several clubs took equivocal positions. The Récollets Society, for example, learned of Cambon's motion on November 19 and voted to place it on its agenda for a future meeting. After the decision was made, however, one member commented that "conformist priests have served the country faithfully and that this should not be forgotten in the discussion." The debates took place on November 22 and 23. Apparently, no consensus was reached; but one speaker argued that the state should continue to pay the salaries of current priests until their deaths, and oblige the faithful to provide for new ones.[45]

La Souterraine was the lone society known to have supported Cambon's motion; but its petition to the Convention was keen-edged and is worthy of being quoted in *extenso*:

> "How much longer must our taxes go to pay a sacerdotal sect, one whose intolerance and perversity are attested throughout the pages of history? . . . As long as it is not annihilated, the clergy will remain dangerous; priests will always be priests. Abolish the Civil Constitution of the Clergy which perpetuates the spirit of intolerance and makes priests believe that they are superior to other Frenchmen. . . . Ought we to tolerate a religion which is by nature intolerant? If some people have need of a mysterious creed, of priests, let them support them. Let the priest, like the businessman, be paid by the consumer. It is absurd that Frenchmen should have to provide for men whose ethics are destructive to the public spirit. Soon, all Frenchmen will think as we do. . . . A good farmer, a brave soldier, a virtuous citizen, these are the saints whose memories we will honor. . . . The name of Beaurepaire [a martyred soldier] should be remembered by the French, not St.-Francis, St.-Anthony or another imbecile who has given no example of the social virtues . . . who has only vegetated and died a useless death.[46]

The remainder of the societies that expressed opinions opposed Cambon's initiative. Toulouse was the first to sound the alarm.

[45] PV, Bordeaux.
[46] *JD*, Nov. 20, 1792.

In a circular of November 21 it blasted the "blind or wicked men" who had concocted this scheme. In Toulouse's view, it was "impolitic" and "unjust": impolitic because it would lead to civil war in the countryside, unjust because the nation had contracted a "sacred debt" to the Catholic clergy when it seized their property. "Undoubtedly the Rabbi should have the same rights as the Catholic minister, but the treasures of other religions were not confiscated to pay off our debt."[47]

Perhaps Aix was influenced by Toulouse's petition, because it used very similar language in an address it printed and circulated a little before December 20. Aix rejected Cambon's motion with "indignation and contempt," charging that it would "enrage three-fourths of the Republic" and would be a violation of the "sacred obligation" contracted by the nation. "We, too, believe that citizens of all religions should be equal. But would equality truly exist if the properties of Protestants have not been touched?"[48]

St.-Hippolyte probably received Toulouse's circular about December 2, for on that date its president denounced Cambon's "unjust" and "impolitic" attempt to "despoil republican priests." The club drew up a petition expressing these sentiments and, in addition, sent an address to the Convention in the name of the "Roman Catholics of St.-Hippolyte." The authors of this address vowed to remain invariably attached to the faith and condemned the "agitators" who were working up sentiment against Catholicism. "Legislators! Beware of those who say that public order and the well-being of the nation can be secured without the benefit of religion . . . , without the sanction of the Supreme Being."[49]

Altogether, about a dozen clubs are known to have demanded that the salaries of priests be conserved. Pont-St-Esprit, for example, declared that the enactment of Cambon's proposal would bring "eternal opprobrium" upon France. Laval sent an address

---

[47] COR: Josselin; Reims; Poitiers.

[48] PV, Toulouse, Dec. 20, 1792. COR: Limoges, L 825; Poitiers, S 1; Bordeaux, 12 L 29.

[49] PV, St.-Hippolyte, Dec. 2, 1792, Jan. 3, 20, 1793. COR, Montpellier, L 5548.

to the Convention which was phrased thusly: "Legislators! . . . It is with sadness that we see you contemplate measures which insult the Divinity. . . . We grieve to see that some wish to annihilate the Catholic Faith. Like Socrates, we will take hemlock if need be, to defend the true god!"[50]

Unquestionably, the majority of clubbists still remained loyal to the constitutional clergy and to the Catholic faith. In the first months of 1793, however, anticlericalism and secularism were to make further inroads. On January 13 a French diplomat, Basseville, was killed by a mob in Rome. This incident, and the fact that the murderers went unpunished, caused the clubs to explode with fury. Someone at Lectoure said that this was the work of the "old idol" and the "hypocritical slaves" who surround him. Jouan le jeune, who was locked in a quarrel with the curé of Tonneins, polemicized that "priests are, in general, bad citizens." Tulle was horrified. A member declared that "priests in all times have done much evil in the name of religion," and he advised his frères to be "on guard against the perfidious insinuations of ministers of all religions." Gardanne called for vengeance against the "tyrant of the Tiber." La Gardelle likened the pope to an aristocrat. "Jesus Christ did not resemble him. He was a true sansculotte. He detested luxury . . . and loved equality. After his death, his disciples shared all of their goods." Louviers organized a parody of a religious procession. At each intersection four sansculottes gave mock lashings to men dressed in the garb of a pope and a cardinal.[51]

By a fateful conjunction, the great military crisis began just as the news arrived of Basseville's murder. This caused Dijon, on February 10, to petition in the name of equality that priests no longer be exempted from military service. Its author (who incidentally was an Episcopal vicar), stated his case in emotional terms: "They invoke the God of Battles from their pulpits, but their arms do nothing. . . . What clauses of the social contract favor them? . . . The time of privilege for the clergy is past. Why

[50] AN, C 250. *ArchP*, Dec. 31, 1792, Jan. 4, 7, 11, Mar. 7, 1793. *JD*, Jan. 25, 1793. PV: Vannes, Jan. 18, 1793; Lille, Dec. 6, 1792.

[51] PV: Tonneins, Jan. 17–28, 1793; Lectoure, Feb. 19, 1793. Forot, *Tulle*, p. 248. AN, C 250. *AP*, Feb. 22, 1793.

should they keep blood in their veins, when others are spilling theirs?"[52]

At the same instant, the Commissaire général des monnaies issued a circular in which he asked the clubs to persuade their communes to sacrifice unneeded bells for the minting of coin. (The reader will recall that the Legislative Assembly had allowed communes to remove and melt down bells, but few had done so.) The clubs immediately began to apply pressure upon municipal officials. Moreover, on February 29, Carcassonne printed and circulated a petition demanding that the number of bells be limited to one per parish. Many clubs adhered, but some added the proviso that the bells be used for making cannon. This was exactly what the Convention decided to do on July 23, 1793.[53]

The most devastating blow to religion in early 1793 was the rebellion of the Vendée. Even the most pious clubbists must have shuddered at reports that priests had precipitated the uprising, and that the rebels had gone into battle shouting "Long Live Jesus Christ!" Although the bulk of the rebel curates were nonjurors, their treason tainted the clergy as a whole. The great historian Aulard believed that the rebellion in the West was the primary cause of de-Christianization during the Terror. "Without La Vendée," he wrote, "there would have been no Worship of Reason."[54]

There can be no doubt that the Vendéen uprising increased suspicion of priests. In addition, it led to more cries for anticlerical legislation. On March 31, Troyes circulated a petition that called for the deportation of clerics who were not salaried by the state or did not hold public office. Those who refused to leave, or tried to return, were to be executed. Only the infirm and aged were exempted.[55] Ten days later, Auxerre distributed a petition that differed from Troyes' only in exempting married priests and in specifying transportation to a "distant isle" where (like the pro-

---

[52] AN, C 247. As far as I can tell, this petition got little support from the clubs; and the Convention, on Mar. 23, exempted bishops and curates from military service.

[53] *JD*, Mar. 15, 1793. COR, Bordeaux, 12 L 30. PV: Aire, Feb. 25, 1793; St.-Servan, Feb. 28, 1793; Tonneins, Mar. 4, 1793; Le Puy, Mar. 7, 1793; Honfleur, Feb.-Mar. 1793; Lectoure, Mar. 30, May 22, 1793; Ingouville, Mar. 15, 1793.

[54] Aulard, *Christianity*, p. 98.

[55] COR, Poitiers, S 34.

verbial scorpions in a bottle) the clerics could destroy each other. Auxerre's language was quite harsh:

> If there are a few virtuous men in the numerous class of ecclesiastics, the total is so small that scarcely one exception is legitimate. . . . The nuance is so slight between the immorality of jurors and nonjurors that we are tempted to call for the destruction of all. If spirit is corrupted in a department and someone asks the cause, the reply is always priests. Let a counterrevolutionary plot be executed, and again priests are at the bottom of it. Where fanatical people have armed themselves against liberty, who has put daggers in their hands? Priests![56]

Several clubs applauded these circulars; and two, Strasbourg and Tonneins, are known to have adhered to Auxerre's.[57] Most, however, were not yet willing to go to such extremes. Gray loathed réfractaires; yet, it refused to adopt Troyes' motion. Bourbonne, Boiscommun, and Provins decided that the best reaction was none at all. Bergerac was shocked by the harshness of Auxerre's words. Gay-Vernon, the brother of the Bishop of the Haute-Vienne, bitterly assailed Auxerre's proposal at the club of Limoges. At Rouen it was victoriously combatted by two members who pointed out that jurors had "rendered great services to the Republic" and should not be lumped with "fanatics and impostors."[58]

On the very day that Auxerre's circular appeared (April 10), Dijon published one urging that all priests and former nobles be barred from holding civil or military office.[59] Reactions varied. At least seven societies (Bourbonne, Nuits, Ornans, Boiscommun, Provins, Besançon, and Nogent) approved it in its entirety. Nogent, in addition, apparently demanded that all priests be gathered in the principal cities of the Republic where they could be kept under surveillance. Valence, Orthez, the Popular Society

---

[56] COR: Reims; Josselin; Poitiers, S 33. *JD*, Apr. 17, 1793.

[57] PV: Tonneins, Jan. 17–28, Apr. 4–6, 1793.

[58] PV: Gray, Apr. 17, 1793; Bourbonne, May 1, 1793; Limoges, Apr. 27, 1793; Provins, Apr. 28, 1793; Boiscommun, Apr. 28, 1793; Rouen, Apr. 25, 1793. Labroue, *Bergerac*, p. 245.

[59] COR, Limoges, L 826.

of Nîmes, Châtillon-sur-Chalaronne, Clermont-Ferrand, and Villéréal favored only a law directed at nobles. Lille and Bergerac initially supported Dijon's motion, but then tabled it. Lons-le-Saunier and Pithiviers, for unknown reasons, refused to consider it.[60]

This review of opinion in the spring of 1793 cannot end without noting a few other incidents that indicate that, despite the Vendée, most clubs remained loyal to the constitutional Church. When the curé of Lectoure pronounced a speech on April 14 in which he demonstrated the "accord between Catholic and republican principles," the club not only listened attentively, but transcribed it in the minutes. Tartas, as late as May 24, still forbade its members to talk about theology. And after the June coup, Ornans expressed pleasure at the fall of the Girondins, saying that they had wished to destroy the faith "to which all good Frenchmen are attached."[61]

[60] Labroue, *Bergerac*, p. 243. Libois, *Lons-le-Saunier*, p. 141. *JD*, Apr. 23, 1793. AN, C 252. PV: Lille, Apr. 18, 1793; Pithiviers, Apr. 19, 1793; Châtillon-sur-Chalaronne, May 10, 1793; Bourbonne, Apr. 19, 1793; Orthez, Apr. 28, 1793; Nuits, Apr. 13, 1793; Boiscommun, Apr. 19, 1793; Provins, Apr. 21, 1793.
[61] PV: Lectoure, Apr. 14, 1793; Tartas, May 24, 1793. *ArchP*, June 25, 1793.

XVI

Symbol and Song

NEARLY A century ago, the great historian Albert Mathiez popularized the idea that a revolutionary religion existed that was analogous to other religions. This revolutionary cult, according to Mathiez, had certain symbols to which the faithful were piously attached. These symbols included tricolor cockades and flags, altars to the fatherland, pikes, Phrygien bonnets, and trees of liberty. All were in use in 1789 and 1790, but it was especially during the Legislative Assembly that the last three won universal acceptance. For this, the clubs were largely responsible.[1]

Pikes achieved cult status in late 1791 and early 1792, amid fears of imminent attacks by émigré armies and anxieties about shortages of arms. On October 20–21, 1791, the *Annales patriotiques* printed a two-part article, signed "DB" (A.-P.-J. de Belair). It included two detailed engravings of pikes along with instructions on their manufacture and use in battle. De Belair argued that pikes were inexpensive and that every village had a blacksmith or ironworker with the expertise to make them. And he exhorted local authorities and clubs to have them forged.

Brissot's *Patriote français* printed engravings of pikes on October 26. Moreover, in the ensuing weeks the editor of the *Annales*, Carra, reiterated de Belair's call in a series of editorials. He vowed not to be silent until two million had been made, and he contended that the French armed with pikes could repel any invasion. "Pikes, more pikes, still more pikes" became the chant of the *Annales*.

Now, Carra was the oracle of the departmental clubs. They were swayed by his columns as reeds by a breeze. After the reading of the *Annales* at Périgueux on October 26, a member proposed that two or three types of "lances" be manufactured and urged each of his frères to acquire one for use in case of an émigré

[1] A. Mathiez, *Les origines des cultes révolutionnaires* (Paris, 1904), pp. 13–35.

attack. A few days later, Périgueux decided to engage the "people of the countryside" to forge pikes. On November 2, Carra printed a letter from Amiens, praising the October 20–21 article and demanding that he intensify his campaign. By the end of November, the club of Bar-le-Duc had announced plans to make pikes.[2]

In December and early January, momentum built. Chalon-sur-Saône and Cognac entreated communes in their districts to manufacture pikes. Rieux boasted that it had made pikes and was unafraid of an assault by the "brigands." Villeneuve-l'Archévêque claimed that several forges were operating in its environs, and Tulle announced that its municipality had ordered the fabrication of 1,200 pikes. On learning of the decision at Tulle, the Récollets Society voted to have 3,000 pikes made. In addition, in a circular of January 2, it urged affiliates to act similarly. On the same date, a "Brother Durand" from Bordeaux advised the club of Bergerac to procure pikes. A little afterward, Grenoble and Pommiers began to collect money for the purchase of *piques à la Carra*, and Courthézon asked its commune to raise funds for the same purpose.[3]

By late January and early February, the snowballing movement had reached Paris. The Paris club published a circular (January 17) advocating the "adoption of pikes"; and popular sheets like the *Courrier des départements* took up the cause. On January 31, at the Cordeliers Club, a woman proposed a collection drive, and listeners rushed forward with donations. Similar scenes occurred in other societies of the capital. As the Parisians armed themselves, the aristocratic press charged that a massacre was imminent. Alarmed, the king summoned the mayor, Pétion, to court; and on February 17, the commune issued a decree forbidding pikes to all except national guardsmen. It came too late to stem the tide.[4]

[2] *AP*, Nov. 2, 30, 1791. PV, Périgueux, Oct. 26, Nov. 17, 1791.

[3] *JD*, Dec. 14, 1791. *JC*, Nos. 3–6. *AP*, Dec, 19, 1791; Jan. 11, Feb. 20, 1792. Le Gallo, "Cognac," p. 244. PV: Chalon, Dec. 6, 1791; Versailles, Dec. 10, 1791; Courthézon, Jan. 26, 1792; Tonneins, Jan. 17, 1792. *Journal de Grenoble*, Jan. 26, 1792. Labroue, *Bergerac*, p. 195.

[4] Cf. *CD*, Jan. 22, Feb. 5, 8, 1792. Aulard, *Jacobins*, III, 328. P.-J.-B. Buchez and P.-C. Roux, *Histoire parlementaire de la Révolution française* (Paris, 1834–38), XIII, 217–224.

The example of Paris caused more departmental clubs to join the movement. After reading the Jacobin circular, Beauvais (January 29) opened a collection drive for pikes. In distributing them, it followed the "prudent policy of the Paris Commune." Honfleur and the Surveillants of Bordeaux adopted plans for the manufacture of pikes on February 5–6. Le Mans did so on February 9. During the next few weeks, Versailles, Sète, Besançon, Blois, Metz, Chalon-sur-Saône, Thionville, Marseille, Givet, Lille, Condrieu, St.-Léonard, St.-Girons, Belleville, Marmande, Lure, and Toulon initiated drives as well.[5]

Fearing popular violence, some communes attempted to forbid the arming of citizens. In so doing, they incurred the wrath of the clubs and the radical Parisian press. A dispute over this issue ended the good relations that had existed between the society and Commune of Metz. Périgueux purged the mayor of Bourdeille from its membership rolls when it learned that he had prohibited the fabrication of pikes. No less a person than the deputy and philosophe Condorcet reminded magistrates in a published letter that every citizen of ancient Rome and Greece had a pike and sword, and that all Frenchmen had the right to bear arms.[6]

Carra, who had not ceased to clamor for pikes, stated on February 19 that 1,500,000 had been forged and predicted that this number would soon double. This was mere journalistic twaddle. Nonetheless, there can be little doubt that hundreds of thousands of pikes were manufactured in early 1792. Their military value was negligible, but psychologically they satisfied the concept of the nation-in-arms. Henceforth, pikes were truly symbols of the Revolution. They were placed as trophies in the clubs, carried aloft in parades, depicted on seals and "artistic" works, and celebrated in song and verse.

THE "bonnet phrygien" or "bonnet de la liberté" was a cloth hat shaped like a cone or éteignoir and usually colored red. Its use as

---

[5] *JC*, Mar. 3–Apr. 14, 1792. *PF*, Mar. 24, 1792. *AP*, May 1, 1792. PV: Blois, Feb. 22, 27, 1792; Beauvais, Jan. 29, Feb. 2, 5, 1792; Condrieu, Apr. 8, 1792; Chalon, Feb. 28, 1792; Le Mans, Feb. 9, Mar. 22, 1792; Honfleur, Feb. 5, 1792; Thionville, Feb. 17, 1792; Versailles, Feb. 13, 15, 1792. COR: Lille, Mar. 3, 1792; Limoges, L 823. Dubois, "Surveillants" (1935), pp. 170–180. Bultingaire, *Metz*, pp. 31–35. *JDM*, Nos. 2–3. *Journal de Provence*, Mar. 3, 8, 1792.

[6] Cf. *JC*, May 3, 1792. *AP*, May 6, 1792.

a symbol dated back at least to the Fetes of the Federation of 1790. And a few clubs of the Constituent (like the Surveillants of Valence) required members to wear them. It was only during the Legislative Assembly, however, that they became a fetish of the Revolutionaries.[7]

That the Phrygien bonnet was rising in popular favor is evident from club minutes of late 1791 and early 1792. Vitteaux and Avallon, for example, voted to erect trophies, consisting of bundles of arms surmounted by these patriotic top hats. On Vitteaux's was a "Hittite" curse: "Whoever touches this will suffer death." Niort decided to substitute a liberty bonnet for a fleur de lys atop a pyramid in the town square. And we must not fail to mention the clubbist of Dijon who pleaded with his "brothers" to substitute cloth bonnets for fur hats. Said he: "Let the innocent beaver in Canada live in peace. . . . The immense tribute that the nation pays for fur will be diminished. Several millions will be saved."[8]

It was especially in February and March, however, that red bonnets became the rage. The reason, apparently, was that they had been worn by the Swiss of the Châteauvieux Regiment during their captivity. In Paris they suddenly popped up like mushrooms. Patriots, and people who wished to pass for patriots, donned them at the least opportunity. They also became accepted wear at the Paris Jacobins. Only Robespierre and a few others refused to wear them.[9]

Even then, Paris was the arbiter of fashion. The Strasbourg club, wishing to be in step with the capital, ruled on February 27 that all members and spectators would have to wear the bonnet rouge. Cognac (March 23) and Périgueux (April 22) made it mandatory dress for the president, secretary, and anyone who took the floor to speak. At Le Mans (March 25), a band of women presented one to the club as a patriotic offering, and it was passed from head to head. A speaker at Amiens (March 18) urged his brothers to wear this "symbol of the people" on promenade and at the theatre, "like the Parisians." He went on to say that red hats

[7] Mathiez, *Origines*, p. 34. PV, Valence, Oct. 2, 1791.

[8] Hugueney, *Dijon*, p. 145. PV: Vitteaux, Oct. 23, 1791; Avallon, Oct. 7, 1791; Niort, Jan. 27, 1792.

[9] Walter, *Jacobins*, pp. 241–242.

had "covered the heads of the Swiss under William Tell" and had been worn by the "American farmers led by Waghinston [*sic*]."[10]

It was not long, however, before a reaction set in. On March 19, Pétion sent a letter to the Paris club urging its members to abandon the bonnets rouges. He contended that they did nothing to advance the cause of liberty, and that bad citizens were using them to discredit the Jacobins. During the reading of this letter, so contemporary accounts assure us, the bonnets disappeared one by one from view. What is more, Robespierre gave a discourse in which he argued that the tricolor cockade was the only outward sign of patriotism needed by citizens. Copies of his speech and of Pétion's letter were printed and sent to affiliates.[11]

Similar scenes were played out in some provincial societies. St.-Affrique adopted a rule forbidding the "indecent" practice of wearing a hat while speaking. On learning that a "true patriot" had been threatened for not having one, Marseille voted to ban them from its assembly hall. At Libourne, a sergeant in a volunteer battalion vehemently combatted this "childish and ridiculous" fad. "It is not," he said, "by frivolous signs and vain ostentation that true Frenchmen ought to display their devotion to liberty." Hardly were these words out of his mouth than the bonnets vanished as if "by magic."[12]

Despite these words and resolutions, the bonnet mania continued to spread; and many clubs fostered it. Rennes (May 13) seems to have originated the idea of putting them ceremoniously on the uppermost part of the bell tower of the principal church. "In order to render the religion of liberty more glorious," Clermont-Ferrand did likewise on May 23. It explained to affiliates that the bonnet would be a warning to aristocrats not to enter the town and a welcome sign to patriots. Lille, Besançon, Chartres, and Rouen soon emulated Clermont and Rennes. It is a shame that we do not know the name of the acrobatic citizen who scaled the tower of the great cathedral at Chartres. When he reached the top, he stood upright on the cross without the aid of hands,

---

[10] Dusevel, *Amiens*, II, 220–222. Le Gallo, "Cognac," p. 247. PV: Le Mans, Mar. 22–25, 1792; Périgueux, Apr. 22, 1792. Heitz, *Strasbourg*, p. 189.

[11] Walter, *Jacobins*, pp. 244–245.

[12] *JDM*, p. 265. Besson, *Libourne*, pp. 161–162. PV, St.-Affrique, Mar. 25, 30, 1792. Forot, *Tulle*, p. 178.

assumed a prone position, and then hung by his knees. All the
while he shouted: "Long live the nation and liberty. To hell with
aristocrats."[13]

As late as September 1792, Châtellerault banned bonnets from
its meeting place on the grounds that "good citizenship . . . is not
dependent upon such a costume." And a member at St.-Hip-
polyte was censured in December for having the "indecency" to
wear a hat indoors. But little by little, clubs adopted rules forcing
members to have the patriotic top-hats or face expulsion. Certainly, by 1793, the vast majority required officers and speakers
to wear them. Some clubbists apparently believed that like the
icons of the Christian faith, they had miracle working powers. A
society of Nîmes reported the story of a baby who had a birth-
mark on his forehead shaped like a Phrygien bonnet. It attributed
this mark to the fact that the mother had looked upon these
"cherished emblems of liberty" during her pregnancy.[14]

FROM time immemorial, on the first of May, French peasants had
held festive celebrations around trees called *mais*. From these folk
rites evolved Revolutionary fetes associated with "trees of liberty." As early as May 1790, a curé near Civray in Poitou had a
mai national planted in a public square and harangued citizens on
the advantages of the Revolution. It was not until two years later,
however, that the liberty tree became universally accepted as a
Revolutionary symbol.[15]

In the clubs the "tree cult" began at almost the same instant as
the "bonnet craze." On March 8, 1792, Strasbourg announced
that it had put up one "in emulation of the Parisians." A week
later Bergues-St.-Winox reported that the people of the countryside had been seized by a "mania" to plant "trees of liberty" and
hold fetes.[16] In April plantings multiplied, although the practice

[13] *JC*, June 4, 1792. *M*, May 18, 1792. Brelot, *Besançon*, p. 103. Babeau, *Troyes*,
I, 489–491. Chardon, *Rouen*, p. 75. PV, Lille, Aug. 26, 1792. A. Bethouart, *Histoire de Chartres* (Paris, 1903), I, 94.

[14] PV: Châtellerault, Sept. 30, 1792; Lectoure, Nov. 23, 1792, Jan. 25, 1793;
Pau, Apr. 21, 1793; St.-Servan, Nov. 20, 1792; Largentière, Apr. 15, 1793; Montreuil, Sept. 3, 1792; St.-Hippolyte, Dec. 21, 1792.

[15] H. Grégoire, *Essai historique et patriotique sur les arbres de la liberté* (Paris, 1792).
M. Dommanget, "Le symbolisme et le prosélytisme révolutionnaire," *AHRF*
(1926). Mathiez, *Origines*, pp. 132–133.

[16] *JC*, Mar. 15, 24, 1792.

was still mainly confined to the north and northeast. By May all regions had been affected. The largest number occurred on Sunday, May 20, although they continued to take place in great quantities right up to July 14.

Most of the fetes were instigated by the clubs, and the clubbists expended much time and money in insuring their success. Sometimes the trees were stripped of bark and roots. Usually, however, a live one was planted. It had to be straight and tall, "a symbol of the strength and duration of the love for liberty"; and arguments sometimes occurred over what variety to choose. The Italian poplar was frequently selected. Special significance was attached to its name, *peuplier*, which was a derivative of "people." But a clubbist of Semur grumbled that its place of origin made him think of "intolerance, fanaticism, and despotism." He favored an oak.[17] Plane-trees, pines, and elms were used as well.

The trees were usually placed in squares. Baskets filled with flowers nestled round the base. Tricolor ribbons adorned the trunks, on which were tacked banners with such phrases as "To Live Free or Die" and "Death to Tyrants." Flags often hung from the branches. Ascending from the crown was a pike. Bound to its handle was a bundle of rods, an ancient Roman symbol of authority. On the pike's tip was a bonnet rouge.

The ceremonies commonly began with a procession. The participants, including local officials, national guardsmen, soldiers, women, and children, often gathered at the club. Then they advanced to the appointed spot as bands played martial music, or while singing revolutionary anthems like "Ca Ira." Floats depicted revolutionary scenes, and patriotic signs were held aloft. At the place where the tree was to be placed, crowds had gathered. Sometimes, paid workmen did the actual planting; but usually it was a collective effort. Speeches were given. Afterward, there was singing, dancing, and feasting.

Once in place, the trees became centerpieces for future Revolutionary fetes. Many times, sessions were suspended so that impromptu celebrations could be held around them. "Aristocrats" were made to do obeissance before them. The *arbres de la liberté* were watched over as though they were sacred. Nonetheless,

---

[17] Henriot, *Semur*, p. 120.

thoughtless citizens allowed their dogs to urinate on them, and they were desecrated by vandals and uprooted in the night.[18]

Because many trees had been planted improperly and at the wrong season, they perished. Their replanting was the occasion for more fetes in the early Convention. By that date the *arbres* had become so popular that one would not suffice. Largentière, which already had three, voted in February 1793 to put up a fourth on which was to be hung a tablet with the last words of the martyred deputy Lepelletier. In the same month, Vaison decided to plant one on each of its five squares.[19]

Religious observances were sometimes held in conjunction with the tree plantings of the spring of 1792. Masses and Te Deums were celebrated in churches, and priests were invited to speak or bless the trees. Valognes declared that its *arbre* was planted "under the auspices of God who created free men." It may be, however, that some clubs were already contemplating the replacement of Catholic rites with civil ceremonies. Douai made a conscious effort to have a purely secular service, publicly proclaiming its planting to be the "first of the civic fetes demanded by Jean-Jacques Rousseau."[20]

Evidence of this phenomenon may be seen more clearly in the memorials for Simonneau, the mayor of Etampes who was killed by a mob on March 3, 1792, after he refused to impose price controls on grain. The Legislative Assembly ordered that ceremonies be held in his honor, and about forty clubs reacted by organizing funeral services in March, April, May, and June. Most, it is true, took place in churches with a priest administering divine offices, but some were rigorously secular in character.

When Honfleur decided to sponsor a service for Simonneau, an altercation erupted between a curé and Taveau, the future Conventionnel. The former desired a blend of civic and religious rites; the latter, whose views were adopted, wanted a strictly civil service. Arras, too, resolved not to mix "Gothic and supersti-

[18] *JC*, Mar. 24, 31, 1792. Adam, *Valognes*, pp. 129–130. PV: St.-Affrique, Nov. 5, 1792; Castres, Mar. 14, 1793. Combes de Patris, *Rodez*, p. 34.

[19] PV: Auray, Dec. 2–25, 1792; St.-Hippolyte, Dec. 6, 1792; Montpellier, Mar. 3, 1793; Largentière, Feb. 28, 1793; Vaison, Feb. 18, 1793. Poulet, *Thann*, p. 379. Deries, *St.-Lo*, pp. 170–171.

[20] Cf. Haize, *St.-Servan*, pp. 75–81. Lefebvre, *Bourbourg*, pp. 100–101. Lecesne, *Arras*, I, 186–187. Adam, *Valognes*, p. 129.

tious religious ceremonies" with civic rites. A eulogy was given at the club by a professor of oratory. The wearing of black was forbidden. At Versailles, "the temple was the hall of the society, the priest was a simple citizen, and the witnesses were a mob of people of all faiths." A young man and woman (representing Simonneau's children) embraced on a mock sarcophagus on which were the words "the French Decius." White-robed women scattered flowers, while a band played lugubrious music. Afterward, a clubbist gave a speech.[21]

Montpellier likewise voted to exclude religious rites after listening to a report by a committee that had been assigned to organize a service. Said the spokesman for this committee:

> Why do we forever have need of priests, of churches, and of services *for the repose of souls?* . . . Citizens! Who among you has the least doubt about the fate of souls of patriotic brothers who have perished because of their love for the fatherland? It is inconceivable that our common father would consign to purgatory his children who have died for liberty and equality, that holy equality which up to now has existed only in heaven! . . . We are no longer Roman Catholics by virtue of our political institutions. Let us cease to be Roman in our fetes and civic ceremonies. For temple, let us have only the Universe; for altar let us have only the one of the Fatherland. . . . All patriots adore the same creator and have the same religion, that of liberty and equality.[22]

Not long after pikes, Phrygien bonnets, and trees of liberty achieved cult status, a stirring, new Revolutionary hymn caught the fancy of the French people. On April 25–26, 1792, at the invitation of Mayor Dietrich of Strasbourg, an army captain named Rouget de Lisle wrote a "War Song for the Army of the Rhine." Dietrich liked the work so much that he printed a number of copies and had them circulated among the local populace. It was not immediately a nationwide hit; but by the early summer of 1792, it had certainly become familiar to some clubs in the Midi. After the decree declaring the "Patrie en Danger," the members of the

---

[21] *CD*, Apr. 7, May 1, 6, 1792. PV, Honfleur, May 22, June 1, 1792.
[22] Duval-Jouve, *Montpellier*, I, 314–316.

society of St.-Hippolyte went to the tree of liberty to renew their oaths, and a Citizen Bontemps sang the hymn that began: "Allons enfans de la patrie; le jour de gloire est arrivé."[23]

In June, a five-hundred-man force of fédérés was organized at Marseille to go to Paris and overthrow the monarchy. On June 22, while preparations were being made for this expedition, a banquet was held at the club, and a Jacobin from Montpellier, François Mireur, gave a rendition of Rouget de Lisle's work. The next day the *Journal* of the club printed the words and music. The fédérés sang it on their march to Paris and in their attack on the Tuileries Palace on August 10. Forever afterward, it was to be called "La Marseillaise."[24]

During the late summer and autumn of 1792, knowledge of "La Marseillaise" suffused throughout the network. In some clubs it was sung first by commissioners of the Executive Branch. Volunteers were also instrumental in facilitating its spread. Club secretaries recount how the hymn "moved all hearts" and everyone joined in singing the "immortal chorus." Often the members cried out for encores, and shouts of "To Arms, Citizens" rang out.[25] Many clubs began to open and close their meetings with the "Marseillaise." It also became customary to sing the anthem in public sessions and revolutionary fetes. As Autun said in a November 4 circular: "The hymn of our brothers from Marseille has made the rounds of the Republic; and everywhere, without shedding blood, it has conquered."[26]

---

[23] Cf. E. A. Arnold, "Rouget de Lisle and the 'Marseillaise,' " *Proceedings of the Western Society for French Historical Studies* (1978). PV, St.-Hippolyte, July 21, 1792.

[24] Kennedy, *Marseilles*, p. 109.

[25] Cf. PV: Châteauroux, Nov. 2, 1792; Pithiviers, Oct. 26, 1792; Aire, Oct. 9–10, 1792; Largentière, Nov. 18, 1792; Limoges, Oct. 7, 1792. Aubert, "Douai," p. 530. Besson, *Libourne*, p. 197. COR, Niort, L 3006 bis.

[26] PV: Castellane, Sept. 4, 1792; Toulouse, Oct. 7, 1792; Lille, Nov. 14, 1792; Bordeaux, Oct. 3, 1792; Périgueux, Oct. 2–21, 1792; Blaye, Oct. 14, 1792; Pau, Apr. 6, 1793; Tartas, Apr. 5, 1793. COR, Bordeaux, 12 L 29.

Part Five

The Fall of the Monarchy

XVII

The Legislators

THE CLUBMAN of 1790 venerated the Constituent Assembly. To be sure, he disliked the deputies of the extreme Right, but they were just so many fungi feeding on a cask of fine wine. By April–June 1791, however, a radical minority of societies had begun to accuse the Assembly of weakness and to call for its disbandment. The decision to pardon the king and the withdrawal of most of the deputies from the Paris Jacobins (July 15–17) increased disillusionment, as did the anticlub legislation of September 29. The result was that many deputies were treated rather shabbily on their retirement. Tributes were mostly reserved for a small knot of Leftists, the "true and sincere friends of liberty," those who had "always served the Revolution faithfully." Poitiers went so far as to circulate a petition asking the Legislative Assembly to erect a monument to these "august and blameless deputies, . . . the fathers of the fatherland."[1]

Two of the ex-Constituents, Pétion and Robespierre, were especially singled out for praise. Fetes were held in their honor; their busts and pictures were placed in club assembly halls, and orators likened them to heroes of antiquity like that Fabricius of whom Pyrrhus said: "It is easier to turn the sun from its course than Fabricius from the path of honor." Barred from service in the Legislative Assembly by a self-denying ordinance, both men left Paris for a time that autumn. Robespierre visited family and friends in the north and was treated like a demi-god by the clubs of Arras, Béthune, and Lille. After his return (November 28), he became once again a kind of high priest at the Paris Jacobins. Pétion, after his English excursion, was elected mayor of Paris, defeating Lafayette. His victory caused the clubs to exult. Chartres erected a statue in his honor. Strasbourg sent him a civic

[1] *ArchP*, Oct. 19, Nov. 24, 1791. *JD*, Oct. 14, 16, Nov. 2, 1791. COR, Poitiers, S 19. PV: Versailles, Oct. 10, 14, 1791; Niort, Oct. 12, 14, 1791; Périgueux, Oct. 14, 1791; Toulouse, Oct. 14, 1791; Beauvais, Oct. 13, 1791.

crown as a sign of its "undying affection." Rochefort equated him to Lucius Junius Brutus, who "delivered his country from despotism and was then elevated to the magistracy." For Versailles he was the new Hercules who would "strangle the serpents around the cradle of liberty."[2]

THE clubs did their utmost to guarantee that what had happened in the Constituent would not recur in the Legislative Assembly. Months in advance they began to campaign for the election of "good" deputies.[3] However, when the electoral assemblies convened in late August and September 1791, the network was atomized by the Feuillant schism. That the majority of those elected were clubmen, there can be little doubt. In some departments (the Corrèze, Gironde, and Côte-d'Or, for example) all of the members of the delegations were "friends of the Constitution." The flipside of this was that many deputies were also moderates whose political views remained static while those of the home societies careened Leftward.

Blois assigned a member to give periodic reports on the conduct of the delegation of the Loir-et-Cher (and urged affiliates to act similarly).[4] But most societies were at first content to read newspaper accounts of the Legislative Assembly and to await reports from the legislators themselves. Some of the deputies had the political savvy to correspond regularly. Pinet wrote to the club of Bergerac every five or six days, on the average. Blois heard often from "brother Chabot," Châtellerault from Ingrand, Cognac from Bellegarde, Limoges from Gay-Vernon, Niort from Ruamps, Périgueux from Lamarque, Lorient from Le Malliaud, Clermont from Couthon, Lille from Duhem, Toulouse from Delmas, Falaise from Vardon, and so forth.

No deputy was more assiduous about corresponding than Brival of Tulle. On his arrival in Paris he dipped quill pen into ink-

[2] Walter, *Robespierre*, I, 199–215. *AP*, Nov. 5, Dec. 9, 1791. *PF*, Oct. 27, Nov. 28, 1791. *CD*, Nov. 26, 1791. *JD*, Oct. 26, Dec. 14, 1791. Bethouart, *Chartres*, I, 83. PV: Lille, Nov. 24, 1791; Libourne, Dec. 8, 1791; Fécamp, Dec. 1, 1791; Tonneins, Nov. 25, 1791; Nuits, Dec. 7, 1791; Montpellier, Dec. 2, 1791; Chalon, Nov. 24, 1791; Honfleur, Nov. 24, Dec. 1, 1791.

[3] Kennedy, *Jacobins*, pp. 218–223.

[4] PV, Blois, Oct. 2, 1791.

well and wrote that he had joined the Jacobins. Thereafter, he dispatched a steady stream of communiqués. Often, he glorified himself and denigrated rivals in the delegation of the Corrèze. Once he promised to send fifty livres per month for the poor of Tulle. Another time he asked anxiously why the club was not responding to his epistles. Always he posed as a zealous defender of the interests of his city. His reward, like the deputies named in the preceding paragraph, was to be elected to the Convention.[5]

Sadly, for every Brival, there were three deputies who failed to keep their fences mended. Strasbourg, which only heard from Ruhl and Kohl, wrote a tongue-in-cheek letter in early 1792 in which it asked if the other legislators from the Bas-Rhin were dead. About the same date a friend warned the deputy, Blanc-Gilly, that he was losing his following in the club of Marseille, and begged him to write more often. "Try, if not in the name of friendship, then in the name of God, to put yourself in the spirit of the people."[6]

The Legislative Assembly, like the Constituent before it, was an incubator of factions. Its meetings were so disorderly that one idealistic representative compared his colleagues to yelping curs. The *Révolutions de Paris* carped: "All the sessions degenerate into clamouring, infighting. Time is consumed; the people suffer."[7] In an effort to bring order from chaos, historians have traditionally divided the deputies into a Left, Right, and Center. On the Left they place the 130 deputies who became members of the Paris Jacobins, on the Right the 236 who joined the Feuillants, in the Center the 350 who enrolled in neither club.

Lists of the 130 Jacobin deputies were printed in the Parisian press and apparently circulated by the "mother society." Chalon-sur-Saône, on reading one, asked its deputy, Joumel, to explain why his name was missing; and Marseille reprimanded the deputies of the Bouches-du-Rhône who had not joined the Jacobins. But Evreux waited for months and never received a list. In January, it begged the Paris club at least to give it details on the status of its six members who were deputies. Niort was also confused

[5] Forot, *Tulle*, pp. 152–220.
[6] *CD*, Feb. 1, 1792. AN, F⁷ 4603.
[7] *Révolutions de Paris*, No. 126.

about party alignments in the Assembly. In December it considered launching an inquiry to determine which deputies of the Deux-Sèvres sat on the Right.[8]

The first months of the Legislative Assembly were a kind of honeymoon period. Several clubs wrote to it in a truckling spirit in late October and early November. And scores of societies, under the guise of "active citizens" of their communes, sent letters of praise following the November 9 decree on the émigrés. Lorient sought to coordinate this effort by circulating a copy of its address and asking affiliates to repeat it in Polyanna style. But the clubs needed no such model. They knew how to speak for themselves. Below is a potpourri of their remarks:

> Wise legislators! This law alone guarantees that you will have public confidence forever. (Clermont-Ferrand)
>
> We facilitate your courage. (Givet)
>
> The decree on the émigrés has crowned all of our hopes. (Calais)
>
> Struck by the energy that you have displayed, we decided to write to you to express our admiration. (Lille)
>
> Legislators! . . . We proclaim you worthy to represent a great people. (Blois)
>
> Count on our love, our patriotism, our arms. (Sezanne)
>
> This severe act . . . recalls the sublime but too infrequent triumphs of your predecessors. (Toulouse)[9]

Another profuse outpouring of homage followed the November 29 decree on the nonjuring priests. By that date, some deputies had become national heroes. Brissot and Condorcet were immensely popular, as were that brilliant trio from the Gironde— Vergniaud, Guadet, and Gensonné. But no one made a greater splash than Isnard of the Var. His speeches were read over and over again by the clubs, and applauded frenetically. Tonneins deemed him to be a "worthy rival of Pétion and Robespierre"

---

[8] AN, F⁷ 4603. *JC*, No. 5. PV: Chalon, Oct. 27, Nov. 10, 13, 1791; Niort, Dec. 2, 1791.

[9] See especially AN, DXL 1–4. On the Lorient circular see: COR and PV, Lorient, Nov. 29–Dec. 2, 1791. PV, Niort, Dec. 11, 1791. Forot, *Tulle*, p. 161.

and declared that if only four other legislators were as courageous, the safety of France would be assured.[10]

Occasionally, however, the deputies did things that caused the
Jacobin brow to knit. Several societies protested when the Assembly, on October 6, voted to address the king as "sire" or
"majesty." Others fumed about efforts of the Right to enforce
the decree depriving the clubs of the right to petition. By the end
of 1791 a few deputies were already in disgrace. Stanislas Girar-
din, the first legislator elected from the Oise and a founder of the
club of Beauvais, was being hooted by the galleries. The club of
Marseille accused the ex-mayor, Etienne Martin, of "eating the
soup of the ministers," destroyed his portraits and memorabilia,
and scratched his name from its rolls.[11]

More reputations were tarnished in early 1792 in the affair of
the naval minister, Bertrand de Molleville. The Constitution had
not established the principle of ministerial responsibility to parliament. The ministers were the king's creatures, and in the view
of the clubs, prime causes of the evils afflicting the kingdom.
Throughout the autumn of 1791 the society of Brest accused Bertrand of embezzlement and treason, and demanded that he be investigated. The Committee of the Marine, after examining these
allegations, proposed that the Legislative Assembly pass a resolution of no confidence in Bertrand. However, when a roll-call
vote took place on February 1, 1792, the motion was defeated by
208 to 196.[12]

After this vote the Assembly was subjected to a cold shower of
criticism by the clubs. Lavaur and Alençon chided it for not dis-
playing an "imposing character" and for letting itself be "dominated" by the Executive Branch. Bort mourned that some deputies had been "ministerialized by the Civil List." Dole chastised
the legislators for their "profound lethargy" and for permitting
the ministers to "act with impunity." Dijon declared that they
were in danger of losing public confidence. Montauban was dis-

---

[10] Le Gallo, "Cognac," p. 244. PV: Tonneins, Nov. 13, Dec. 29, 1791, Jan. 29,
1792; Niort, Dec. 7, 1791, Jan. 11, 1792; Sète, Nov. 22, Dec. 8, 1791; Chalon,
Dec. 8, 1791; Falaise, Nov. 14, 1791; Honfleur, Dec. 4, 1791.

[11] Kennedy, *Marseilles*, pp. 104–106. *CD*, Oct. 28, 1791. *PF*, Oct. 25, 1791.

[12] Cf. *ArchP*, Dec. 3, 8, 18, 29, 1791, Jan. 2, Feb. 1, 1792.

tressed that over three hundred deputies had not voted, and it asked the Paris Jacobins to publicize their names. Montpellier demanded more roll-call votes so that the nation would know who was "doing his duty."[13]

Lists of the deputies who voted *oui* and *non* and of the absentees were printed by the Paris Jacobins and by several newspapers.[14] Those who had voted against the motion of no confidence were given such appellations as "False Friends of the Fatherland Unmasked." The publication of these lists provoked much comment from the clubs. Letters of congratulation were sent to deputies who had supported the "just cause." Sadness, dismay, and anger were expressed about native sons who had voted "wrongly" or not at all. The fall-out was so great that several deputies issued statements justifying their conduct.[15]

The Assembly refurbished its image somewhat on March 10 when it voted by an overwhelming majority to cite the foreign minister, Delessart, before the High Court at Orléans. Commendations poured in from the clubs; but some were rather churlish. The Popular Society of Nîmes wrote: "At last we can give you honest praise. Be careful to continue this course."[16]

In truth, although the majority of societies still danced attendance to the Assembly, criticism of it and individual deputies continued to build in April-May 1792. Jeanbon St.-André, who was a lobbyist in Paris, called the legislators "petty" in his letters to Montauban. Marseille denounced a "part" of the Assembly in a letter to Parisians. Bourg St.-Andéol burned some "Reflections" written by Delmas of the Ardèche. The deputy Guillois was censured at Lorient. And nearly all of the clubs of the Tarn, save for Gaillac, condemned an "iniquitous work" published by six deputies of that department.[17]

[13] *JD*, No. 138. *CD*, Feb. 4, 1792. *AP*, Feb. 5, 1792. *Révolutions de Paris*, No. 134.

[14] *JC*, Mar. 1, 8, 15, 26, 1792. *AP*, Feb. 23, 1792. Levy-Schneider, St.-André, p. 124. PV, Montpellier, Mar. 17, 1792.

[15] *JC*, Mar. 17, 22, 31, Apr. 9, 1792. *CD*, Feb. 11, 20, 1792. *AP*, Feb. 9, 15, Mar. 9, 1792. *PF*, Mar. 10, 1792. *M*, Feb. 25, 1792. AN, F⁷ 4603. PV: Tulle, Feb. 14, 1792; Bourbonne, Feb. 12, 1792; Toulouse, Feb. 8, 11, 1792.

[16] *JC*, Mar. 26, 29, Apr. 9, 1792. *PF*, Apr. 4, 1792. Ligou, *Montauban*, p. 265. PV: Chalon, Mar. 15, 1792; Le Mans, Mar. 29, 1792; Blaye, Mar. 18, 1792; Montpellier, Mar. 18, 1792.

[17] *ArchP*, June 4, 1792. BN, Lb 39, 10484. *PF*, May 14, 1792. PV: Gaillac, Apr.

The passage of the decree of May 27 on nonjuring priests and another on June 8 establishing a camp of twenty thousand national guardsmen near Paris temporarily raised the Assembly's popularity quotient. Messages of praise flowed in once more. Moreover, when the king vetoed these acts and dismissed the popular "Girondist" ministers, the clubs expressed their readiness to fly to the assistance of the Assembly. Alas, there was a sharp erosion of support in the six weeks preceding August 10. The reasons were threefold: indictments of the clubs in the Assembly; its mollycoddling treatment of Lafayette; and the reluctance of the majority of deputies to modify the Constitution or dethrone the king.

Following the invasion of the Tuileries on June 20, there was a royalist backlash in the Assembly. The right wing blamed the Jacobins for this insult to the person of the king. Delfau of the Dordogne, for example, characterized the network as a "menacing colossus" and demanded its dissolution. Blanc-Gilly (Bouches-du-Rhône) described June 20 as an "atrocious . . . incident which dishonored the Revolution." Such diatribes brought the societies to a boil. Delfau was denounced by several clubs of the Dordogne. Marseille expelled Blanc-Gilly from membership and warned affiliates that he was in league with the king and Lafayette.[18]

In fact, the views of Delfau and Blanc-Gilly were congruent with Lafayette's. The latter had once been admired by the clubs, and as late as May 1792, Douai and Gaillac still regarded him as one of the "heroes of the Revolution"; but most societies, by that date, distrusted him. Courtenay, for example, had heard that he wanted to close the clubs and wondered if he desired to be a "new Caesar." Besançon postulated that Lafayette had "had himself named general so that he can betray us."[19]

Perhaps Besançon was psychic, for on June 16, from his camp at Maubeuge, Lafayette wrote a letter to the Legislative Assembly in which he villified the clubs. Then, on the night of June 27, he suddenly showed up in Paris. The next day, before the Assem-

---

26, 1792; Périgueux, May 14, 1792; Toulouse, Apr. 28, 1792; Lorient, Apr. 23, 1792. Levy-Schneider, *St.-André*, pp. 134–135. *JDM*, p. 93. *JC*, May 3, 17, 1792.

[18] *ArchP*, June 25, 1792. *PF*, July 30, 1792. Kennedy, *Marseilles*, pp. 105–106.

[19] Cf. *JC*, May 11, 14, June 11, July 5, 1792.

bly, he demanded the dissolution of the network and the severe
punishment of those responsible for the affair of June 20. He
probably hoped that he would be named to lead the repression.
But the queen despised him; and he was unable to rally enough
support from the national guard in Paris, so he had to return to
his army command.

Gaillac's faith in Lafayette could not be shaken. As late as July
11 it burned a condemnation of him written by the deputy Lasource. But for most societies, Lafayette's behavior in June removed any shadow of a doubt about his "bad" intentions. Tonneins was horrified by the "abominable letter of the insidious
traitor." Tulle was also incensed by the "cowardly letter" of June
16 and drew up an address in which it described Lafayette alternately as a "Cromwell," "Marius," and "Sulla."[20] After his
speech of June 28, at least fifty-seven clubs wrote to the Legislative Assembly to denounce him and/or demand his arrest.[21]

At the June 28 session, Guadet had moved that Lafayette be
censured for leaving his post without authorization; but the Assembly voted down this motion by 339 to 234, proving, said the
historian Michelet, that it "had not the will to combat the enemies of the Revolution." Leftists in Paris assailed this action. The
reaction of the clubs was akin to that which had followed the vote
on Bertrand. Vire purged its former leader, R. R. Castel, for
"failure to do his duty as a deputy." Lorient described the June 28
session as a "triumph for aristocracy." Lannion was "anguished"
at the conduct of the legislators. Angers told them that they
should "blush with shame."[22]

Calls for the indictment of Lafayette in July and early August
were often linked with demands for constitutional reforms or the
dethronement of Louis XVI. The failure of the Assembly to comply brought a tidal surge of reproach from the clubs. It ranged
from mild declarations of impatience, to expressions of contempt, to threats of violence. Grenoble charged that the deputies
were all talk and no action: "You say that you will die at your
posts like Spartans. But the Fatherland demands more sublime

[20] Cf. AN, C 152. *JC*, July 7, 1792. PV: Gaillac, July 11, 1792; Tonneins, June
26, 1792.

[21] See especially AN, DXL 7–9, C 152–153.

[22] Nicolle, *Vire*, p. 99. COR, Poitiers, S 26; Lorient, July 9, 1792.

efforts of you than merely dying." Autun fussed that the Assembly spent all of its time on minutiae. Marseille stated flatly that "three-fourths of the deputies are sold to the Civil List." Bédarieux warned that "the people may be forced to act themselves." Lavaur, in an address to the Parisians, said that "if the Assembly remains inert, our only choice is a general insurrection or death." Châtellerault urged affiliates to petition for the convocation of primary assemblies to elect two additional deputies per department. Limoux, Sarrelouis, and Strasbourg demanded a National Convention. Montdidier declared that those legislators who were "gangrened with aristocracy were more guilty than the king" and ought to be imprisoned in the Abbaye.[23]

On August 8, in defiance of public opinion, the Assembly defeated a motion to indict Lafayette by a vote of 406–224. After the session some of "Fayettists" were jostled by menacing crowds, and the following night a great insurrectionary movement occurred. The Revolution of August 9–10 was an assault on the Assembly as well as the king. Afterward, only a small percentage of deputies, mainly Leftists, continued to show up at the sessions. Most cowered in their residences writing protests about the treatment that they had received.

Lists of the deputies who had voted for and against Lafayette on August 8, were printed in the Parisian press. On reading them, several clubs hissed their displeasure with the majority in the Assembly. Castres, for example, publicly declared six deputies of the Tarn to be "traitors." Le Mans and Périgueux each purged two deputies from their membership rolls. Lille placarded the names of the "good" and "bad" legislators of the Nord for everyone to see.[24] Later in August the Paris Jacobins published and circulated a *Tableau comparatif* of seven crucial roll call votes in the Legislative Assembly. The effect of this action on the elections to the Convention will be examined in a subsequent chapter. Suffice it to say that the *Tableau* ended many political careers.

The clubs differed about whether the blacklisted deputies should be subjected to reprisals on their return home. When it learned that Barennes had been threatened with physical harm,

---

[23] Cf. AN, C 151–153, DXL 7–9. On Châtellerault see COR, Poitiers, S 23.
[24] PV: Lille, Aug. 15, 1792; Le Mans, Aug. 15, 1792; Périgueux, Aug. 15, 1792; Castres, Aug. 23, 1792.

the Récollets Society magnanimously sent him a letter of "consolation and fraternity." Toulouse first voted to burn the mannequins of nine former deputies, but on second thought simply stripped them of membership. Later it intervened to protect them from "popular fury." The society of Uzerche readmitted the moderate Chassaignac; but Rouen, after long debates, expelled its ex-deputies. Metz, in a printed circular, brutally condemned six ex-legislators of the Moselle. Following the example of Metz, Tonneins expressed contempt for seven ex-deputies of the Lot-et-Garonne and called upon the other clubs of the department to ostracize them. But Agen and Clairac thought that Tonneins was being unjust, broke off relations with it, and offered asylum to the seven.[25]

[25] Forot, *Tulle*, pp. 192, 227. PV: Bordeaux, Sept. 15, 1792; Blaye, Dec. 5, 1792; Toulouse, Sept. 17, 22, Oct. 4, 1792; Rouen, Sept. 26, 1792; *AP*, Oct. 30, 1792. COR: Reims; Poitiers, S 26.

XVIII

The First Vetoes

THE PROTOTYPAL club member was a staunch monarchist. What is more, he had a high regard for Louis XVI, whom he hailed as "the best of kings" and "the restorer of liberty." He might sometimes make surly noises about "the Executive Branch," the queen, or the ministers, but never the crowned head. The Jacobin of 1789–90 was also quite literally a "friend of the Constitution." He had the right and duty to comment on pending legislation; but once laws were enacted, obedience was mandatory.

Signs of a change in attitudes first bubbled up in March–June 1791. A few societies began to inveigh against "bad" parts of the Constitution, and to campaign for the abolition of the royal veto and the reduction of the Civil List. In addition, rumors of plots at Court caused Brest to launch a petition drive aimed at forcing Louis XVI to affirm his attachment to the Revolution. Nonetheless, at this date the vast majority of clubs remained devoted to Constitution and king. Not one associated itself with the tiny republican party which was developing in Paris.

Even after the flight to Varennes, republicanism made little headway. When Montpellier circulated a petition calling for an end to the monarchy, just two clubs are known to have adhered. Most tabled Montpellier's suggestion or repudiated it. Those who bothered to print responses reasoned from the theories of Montesquieu and seventeenth-century English history that a republic was unsuitable for a country the size of France and would lead inevitably to party strife and to dictatorship.

There is no question, however, that the affair of June 20–21 grievously undermined the popularity of Louis; for he had not only tried to flee, but had left behind prima facie evidence of his dislike for the clubs in the form of a proclamation. In late June and early July, at least sixty societies advocated judicial proceedings against the king. Others petitioned for the rule of the Dauphin, the creation of a board of regents, or the institution of an elective monarchy. Parts of the Constitution again came under attack, including this time the provisions allowing the monarch to appoint ministers and ambassadors, and to declare war.

At the last minute, several societies tried to avert a pardon of Louis by demanding a national referendum on his fate. Once the pardon was issued (July 15–16), the clubs acquiesced in the fait accompli. One hundred and thirty-six, to my knowledge, wrote to the Constituent in late July and August to pledge allegiance to its decision. Some did so with enthusiasm, signifying their hatred of "republicans," "anarchists," and other "infernal sects." Others submitted sullenly, reaffirming their oaths to obey the laws, but taking parting shots at the king.[1]

As summer edged toward autumn, the nation waited anxiously to see whether Louis would sanction the Constitution. He really had little choice. To have refused would have almost certainly meant the end of his reign, and might have endangered the dynasty. On September 14, 1791, therefore, he appeared before the Constituent Assembly and signified his acceptance. This news caused joy and relief in the clubs. Shouts of "Vive le Roi" rang out. Once again the king was wrapped in a mantle of adulation. Cognac told Louis: "Twenty million Frenchmen cherish you because you are just."[2]

There was also a great round of public celebrations in honor of the Constitution. Henceforth, many clubs opened their sessions with readings from it, and members stood in sign of respect. Libourne referred to it as the "Holy Constitution." It was Issoudun's "tutellary divinity." Le Mans begged its department to print enough copies so that every citizen of the Sarthe could have one.[3]

---

[1] For a fuller account of the material in the preceding paragraphs see Kennedy, *Jacobins*, pp. 253–279.

[2] On Cognac see AN, F¹ C III (Charente 12).

[3] Cf. PV: Le Havre, Oct. 6, 1791; St.-Affrique, Oct. 9, 1791; Courthézon, Oct. 13, 1791; Tain, Sept. 18, 1791; Gaillac, Sept. 23, 1791; Sète, Sept. 14, 1791; Tonneins, Sept. 19, 1791; Montauban, Sept. 19, 23, 1791; Le Mans, Oct. 2, 1791. Besson, *Libourne*, p. 146. Le Marchand, "Le Havre," p. 80. Poulet, "Thann," p. 237.

It would be folly to presume, however, that the clubs were now completely satisfied with the Constitution or that the treason of the king had been totally forgotten. At Aiguesvives' fete in honor of the Constitution, its president, the Pastor Ribe, made allusions to the "weaknesses" of the "Roi." An orator at Lorient intoned: "How sweet it is to see the chief of the executive branch return to the road which he never should have left!" Blois said puckishly to Louis: "We venerate the supreme head of the executive branch, but we do not recognize you as our sovereign. We are the subjects of the law, not you. The nation alone is sovereign."[4]

THE Legislative Assembly was not yet a week old when a row occurred over the constitutional position of the king. On October 6, on the eve of a royal session, the deputies reversed an earlier decision by voting to address Louis as "Sire" or "Your Majesty," rather than "King of the French." In so doing, they irritated radicals in the capital. The *Révolutions de Paris* had the gall to compare this action to the Revocation of the Edict of Nantes.

Three clubs are known to have registered protests. Longwy described the Assembly's action as "base adulation." Marseille categorized it as an "attempt to revive feudalism." Etain observed that the whole nation had been waiting to see if the new representatives would be "worthy successors of the Pétions and Robespierres," and had been disappointed.[5] Most societies, however, seem to have been unmoved by the "flap" in Paris; and some reacted positively to the royal session of October 7 in which the king was greeted with traditional deference. Tonneins was deeply touched by the speech of Louis. The recorder of its minutes wrote: "Despotism with its iron scepter has never heard such language. It was reserved to Louis XVI to demonstrate this phenomenon to Europe."[6]

A much more serious controversy welled up in November 1791 when the king, for the first time, used the right of veto guar-

---

C. Charton, "Le Club d'Epinal," *Annuaire statistique des Vosges pour 1847* (Epinal, s.d.), pp. 83–104.

[4] PV: Aiguesvives, Oct. 2, 1791; Lorient, Oct. 6, 1791. *AP*, Oct. 2, 1791.

[5] Cf. Kennedy, *Marseilles*, p. 106. *CD*, Oct. 28, 1791. *PF*, Oct. 5, 1791.

[6] PV, Tonneins, Oct. 14, 1791.

anteed to him by the Constitution. On the twelfth he rejected the decree on the émigrés passed three days before by the Assembly. He maintained that the law was too severe and incompatible with the principles of a free constitution. He announced that he had written to his brothers to urge them to come back to France. Finally, he claimed that emigration had slowed and that many expatriots were returning.

Radicals in Paris responded to the veto with thinly veiled attacks upon the king. Carra, for example, contended that it was proof that the "Court is not just the accomplice of counterrevolutionaries. It is the center of counterrevolution." In comparison, the comments of the clubs were at first relatively mild. Blaye huffed that the king's action was "unworthy of the chief of a generous people." And Givet puffed that "24,000,000 individuals should not be victims of royal caprice. . . . The Assembly ought to hold him responsible for the evils that the veto of this decree will cause."[7] But most of the clubs, although angered and shocked, refrained from criticizing the head of state.

Some kept silent because of their "profound respect for the Constitution." Others wanted to believe that the king's motives, although misguided, were "pure." Many blamed Louis' "perfidious" counsellors for "deceiving" him. Another popular theory was that the chief of state was trying to demonstrate that he was not a prisoner. Artonne rationalized that "the veto shows at least that those people who say that the king is unfree are liars." Douai actually voted to congratulate Louis for "proving his liberty to the whole universe"; but it rescinded this vote after two members protested that "our mad love of kings will put us back in chains."[8]

While the clubs generally refrained from casting aspersions on the king, many nonetheless strove to undo the veto. Parrotlike, they repeated the Rousseauistic dictum that the veto was "a violation of the supreme law, the *salut du peuple.*" At least nine societies petitioned the Assembly for a *décret d'accusation* (act of indictment) against the émigré chiefs. This, they reasoned, would

[7] *ArchP*, Dec. 5, 17, 1791.

[8] AN, DXL 1–4. *ArchP*, Nov. 24–Dec. 17, 1791. *JD*, Nov. 23, 1791. Aubert, "Douai," pp. 228–229.

place the matter in the courts and beyond the reach of the Executive Branch. Eventually (January 1) the Legislative Assembly did indict the king's two brothers, the counts of Provence and Artois.[9]

A few clubs took the tack that the veto was unconstitutional. "If the one which has just been applied is in the Constitution," said Héricourt, "it is a vice." Angoulême protested that the veto was intended to be suspensive, but "is in fact absolute." Pontoise stated defiantly that it was going to regard the November 9 decree as law. Niort suggested that the veto ought not to apply to *décrets de circonstance* (laws the prompt execution of which were essential to the good of state). In a debate on the same subject at Versailles, one member compared France to a house on fire and exclaimed that it was inconceivable for someone to have the power to prohibit residents from putting out the flames.[10]

Most emphasis was placed, however, on trying to persuade the king to change his mind. Strasbourg may have been the first to ask the king to sanction the decree. Its address of November 15 was reported in several Parisian papers. Another widely publicized appeal, that of thirty "Friends of the Constitution" of Versailles, was read before the Legislative Assembly on November 29. The Versaillais declared that although they respected the powers given to the king by the Constitution, it was their "right and duty" to say that they did not approve of the use of the veto in this case. "We are doing so in order that the prince will know public opinion and obey it."[11]

Inspired by a speech of Dubois-Crancé at the Paris Jacobins, Toulouse voted on December 2 to send an address to the king telling him that he was in opposition to the "national will." One thousand copies were printed and circulated to affiliates.[12] This address made quite an impact. From all over the country Toulouse received adhesions. Circulars of the same type were pub-

[9] Dijon, Givet, Angoulême, Clermont-Ferrand, Marseille, Cherbourg, Niort, Orléans, Valognes.
[10] AN, DXL 1–4. *ArchP*, Dec. 5–17, 1791. PV, Versailles, Dec. 12, 1791. *JD*, Nov. 29, 1791.
[11] *ArchP*, Nov. 29, 1791. Heitz, *Strasbourg*, p. 167. *M*, Nov. 24, 1791.
[12] Toulouse Minutes, Dec. 2, 7, 1791.

lished by Bordeaux and Aix. Altogether, about thirty clubs are known to have written to the king to ask him to retract his veto.[13]

Tonneins, however, refused to adhere to Toulouse's address. When it was read on December 9, three members spoke against it. One accused Toulouse of subverting the Constitution by "demeaning the Executive Branch." Moreover, many of the clubs that did write to the king behaved more like postulants at a shrine than free citizens. Toulouse was quite displeased by the servile letters of some societies of its vicinity. It told Rieumes that the use of the word "subjects" was "offensive to regenerated ears." Carla's epistle contained expressions "unsuitable for free men." Bédarieux was urged to delete such phrases as "listen to the will of your children," which were "too humble for a sovereign people."[14]

In a crafty public relations move, the king went before the Legislative Assembly on December 14 to announce that he had given an ultimatum to the Elector of Treves, to cease harboring the émigrés. The reaction to this ultimatum proved again that royalism was deeply entrenched in the societies. At Libourne, Le Havre, and St.-Hippolyte the audience applauded and cried out "Vive le Roi." Douai noted in its minutes that this action proved that "the king of the French will always be loved by citizens and that he loves the Constitution." Gaillac, which was ardently royalist, praised the monarch for his "vigorous, noble, and worthy" act.[15]

By mid-December, however, concern was building rapidly over another issue. On November 29 the Assembly had approved a punitive law against refractory priests. The societies had long clamored for such a decree, and they thanked the Assembly effusively for its passage. Imagine, therefore, their wrath on learning that ten administrators of the Department of Paris had petitioned the king to veto it. The petitioners professed them-

---

[13] See especially F¹ C III. Ligou, *Montauban*, p. 267. Forot, *Tulle*, p. 160. PV, Toulouse, Dec. 10, 1791–Jan. 5, 1792.

[14] PV: Tonneins, Dec. 9, 1791; Toulouse, Dec. 19–28, 1791. AN, F¹ C III (Ariège 8).

[15] PV: St.-Hippolyte, Dec. 27, 1791; Le Havre, Dec. 18, 1791. Besson, *Libourne*, p. 147. Aubert, "Douai," p. 238. Rossignol, *Gaillac*, p. 68.

selves to be in favor of liberty of conscience and argued that persecution would only increase fanaticism and public disorders.

Copies of this petition appeared in the Parisian press on December 9–10. On the eleventh the Paris Jacobins voted to print and circulate an address of Robespierre, condemning the administrators.[16] The clubs responded with a multitude of letters to the Assembly denouncing the ten "vetogogues" and demanding their indictment. The administrators were accused of setting a bad example for public officials, unconstitutional behavior, collusion with the "black hordes," combatting "the will of the people," and inciting civil war.[17] As always, there were one or two oddball clubs. Marmande was at first "revolted" by the petition but on closer examination found it to have "good principles." Yet, even Marmande wondered if the times did not warrant the abandonment of such principles.[18]

In addition to denouncing the ten administrators, the clubs tried to negate the effect of their petition upon the king. A number of circulars appeared between December 15 and 20. Tulle, Brest, and Tours, for example, exhorted affiliates to ask Louis XVI to lift his veto of the law on émigrés and to sanction the decree on réfractaires. Clermont announced that the Department of the Hérault had drawn up a petition in opposition to the one of the ten Parisian administrators. Chalon-sur-Saône urged its sisters to get their departments to do the same.[19]

Few departments emulated the Hérault, but many clubs made known to the king the "supreme will of the people." Some of their letters were vaguely menacing. Arras told Louis "that whosoever tries to prevent the punishment of the assassins of the country is an assassin himself, and subject to punishment like them." Valognes wrote: "Sire! It is in your interest to be king.

---

[16] Cf. *PF*, Dec. 12, 1791. Labroue, *Bergerac*, p. 193. PV: Montauban, Dec. 21, 1791; Perpignan, Dec. 22, 1791; Versailles, Dec. 19, 1791; Toulouse, Dec. 23–24, 1791.

[17] AN, DXL 1–4, F¹ C III.

[18] *JD*, Jan. 4, 1792.

[19] Labroue, *Bergerac*, pp. 194–195. PV: Tonneins, Jan. 2, 1792; Niort, Jan. 4, 1792; Lille, Dec. 29, 1791; Versailles, Dec. 30, 1791; Toulouse, Dec. 17, 1791, Jan. 5, 1792; Chalon, Dec. 18, 1791. Forot, *Tulle*, p. 164.

The way to remain king is to preserve public confidence." Ste.-Marie-aux-Mines declared: "If the king vetoes the decree on priests, he will, in effect, renounce the title of 'Restorer of Liberty.' And royalty . . . will be looked upon as a scourge." Brest put it neatly: "Sire, you still reign; but if you yield to certain impulsions, you will reign no more."[20]

The veto of the decree on refractory priests, which came on December 19, was a turning point in the Revolution. Admittedly, it made only a faint impress on small, conservative clubs like Gaillac and Neuville. But at others the second veto had a more decisive impact on opinion than the flight to Varennes. To use a phrase that was popular with the clubs, "the veil was torn." The "Restorer of Liberty" had become "Monsieur Veto." Everywhere, his supporters were put on the defensive.[21]

Marvéjols wrote to Montpellier on January 1 to say that although it had approved of the decree of November 29, "the new veto prohibits all discussion of the matter." But most societies were unwilling to remain mute as they might have done in the past. On the contrary, the veto of December 19 set off an avalanche of resolutions, addresses, and petitions. Once again, the club of Toulouse provided key leadership, circulating addresses of its commune to the king and to the Legislative Assembly. Both demanded the revocation of the vetoes. Louis, referred to throughout as the "king of the French," was given this choice: "The love of a great people or its implacable hatred."[22]

A raft of societies adhered to Toulouse's address to the king. Montpellier voted to reprint it.[23] Another circular that picked up many endorsements was printed by Caen on December 29. It too included addresses to the Legislative Assembly and to the king. From the Assembly Caen sought acts of indictment against the émigré chiefs and the king's advisors. Louis XVI was given an ul-

---

[20] *CD*, Dec. 13, 23, 30, 1791. La Gorce, *Histoire*, II, 58.

[21] Cf. Ligou, *Montauban*, pp. 266–267. Levy-Schneider, *St.-André*, pp. 119–122. Nicolle, *Vire*, pp. 96–97. PV, Beauvais, Dec. 25, 27, 29, 1791.

[22] COR, Montpellier, L 5544. *JD*, No. 129.

[23] Ligou, *Montauban*, p. 267. Rouvière, *Gard*, II, 83–84. PV, Montpellier, Jan. 1, 1792.

timatum: "You are betrayed and are betraying us! . . . Withdraw your vetoes. . . . Two roads are open to you. The choice is yours. One leads to the love and gratitude of the French people, the other to the loss of the throne."[24]

Altogether, fifty-two clubs are known to have petitioned the king to lift the vetoes. Most of the letters, it is true, were gentler than Caen's. Chalon-sur-Saône, for instance, expressed confidence that Louis would change his mind once he learned "the true will of the people." Beauvais persisted in believing that, at bottom, the monarch was "good and sensible." Montauban asked the king if he had been duped by his advisors, if they had abused the "natural goodness" of his character. Lille and Bordeaux reminded Louis that the people were his "only true friends."[25]

But many of the words of the clubs were diamond-tipped. La Flotte gave the king a "last warning." Ste.-Foy cautioned Louis that the "anger of a powerful nation is more terrible than you think." Héricourt recalled the generosity of the French people after the flight to Varennes and indicated that they would not be so forgiving again. Béziers concluded that the monarch was either "simple-minded or perfidious." Lons-le-Saunier charged that throughout the Revolution Louis had been guilty of perjury and "attempts to restore despotism."[26]

Some interesting suggestions were made to the Legislative Assembly. Béziers, for example, demanded a constitutional amendment freeing *décrets de circonstance* from the royal veto (and received a number of adhesions from affiliates). The most daring proposition was advanced in late December by Langres. The Langres club, which was quite vocal at this time, declared that Louis had violated article 6, section 1, chapter 2 of the Constitution. It read: "If the King places himself at the head of an army and directs the forces thereof against the nation, or if he does not,

[24] *JC*, Jan. 26, 1792. *CD*, Jan. 18, 1792. PV: Tonneins, Jan. 22, 1792; Niort, Jan. 22, 1792.
[25] PV: Chalon, Dec. 24, 1791; Beauvais, Dec. 25, 1791. *PF*, Dec. 27, 1791. *JC*, No. 3.
[26] *CD*, Jan. 20, 1792. *AP*, Feb. 25, 1792. *JC*, Feb. 14, 1792. AN, F¹ C III (Hérault).

by a formal statement, oppose any such undertaking carried on in his name, he shall be deemed to have abdicated the throne."[27]

In vain did the minister of justice, Duport, issue a circular on January 10 trying to justify the second veto. And only the Gaillac society, to my knowledge, was enthused about the king's exhortation to refractory priests to stop causing troubles. This time the clubs were not quick to forgive Louis. On the contrary, some continued to insult and threaten him. Besançon (February 25) instructed "the people of the countryside" that the king "is suspected of being the most dangerous enemy of France." Dijon (January 23) warned Louis to declare war immediately upon the foreign powers: "If you refuse to yield to the wish of the people, your sovereign. Ah! Fear our awakening. . . . Tremble that in the legitimate fury which overcomes us, your fall will be only a prelude to the punishment that we inflict upon tyrants."[28]

By February a few societies were already whispering of the need for a "second revolution." Autun, in an address to the Parisians, declaimed: "The time has come to cut the evil at the roots. It's the court, the agents of the executive branch which are causing all of the evils in France. Have the men of July 14, of October 5 perished? Awaken! Rise up brave Parisians; the whole empire will sustain you." The attitude of the clubbists of Marseille was summed up in the following letter: "We await a coup from the Parisians whom the Marseillais will second marvelously; . . . provided that the patriotic deputies are informed, my friend, is it not essential that the Tuileries suffer the same fate as the Bastille?"[29]

On the other hand, evidence indicates that the societies were not yet ready for a republic or to abandon the Constitution. On January 14, the Legislative Assembly took an oath "to regard as traitors to the fatherland any Frenchmen who would try to bring about the slightest modification in the Constitution." This reso-

[27] *JD*, Dec. 26, 1791. AN, DXL 2. PV: Toulouse, Feb. 13, 1792; Versailles, Feb. 23–Mar. 5, 1792.

[28] PV, Gaillac, Jan. 26, 1792. Brelot, *Besançon*, p. 90. Hugueney, *Dijon*, p. 137. COR, Reims. Many clubs reacted enthusiastically to Dijon's circular, but Perpignan burned it, fearing that it might "exalt spirits."

[29] *JC*, Mar. 1, 1792. AN, F⁷ 4603.

lution was directed at the émigrés and suspected traitors in the Executive Branch rather than republicans; nonetheless, the reaction of the clubs is illuminating. At the instant that they heard the news of this oath, the clubbists raised their arms and cried out "I so vow." Societies throughout the kingdom adopted this motto: "All of the Constitution or death!"[30]

[30] Cf. PV: Lectoure, Jan. 27, 1792; Le Mans, Jan. 22, 1792. AN, DXL 5. *PF*, Feb. 11, 1792. *AP*, Feb. 25, 1792. Labroue, *Bergerac*, p. 199.

XIX

The Jacobin Ministers and the Second Vetoes

O N MARCH 9, 1792, Paris was rocked by the news of the decease of Leopold and the king's dismissal of his bellicose war minister, Narbonne. Buoyed by the death notice and peeved by the firing, the warmongers in the Legislative Assembly struck decisively the next day. On a motion of Brissot, Narbonne's ministerial rival, Delessart, was indicted. The remaining ministers resigned. Moreover, threats of reprisals were made against the queen and the "Austrian Committee" at the Tuileries. Seriously alarmed by this *coup de théâtre*, the king appointed a new cabinet composed of men acceptable to "the popular party" in the Assembly. This was a smart move on his part. One historian has described it as "the first statesmanlike thing Louis had done since the beginning of the Revolution."[1]

The new cabinet is known in Revolutionary history as the "Brissotin" or "Girondist Ministry," but contemporaries with good reason called it the "Jacobin Ministry." Almost all of the ministers were clubmen;[2] and after taking office, they cultivated the good will of the network. Dumouriez appeared at the "mother society" wearing a red hat. Clavière gave a speech at the Jacobins which was circulated to affiliates. Roland sent addresses to the clubs in which he described them as "indefatigable sentinels" of the Revolution.[3]

The clubs doted upon the appointees but, surprisingly, gave scant credit to Louis XVI for designating them. Coutras,

[1] J. M. Thompson, *The French Revolution* (Oxford, 1945), p. 282.

[2] Clavière was an early member of the Paris Jacobins. Roland founded the Popular Society of Lyon. Servan sired the club of Condrieu. Duranthon was one of the "fathers" of the society of Brest.

[3] On Roland cf. *JC*, May 21, 1792. PV: St.-Affrique, Apr. 13, June 4, 1792; Le Havre, May 22, 24, 1792; Valence, May 27, 1792; Lons-le-Saunier, May 24, 1792; Honfleur, June 3, 1792. Heitz, *Strasbourg*, p. 200. *M*, May 22, 1792.

Langres, and Marseille suspected a trick and advised the Paris Jacobins to beware. Tulle was also dubious of the king's intentions. On March 19 it asked the Assembly "to no longer require of him any type of oath, on the grounds that it is for him only a means to deceive the people."[4]

There was somewhat more commendation for the king after the Declaration of War. Angoulême, for example, said that if he continued to follow the counsel of the patriotic ministers and the people, he would soon be able to call himself "the first king of the universe."[5] But attitudes changed quickly after the defeats in Belgium. The underlying cause of this disaster was the haste with which the new ministers, pressed by the jingoistic press, had ordered an attack; but the warmongers could not admit the bankruptcy of their strategy. They attributed the reverses to the "Austrian Committee" at the Tuileries, which, they claimed, had warned the enemy in advance.

No one propounded the treason theory with more fervor than the journalist Carra. "I am going to demonstrate geometrically, mathematically, and geographically that treachery occurred," he ejaculated at the Jacobins on May 2. In his *Annales patriotiques* he repeatedly denounced the Austrian Committee.[6] When two of the alleged ringleaders of the committee, the former ministers Bertrand and Montmorin, hailed him before a Parisian justice of the peace, his case became a cause célèbre. At the audience, Carra proclaimed that the Tuileries was plotting to massacre patriots, and that the time had come "to sound the alarm bells and build signal fires on the heights." When proof was demanded of the existence of the Austrian Committee, he said that he had obtained his evidence from three members of the Surveillance Committee of the Legislative Assembly, Merlin de Thionville, Chabot, and Bazire. The hapless judge subpoenaed the deputies to appear and was himself sent before the High Court at Orléans for venturing to infringe upon the inviolability of the Legislature.[7]

This affair made the already popular Carra a hero of the clubs.[8]

[4] *JC*, Apr. 23, 1792. Forot, *Tulle*, p. 177.
[5] AN, F^1 C III (Charente).
[6] *JD*, Nos. 189, 191. *AP*, May 5–10, 1792. *Gazette universelle*, May 4, 1792.
[7] AN, W 242, No. 5, and F^{17} 1083. *M*, May 4–21, 1792. *AP*, May 8–22, 1792.
[8] Cf. PV: Montauban, May 20, 1792; Périgueux, May 25, 1792.

In addition, it reinforced the belief that there was, in fact, an "Austrian Committee." The committee became a kind of devil fixation. Dark references to it tinted club correspondence of May and early June. Port Louis, for example, warned the mayor of Paris, Pétion, to be on guard against it. Strasbourg charged that the "infernal committee" was in league with its mayor, Dietrich. Givet moaned: "When a Marie Antoinette . . . knows the plans of war operations, what does this augur for patriots?"[9]

Perpignan circulated a call to arms against the committee. Lons-le-Saunier, one of many clubs that read and applauded this circular, described it as being "so full of energy that it makes tyrants pale." It began by saluting "the virtuous Carra, that rock of patriotism." Then it posed a series of rhetorical questions. "Brothers and Friends, where are we? What has become of the conquerors of liberty? Is July 14 today only a vague memory? Has the Bastille been rebuilt? Does the popular lion sleep?"[10]

What of the king in all of this? The answer is that occasionally he too was assailed. In a jeremiad at the Besançon club an old soldier lamented: "What is to be done when the king, to recover his despotism, arms all of the powers of the earth against the nation?" Langres grouched that Louis loved his kinsmen more than his people. Toulouse, Lorgues, and Nîmes demanded that he be stripped of his war powers. Bouzonville gave him this sharp warning: "It is notorious that the Château of the Tuileries is the residence of counterrevolutionaries. You must not permit it. Either quit the throne or sustain the independence and sovereignty of the nation."[11]

The furor over the Austrian Committee heightened fears that brigands were plotting a coup in Paris. In February and March there had been a rash of reports that aristocrats and priests were headed to the capital with the intention of doing mayhem or kidnapping the king.[12] Although the Paris club tried to dispel such rumors,[13] they built to a crescendo after April 20 and caused the

---

[9] *JC*, May 24–June 9, 1792.

[10] COR, Niort, 3003. PV: Montreuil and Lons-le-Saunier, June 16, 1791.

[11] *ArchP*, June 15, 1791. AN, DXL, 10, 15. *JC*, May 24–June 14, 1791.

[12] Cf. *JC*, Feb. 16, Mar. 3, 22, 31, 1792. *AP*, Mar. 23, 1792. PV, Le Mans, Mar. 25, 1792.

[13] Cf. COR, Le Mans, L 1007.

great Récollets Society of Bordeaux to issue two important circulars. The first, dated May 2, stated that enemies of the Revolution were going to Paris with the aim of enrolling in the national guard and, at a specified moment, falling upon the Legislative Assembly and the Jacobins. The way to foil this conspiracy, it added, was for the clubs to get their Communes to send Pétion duplicates of all travel permits that had been issued. With these in hand, the worthy mayor would supposedly be able to identify the traitors. Twenty-three societies are known to have carried out Bordeaux's instructions.[14]

Three weeks later (May 19–24) the Récollets Society circulated a second letter together with a placard called the *Eveil du peuple*.[15] In them it further outlined the plans of the Austrian Committee and the "evil-doers" who were congregating in Paris. Their goal, Bordeaux said, was nothing less than to restore nobility by destroying the Legislative Assembly and installing a new assembly with two chambers. They would commence by seizing a strong point within the kingdom to which the king would flee under cover of an insurrection in Paris. Whether Louis was the "accomplice or victim of this crime," the Bordelais did not know.

The *Eveil du peuple* was, in fact, a call to the French to awaken and defend liberty. The clubs were charged to instruct citizens, "thunder against any system of inequality," and form surveillance committees. Few works of the Revolution had a greater impact. It was applauded and applauded, read and reread. Marseille, Pézenas, Poitiers, Autun, Chalon-sur-Saône, Caen, Rouen, and Lille voted to print it and distribute copies to affiliates. Le Mans had the *Eveil*'s concluding words, "Liberty, equality, never two chambers," inscribed on its walls. At Libourne the members vowed to die rather than allow the "plot of two chambers" to succeed. A score of societies wrote to the Bordelais to laud their courage and eloquence. Argentat gushed: "One would have to be as cold as marble not to feel the fire in this address."[16]

[14] COR: Niort, 3001; Bordeaux, 12 L 29–32, 38–40. *JC*, May 19–June 18, 1792. PV: Le Mans, May 13, 16, 1792; Périgueux, May 4, 1792; Chalon, May 11, 1792; Castres, May 12, 1792.

[15] Flottes, "Bordeaux," pp. 353–354. COR: St.-Zacharie; Poitiers, S 26.

[16] COR: Bordeaux, 12 L 29–32, 38, 40; Poitiers, S 23; Aix, L 2038; St.-Zacharie; Lille. PV: Tonneins, June 10, 1792; Toulouse, May 21, 1792; Chalon, June

As early as February 17, Périgueux voted to ask the Legislative Assembly to levy thirty thousand men from the departments to guard Paris. On April 6, Falaise demanded the formation of a camp of twenty thousand provincials on the Champ de Mars. In May and early June, the clamor increased. Nantes, for instance, issued this manifesto to affiliates on June 2:

> A storm rumbles over the capital. . . . Paris is threatened. Well! It is to Paris that we must march. Such is the resolution that we have just taken. We have collected the men and money. The moment of departure approaches. Friends! The alarm has sounded. Let good citizens rise up! . . . Our Commune, applauding our zeal, has just asked the Legislative Assembly to call up a force from all parts of the country to protect the capital.[17]

Throughout much of the spring of 1792 the prevailing political winds had blown from the southeast, from the direction of Marseille. The Marseille club was not only the most powerful in all of provincial France, it was also one of the most radical. Orally and in print its members blasted the Legislative Assembly, the Constitution, and the king. On May 23, one blustered that the inviolability of legislators merely allowed them "to outrage reason and justice with impunity." The June 12 number of the *Journal des départements méridionaux* blared: "We Marseillais do not believe that all parts of the Constitution are good. The Civil List, the absurd and fatal veto, the right of peace and war are murderous provisions." The editor of the *Manuel du laboureur et de l'artisan* (June 4) went so far as to defend republicanism: "Who is a republican? It is a man who has virtue, who has vowed to exterminate traitors and tyrants . . . and to defend his fatherland to the death."

The Marseille club was spoiling for a chance to send an expeditionary force to Paris. On May 27, in a letter to Paris, it expressed concern about the "lethargy" of the Parisians and said: "Here and at Toulon we have debated the possibility of forming

1, 1792; Lons-le-Saunier, May 31, 1792; Le Mans, May 28, 31, 1792. *JC*, June 14, 23, 1792. Besson, *Libourne*, pp. 169–170.

[17] PV, Périgueux, Feb. 17, 1792. *JC*, May 7, June 7, 1792. COR: Poitiers, S 26; Niort, 3003.

a column of 100,000 men to sweep away our enemies." On June 1 it informed Pétion: "Paris may have need of help. Call on us!" A few days later it sent this summons to the Legislative Assembly: "Liberty is in peril! . . . We demand a decree requiring the people to march in strength to the capital and to the frontiers. Do not refuse us!"[18]

At least two clubs of the Var ached to march alongside the Marseillais. On May 27 Toulon and La Seyne petitioned the department to begin preparations to send five hundred men to Paris. Toulon also told the Legislative Assembly that a great plot was afoot and could only be foiled by assembling forty thousand men in the capital, five hundred from each department. Several clubs of the Gard likewise adhered to "the wishes of Marseille." The Popular Society of Nîmes (June 1) petitioned for a camp of twenty thousand in Paris, consisting of 250 men per department and drawn mainly from the popular societies. Aiguesvives and Vauvert (June 5–6) made similar pleas.[19]

The Legislative Assembly reacted with unaccustomed vigor to the rumors of plots and to popular demands. On May 27 it approved a law making nonjuring priests liable for deportation. The next day it declared its sessions to be permanent, and the day afterward it voted to disband the king's constitutional guard, which was suspected of aristocracy. On June 4 the minister of war, Servan, proposed the formation of a camp of twenty thousand provincial fédérés outside the walls of Paris. (The plan was for the men to take part in the Fete of Federation of July 14, hence the name "fédéré.") This motion was approved on June 8, and the site of the encampment was fixed at Soissons.

A struggle ensued for the mind and heart of the king. Conservatives at Court advised Louis to refuse his sanction to the decrees, contending that the Jacobins planned to use the fédérés to topple the throne. The national guard of Paris, which regarded the camp of twenty thousand as an insult to its patriotism, also petitioned for a veto. But Roland (June 10) sent an open letter to the king stating that any delay in sanctioning the decrees of May 27 and June 8 would lead to an upheaval. "No more temporizing.

[18] *JC*, June 7, 1792. *JDM*, p. 165. *PF*, June 22, 1792. BN, Lc 34, no. 92.
[19] AN, DXL 15. COR, Marseille, L 2075. Rouvière, *Gard*, II, 327. PV, Aiguesvives, June 5, 1792. Poupé, *Var*, pp. 156–157. *ArchP*, June 21, 1792.

The Revolution is made in men's minds. It will be consummated in blood if you do not act wisely. If you tarry, the people will decide that their king is the friend and accomplice of conspirators."

Piqued by such insolence, the king dismissed Roland, Servan, and Clavière on June 13. The same day the Legislative Assembly adopted a resolution praising the three ministers and expressing regret over their firing. Dumouriez, who had quarreled with Servan, at first agreed to be minister of the interior, but he too resigned on June 16 after Louis refused to follow his recommendations and approve the decrees. A "Feuillantist" ministry was appointed, and on June 19 the king made the fateful announcement that he had vetoed the decrees on the nonjurors and the camp of twenty thousand.

For the clubs this three-week period was an emotional roller coaster ride. The events of May 27–June 8 produced a tremendous high. Blessings were bestowed on the Assembly, on Servan, and on Pétion for his speed in disbanding the constitutional guard. Preliminary registrations began for volunteers for the camp of twenty thousand.[20] Then anxiety set in at the prospect of royal vetoes and at the news of the petition of the Parisian national guard. But spirits were lifted by Roland's letter of June 10. It was accorded multiple readings, reprinted, and lauded to the skies.[21] Finally, came the black days of June 13 and 19. Reactions ranged from sadness to fury. Calls for unity went out. Sympathy was expressed for the fallen ministers. And stupendous quantities of letters, addresses, and petitions were sent to the "mother society," the Assembly, and the "people of Paris." So much was written that it almost defies analysis.

As they had done in the past, some societies affixed the blame for the royal actions on the queen and the Austrian Committee. "The king's conduct is the result of perfidious counsel," soliloquized Morlaix. Besançon concluded that Marie Antoinette was "the most wicked and arrogant woman there ever was." Nancy fulminated: "The Austrian Committee has dictated the vetoes. Strike it down!" Laval said: "The author of all of our troubles is

[20] AN, C 152. *JC*, June 9–23, 1792. PV, Lorient, June 7, 1792. *PF*, June 18, 21, 1792. Rouvière, *Gard*, II, 327–328. Besson, *Libourne*, p. 175.
[21] Cf. PV: Montauban, June 19, 1792; Honfleur, June 7, 1792; Lorient, June 26, 1792; Blaye, July 11, 1792; Limoges, June 17, July 8, 1792.

Marie Antoinette. Send her to Orléans, and the empire is saved!"[22]

But most of the clubs held Louis XVI responsible. Confidence in him was shattered, as the following excerpts show:

It is evident that the chief of the executive branch marches in a direction contrary to the Revolution. (Carcassonne to affiliates)

The head of the executive branch is not only a perjuror but the chief of our enemies. (A speaker at Condrieu)

Louis XVI has just proved that he does not want the Constitution. (Lorient to the Paris Jacobins)

The king can dissimulate no more. He is a traitor to his oaths. (Clermont-Ferrand to the Assembly)

We are no longer deceived. The king does not want the constitution. (Dijon to affiliates)

It is time to tear the veil away from the eyes of citizens. The king has always acted contrary to his words. (Domfront to the Paris Jacobins)

You could have been adored by the people if you had listened to them. Instead of the love of a free people, you prefer its hatred and contempt. (Rodez to the king)

We have been constantly deceived by the king. (The Club National of Bordeaux to the Paris Jacobins)

Your flight of a year ago disturbed us greatly, but we were reassured by your oath and by the appointment of the patriotic ministers. One lone instant has destroyed these illusions. (Pontivy to the king)

We have always been attached to the king; thus, we are quite disturbed about his conduct. (Le Faouet to the Paris Jacobins)

We feel that the king oppresses us. How could we feel otherwise? (Bergerac to the Assembly)

The king has concurred in bringing about the misfortunes which afflict the country. (A member at Senlis)

The dismissal of the patriotic ministers destroys all confidence in Louis XVI. (Beaugency to affiliates)

Louis XVI is . . . an ingrate. A less generous nation would

[22] *JC*, July 12, 1792. AN, C 152, 158. COR, Poitiers, S 23.

have long since toppled his throne. (St.-Girons to the Assembly)[23]

As to what should be done, there was disagreement. Many societies thought that the solution to the problem was to restrict the king's power to do evil. Autun, Nancy, Reims, Avallon, Rennes, Toulouse, and Falaise demanded from the Assembly a constitutional amendment prohibiting vetoes of *décrets de circonstance.* Moulins and Lons-le-Saunier wanted vetoes abolished altogether and the Civil List reduced to 1,500,000. Langres proposed the formation of an Executive Council, presided over by the king but responsible to the nation. No veto could be imposed except by vote of its members.[24]

A few clubs urged the deputies to consult the "people." Orléans and the Popular Society of Lyon demanded a national referendum to determine whether the vetoes should be suspended. Montauban counselled the Assembly to use "all constitutional powers available to it" to fight the enemies of the fatherland. "If these are not enough, . . . indicate to the country how to form a new representative assembly with great powers and short duration."[25]

A significant minority of societies (about one-fifth) called for the Assembly to take punitive action against the king. Nérac, for example, enjoined the legislators to interpellate Louis to see if he "wants to abdicate." Mâcon said: "Let the welfare of the people guide you. Strike with decrees, if need be, the crowned head who opposes the popular will." Several clubs implied that Louis should be dethroned. "Give to kings a terrible lesson. . . . We can get by without a monarch but not without liberty" (St.-Paul-Trois-Châteaux). The Popular Society of Lyon got 6,620 citizens to sign the following address: "Traitors dominate the Tuileries, and the king, as cowardly as he is inconsequential, allows himself to be controlled by them. The time has come for action. Louis

---

[23] COR: Poitiers, S 23, 26; Lorient, June 25, 1792; Reims. PV: Condrieu, June 24, 29, 1792; Senlis, June 20, 1792. AN, F¹ C III (Morbihan), DXL 8–9, C 152. Combes de Patris, *Rodez*, pp. 165–166. Labroue, *Bergerac*, pp. 205–206. *JC*, June 25, July 9, 12, 1792. *ArchP*, June 25, 1792.

[24] PV: Lons-le-Saunier, June 26, 28, 1792; Toulouse, July 2, 1792; Falaise, June 20, 1792. AN, C 152, DXL 7. *JC*, July 2–12, 1792. *CD*, June 29–July 13, 1792.

[25] PV, Croix-Rousse, June 26, 1792; COR, Poitiers, S 26.

XVI has deceived you. Louis XVI has favored enemies and fanatical priests. Louis XVI does not want the Constitution."[26]

Arras articulated its feelings more clearly. It told the Assembly:
"Do not sacrifice the interests of the nation for one man. He must
not frustrate the general will. If the king has not done his duty, he
must be removed." Blois was more explicit still. Like Langres six
months before, it took the stand that the king had abdicated the
throne by not opposing by "a formal act any enterprise under-
taken in his name against the Constitution" (article 6, section 1,
chapter 2, title 3 of the Constitution). "Act in consequence," it
charged the deputies. "Bring back the ministers. Deprive Louis
of the crown. Prosecute Marie Antoinette."[27]

At least forty-nine clubs wrote directly to the king to ask him
to revoke his vetoes and to recall the ministers. Few, however,
addressed the king as supplicants. The letters were written in the
spirit of Roland's. More often than not, Louis was given a
tongue-lashing. "King! Your flatterers will be your downfall.
There is only one way to regain popular confidence" (Angers).
"The French are tired of your vexations. It is time that you declare whether you wish to be the king of traitors and conspirators, or of a free people" (Rennes). "The people pardoned you a
year ago, but its irritation is increasing now" (Les Dorades).
"March loyally in the way of the Revolution or descend from the
throne" (Aix).[28]

Limoges advised Louis to read and ponder article 6, section 1,
chapter 2, title 3 of the Constitution. Grenoble warned the king
to beware, that the people would deprive him of his throne. St.-
Paul-Trois-Châteaux raged: "The love that we felt for you in the
past is changing into a terrible, implacable hatred. . . . Remember! Lightning strikes the tallest edifices." Marseille, Langres,
Narbonne, Montpellier, Grenoble, Condrieu, St.-Paul, and Ampuis, among others, implored the Parisians to rise up and combat
the vetoes and the firings. Finally, a host of societies offered or
threatened to send armed forces to Paris. In addresses filled with

[26] COR, Poitiers, S 23. AN, C 152, DXL 15. *AP*, July 5, 1792.
[27] *ArchP*, June 28, 1792. PV, Blois, June 15–22, 1792.
[28] Cf. COR: Poitiers, S 26; Bordeaux, 12 L 29. *JC*, July 5, 1792. *CD*, June 28,
July 6, 1792. Combes de Patris, *Rodez*, pp. 165–166. AN, C 152, F¹ C III.

confused, dark augury, they declaimed that the nation must rise up "toute entière." Little Montbron summed up the feelings of many when it proclaimed: "The time of vengeance approaches. The entire nation is going to rise up. Its first cry will be 'War to Tyrants.' "[29]

[29] AN, C 152. *AP*, July 3, 5, 1792. *JC*, June 29–July 9, 1792. *CD*, June 28–July 10, 1792. PV: Montbron, June 18, 1792; Cognac, June 26, 1792.

XX

The Fédérés

MANY CLUBS went beyond mere threats to "fly" to Paris. In defiance of the veto of June 19, they organized and sent corps of fédérés to the capital. There was no single, guiding hand behind this movement. It seems to have begun spontaneously in dispersed regions between June 19 and June 23. Once under way, it was nurtured by the Paris Jacobins, the radical press, and the deputies of the Left. By July most parts of the country had become involved.

The club of Brest kicked off the movement in the west and northwest. As early as June 17, in the name of 336 citizens, it commended the Legislative Assembly for the decision to create a camp of twenty thousand fédérés. In addition, the Brestois intimated that, veto or not, they planned to enforce the decree: "We know that the king can impose his veto. But legislators, it matters not! He has no veto over our hearts and minds. Say one word and you will be surrounded by a forest of arms."[1]

After receiving news of the June 19 veto, Brest pronounced its sessions permanent and set about to form a company of one hundred fédérés to march to Paris. Twenty thousand livres were raised to pay for the costs of the expedition. Couriers sped off to the other districts of the Finistère to ask them to provide men and money; and the department, which was initially hesitant, was persuaded to approve the levy. Altogether, about 154 fédérés from the Finistère set out for Paris. After more than a fortnight's march, they reached their destination on July 25.[2]

Brest broadcast its decision to affiliates in other departments in a terse, dramatic circular of June 22. "Friends!" it enunciated. "The fatherland is in danger. If you love it like we do, follow our

[1] *CD*, June 26, 1792. *PF*, June 25, 1792.
[2] J. Savina, *Les Volontaires du Finistère et la prise des Tuileries* (Quimper, 1909), pp. 30–39. *JC*, July 14, 1792. *CD*, July 2, 1792.

example. The rendezvous is under the walls of Paris." The clubs of the neighboring Morbihan were the first to respond to this challenge. Vannes may have been cognizant of Brest's actions on June 22 when it published this exhortation: "Citizens! Rise up! One lone man is responsible for our misfortunes, one man. . . . We must not allow him to succeed. We must have a federation, a camp of ten, twenty, even forty thousand men if necessary." Certainly, Hennebont knew of Brest's circular when it vowed on June 25 to send "men of good will" to Paris. By July 7 a small band from Hennebont was on its way to the capital to foil the "conspiracy which had been made manifest by the conduct of the king and Lafayette."[3]

Lorient decided to emulate Hennebont on June 26. It named eight members to go door-to-door through the city's four sections, to sign up volunteers. These commissars reported success on July 2, although the club was "pained to hear that the indigent classes had shown more ardor and good will than the well-to-do." The club examined the volunteers to see if they had "the required moral and physical attributes," and to try to prune their number to twenty. Each fédéré was given fifty livres for travel expenses, and two livres per diem while in Paris.[4]

Documentation is not as good in the other departments of Brittany. We do know that Guingamp twice petitioned the administrators of the Côtes-du-Nord to authorize volunteers to accompany the Brestois to Paris. Also, the club of St.-Servan (Ille-et-Vilaine) transmitted a copy of Brest's circular to communal officials and undertook to muster a troop of fédérés. Although there was no mass exodus from St.-Servan, six clubbists had taken to the roads by July 12, and the others boasted: "We all would have gone if we could."[5]

Brest's circular reached the Maine-Anjou region on June 28. The club of Le Mans hurrahed it lustily, voted to invite citizens to go to the Fete of the Federation, and vowed to subsidize those who did. Le Mans also issued an address to "The Patriots of the

---

[3] COR, Colmar, B 34. *M*, June 29, 1792. *PF*, June 30, 1792. *CD*, June 28, 1792. *JC*, July 5, 21, 1792. PV, Lorient, June 26, 1792.

[4] PV, Lorient, June 26–July 3, 1792.

[5] Dobet, "Guingamp," p. 38. PV, St.-Servan, June 26–July 12, 1792.

Empire" urging them to "rise up and teach Louis XVI that it is up to the nation to provide for its defense and demand reparations for anything that strikes at the social compact." The clubbists of Angers (June 29) responded to Brest thusly: "Nous partons!" In addition, they circulated a letter asking members of affiliated societies to meet them at the Fete of the Federation. Incidentally, Angers employed Brest's phrase: "The rendezvous is under the walls of Paris." Blois published a manifesto on June 28. It admonished affiliates: "Let us prove that the entire nation is upright. The Federation in Paris gives us the opportunity to make an imposing demonstration that will cause despots to tremble. We will all be there."[6]

The clubs of Le Mans and Angers became absorbed in a related project in July. This was to recruit volunteers who would first go to the "Camp of Soissons" and thence (when Paris was safe) on to the frontiers to join army units. Angers, by mid-July, claimed to have raised sixty-six men and 1,800 livres for this purpose. Le Mans, on July 5–6, persuaded its commune to open registers for men and money, and on July 28, it published the names of those who had inscribed.[7]

Brest's circular also fired the zeal of the Norman clubs. Domfront, a little before June 28, boasted that it was expediting "a double contingent" to the "camp" in Paris. Falaise deputed a member to the Paris Jacobins to report that fédérés from its district were on the march. Moreover, it asked clubbists of Vire to join with the "several citizens of Falaise, Argentan, Verneuil, Domfront, and L'Aigle who were going to dance with the Parisians on July 14 on the ruins of the Bastille." Several Virois immediately volunteered and others gave money. Caen, Rouen, and Coutances likewise sent fédérés to Paris.[8]

Most of the clubs of the north were fearful for their own safety and had no men to spare for the defense of Paris. Apparently, however, Bergues sent fédérés to the capital. And Arras (early

[6] PV: Le Mans, June 28–29, 1792; Blois, June 28, 1792. COR: Bordeaux, 12 L 29; Poitiers, S 23. *CD*, July 5, 1792.
[7] PV, Le Mans, July 5–28, 1792. *AP*, July 17, 1792.
[8] Nicolle, *Vire*, pp. 100–101. *CD*, June 28, July 13, 1792. *AP*, July 1, 1792. *ArchP*, July 13, 20, 1792.

July) disclosed that it was following "the example of Brest and the other cities of the empire" and appealed to affiliates in the Pas-de-Calais to do likewise. At least one club, Aire, responded affirmatively. The Directory of the Pas-de-Calais, in league with the minister of interior, Terrier, declared the march of fédérés to be unlawful. But Arras defended the legality of this exercise and denounced the Directors to the Legislative Assembly.[9]

Elsewhere in France Brest's circular arrived too late to have much practical effect. The recruitment of fédérés had already begun. In the Paris region one of the first to sound the bugle call was the club of Versailles. In an address read before the Legislative Assembly on June 21, it suggested that in spite of the veto of the camp of twenty thousand, national guardsmen from all departments should come to the Fete of the Federation. What steps Versailles took to implement this proposal are unknown, but there were some fédérés from the Seine-et-Oise in Paris at the time of the fete.[10]

Langres gets top billing in the east. On June 22 it published an address condemning the vetoes and announcing that it had just opened a register on which members who wished to go to the fete of July 14 could inscribe. It also pledged to provide arms and uniforms to the volunteers and begged affiliates to follow its lead. This notice was distributed far and wide. Strasbourg adhered to it, and Gray certainly knew of Langres' address before it sent delegates to the July 14 fete.[11]

But in the other parts of the east it has not been possible to establish cause-and-effect relationships. All that is known is that a number of societies were smitten by the desire to send fédérés to Paris. Lons-le-Saunier and Grenoble announced very early (June 26) that their fédérés were "on the march." Several clubs of Burgundy, including Autun, Beaune, and Chalon-sur-Saône, were represented at the fete. Autun gave fifty livres to its members who made the trip. In July, Besançon and Avallon recruited volunteers for the "camp of Soissons." Clubbists of Ornans wanted

---

[9] PV, Aire, July 4–9, 1792. *JC*, July 19, 1792. AN, F ^{1} *C III (Pas-de-Calais)*.
[10] AN, C 152.
[11] Heitz, *Strasbourg*, p. 223. *JC*, July 7, 1792. COR, Reims. PV, Gray, June 26–July 8, 1792.

to go but could not because of "pressing obligations in the countryside."[12]

It is possible that some eastern clubs were influenced by the example of Montpellier and Marseille. Certainly, these two societies were prime movers in the southeast, the region that produced the greatest numbers of fédérés. On June 19, the day that it learned of the ministerial firings, Montpellier resolved to send three addresses to the capital. The first, in stirring cadences, admonished the Legislative Assembly to be strong. The second cautioned Louis XVI to "read and reread" Roland's letter. The third advised the "people of Paris" that the "reunion of July 14 is decided."

That very evening at 10 P.M. the Department of the Hérault met at the goading of the Montpellier society and approved an address and a decree. The address (to the Legislative Assembly) indicated that the Hérault was taking steps to raise its contingent for the camp of twenty thousand. The decree (which the club circulated nationally along with the aforementioned addresses) ordered each commune of the department to open up a register for volunteers. "This is not just a question of a simple patriotic mission, but of assembling under the walls of Paris 20,000 Spartans to save the republic from attacks by foreigners and plots by conspirators. . . . We must have men whose physical strength corresponds to their moral strength."

Recruitment began immediately in the Hérault and was not halted by the news of the veto. By early July a contingent of 250 men was on route to Paris. Eighty came from the district of Montpellier, eighty-five from Béziers, fifty from Lodève, and thirty-five from St.-Pons. Almost all were club members. Each one had been given fifty-eight livres. Even as this force was being assembled, the Montpellier society had begun to promote another scheme designed to "get around the veto." It mailed out copies of a June 26 petition of the Department of the Hérault asking the Legislative Assembly to order each department to levy,

---

[12] *ArchP*, July 13, 16, 1792. *AP*, July 15, 1792. PV: Ornans, July 4, 1792; Avallon, July 31, 1792. *JC*, July 19, 1792.

arm, and train six thousand reserves to be ready to fly to Paris or wherever danger threatened.[13]

Special messengers of the Montpellier club carried copies of the June 19 addresses and decree to the societies of Marseille, Nîmes, Toulouse, and Lyon. When two of these envoys arrived at Marseille on June 21, they found that the club there was already feverishly active. Supposedly, on June 19, it had received a note from Paris in which the Marseillais Barbaroux pleaded: "Send six hundred men who know how to die." Certainly, on June 20, the day that it learned of the dismissal of the ministers, it petitioned the commune to open up a register wherein citizens might volunteer to go to Paris. On June 23, after consultation with the club, the commune voted to dispatch five hundred men to the capital. Twelve clubbists supervised their selection. Most were Marseillais and members of the society, although some came from nearby villages like Allauch and Aubagne. On July 2, the day of their leave-taking, the vice-president of the club charged the volunteers to "blend their courage with the Parisians. Frighten the tyrant on a throne he no longer merits! Tell him that the sovereign people have come to sanction the decree that he has struck down with his monstrous veto."[14]

Marseille announced the departure of its battalion in a circular dated July 3, "the first year of liberty or death." The Parisian press printed this notice along with news of the battalion's progress. All along their route, the Marseillais were feted by the clubs. Meanwhile, Paris waited anxiously for the men from the south. Blanc-Gilly, a royalist deputy from the Bouches-du-Rhône, published a pamphlet in which he portrayed the Marseillais as a "horde of brigands." Certainly, they were a colorful bunch. Another royalist, recounting their triumphal arrival in Paris on July 30, wrote: "Their red hats, the daggers and pistols stuck in their woolen waistbands, the bizarre variety of their clothing, their

---

[13] On Montpellier and the Hérault cf. Duval-Jouve, *Montpellier*, I, 212–215. COR: Poitiers, S 26; Niort, 3003. *M*, July 2, 1792. PV, Montpellier, June 19, 1792.

[14] Kennedy, *Marseilles*, pp. 108–109. J. Pollio and A. Marcel, *Le Bataillon du 10 août* (Paris, 1881), pp. 55–125.

sun-burned faces . . . gave the battalion of Marseillais the air of a gang of bandits."[15]

As soon as the Antipolitiques of Aix learned of the decision of Marseille, they assembled and dispatched a troop of fédérés to Paris. Likewise, the Monnaidiers of Arles leaped at the chance to share in the glory of the "Invincible Marseillais." In a circular of July 2 Arles proclaimed: "The alarm has just rung. The French are upright. Fifteen of our brothers have just left. They are resolved to shed the last drop of their blood in defense of our rights."[16]

All the while, *commissaires* from Marseille were barnstorming Provence, promoting the cause in smaller clubs. One went to the Vaucluse. Another later claimed to have caused four hundred to volunteer in the Basses-Alpes. A third, accompanied by two recently recruited fédérés from Peynier, made a salesmanlike pitch at St.-Zacharie (Var) on July 10. He proclaimed liberty to be in peril and the king to be a traitor.

> His many forfeits have obliged the citizens of the great cities to march to the capital. Five hundred have left from Marseille. . . . We reckon that there will be 150,000 citizens in Paris. . . . Come brothers and friends; come join us. . . . The moment has arrived; . . . let us demand that the royal family be proscribed, that this family which is the cause of our troubles be annihilated.[17]

Marseille's recruitment efforts in the Var were ably seconded by the club of Toulon. On June 21, the day after learning of the dismissal of the ministers, Toulon persuaded its municipality to send fifteen national guardsmen to Paris to "offer their arms, their blood, and their lives in defense of the Constitution." Two days later the Toulon society published a circular to affiliates asking them to take similar steps. Like Marseille, Toulon was con-

---

[15] *JC*, July 19, 1792. COR, Poitiers, S 26. *CD*, July 13, 15, 1792. Pollio and Marcel, *Bataillon*, pp. 135–183. *AP*, July 13, 25, 1792.
[16] Ponteil, "Antipolitiques," pp. 471–472. COR, Bordeaux, 12 L 29. *ArchP*, July 14, 1792. *JC*, July 14, 1792. *CD*, June 29, 1792.
[17] Kennedy, *Marseilles*, p. 110. E. Poupé, "Une brochure de propagande révolutionnaire en 1792," *RF* (1905), pp. 328–332.

temptuous of the king, whom it described as "M de Varennes, the first of the crowned imbeciles."

Sixteen fédérés from Toulon actually made the long journey to Paris. They arrived far in advance of the Marseillais, on July 9. By mid-July, at least twenty-five other communes of the Var had pledged to send men to the capital. If all fulfilled their commitments, there would have been about one hundred "fédérés Varois" in Paris by August. Sixty-five took part in the attack on the Tuileries on August 10. Most were young farmers or artisans, and club members.[18]

The Gard department, which borders on the Hérault and on the Bouches-du-Rhône, was powerfully influenced by the example of both. On June 21, the Popular Society of Nîmes gave cordial welcome to two commissars from the Montpellier club and adhered to its addresses of June 19. Then, on June 24, after being apprized of Marseille's actions, the Nîmes society engaged all of the clubs of the Gard to set up registers on which citizens could inscribe to go to the federation of July 14. In addition, it petitioned the department to authorize districts to set up registers.

The Directors of the Gard, abetted by the minister, Terrier, did their utmost to avert the march of the fédérés. They rejected the petition of the Popular Society of Nîmes (and similar ones from Calvisson, St.-Hippolyte, Clarensac, and Quissac). In addition, they decreed on July 2 that it was unlawful for national guardsmen to set off under arms without their express authorization. Their efforts were partially successful. Several clubs, including the Friends of the Constitution of Nîmes, the three societies at Alès, and the one at St.-Hippolyte, refused to join the movement.

But the passage of the fédérés from the Hérault, the exhortations of commissaires from Marseille, and the inspired leadership of the Popular Society of Nîmes caused some clubs of the Gard to defy the department. The Popular Society collected enough money to give sixty livres to each of the men for travel and subsistence. The first batch of fédérés left on July 4. They put their

[18] E. Poupé, "Les fédérés varois du 10 août," *RF* (1904), pp. 305–325.

weapons and packs in carts so that they were not technically "armed" and in violation of the law.[19]

The patriotic currents coming from the southeast swept up the Rhône valley and into parts of the Massif Central. The Montélimar club, for example, drew up addresses to the Assembly, the king, and the Parisians modelled on those of Montpellier. St.-Paul-Trois-Châteaux first summoned the Department of the Drôme to emulate the Hérault, and then, on its own, recruited three fédérés and paid for their trip to Paris. Tournon (Ardèche) furnished one fédéré, although it made clear that it wanted "no modification of the Constitution." Marvéjols asked the Department of the Lozère for permission to send fédérés to Paris but was rebuffed. The Department of the Rhône-et-Loire (July 3) rejected a similar plea from "150 citizens of Lyon." Nonetheless, some Lyonnais went to the capital anyway and took part in the attack on the Tuileries.[20]

Impulses from Montpellier also radiated southwestward. Narbonne (June 23) was moved by Montpellier's June 19 circular to petition the Department of the Aude to raise a contingent for the camp of twenty thousand. On June 21, after the arrival of the special envoys from Montpellier, the club of Toulouse asked the department to authorize the formation of a corps of fédérés from the Haute-Garonne. When the department acquiesced, the Toulouse society sent advancemen to Paris to arrange for the lodging of the fédérés; and on July 3, it called an emergency meeting to procure last-minute donations of arms and money.[21]

In a circular of June 23 Toulouse bruited the news that "some citizens of the Haute-Garonne have vowed to fly to the capital." On receiving this imprimé St.-Affrique petitioned its department to authorize the creation of a force of fédérés and invited other societies of the Aveyron to follow its example. By July the whole region from Quercy south to the Pyrénées was in ferment. Montauban persuaded its commune to dispatch fédérés to the capital and collected 1,200 livres to pay for their expenses. Limoux re-

---

[19] Rouvière, *Gard*, II, 329–346. *JC*, July 7, 19, 1792. PV, St.-Hippolyte, June 20–July 2, 1792.

[20] COR, Montpellier, L 5544. *JC*, July 19, Aug. 4, 1792. Wahl, *Lyon*, pp. 539–542. *AP*, July 5, 1792.

[21] *JC*, July 7, 1792. *CD*, July 12, 1792. PV, Toulouse, June 20–July 3, 1792.

cruited fifteen to twenty fédérés, funded their passage to Paris, and provided for their dependents in their absence. Perpignan entreated the clubs of the Pyrénées-Orientales to give offerings for volunteers enrolling for the "camp of Soissons." Pau and Orthez tried to get the Department of the Basses-Pyrénées to adopt the Hérault's June 26 proposal for the training of six thousand reserves in each department.[22]

Some clubs of the Lot-et-Garonne and Gironde began preliminary registrations of volunteers as soon as they heard of the June 8 decree. What is more, they announced their intention of defying the veto quite early, before they could have known of the actions of Brest, Montpellier, or Marseille. In a circular of June 24 Nérac asserted that it was sending fédérés to Paris. The same day the Récollets Society bragged that four thousand Bordelais had volunteered to "succor their brothers in the capital," that a drawing would be held to determine the lucky ones, and that contributions were pouring in.[23]

Both the Récollets Society and the Club National issued special appeals to the clubs of the region. Blaye responded by sending five fédérés to Paris. Estaffort furnished eight and promised to cultivate their fields in their absence. Libourne opened up two registers: one for money, the other for men. Enough cash came in to provide seventy livres for each man. And the number of volunteers exceeded the quota of twenty that had been set. To whittle down the number, the club voted to give bachelors priority; but it rescinded this action when a married man protested: "I prefer death to the decision that you have just taken." A last-minute appeal to citizens brought in a monstrous quantity of arms. The squad departed on schedule in the wee hours of July 3.[24]

On the road north to Paris the Libournais might have linked up with fédérés from the Dordogne, for several societies of that department, including Périgueux, Montpont, and Bergerac, participated in the movement. Bergerac acted at the behest of its deputy in the Legislative Assembly, Pinet. In a letter of June 12 Pinet ex-

[22] PV: Orthez, July 5–6, 1792; Perpignan, July 15, 1792; Toulouse, June 23, 1792. *JC*, July 5, Aug. 2, 4, 1792. Ligou, *Montauban*, pp. 268–269.

[23] *CD*, July 2, 1792. Besson, *Libourne*, p. 175. PV, Tonneins, June 17, 1792. COR, Poitiers, S 23.

[24] PV, Blaye, July 4–5, 1792. Besson, *Libourne*, pp. 175–176. *AP*, July 17, 1792.

pressed the hope that the Dordogne would fill its contingent for the camp of twenty thousand. After the veto (June 20) he offered to feed and lodge any clubbists who came to Paris. In response to this offer, Bergerac raised a force of thirty young men. They left on June 29 with borrowed guns for which the club was the guarantor.[25]

Clubs in the west-central departments were also bitten by the bug. The June 19 circular of Montpellier caused Tulle (June 27) to petition its Department to form a battalion. Later (July 4), after reading Toulon's circular, Tulle decided to invite every club of the Corrèze to send members to Paris. A collection was started to finance this enterprise. By July 15–16 some fédérés from Tulle had reached Paris, and others were on their way.[26]

Angoulême (June 29) petitioned its department to implement the June 19 decree of the Hérault. The department refused to do so without written authority from Paris, but it did permit communes to sign up volunteers who would be ready to march when the official call came. At least one club of the Charente (Ruffec) sent fédérés to Paris anyway. And La Rochelle (Charente-Maritime) asked its commune rather late (July 6) to set up a register on which volunteers could inscribe their names, contending that even after July 14, the presence of fédérés in the capital would be "useful."[27]

Niort (Deux-Sèvres) was egged on by its deputies in the Legislative Assembly, Ruamps and Baudry. Both wrote in early July to urge it to emulate the clubs of the Midi. Whereupon, Niort offered a bonus of thirty livres for any citizen who would enroll to go to the "camp of Soissons." Poitiers also furnished a detachment of fédérés which arrived in Paris about July 28.[28]

Thus, from all points of the compass, fédérés converged on Paris. Pétion said on July 18 that 2,960 had registered at the commune, but this was before the arrival of some of the largest contingents. It is unlikely that anyone will ever know the exact number. Some of the volunteers never reached Paris. Others only stayed briefly before heading to the battle fronts. Finally, to the chagrin of the clubs, a sizable number of the fédérés neither remained in Paris nor joined the armies, but returned home. Ruffec was terribly distraught when it heard that its fédérés were coming back. Motions were made to censure them and to demand the refund of the one hundred livres that each had been given; and they were subjected to interrogation. Tumultuous scenes also occurred at the club of Aire when its three fédérés suddenly reappeared. When twelve of the fifteen Monnaidiers returned, the club of Arles branded them as cowards.[29]

This brings us to another question for which there is no precise answer. That is, how many fédérés left their hearths with the intention of overthrowing the king? We may safely assume that this was the intention of Marseille and its allies in the southeast. But others who took part in the assault on the Tuileries were converted to the cause after their arrival in Paris. The deputy Pinet flatly stated in a letter that he had persuaded the fédérés of Bergerac to stay in Paris because "they would be useful in provoking various measures, notably the overthrow of the king." The correspondence of the Brest fédérés also suggests that they were convinced to tarry against their better judgment.[30]

Those who did pitch camp in Paris established their headquarters at the Paris Jacobins. There they formed a "central committee" which published addresses in their name. By July 26 they also had a "Secret Directory" which was scheming with Parisian radicals to overthrow the king. The fédérés in Paris corresponded with clubbists back home. Many of their letters survive in archival collections and show clearly how they were prey to rumors. The fédérés of Aix, for example, recounted tales of plots to assassinate Robespierre and Pétion, and an attempt by the king to escape disguised as a groom.[31]

[29] PV, Aire, July 30, Aug. 1, 1792. Chambon, "Charentais," p. 22. *JC*, Aug. 23, 1792.

[30] Cf. Labroue, *Bergerac*, pp. 212–213.

[31] Ponteil, "Antipolitiques," pp. 471–472.

XXI

Dethronement

O N THE morning of June 20, 1792, masses of armed men assembled in the working-class quarters of eastern Paris. About noon, headed by the popular brewer, Santerre, the mob marched on the Legislative Assembly where it interrupted the debates and vowed to avenge the vetoes and the ministerial firings. Next, unhindered by Pétion or municipal officials, the rioters surrounded the Tuileries. Toward 4:00 P.M. they burst into the palace through an unlocked door. Louis XVI was trapped in the embrasure of a window, and compelled to don a red cap and drink a toast to the nation. However, he courageously refused to recall the ministers or lift his vetoes. His kingly demeanor cowed the invaders, and, after two tense hours, they were finally persuaded to withdraw.

Louis struck back peevishly the next day, curtly silencing Pétion and turning his royal back when the mayor showed up for an audience. Then, on June 22, he issued a defiant proclamation to the nation. Meanwhile, royalists in Paris threatened reprisals against the Paris Jacobins and others who were deemed responsible for the attack. The "mother society" was so alarmed that it wrote to affiliates on June 21 asking for their loyalty and support.

The treatment accorded to the king, and the bravery that he had shown, also provoked a royalist, anti-Jacobin backlash in the provinces. More than one-third of the departments manifested their horror at the riot and demanded punishment of the rioters. Some advocated the dissolution of the clubs to boot. A number of districts and municipalities emitted protests too. The Commune of Strasbourg, for example, sought the passage of a law against the "anarchist corporations known under the name of Jacobins." In addition, groups of citizens in many towns petitioned for punitive action against the clubs.

A few of the clubs themselves were displeased by the assault on the king. Neuville-sur-Saône sundered all ties with the Paris Jacobins and expressed its indignation to the Legislative Assembly. Gaillac approved of a letter in which the Department of Paris branded the Jacobins as "factionalists"; it also applauded the royal proclamation of June 22 and assured the king of its devotion. Ploërmel reprimanded Lorient for demanding the deportation of the Department of Paris. The Auditoire Society of Strasbourg voluntarily disbanded; Confolens may have done likewise.[1]

Agen, in a letter of July 2 to the Récollets Society, railed at the "ambitious and dissimulating men who exert the greatest efforts to undermine royal authority." It went on to say that it respected the Constitution and regarded the king as "the dupe of rogues" rather than "the soul of conspiracy." Agen, moreover, sided with the Department of the Lot-et-Garonne when the latter assailed "republicans" in Paris and advised the Legislative Assembly to quit the capital. In so doing, the Agen club drew fire from the societies of Tonneins, Marmande, Nérac, Villeneuve, and Monflanquin.[2]

At Melun, a minority of "patriots" withdrew when the majority hooted down a Jacobin from Paris and accused the "mother society" of preaching anarchy. Bourbonne took a more moderate but nonetheless conservative stand. It first decided to draft an address in protest of June 20. Then it reversed this decision since this incident "did no injury to life and property" and voted instead to chasten the Paris society because some of its members had demanded the "revision of the Constitution."[3]

At Rouen a great many clubbists signed a June 27 address of "active citizens" to the king. "Sire," it began, "the outrage committed against your majesty has filled us with horror and indignation." And it proceeded to endorse the opinions of Lafayette and the Department of Paris. This address set off a struggle within the society between defenders and opponents of June 20. By July 21 the former had gained the upper hand, and the latter began to resign in droves. On July 29 the address to the king was

[1] PV: Neuville, June 23, 1792; Gaillac, June 28–July 11, 1792; Lorient, Aug. 8, 1792. ArchP, July 20, 1792. AN, DXL, 14. Babaud-Laribière, *Etudes*, I, 95. Heitz, *Strasbourg*, p. 223.

[2] COR, Bordeaux, 12 L 29. PV, Tonneins, June 16–Aug. 5, 1792.

[3] Noiriel, "Melun," pp. 339–343. *JC*, July 12, 1792. PV, Bourbonne, June 24, July 1, 4, 1792.

torn into "a thousand pieces" to the applause of those in attendance.[4]

The Le Havre club was also deeply split. On June 22 it learned that some citizens were gathering signatures for an address that deplored the events of June 20 and damned the "faction jacobite." The club denounced this address. Alas, it soon became apparent that many of the signers were clubbists. On the twenty-third, a prominent member resigned, stating that he no longer wished to be a part of a body that was affiliated with the Paris Jacobins. A wave of resignations followed. By the end of July Le Havre was so depleted in strength that it closed temporarily.[5]

Such troubles were by no means confined to the Seine-Maritime. Aurillac lost many members due to resignations. A large number of clubbists at Abbeville affixed their names to an address condemning the "criminal assemblage" that had invaded the Tuileries. Orléans announced that it had purged a faction that had "just sent a perfidious letter to the king." Avallon purified itself of certain members who, after June 20, signed a statement accusing the societies of "excesses."[6]

There were also numerous reports of failed royalist motions. Orange, for instance, indignantly refused to allow one of its members to read the king's proclamation of June 22. At Castres, on June 28, an orator was heckled and interrupted when he argued that the "safety, repose, and liberty of the first citizen of the empire were at the mercy of a horde of brigands and anarchists."[7]

Almost always, as at Castres and Orange, friends of the king were in the minority. Of those clubs that enunciated opinions, the vast majority approved of or excused the invasion of the Tuileries. Many spoke up in defense of the Parisian people and the "mother society." Pontlevoy was ready to shield the Paris Jacobins with "blood and arms." Falaise saw in the rioters of June 20 "only a just and benevolent people who wanted to save the king and the fatherland at the same time." Châteauroux prattled: "The

[4] BN, Lb39 10656. Chardon, *Rouen*, pp. 73–75. Mazauric, "Rougemaure," pp. 62–64. PV, Rouen, June 27–July 29, 1792.

[5] Le Marchand, "Le Havre," pp. 86–87. PV, Le Havre, June 22–July 31, 1792. *ArchP*, July 6, 15, 1792. *JC*, July 5, 1792.

[6] *JC*, July 19, 1792. AN, DXL 12, 14. COR, Poitiers, S 26.

[7] *JC*, July 21, 1792. PV, Castres, June 28, 1792.

good citizens went to the Palace of the Tuileries to recall Louis to order. They had no bad intentions."[8]

The clubs also led the counterattack against conservative local officials. Langres, St.-Girons, Laon, Sommières, Lyon, Monflanquin, Carcassonne, Metz, Amiens, Lons-le-Saunier, Montdidier, Abbeville, St.-Maixent, Le Beausset, Bourges, Nérac, Tonneins, Marmande, and the Popular Society of Nîmes, among others, publicly disavowed royalist, anti-Jacobin pronouncements of their departments. Soissons, in addition, purged five directors of the Aisne. Versailles and Limoges demanded that directors of their departments be removed from office. Nérac, Orléans, Solliez, Montdidier, and Perpignan petitioned for national elections to replace officials at all levels.[9]

Much criticism was aimed at the king's proclamation of June 22. Lons-le-Saunier burned it on a public square. Le Mans was gleeful when it learned that the Commune of Chartres had refused to publish it. Dijon lectured Louis: "You were wrong when you wrote to the Legislative Assembly that France would learn with sadness and astonishment of June 20. The whole of France applauds the zeal of the Parisians." Aiguesvives mused: "What a strange species of character is the king of the French. He covers his head with the red cap and keeps it in place with one hand while . . . with the other he signs the veto." Cognac wrote: "Sire! You should be cognizant of the true public spirit. . . . You have violated the rights of man in forbidding Pétion to speak. . . . As for your proclamation of June 22, we regard it as contrary to the Constitution."[10]

A host of societies wrote to Pétion after June 20 to congratulate him on his "wise and prudent conduct" and to pledge their support. Great were the lamentations when Pétion was suspended by

[8] *JC*, July 6, 7, 19, 1792.

[9] PV: Le Mans, July 18, 1792; Limoges, July 15, 16, 27, 1792; Tonneins, July 15–19, 1792. AN, DXL 7, 14, 15. *JC*, July 7–30, 1792. *AP*, July 10, 30, 1792. *M*, June 30, 1792. *ArchP*, June 27–Aug. 12, 1792. *CD*, July 2, 5, 24, 1792. BN, Lb39 6011. COR: Reims; Poitiers, S 26. Arnaud, *Ariège*, pp. 296–297. Rouvière, *Gard*, II, 322–323. Nicolle, *Vire*, p. 98. Henriot, *Lyon*, I, 43. Bultingaire, *Metz*, pp. 38–39. Heitz, *Strasbourg*, p. 229.

[10] Sommier, *Jura*, p. 103. AN, F¹ C III (Charente). Le Gallo, "Cognac," p. 251. Hugueney, *Dijon*, p. 138. *JC*, July 12, 1792. COR: Bordeaux, 12 L 29; Le Mans, L 1007. PV, Le Mans, July 11, 1792.

the Department of Paris on July 7. On that occasion he published an apologia that evoked emotional outbursts. "O Pétion, Pétion," keened Limoux, "the people honor and love you." Ornans compared him to Cicero and had a plaque engraved with these words: "Long live Pétion, father of the fatherland. Chance makes kings. Virtue makes great men." When the Legislative Assembly lifted the suspension, Eguilles exulted: "The incorruptible defender of the Rights of Man in the Constituent is today the cornerstone of the welfare of the French empire."[11]

By early July Paris hummed with talk of dethronement. Before the Legislative Assembly, on July 3, Vergniaud gave a famous speech in which he implied that Louis XVI had violated article 6, section 1, chapter 2 of the Constitution. In so doing, says the historian Mathiez, he "put the idea of deposing the king into the minds of the public." Actually, he was but a retailer of second-hand opinions. The club of Langres had advanced this theory seven months previously, and by early July it was becoming rather shopworn.

At the Paris Jacobins a parade of orators stepped to the rostrum to call for the removal of Louis. On July 8 Audouin cited this same constitutional article to prove that the king could be deposed. Three days later Robespierre pointedly asked fédérés in attendance if they had hastened to Paris "for a mere ceremony." Carra (July 6, 13) twice called for the king's suspension. Meanwhile, the Leftist Parisian press was filled with clamorings.

The Declaration of the Fatherland in Danger, the daily arrivals of the fédérés, shortages of foodstuffs, and the shilly-shallying of the Assembly raised political temperatures in Paris to the flash point. By the end of July a secret "Insurrectionary Directory" had been formed and the sections were in "permanent" session. On August 3, in the name of forty-seven sections, Pétion presented a petition to the Assembly seeking the dethronement of the king and the election of a National Convention. The next day

[11] Cf. *JC*, July 6–Aug. 4, 1792. *CD*, July 4, 14, 1792. *AP*, July 9, 24, 1792. *Courrier de la Gironde*, July 15, 1792. PV: Ornans, July 10, 1792; Lorient, July 5, 12, 1792; Périgueux, July 21–22, 1792; Perpignan, Aug. 4, 1792; Le Mans, July 18, 1792; Rouen, July 19, 1792. Bellanger, *Provins*, p. 41. COR, Niort, L2ᶜ supp. M 1.

the Quinze-Vingts section issued an ultimatum giving the deputies until 11 P.M. on August 9 to implement this demand.

Paris was set for revolution, but what about the clubs? What was their attitude on the eve of August 10? A little less than four hundred societies are known to have met in the period from June 20 to August 10. Data on about one-third are so scanty that no judgment can be made about their opinions. A dozen for which there are good records refrained from comment on the subject. Most of these were small, rural, and inarticulate, or near extinction.[12] Only a few (like Gaillac, Neuville-sur-Saône, and Melun) were staunchly loyal to Louis XVI. But several others (including Loudun, La Réole, Bourbonne, Agen, Barsac, Confolens, Château-Thierry, Ploërmel, Tournon, and Annonay) seem to have been basically sympathetic to the king.

Approximately 150 clubs voiced criticism of the king but did not, to my knowledge, call for his removal. These manifestations of ill will ranged from simple rebukes, to suggestions that Louis step down voluntarily, to vaguely revolutionary pronouncements. The two latter types of utterances increased in July and early August. Aigre, for example, told the king: "Either you must quit the throne or march with your sovereign, the nation." Le Puy used the familiar as though speaking to a child: "If you do not feel strong enough to uphold the weight of royalty, put it in more vigorous hands." Narbonne exhorted Parisian sansculottes to watch the king sharply: "It is up to you to survey the pilot and throw him into the sea if he threatens to sink the ship."[13]

As their minutes show, some of these 150 clubs considered calling for dethronement. A motion for *déchéance* was debated at Castres (August 12) and tabled. Cherbourg first approved an address demanding suspension (July 27) but then adjourned this decision when someone observed that this might lead to civil war. Bourg-en-Bresse was also afraid of the "leap into the dark." On June 24 one of its members attacked Louis violently, arguing that he had violated article 6, chapter 2, section 1 of the Constitution and was guilty "at least of a felony, at worst of a felony and trea-

[12] Cf. PV: Courthézon, Eymoutiers, Tulette, Monpazier, Lectoure, Vitteaux, Nuits, Ars-en-Ré, Châtillon-sur-Chalaronne, Montreuil, Lauris. Lefebvre, Bourbourg.

[13] AN, F¹. C III (Charente). *JC*, July 23, Aug. 2, 4, 1792.

son." But the club contented itself with calling for the modification of certain constitutional articles. Two weeks later, in a letter to the Paris Jacobins, it stigmatized the king "as the cause of all of the calamities threatening the nation." On July 13 a speaker called for the "end of the monarchy or at least the right of the king to sanction the laws." Finally (August 4) Bourg gave a warm reception to four commissars from Marseille who advocated the deposition of Louis, but again declined to take any formal action.[14]

However, eighty-three clubs, at least, declared for dethronement or suspension.[15] Now, it is true that some of these declarations were qualified or tepid. Perpignan and the Surveillants of Bordeaux, for example, summoned the Legislative Assembly to investigate the king's conduct and to deprive him of the crown if he was judged guilty of treason. Montastruc told the deputies to "dethrone the king if you judge it necessary." And Rouen, after a discussion of the petition of the forty-seven sections of Paris, simply concluded that the Assembly had the "power to pronounce the deposition of Louis."[16] Yet, when all allowances are made, eighty-three is still a very high figure; and the actual total was probably much higher.

As we have seen, the first cries for deposition had been loosed after the ministerial firings and vetoes in June. Arras (June 24) insinuated that the king had not done his duty and should be removed. Blois (June 22) stated categorically that he had violated article 6, section 1, chapter 2 of the Constitution and should be

[14] Dubois, *Ain*, II, 322–326, 341, 344, 491. Galland, "Cherbourg," p. 342. PV, Castres, Aug. 12, 1792.

[15] Aiguesvives, Aix, Alençon, Ampuis, Angers, Arras, Arles, Aubagne, Bar-le-Duc, Beaucaire, Beaumont-de-Lomagne, Bédarieux, Bergerac, Béziers, Blois, Bordeaux (Club National, Surveillants, and Récollets), Bourgoin, Caen, Carhaix, Chalon-sur-Saône, Champlitte, Châtellerault, Clarensac, Condé-sur-Noireau, Dampierre, Digne, Dole, Draguignan, Falaise, Forcalquier, Héricourt, Honfleur, Langres, Lavaur, Le Mans, Libourne, Lille, Lons-le-Saunier, Lyon, Mâcon, Marseille, Montastruc, Montbard, Montdidier, Montflanquin, Moulins, Nantes (Club Mirabeau), Nérac, Nîmes (Friends of the Constitution and Popular Society), Ollioules, Orléans, Orthez, Pauillac, Pennes, Périgueux, Perpignan, Rennes, Rieumes, Riom, Rouen, Ruffec, St.-Ambroix, St.-Fargeau, St.-Girons, St.-Hippolyte, St.-Jean-de-Luz, St.-Jean-du-Gard, St.-Nicolas (T-et-G), St.-Pierre-sur-Dives, Sarrelouis, Sète, Sezanne, Solliès, Strasbourg, Tonneins, Toulon, Toulouse, Tulle, Valence (Gers), Vesoul.

[16] COR, Colmar, B 34. PV, Toulouse, Aug. 13, 1792. Dubos, "Surveillants" (1933), pp. 185–188. Chardon, *Rouen*, p. 75.

put aside. Caen (June 22) may have also plumped for dethronement.[17]

Of special importance among the early petitions was one that was circulated by the Club National of Bordeaux. It was conceived about June 20, but the covering letter was dated June 23. Clubs as far away as Le Mans adhered to the Bordeaux circular, but it had its greatest impact in the southwest. Libourne agreed on June 26 to demand dethronement. Ruffec, by July 3, was for suspension. Orthez adhered on June 29, reversed itself on July 22, but adhered again on August 9. On the last date it informed the Club National that it supported "its efforts to destitute the perjurious and traitorous executive branch."[18]

It is possible that the Club National circular was also the stimulus behind petitions of early July from Nérac and Monflanquin (Lot-et-Garonne). Nérac, which was quite prolix and radical at this date, declared on the seventh that the king was "acting in good or bad faith." If the first was true, he had proven himself incapable of governing France and a regency ought to be established by virtue of article 18, section 2, chapter 2 of the Constitution. If the second was the case, he was guilty of violating his oaths and of not opposing enterprises executed in his name and should be deposed according to articles 5 and 6 of section 1, chapter 2.[19]

Unbeknownst to Nérac, an almost identical petition was drawn up at St.-Girons (Ariège) on July 4. It was the work of four clubbists but purported to represent the views of the great mass of citizens of that place. It cited the same three articles and left it up to the deputies to decide which course to take. They could declare Louis to be insane and set up a regency, or they could rule that he had betrayed his oaths and forfeited the crown.[20]

In the second half of July and early August the movement mushroomed. Indeed, over 50 percent of the clubs that declared for dethronement or suspension did so in the two weeks preced-

[17] On Caen cf. A. Aulard, *The French Revolution* (New York, 1910), II, 45.

[18] COR: Poitiers, S 26; Niort, 3001. PV: Le Mans, July 3, 5, 8, 1792; Orthez, June 29, July 22, Aug. 9, 1792.

[19] *JC*, July 26, 30, 1792. *AP*, July 29, 1792. AN, DXL 12. *CD*, Aug. 3, 1792. PV, Tonneins, July 16, 19, 1792.

[20] AN, DXL 7.

ing August 10, or in the days immediately afterward (before hearing the news).[21] The reading of Vergniaud's oration at the Assembly, the speeches in the "mother society," and the editorials of the radical Parisian press won many converts. The petition of the Paris sections had a tremendous impact.[22] Lastly, the clubs themselves did much to promote the cause.

In mid-July the Ampuis society circulated a parable for the people. Once upon a time, so it began, an African tribe threatened by wild beasts resolved to build a *maison commune*. After much debate the tribesmen decided, on the advice of an old man, that it would be supported by three wooden pillars called the columns of the law, the people, and the king. In the interests of tribal unity everyone took an oath to observe this plan for ten years. Four years passed; then a storm came and the pillar of the king nearly fell. On examination, it was found to be infested by millions of termites. Some tribesmen demanded that it be replaced; but the old man reminded everyone of their vows, and nothing was done. Sure enough, the pillar collapsed; and all of the women and children, "the hope of the people," were buried in the ruins of the communal house.[23]

Several circulars of a more conventional type appeared at the end of July. Caen (July 21) sought the elevation of the Dauphin to the throne. The Central Committee of the Gironde (July 30) urged all of the clubs to demand the king's suspension and the election of a Convention to decide whether he should be dethroned. Nérac (July 26) again called for suspension. Forcalquier (July 30) wanted each society to send one envoy to Paris to lobby for dethronement. Nîmes (July 27) advocated the suspension and trial of Louis.[24]

Nîmes in its circular stated that it shared the opinions of Marseille. Certainly, the club of that city was avidly for dethronement. It has been shown how its commissars abused the king in the small societies of the southeast. And on July 23, in conjunc-

---

[21] St.-Hippolyte, for example, had not yet heard the news when it decided for dethronement on Aug. 14.

[22] Cf. Maintenant, "Alençon," pp. 121–122. AN DXL 15. Chardon, *Rouen*, p. 75.

[23] PV, Le Mans, July 29, 1792. *PF*, July 19, 1792.

[24] AN, DXL 7. COR, Poitiers, S 23. *JC*, Aug. 6, 9, 1792. PV, Perpignan, July 30, 31, 1792. *ArchP*, Aug. 6, 1792. Rouvière, *Gard*, II, 412–413.

tion with local authorities, it appointed a task force of thirteen members to tour the "southern departments." Their ostensible aim was to raise an army of men to defend the Midi; but everywhere they went, they called for the overthrow of Louis.[25]

Some of the Marseillais made so bold as to advocate a republic. The future Conventionnel Moyse Bayle, for example, published an address on August 2 "On the Uselessness and Danger of a King in a Free and Representative State."[26] Usually, however, those clubs that wished to be rid of Louis XVI underscored their desire to retain a monarchical constitution. Condé-sur-Noireau's petition of July 29 is typical: "We recognize the Constitution and the principles which declare France to be a monarchical state. But we are convinced that Louis XVI has done everything in his power to favor the designs of our enemies, and we demand his dethronement. So that his successor will not abuse his position, we also demand the abrogation of the veto, the reduction of the civil list."[27]

One of the most famous incidents of the summer of 1792 was the "kiss of Lamourette." On July 7 Lamourette, Bishop of the Rhône-et-Loire, appeared before the Legislative Assembly, called for unity, and urged all of the deputies to renounce any intention of instituting a republic or a system of "two chambers." The deputies rose as one to take the oath and embrace. Moreover, the king was called to the hall to take part in this love feast. He expressed his gratitude and was cheered by the deputies and the galleries.

The reaction of the clubs to this incident is interesting. Although some suspected a plot and warned the "good deputies" to beware, many more adhered with seeming enthusiasm to the oath taken by the deputies. Arras, which had suggested that Louis be deposed, nonetheless solemnly anathematized a republic and a system of two chambers. Besançon also made clear that it did not want a republic. Loudun said: "We prefer the tomb to the system of two chambers, we will dig one for the republican system." The members at La Souterraine inscribed the words "the

[25] Cf. Fochier, *Bourgoin*, pp. 451–453. Dubois, *Ain*, II, 344, 493. Allemand, "Draguignan," p. 44. Kennedy, *Marseille*, p. 111.

[26] AN, AFII 90 664.

[27] AN, DXL 7.

constitution or death" on their doors.[28] Republicanism was not to triumph in the clubs until September.

ABOUT midnight on August 9–10, Paris exploded in rebellion. An army of sansculottes and fédérés marched on the Tuileries. In the general hubbub representatives of the sections went to city hall and established an Insurrectionary Commune. Early in the morning the attack on the Tuileries commenced. The battle raged for two hours and resulted in the death of 376 of the attackers and the massacre of the royal guards. The king and his family sought sanctuary in the Legislative Assembly. There, under pressure from the populace, the deputies suspended him from office.

The response of the clubs was overwhelmingly favorable. Almost all adhered promptly to the decree of suspension, and many were positively euphoric, chortling that the day of August 10 had "saved France," "put the seal on our liberty," "completed the victory over tyranny." Louis XVI was painted as the blackest of traitors. The blessings of God were invoked upon the Jacobins, the "brave Parisians," and the fédérés. Funeral services were held for sansculottes and fédérés who had died in the assault. Money was raised for their widows and children. Mont-de-Marsan asked for the names of all of the attackers who had perished so that they could be inscribed in a plaque in its hall. It urged affiliates to do the same so that these glorious heroes would never be forgotten.

There was nothing surprising about this reaction. The number of societies favoring deposition was large and growing rapidly by early August. Moreover, it was inherent in the nature of moderate clubs like Bourbonne to acquiesce in the fait accompli, readily to pledge allegiance to actions taken by the assemblies in Paris. Doubtless, many clubbists felt like one at Châteauroux. In the session of August 15 he stated that he had always been devoted to the Constitution and was, therefore, saddened that "the fatherland could only be saved by the violation of the laws." Nonetheless, he recommended that the club send an address of adhesion to the Assembly.[29]

Apparently, Annonay was so shocked by August 10 that it al-

---

[28] Lecesne, *Arras*, II, 2–5. Brelot, *Besancon*, pp. 90–91. *ArchP*, Aug. 4, 1792. PV: Limoges, Aug. 7, 1792; Toulouse, July 12, 1792. Forot, *Tulle*, p. 198.

[29] PV: Bourbonne, Aug. 15, 1792; Châteauroux, Aug. 15, 1792.

most closed. Laval and Vienne also experienced troubles. Only a few societies, however, protested openly. Réalmont took a stance in opposition to the suspension and was ostracized by Lavaur and other clubs of the Tarn. On learning of the "disastrous news" from the capital, the clubbists of Gaillac voted to send a copy of their profession of faith to "our unfortunate king." Not until late August did Gaillac take an oath of allegiance to the new regime, and only then after reading some of the documents found in the king's cabinet which exposed "the immensity of dangers run by patriots in the capital." Agen also seems to have been slow about adhering. On August 28, however, it wrote to the Paris club to say: "Jacobins! Henceforth you will be our rallying point."[30]

[30] *JC*, Sept. 8, 1792. Rossignol, *Gaillac*, pp. 75–76.

Part Six

Girondins and Montagnards

XXII

The Girondin-Montagnard Schism to the Trial of the King

O N AUGUST 10 the rump in the Legislative Assembly consented to summon a National Convention into session to
write France a constitution and to decide the fate of the king. The
new body was elected by universal manhood suffrage, but indi-
rectly. Roughly six thousand primary assemblies convened on
August 26 to choose electors. Then, commencing on September
2, the electors met in designated cities of each department to
nominate deputies.

The clubs were practically the only groups in a position to af-
fect the outcome of the elections; and as soon as they learned of
the August 10 decree, some began to plan for the primary assemblies. Montauban set up a special committee and, along with
Strasbourg, declared itself in permanent session. At Tonneins,
St.-Germain, Eymoutiers, Le Mans, Cherbourg, and Château-
du-Loir, clubbists expounded on the "necessity of making good
choices." Castres, La Rochelle, Montauban, Perpignan, Rodez,
and Lons-le-Saunier published and circulated "opinions" to
voters. Angers and Rouen called for the disenfranchisement of
persons who had not demonstrated their loyalty to the Revolution. Montauban and Lons-le-Saunier drew up slates of approved
candidates. Limoges followed the example of the Paris Commune and demanded that the electors be chosen by voice vote.[1]

On the eve of the primary assemblies, Semur, Douai, and
Castres held extraordinary meetings to discuss strategy, and La

[1] *JC*, Aug. 23, 27, 30, 1792. *JD*, Aug. 22, 1792. *ArchP*, Aug. 23, 1792. David,
La Rochelle, p. 57. Ligou, *Montauban*, p. 280. Lévy-Schneider, *St.-André*, p. 156.
Combes de Patris, *Rodez*, pp. 169–170. Chardon, *Rouen*, p. 80. Heitz, *Strasbourg*,
p. 236. COR, Bordeaux, 12 L 39. PV: Eymoutiers, Aug. 23, 1792; Limoges, Aug
24, 1792; Tonneins, Aug. 19–22. 1792; Toulouse, Aug. 22, 1792; Lons-le-Saunier,
Aug. 18, 22, 23, 1792; Le Mans, Aug. 19, 23, 1792; Perpignan, Aug. 20, 22, 1792;
Castres, Aug. 20, 25, 1792.

Bassée flatly predicted that all of its electors would be "good Jacobins." Turnouts of voters were low, increasing opportunities
for electioneering. At Tonneins, allegedly, Jouan le jeune showed
up at the assemblies in the company of armed men and delivered
harangues. In this case, as in others, it is impossible to separate
fact from fiction. The lone certainty is that clubbists won many
election victories. At Douai, Montauban, Eygallières, and Gour-
nay the entire slates were *sociétaires*. Six of seven electors at Semur
were Jacobins. Le Havre boasted that twelve of twenty-one electors were its members, that six shared its "principles," and that
only three were "doubtful."[2]

The next step was the choice of deputies, and on this crucial
matter several clubs sought direction from the Paris Jacobins. As
early as August 19, Montdidier asked the "mother society" for a
list of deputies who had good records in the Legislative Assembly. Argenteuil thought it would be useful to have the names of
the legislators who had voted for or against the suspension of the
king. The Paris club responded to (or anticipated) these requests
by voting on August 22 to print a *Tableau comparatif* of seven crucial roll call votes in the Legislative Assembly.[3] Copies were sent
to affiliates with admonitions to pass them along to the electoral
assemblies. Not only did the *Tableau* identify "the friends of the
fatherland" in the Legislative Assembly, it also called for the election of Pétion, Robespierre, and the "forty immortals" of the
Constituent.

This *Tableau* was published about August 29. The club of Le
Havre received a copy on August 30 and resolved to follow the
directives of the "mother society." Le Mans (September 2) forwarded it by special messenger to the electoral corps meeting at
St.-Calais. At Auray someone read the *Tableau* on September 3
before visiting electors. Libourne (September 5) assured Paris
that the *Tableau* would be used with "great profit" in the
Gironde. The next day, the electoral assembly of the Gironde

[2] Caubet, "Jouan," p. 171. *JC*, Sept. 3, 8, 13, 1792. Aubert, "Douai," pp. 524–
529. PV, Castres, Aug. 20, 25, 1792. Ligou, *Montauban*, p. 280. Henriot, *Semur*,
pp. 156–157.

[3] *JD*, Aug. 21, 24, 29, 1792. *JC*, Aug. 25, 27, 30, 1792. PV: Le Mans, Aug. 24,
1792; Périgueux, Aug. 15, 1792; Castres, Aug. 23, 1792; Tonneins, Aug. 16, 19,
1792. A published record of the voting on the motion to arrest Lafayette (August
7) was already in circulation.

thanked the Récollets Society for giving it a copy.[4] The electoral assemblies of the Haute-Vienne and Mayenne expressed their gratitude directly to the Paris Jacobins. Beaugency and Montargis gloated that the reading of the *Tableau* had caused the electors of the Loiret to honor one legislator and censure the remainder for "betraying their constituents." Altogether, the *Tableau* reached at least one-half of the electoral assemblies. In many, the first deputies chosen were ex-Constituents or former legislators "who had been faithful to the cause of liberty."[5]

The degree of influence that local clubs exerted over electoral assemblies is hard to measure. According to Alison Patrick, twenty-six of the official "proceedings" mention addresses or deputations from societies. In only two departments, however, is she able to reconstruct accounts of clubs trying to impose opinions on the electors. One succeeded; the other failed.[6] Of course, the official proceedings do not tell the whole story. To get a fuller picture of the activities of societies, one must also look at their papers, and the letters and reminiscences of electors.

Lons-le-Saunier discussed a range of issues with the intention of giving specific charges to the deputies of the Jura. Electors from the club of Tulle set off for Brive bearing "instructions." The Récollets Society kept in constant touch with its electors at Libourne. Two of its members, Boyer-Fonfrède and Marandon, were the president and secretary of the electoral assembly, and six of the twelve deputies chosen were on its rolls. Valence published an "opinion" of an elector to his colleagues. Montauban and Tarbes helped to persuade the electors of their departments to admit the public and vote aloud. The electoral assembly of the Var met at the headquarters of the club of Grasse. The societies of Coutances, Auray, and Orthez served as after-hours social centers for the electors of the Manche, Morbihan, and Hautes-Pyrénées. Limoges ordered its members who were electors to re-found the club of Le Dorat so that it could be an election center. In the Gard, a *comité central* representing twenty-five clubs moved its headquarters from Nîmes to Beaucaire, where the electoral as-

[4] PV: Le Mans, Auray, Libourne, Bordeaux. *JC*, Sept. 15, 29, 1792.

[5] *JC*, Sept. 10–29, 1792. A. Patrick, *The Men of the First French Republic* (Baltimore and London, 1972), pp. 145, 148.

[6] Patrick, *Republic*, p. 155.

sembly was to convene. Delegates from the committee showed up at the assembly and inveigled it into adopting a resolution of no confidence in the department.[7] Marseille urged the clubs of the Bouches-du-Rhône to work together for the selection of good deputies. At the electoral assembly, according to Durand de Maillane's memoirs, "The four hundred electors from Marseille permitted no one to raise a voice against them." Of the six Marseillais selected, all were clubbists.[8]

Tonneins was disgruntled about the results of the elections in the Lot-et-Garonne. In a letter to the Paris Jacobins it sobbed that only two "good patriots" (Paganel and Vidalot) had been chosen. However, most of the clubs expressed pleasure at the outcomes and congratulated the victors. The latter, in turn, went to the societies to bid emotional adieux to their frères. Exact figures are unobtainable, but there is no doubt that the overwhelming majority of Conventionnels, at the time of their elections, were members of the Paris society or one of its affiliates.[9]

After taking their seats in the Convention, the deputies remained in touch with their clubs. Sometimes local authorities, friends, or relations served as go-betweens. Frequently, however, they wrote directly to the societies. In the first four months of the Convention, the deputy Pinet sent an average of two letters per week to Bergerac. Moreau wrote twelve times to Chalon-sur-Saône between November 3 and January 21. The Récollets Society received dozens of communiques from Boyer-Fonfrède, Grangeneuve, Ducos, Guadet, Vergniaud, and Gensonné before their purge. Each week, the delegation from Clermont-Ferrand designated one of their number as official correspondent. The deputies from Rennes rotated the assignment monthly.[10]

[7] PV: Limoges, Aug. 30, 1792; Lons-le-Saunier, Aug. 22–23, 1792; Bordeaux, Sept. 3–10, 1792; Auray, Sept. 3–10, 1792. Rouvière, *Gard*, II, 430–447. *JC*, Sept. 13, Oct. 27, 1792. Forot, *Tulle*, p. 219. Lévy-Schneider, *St.-André*, pp. 158–160. Sarot, *Coutances*, p. 47. Planté, "Orthez," pp. 57–61.

[8] Kennedy, *Marseilles*, pp. 113–114. PV, Lauris, Aug. 31, 1792.

[9] Cf. *JC*, Sept. 20, 24, 1792. Besson, *Libourne*, p. 196. Guillemaut, *Louhans*, p. 40. Heitz, *Strasbourg*, p. 238. PV: Provins, Sept. 13, 1792; Montauban, Sept. 15, 1792; Toulouse, Sept. 7, 1792; Châteauroux, Sept. 18, 1792; Avallon, Sept. 18, 1792; Honfleur, Sept. 15, 1792.

[10] Labroue, *Bergerac*, pp. 32, 214–216. PV, Châteauroux, Sept. 18, 30, 1792. P. Caron, "Lettres de la député Moreau à la Société populaire de Chalon-sur-Saône," *RF* (1933), pp. 55–74. F. Mège. *Le Conventionnel Bancal des Issarts* (Paris,

Sometimes the clubs were the dominant partners in this relationship. The deputies sought advice on sensitive issues and fretted about losing the esteem of the home society. The Conventionnels went to Paris thinking that their tenures would be short ones. For those who had political ambitions, it must have seemed vital to maintain local bases of support. Louchet went so far as to ask the Rodez society to do as the slave of Philip of Macedonia had done, and remind him that he was "only a man."[11]

Usually, however, the club was obsequious to the deputy. In Paris he might be regarded as one of the "toads of the Marsh," but his old comrades recalled his past services to the Revolution and accepted his reports as incontestable truths. Generally speaking, the smaller the society, the greater the ascendancy of the deputy-correspondent. Large clubs, which had sent several members to the Convention, were more likely to be confronted with the problem of split delegations.

MOST accounts of the early Convention focus on the power struggle between the "Girondins" and "Montagnards." However, there is much disagreement over the meaning of these terms. The great liberal historian Aulard viewed the conflict as essentially one between Paris and the departments. Marxist theory, best illustrated in the works of Mathiez, Lefebvre, and Soboul, holds that the dispute was political at first but eventually became social as well. Both factions were bourgeois, so the argument runs; but the Montagnards, who relied upon the support of the Commune and radical sections of Paris, were forced to adopt parts of the social program of the sansculottes. M. Sydenham, in a book published in 1961, challenged the very existence of a Girondist party, asserting this to be a myth fabricated by extremists for propaganda purposes. The ensuing debate prompted A. Patrick to do a detailed study of voting patterns in the Convention. Her evidence suggests that there were *four* distinct blocs of deputies: an extreme Right which was strongly anti-regicide and anti-Parisian; the Girondins, who were moderately anti-reg-

1887), p. 240, and *Correspondance de Georges Couthon* (Paris, 1872), p. 198. R. Dupuy, "Aux origines du 'federalisme' breton: Le Cas de Rennes," *Annales de Bretagne* (1975), p. 351. PV and COR, Bordeaux, 12 L 13, 19–20.

[11] Combes de Patris, *Rodez*, pp. 171–172.

icide and anti-Parisian; the Mountain, which was pro-regicide, pro-Parisian, and anti-Gironde; and the moderate center ("Marsh" or "Plain").[12]

At best, the Girondins and Montagnards were ill-defined entities, fairly solid at their cores but ragged around the edges. Those identified with the two blocs came from all parts of France. However, Gascony, Brittany, Provence, and Normandy were Girondist strongholds. The Montagnard deputies tended to represent the Paris region, the north, and east. Both groups had rich men, but the Girondins were slightly wealthier and more likely to derive from the *haute bourgeoisie*.[13]

As we have seen, the origins of the Girondin-Montagnard schism may be traced to the end of 1791, and to the rhetorical feuds of Robespierre and Brissot on the war. From March–May 1792, the rivalry between the two men and their partisans worsened. Some have attributed this to the appointment of a "Brissotin" ministry and the jealousy of the "Robespierrists." Whatever the case, there were clashes at the Jacobins. Robespierre, Chabot, Desmoulins, and Collot-d'Herbois charged the Brissotins with putting their friends in government posts and aiming to establish a protectorate under Lafayette. Brissot, Guadet, Réal, and Louvet accused Robespierre of perversity and tyranny. Inevitably, the conflict spilled over into the press. Robespierre, who had been denigrated in the *Patriote français*, the *Chronique de Paris*, and the *Courrier des départements*, founded his own paper, the *Défenseur de la Constitution*. The first number attacked Brissot. Later ones defamed Condorcet, and the deputies of the Gironde (Guadet, Vergniaud, and Gensonné).

Two clubs, at this date, sided with the Brissotins. Douai deplored the influence of Robespierre over the Jacobins, stating that "his exaggerated principles are threatening to lead France to anarchy." Lons-le-Saunier encouraged Brissot to "march with a firm heart, to thunder against the factionalists and conspirators" who had calumniated him. The remainder of the societies

---

[12] Cf. Soboul, *Colloque Girondins*, pp. 7–9. Patrick, *Republic*, pp. 5–7, 295–297. Sydenham, *Girondins*.

[13] A. Aulard, *The French Revolution* (New York, 1910), III, 39–43. J. Chaumié, "Les Girondins" and F. Brunel, "Les députés Montagnards," in *Colloque Girondins*, pp. 343–361. Patrick, *Republic*, pp. 318–371.

mourned the dissension and called for a reconciliation. Bisch-willer, Civrai, and Beaugency declared their solidarity with Pétion, who had appeared at the Jacobins on April 29 to urge peace and concord. Cherbourg and Besançon twitted the Jacobins for setting a bad example. Toulouse said that only the enemies of France would profit. Le Havre keened that the loss of a battle could not have affected it more. Many reminded the feuding parties that France was at war. Effiat repeated Demosthenes' words: "Athenians: Philip is at your gates." Toulon recalled the fable of the oyster that had been eaten by a third party when two companions took to quarreling.[14]

News of a "reunion" at the Jacobins on May 20 had a sedative effect; many clubs concluded that the feud was over. It blazed up again, however, at the time of the fall of the monarchy. On August 9–10, radicals from the sections seized control of the Paris Commune. Not content with governing the city, they tried to run the country as well, thereby rousing the ire of the interior minister, Roland, and the Brissotins in the lame-duck Legislative Assembly.

In the nightmarish, Kafkaesque days of early September, the latent hostility burst into mortal conflict. While fear-crazed Parisian mobs were invading the prisons and massacring 1,100 to 1,400 inmates, the Montagnards apparently attempted a coup. On September 2, at the Commune, Robespierre pointed an accusing finger at a "party" seeking to put a foreign prince on the throne. According to one account, he named Brissot and the "faction of the Gironde." The same day Marat's Surveillance Committee issued warrants for the arrest of Brissot and thirty others. If Danton (then the justice minister) had not intervened, the Brissotins might have shared the fate of the prisoners of the Abbaye.

At this juncture, the war and the elections monopolized the time of the provincial societies. Most ventured no comment on the Massacres or the attempted proscriptions. In Bordeaux, however, these incidents had serious repercussions. The Récollets Society received letters from Paris decrying the "perfidious maneu-

[14] *JC*, May 7–July 2, 1792. *CD*, Apr. 26–May 12, 1792. *PF*, May 10, June 10, 20, 1792. Dubois, *Ain*, II, 315–316. Aubert, "Douai," p. 242. COR, Poitiers, S 26. PV: Limoges, May 25, 1792; Lorient, May 29, 1792.

vers of Robespierre," and on September 18 it issued a statement expressing full confidence in the Gironde delegation. The Club National, on the other hand, defended the Massacres and demanded that the sections of Bordeaux emulate those of Paris and remain in permanent session. On September 28 the Récollets Society censured the Club National, saying that its motion on the sections "promoted a spirit of discord and was conceived by factionalists." Henceforth, the two bodies were to be almost constantly at odds.[15]

The Eastern Society of Angers (the Angevin equivalent of the Récollets Society) also took an early stand against the Massacres and the Montagnards. In a circular of September 24, it urged affiliates to demand the arrest of Marat, Robespierre, Desmoulins, and Danton, the chiefs of the "new faction" which "thirsts for blood and pillage." Danton's inclusion is noteworthy, because most historians have him, at this time, playing the role of peacemaker. Angers singled him out because of a "poisonous" pamphlet called the *Compte rendu au souverain* being circulated in his name. Actually, this work, which justified the September Massacres, may have been penned by Fabre d'Eglantine.[16]

Affiliates refrained from commenting on Angers' circular. Doubtless, most at this early date were loath to believe in the guilt of Robespierre and Danton. Marat was another matter, for the clubs looked upon him as a pockmark on the profile of Jacobinism. In a placard of September 8 he had accused all of the ministers, save for Danton, of collusion with the Prussians. Roland retaliated on September 12 with a *Lettre aux Parisiens* in which he defended his policies and alleged that Marat wished to install a dictatorship. Now, Roland was immensely popular. Many societies had congratulated him on his reinstatement after August 10, and he (or Madame Roland) always responded with thank-you notes and copies of official pronouncements.[17] Given these attitudes, it is hardly surprising that the clubs sided with him against

[15] PV, Bordeaux, Sept. 13, 18, 1792. Dubos, "Surveillants" (1932), pp. 99–104. A. Forrest, "L'Exemple de Bordeaux," *Colloque Girondins*, pp. 155–160.

[16] COR, Niort, 3001; Poitiers, S 1, 26. Bellanger, *Provins*, p. 49. PV, Périgueux, Oct. 3, 1792.

[17] PV: Rouen, Aug. 15, 1792; Limoges, Aug. 16, 1792; Béziers, Aug. 20, 1792; Périgueux, Sept. 25, 1792. Planté, "Orthez," pp. 53–54. *JC*, Sept. 8, 1792. Dubois, *Ain*, III, 46. AN, F¹ C III, Charente 12.

Marat. Even Strasbourg, which soon became violently pro-Montagnard, assured Roland that he had "the confidence of citizens." Courtenay sniffed: "If the machine of state is not to be entirely disrupted, we must end denunciations of patriotic public servants." Villefranche (Rhône) and the Récollets Society engaged the interior minister to remain at his post, while the Surveillants of Bordeaux hailed him as the "French Aristides." Moissac, in a widely circulated communique of October 1, scolded the sections of Paris for permitting "conspirators" to sow distrust of "worthy" officials. Vowing never again to live under tyranny, it announced that two hundred of its citizens had armed themselves and were headed for Paris.[18]

Another irritant in September was the election of deputies to the Convention from Paris. On the eve of the electoral assembly, Louvet had published a list of fifty "suitable" candidates. The names of both Girondins and Montagnards on this slate prove that factional lines were not yet rigidly drawn. Again, however, Marat fanned the flames of dissension by publishing a malignant critique of Louvet's list under the title of "Unworthy Candidates." The Girondist press published counterlists, railed against the "cabal" in the Paris electoral assembly, and branded Marat alternately as a criminal, a madman, and a mad dog. Nonetheless, it could not prevent the election of Marat, Robespierre, Danton, and other nominees of the Commune.

A sign that the Paris club was tilting to the Left came on September 12 when it issued a circular praising the Paris electoral assembly and asking affiliates to adhere to its resolutions. These included provisions for the impeachment of "suspect deputies." Despite the prestige of the "mother society," the vaporings of the Girondist press seem to have had more effect upon the network. Only two clubs are known to have responded to the circular, and both did so adversely. Villefranche (Aveyron) was aghast that the electoral corps of Paris was offered as an exemplar. How could anyone emulate a body, it ranted in a published letter of October 3, that had elected the "demagogue" Marat? Quimper, in a circular of October 2, called upon affiliates to surround the minis-

[18] Heitz, *Strasbourg*, p. 238. *JC*, Sept. 15, Oct. 15, 20, 1792. AN, F¹ C III, Rhône 8. PV, Bordeaux, Sept. 28, Oct. 7, 1792. Dubos, "Surveillants" (1933), pp. 185–188. *PF*, Oct. 23, 1792.

ters and deputies of the nation with an "impenetrable rampart," if this was necessary to insure their "latitude of action." It also made an oblique, critical reference to the Paris Jacobins, asserting that "no popular society" had the right to obstruct the "general will."[19]

After the opening of the Convention, the party strife became endemic. On September 21 Fauchet was expelled from the Paris club. Two days later, the *Patriote français* charged that the Paris Jacobins had become the abode of a "disorganizing party." That night the club adopted a motion commanding Brissot to explain his conduct or face condemnation as "the greatest of criminals." On the twenty-fourth and twenty-fifth, the Girondins launched a major offensive in the Convention. Buzot proposed the creation of a guard recruited from the departments to protect the deputies from "anarchists" and "disorganizers." Lasource voiced his apprehension about the "schemers" who wanted Paris to become a new Rome, and argued that its influence should not exceed that of a single department. Barbaroux snapped that Robespierre was aiming at dictatorship. Brissot and Vergniaud laid responsibility for the September Massacres at the door of the Commune. The Montagnards countered that their denouncers were conspiring to institute a federalist republic.

The next few weeks were fateful ones for the Paris club. The Girondins, along with most of the other deputies, ceased to attend. In retrospect, it is clear that this was a mistake. They should have fought for control of the society. By gathering separately and in secret, they exposed themselves to charges of conspiracy. One of the Jacobins, on October 5, likened them to ungrateful children "tearing at the bosom" of their "tender mother." Their names were gradually stricken from the rolls. The first to go was Brissot on October 10.

The flight of the Girondins from the nest allowed it to be taken over by a tiny brood of militants—men like Bentabole, Chabot, Collot-d'Herbois, Fabre, Billaud-Varenne, Tallien, Merlin de Thionville, and Robespierre. Marat also appeared at the sessions occasionally and was greeted politely. The intemperate assaults

---

[19] COR: Niort, 3005; Poitiers, S 26. *CD*, Nov. 1, 6, 1792. *PF*, Oct. 30, 1792. *JC*, Oct. 13, 29, 1792.

of the Girondins soon threw Danton into an uneasy alliance with Marat and Robespierre (henceforth dubbed the "triumvirs"). Montagnard ranks were also swelled somewhat by deputies like Couthon and St.-André, who were resentful that the Girondins held the key positions in the Convention.

The schism caused anguish in the clubs. Lisieux, for example, was faced with the decision of whether to give its allegiance to the "mother society" or to its bishop and deputy Fauchet, who had published an apologia entitled *Claude Fauchet à trente Jacobins qui s'intitulent la Société*. Deeply troubled, it announced on October 10 that it planned to study the matter. The clubbists of Perpignan, whose knowledge of Parisian politics came mainly from the Girondist deputy Birotteau, begged the "mother society," on October 25, to reexamine Fauchet's case and expressed disquiet over all the talk of "dictators, assassins, and triumvirs." A bewildered Castres asked the deputy Lasource why he had ceased to attend the Paris club. Lasource replied that the "criminals who ordered the assassinations of September 2" ruled there, and that his life would be in danger if he went.[20]

On October 10 at the Récollets Society, Grangeneuve, whose brother was a Girondist deputy, read a letter from Paris. Immediately afterward, those present decided to tell the Paris club that they would cease to fraternize with it unless it "conformed to the law." A letter to this effect was approved on October 17, and copies were sent to affiliates.[21] As yet, not many societies were willing to go so far; on the other hand, very few pledged undying loyalty to the Paris Jacobins. Auxerre, which may have been influenced by the Montagnard deputies Maure, Bourbotte, and Lepelletier, vowed on October 17 that it would remain attached to the "mother society" in spite of "all the Brissotins in the world." Strasbourg (October 30) fretted about the "inquisitorial tactics" that the "tyrants" who led the Convention were employing against the Commune, the Paris delegation, and the "incorruptible Robespierre." It implored the Paris society to awaken affiliates from their "dangerous sleep."[22]

---

[20] *JD*, Oct. 12, 1792. *JC*, Nov. 15, 1792. PV, Perpignan. C. Rabaud, *Lasource* (Paris, 1889), pp. 138–139. Charrier, *Fauchet*, p. 195.
[21] PV, Bordeaux, Oct. 10–19, 1792.
[22] *JC*, Oct. 27, Nov. 9, 1792.

In October at the Convention the battle lines continued to follow those set down on September 24–25. The Montagnards harped on the federalist issue and the "new tyranny" of the Girondins. The Girondins waxed indignant about the September Massacres, the "anarchists" in the Paris Commune and sections, and the dictatorial ambitions of the triumvirs. A major bone of contention was the departmental guard. Lanjuinais declared on October 5 that it should consist of 24,000 men. Merlin countered that only a Feuillant would make such a proposal, and the next day the Temple section voiced its disapproval. On October 8, Buzot presented a plan for a 4,470-man force selected by departmental administrators. The Girondist press campaigned for it. The Paris club printed and circulated negative opinions. And on October 19 and 21, emissaries from the sections showed up at the Convention with antiguard petitions. The Commune printed forty thousand copies of these petitions with the intention of sending them to all the clubs and communes of France. In the end, the Convention took no action on Buzot's plan.

Support for a departmental guard is usually regarded as one of the litmus tests of Girondism. It is noteworthy, therefore, that by the end of October, at least fifteen clubs had espoused Buzot's project.[23] Most did so in the form of petitions to the Convention. Agen sent two and, along with Bayonne, Beaune, and Brive, forwarded copies to journalists and to affiliates. Perpignan manifested reprobation for the petitions of the sections. Quimper published a proguard manifesto of the administrators of the Finistère. The Récollets Society announced in a circular of October 18 that it was not waiting for authorization from the Convention but was sending an armed force to Paris.[24]

In contrast, just four clubs (Auxerre, Châteauroux, Sezanne, and the Popular Society of Lyon) had sent antiguard petitions to the Convention by October 31. Sezanne's was printed and cir-

---

[23] Quimper, Bordeaux, Lorient, Perpignan, Agen, Marmande, Lisieux, Alençon, Brive, Beaune, Honfleur, Avranches, St.-Malo, Pontivy, Bayonne.

[24] AN, DXL 18–23. H. Wallon, *La Révolution du 31 mai et le fédéralisme en 1793* (Paris, 1886), I, 394–395. COR: Reims; Lorient, Oct. 24, 1792; Poitiers, S 26; Bordeaux, 12 L 29. *ArchP*, Oct. 25, Nov. 1, 1792. PV: Lorient, Oct. 15, 29, 1792; Honfleur, Oct. 28, 31, 1792; Alençon, Oct. 15–17, 1792; Bordeaux, Nov. 8, 9, 1792; Châteauroux, Nov. 18, 1792. *PF*, Nov. 19, 1792. *JD*, Nov. 9, 1792. *M*, Oct. 26, 1792. *JC*, Nov. 5, 1792.

culated nationally by the Paris Jacobins. Henceforth, these four gave dog-like devotion to the Paris club. Lons-le-Saunier was, at this stage, befuddled by the factionalism in Paris; nonetheless, it too opposed a guard. Castres (October 25) considered a motion to endorse Buzot's project but tabled it for unknown reasons. Rouen (October 21) refused to air an opinion, even though three of its deputies asked it to do so. It deferred, instead, to the "wisdom of the Convention."[25]

Toulouse got contrary advice from its delegation in the Convention. The deputy Estadens was a proponent of a guard; his fellow representative Julien was a militant adversary. At one point (October 24) it seemed as though Julien would be censured; but the club opted instead to demand an explanation from him, and to set up a committee to study the newspapers and report on "the divisions in the Convention." For three weeks the issue hung in the balance. The club read proguard circulars from Agen and Perpignan and considered motions to denounce Robespierre and Marat, and to break off relations with the Paris Jacobins. An eloquent apologia from Julien and two ringing endorsements from his colleagues, Drulhe and Pérès, finally decided the issue. On November 8–10, Toulouse voted to keep corresponding with the Paris club, to send an antiguard petition to the Convention, and to distribute copies to affiliates.[26]

Apparently Arras also went through a period of indecision, although three of its deputies, the two Robespierres and Guffroy, were antiguard. Its leader, Joseph Le Bon, grumbled: "I still do not know what I will propose on the subject of a guard from the eighty-three departments; because, truthfully, men are dirty b_____s, and I know not whom to trust." Finally, in November, the Arras society published a memorandum derogating Buzot's project.[27]

Pithiviers kept getting sidetracked by extraneous issues. On November 4, a certain Bidault recommended that the society align itself with the "great majority" of the Convention which

---

[25] AN, DXL 23. *ArchP*, Oct. 23, 27, 31, 1792. *M*, Oct. 26, 1792. PV, Châteauroux, Oct. 28, 1792. Chardon, *Rouen*, p. 98. COR, Reims. *JD*, Nov. 4, 1792.

[26] Toulouse Minutes, Oct. 24–Nov. 10, 1792. COR, Poitiers. PV, Bordeaux, Nov. 17, 1792. *ArchP*, Nov. 23, 1792. *JC*, Nov. 26, 1792.

[27] Lecesne, *Arras*, I, 314. PV, Blaye, Nov. 10, 14, 17, 25, 28, 1792.

wanted a "departmental force." To objections raised by the president, he replied that the deputies belonged to all of France and that their predecessors in the Constituent and Legislative Assemblies had been coerced into enacting "bad decrees." When some supercilious soul clucked that "good citizens" ought not to complain about the Revolution, Bidault said that he had nothing against the Revolution, only the new tax system which was "onerous and labyrinthine." Whereupon, discussion turned to Revolutionary taxes. Much the same thing happened in the next session. At last, on November 10, Pithiviers approved a pro-guard petition.[28]

Altogether, in November, twenty more clubs formally approved the concept of a departmental guard,[29] bringing the grand total to thirty-five. Several others vowed to defend the Convention against agitators and anarchists. Thirteen more societies registered "nos,"[30] raising that total to eighteen. Notable nay-sayers were Lille, La Rochelle, Montauban (which was influenced by the deputy St.-André), the Popular Society of Nîmes, and the Club National of Bordeaux. At the risk of being repetitive, the consistency with which popular societies took Montagnard positions must be reemphasized.

Antiguard clubs maintained that the deputies had nothing to fear, and that a security force was an unnecessary extravagance. (Auxerre estimated the cost at twenty thousand livres per day.) Besides, they argued, honor guards contravened egalitarian principles and were a threat to liberty. Every schoolboy knew of the excesses committed by Rome's Praetorian Guard! Who could forget the Massacre of the Champ de Mars perpetrated by Lafayette's myrmidons? At bottom, contended the dissenters, the proposal was an "apple of discord" thrown into national politics by "ambitious men who wish to divide the Republic." Rather than being reviled, the Parisians ought to be commended for "meritorious service to the Fatherland."

[28] PV, Pithiviers.

[29] Cherbourg, Libourne, Moissac, Maringues, Vitré, Dinan, Castelsarrasin, Viens, Nevers, Lorgues, Vienne, Coutances, Alès, Ollioules, Ampuis, Pithiviers, Brest, Beaumont, Le Puy, and Sommières.

[30] Club National of Bordeaux, La Rochelle, St.-Florentin, Lavaur, Civray, Arras, Blaye, Toulouse, Châteaudun, Popular Society of Nîmes, Lille, Salon, and Montauban.

Proguard clubs wanted to guarantee the freedom of the legislators and to exterminate the "agitators," would-be "dictators," and "assassins of September 2." They acknowledged the debt owed by France to the sansculottes of Paris but warned the Parisians to beware of the artifices of "a few ambitious men." The sectionnaires who composed "senseless petitions" demanding that Paris alone should guard the deputies were reminded that provincial fédérés had also fought and died on August 10. Many clubs quoted the passage in Buzot's October 8 report which said that the Convention belonged to all the departments. Others paraphrased Lasource's speech of September 25, saying that Paris was one eighty-third of the Republic and no more, and averring that the Commune was intent on making it a new Rome. Lorient described Paris as the center of "enlightenment and *intrigue*" and backed Lanjuinais' motion for a twenty-four-thousand-man force. Beaumont added the phrase "no privileged city" to its vow of "no dictators or triumvirs." Proguard clubs generally expressed aversion to federalism. But Perpignan vowed that if the deputies were endangered, the departments would recall them and "create a truly free republic." Auray invited the Convention to hold its meetings in another city. Villefranche (Aveyron) growled that Paris should lose the right to host the Convention until it meted out justice to the "murderers of September 2."

The Récollets Society, which had vowed not to wait for the Convention to approve a guard, labored feverishly to organize a force of three hundred men to send to Paris. Under its influence Libourne recruited a squad of 109 fédérés "to save the Convention." In the end, however, these efforts went for naught. On November 9 the Récollets advised the societies of the Gironde, including Libourne, to disband their forces. One reason for the failure of this initiative was the obstinate resistance of the Club National. Led by J.-B.-M. Lacombe, it raised questions about the legality of the expedition, and it published an antiguard address which was printed and circulated by the Paris Jacobins.[31]

Despite this setback and the adjournment of Buzot's plan in the Convention, groups of fédérés converged on the capital in Oc-

---

[31] PV, Bordeaux, Oct. 21–Nov. 9, 1792. COR, Poitiers, S 26. Besson, *Libourne*, pp. 198–200.

tober. The most celebrated was a six-hundred-man battalion organized by the club of Marseille. It had set off on September 16 with the intention of defending Paris against the Prussians. By October 20, when it entered Paris, the foreign menace had subsided, and it became a pawn of the Girondins. On October 21 its spokesmen appeared at the Convention to read a polemic against the "dictators" and "triumvirs" written by the deputy, Barbaroux. Ten days later some of its members were involved in a menacing demonstration before the domicile of Marat. A *club des fédérés* was formed at its barracks on the rue du Bouloi and became a gathering spot for thousands of volunteers in the capital.[32]

The arrival of fédérés from the "land of Barbaroux" perhaps inspired the Girondins to attempt a coup. On October 29, Roland submitted a memorandum to the Convention which purported that Robespierre was contemplating a dictatorship and proscriptions. Then Louvet delivered a philippic in which he called for the arrest of Marat and declared that Robespierre was intent on making himself an "object of idolatry." Robespierre asked for and was granted time to prepare a defense. A week later, November 5, he presented an eloquent rebuttal. The Convention, in effect, dismissed Louvet's charges.

If anything, these events made the Montagnards more uncompromising. When Robespierre showed up at the Paris Jacobins after his speech, he was greeted like a conqueror. Garnier gushed that this was "the most glorious day since the dawn of liberty" and demanded a purification to rid the society of "Janus-faced" members. Collot d'Herbois boldly defended the September Massacres, saying that without them "liberty would not exist." And six clubbists were assigned to draw up a précis of events since August 10 in order to document the "perfidy of the Brissotins."[33]

By this date a veritable propaganda war was in progress. In this contest for the souls of the clubs, the Girondins, at first, held the trump cards. As has been seen, they had many popular newspapers, and the Montagnards had none. In addition, they controlled a number of government agencies. Through the *bureau de l'esprit*

---

[32] Cf. F. Portal, *Le Bataillon marseillais du 21 janvier* (Marseille, 1900). S. Vialla, "Le Bataillon aixois du 21 janvier," *RF* (1911), pp. 27–49.

[33] *JD*, Nov. 7, 1792.

publique that he administered, Roland inundated the departments with their writings.[34] Add to this the fact that only a few deputies still attended the Paris society, and the sum is that many clubs got just one side of the story. Alençon was almost completely insulated from Leftist impulses. Virtually all of its correspondence came from Roland or the Girondist deputy Valazé. Louhans accepted the word of the deputy Guillermin as gospel and concluded that the Paris club was filled with "intriguers." At Libourne, on November 4, Gaston Lacaze read a letter from his brother Jacques, the Conventionnel, in which the latter said that the Paris society was a "rendezvous of criminals." Whereupon, the president recommended that Libourne "cease all correspondence with these agents of satan."[35]

One of the gravest liabilities of the Paris society was its association with Marat. When the latter, in late October, circulated some vicious attacks upon the Girondins, the clubs recoiled in disgust. Cherbourg and Lesparre incinerated them. Annonay demanded that Marat be drummed out of the Convention. Perpignan and Morlaix howled for the Paris club to eject this "malevolent being." The Récollets Society compared Marat's works to the "robe of Nessus, which . . . infected all that it touched." And Lisieux, on October 30, issued a circular in which it summoned affiliates to petition for the arrest of this "monster" and his "detestable accomplices," on the grounds that they were conspiring to proscribe "the Buzots, Guadets, and Vergniauds."[36]

These salvos were followed in early November by a barrage of addresses to the Convention against the "Maratists." Honfleur adhered to the wishes of its neighbor, Lisieux. Condrieu demanded the punishment of the "incendiary writer, Marat," and "the whole cursed caste of agitators." Provins wanted them to be "hurled from the Tarpeian rock." Périgueux, after listening to the Lisieux circular, voiced its alarm about "agitators who are

---

[34] Cf. AN, F¹ C III, Rhône-et-Loire, Charente. COR, Poitiers, S 23–24. PV: Eu, Sept. 21, 1792; Pithiviers, Oct. 28, 1792; Bordeaux, Oct. 18, Nov. 20, 1792; Montreuil, Nov. 3, 1792. *JC*, Nov. 12, 1792. Poupé, "Callas," p. 483.

[35] Maintenant, "Alençon," p. 26. P. Nicolle, *Valazé* (Paris, 1933), pp. 119–120. Guillemaut, *Louhans*, II, 47. Besson, *Libourne*, pp. 198–200.

[36] PV, Bordeaux, Oct. 26, 1792. *PF*, Nov. 7, 13, 1792. *AP*, Nov. 1, 17, 1792. *CD*, Nov. 1, 2, 1792. Rostaing, *Annonay*, p. 182. COR, Poitiers, S 26. *ArchP*, Nov. 8, 1792. *JD*, Nov. 11, 1792.

spreading anarchy in Paris." A Jacobin of Marseille quipped that Marat should be certified insane and sent to the "petites maisons." Villamblard said that it would not try to choose between the "two parties," but could not help being outraged by the agents of the Commune who "preach murder and the principles of the agrarian law . . . , and the monster who dares to say that 260,000 more heads must fall in order for liberty to be consolidated."[37]

Two of the most publicized indictments of the "Maratists" came from Orléans and Coutances (November 7 and 13). Coutances maintained that to be truly successful, a Republic must rely upon the "virtue" of its citizens and be constantly on guard against "ambitious, turbulent, and perverse factions." It prescribed swift action against the "infamous sect and the monster who leads it" and reminded the deputies that "if the execrable Catiline had not existed, Cicero would never have been named father of his country." Orléans also used the Catiline-Cicero analogy. In addition, it appealed plaintively for an end to insurrections. "Revolutions have their limits; let us not go to extremes."[38]

Guided by the herd instinct, Beaugency quickly adhered to the Orléans circular and asked other clubs of the Loiret to demand the expulsion of Marat from the Convention. Boiscommun decided to reflect upon the matter. It read a letter from the Paris Jacobins describing Marat as "impetuous and headstrong, but precious because of his zeal for the Republic." It also listened with "scrupulous attention" to an "opinion" of Brissot. Finally, it determined that Marat was "dangerous to the Republic" and voted to conform to Beaugency's wishes.[39]

Increasingly, Robespierre's name was linked to Marat's. After hearing "the news of the day" on November 4, the clubbists of Cognac grieved that the men for whom they had "the greatest respect" had been placed in the demeaning position of having to defend themselves against "miserable personalities such as Robespierre and Marat." A little later, Grasse, in a national circular,

---

[37] PV: Honfleur, Nov. 2–4, 1792; Condrieu, Nov. 1, 10, 1792; Périgueux, Nov. 11, 1792. *JDM*, Dec. 6, 1792. *JC*, Nov. 26, 1792.

[38] AN, DXL 19, 21. *JC*, Nov. 21, 24, 1792.

[39] PV, Boiscommun, Nov. 11–28, 1792.

demanded judicial action against "Marat, Robespierre, and their accomplices." Dieppe let all the Republic know that it was no longer duped by "the false virtue of Robespierre." Falaise informed the Paris club that it did not wish to receive copies of Robespierre's or Marat's works. Villeneuve-sur-Yonne was repulsed by the "imprecations" of Marat and the "vomitings" of Robespierre. Perpignan swore by the "dagger of Brutus" to combat men like them.[40]

Criticism of the Paris society also rose steeply in November. Several clubs reacted negatively to a circular of October 15 justifying the purge of Brissot. The Récollets Society (November 1–3) made Brissot an honorary member and affirmed its abhorrence of the "insolent and anarchistic principles" in the October 15 encyclical. Cherbourg (November 4) reproached the Paris society. Speaking as "brothers," the clubbists of Riom (November 6) contrasted the differences between the Jacobins of 1789 and 1792. "Did you work so hard to overthrow despotism," they queried, "only to become heads of a band of anarchists?" Chalon-sur-Saône (November 3) likewise drew up a rebuttal. "Jacobins," it began, alluding to Louvet's speech of October 29, "the veil has been lifted and the faction of Robespierre laid bare." It then imputed these sins to the Paris club: calumniating Brissot, Guadet, Vergniaud, and other "defenders of the people"; undermining a ministry composed of "wise and useful men"; dividing France when it was threatened by foreign enemies; "burning incense to a man regarded with contempt" (Marat) and to the "so-called Incorruptible" (Robespierre); sustaining "a disorganizing Commune"; and shielding the men responsible for the September Massacres. The letter ended with a call for repentance.[41]

About November 1, the Eastern Society of Angers published a letter in which it vowed to sever relations with Paris if Marat and Robespierre were not expelled. It asked affiliates to do likewise so as to "dissipate the pestilential miasma" overhanging the

[40] PV: Cognac, Nov. 4, 1792; Falaise, Nov. 26, 1792; Bordeaux, Nov. 12, 1792. Wallon, *Fédéralisme*, II, 250. COR: Poitiers, S 1; Lorient, Dec. 12, 1792. *JD*, Nov. 27, 1792. *JC*, Nov. 29, Dec. 1, 27, 1792.

[41] *JC*, Nov. 15, 1792. *JD*, Nov. 14, 1792. PV: Bordeaux, Oct. 27–Nov. 3, 1792. *PF*, Nov. 13, 1792. *AP*, Nov. 15, 1792. Caron, "Moreau," p. 59. Carraz, "Chalon," p. 174.

"mother club." Crémieux denounced this circular. Aire at first applauded it, but was finally persuaded by certain members to continue to correspond with Paris. Limoges adjourned action and never took up the matter again. Lons-le-Saunier decided to write to Paris to urge unity. Elsewhere, however, Angers' address received much support. Périgueux, Avranches, and Lorient definitely adhered.[42] And at least fifteen other clubs wrote to Paris in November to demand a housecleaning.[43]

About a week after his expulsion from the Jacobins, Brissot published an *Adresse à tous les républicains de France*. For some reason, however, this address did not reach the departmental clubs until November. In it Brissot counseled them to be guided by the principles of "respect for the Convention" and "hatred of anarchists" and advised them to cease regarding the Paris society as a kind of Holy See. "There should be no Jacobin metropolitan, just as there is no longer a capital of the republic. Affiliation ought to disappear; it is a sign of inferiority, of subordination."[44]

Chartres was the birthplace of Brissot and had elected him to the Convention. And its club seems to have been the first to follow his advice and actually break with Paris. In a statement of November 9 it declared affiliation to be a "sign of inferiority and subordination." Two days later, Meaux annulled its affiliation and vowed that it would no longer use the term "mother society." Béziers (November 20) and Fécamp (November 29) interdicted correspondence with Paris until it ousted Marat. Fécamp also expressed admiration for "Roland, Clavière, Louvet, the Girondists, and the Brissotins." Nantes, in late November, set the purge of the "vile provocateur," Marat, and the "adroit intriguer," Robespierre, as its condition for renewing the bonds of fraternity. Chalon-sur-Saône announced its intention of ending relations with Paris. Niort told the Jacobins that they were now the primary source of "discord" in France:

---

[42] *JC*, Dec. 1, 6, 1792. PV: Périgueux, Nov. 15, 1792; Lorient, Nov. 12–29, 1792; Aire, Nov. 18–21, 1792; Bordeaux, Nov. 15, 1792; Limoges, Nov. 14, 1792. COR: Lorient, Nov. 30, 1792; Limoges, L 828; Poitiers, S 26. *PF*, Nov. 13, 1792. *CD*, Nov. 13, 1792. *JD*, Nov. 11, 1792. Libois, *Lons-le-Saunier*, p. 74.

[43] Louhans, Perpignan, Agen, Libourne, Honfleur, Pontivy, St.-Pierre (Charente-Maritime), Castres, Mâcon, Angoulême, Grasse, Falaise, Fécamp, Villeneuve-sur-Yonne, Bayonne, and Bordeaux.

[44] *Chronique du mois*, pp. 72–75.

You endure the presence of a creature [Marat] justly abhorred in all the departments, whose words and writings exude only blood. . . . You are chained to the chariot of another ambitious individual [Robespierre] who is using his past services to attain the supreme power that he craves. . . . Cease to believe that you are above the other societies, your affiliates; henceforth, we will correspond with you only as equals.[45]

The Popular Society of Nîmes, on the other hand, decided that Brissot's address must have been motivated by some "secret intrigue." Fontenay burned the *Adresse* and sent the ashes to the author. Even Lorient, which had some members who were rabidly anti-Montagnard, found it too offensive to read. Steadfast Auxerre praised the Paris club for its circular of October 15 justifying Brissot's ouster, and said that the "name agitator, like *enragé*, is soon going to become an honorable appelation." Lavaur announced that the October 15 encyclical merely "confirmed" its suspicions of the "faction of Brissot." Beausset thanked the Jacobins for warning it about the "Machiavellians," adding that if Brissot was "truly guilty," his punishment was deserved. Somewhat belatedly, Montréjeau also expressed gratitude to Paris for telling it about a "certain faction."[46]

Pro-Montagnard clubs were jubilant about the outcome of the Louvet-Robespierre debates. The Girondist deputy Vitet, who was in Lyon, has left a record of their effect on that city. In a letter of November 10 he exulted over Louvet's speech and the "fall of Robespierre's faction that the Central Club [of the Popular Society] has sustained." But two days later his joy had turned to ashes. "The news of the triumph of Robespierre," he lamented, "has made the Central Club and its agents more audacious." As though to prove Vitet's assessment, the Central Club, on November 16, suggested that electoral assemblies be convoked to replace "unfaithful deputies."[47]

[45] *JC*, Nov. 24, 25, Dec. 6, 1792. Caron, "Moreau," pp. 65–66. *CD*, Dec. 3, 1792.

[46] *JC*, Nov. 15, Dec. 15, 1792. *JD*, Nov. 11, 27, 1792. PV, Lorient, Nov. 19, 1792.

[47] AN, F^{12} 501 B. *JC*, Nov. 29, 1792.

XXIII

The Trial of the King

O^N SEPTEMBER 21, in its inaugural session, the Convention unanimously proclaimed France to be a republic. This decree caused seeming rejoicing in the clubs, despite the fact that just a couple of months before, most had been leary of republicanism. Cries of "Vive la République" went up. Fetes of thanksgiving were held; and more than 250 societies sent letters of approbation to the Convention.[1] These addresses gave fulsome praise to the deputies. Their action was described as "wise and just," a "sublime debut," a "glorious first step" toward a recrudescence of "the beautiful days of Sparta and Rome." One club predicted that by the end of the century monarchy would have vanished from the earth. Others demanded the death penalty for anyone who proposed a royalist restoration. Much was said about the crimes of kings.

It is true that a few clubs were slow about endorsing the decree of September 21. And at Montauban and Toulouse the societies let it be known that those who failed to sign addresses to the Convention would be dropped from the rolls. For the most part, however, the expressions of satisfaction seemed to be heartfelt and spontaneous. When the Récollets Society issued a circular urging the network to show its support for the deputies, many affiliates responded that they had already done so.[2]

The decree of September 21 left unanswered the question of the fate of the king. For six weeks the nation waited while a special commission examined the evidence against Louis, and the Legislation Committee of the Convention grappled with the legal complexities of the case. During this period, only a smattering of comments came from the clubs. Langres said that winning the

---

[1] See especially *JC*, Oct. 4–Nov. 15, 1792. AN, C 233–238, DXL 18–23. *ArchP*, Sept. 27–Dec. 9, 1792.

[2] PV: Bordeaux, Sept. 25–Nov. 6, 1792; Toulouse, Sept. 28, 1792. COR, Bordeaux, 12 L 29–30. Ligou, *Montauban*, p. 277.

war should be France's first priority; and Mazin bleated that Louis deserved "pity" rather than "vengeance." But Auxerre demanded a trial, and Pithiviers voted to do the same. Debates on this issue also took place at Paris, Semur, and Toulouse.[3]

The next phase in the proceedings opened on November 7, when the deputy Mailhe proposed in the name of the Legislation Committee that Louis be tried by the Convention. Debates on this motion began in the Convention on the thirteenth and went on intermittently for the rest of the month. A portion of the deputies, including some Girondins, tried to avert a trial, arguing that the king was inviolable, forecasting a backlash against the Revolution in Europe, and raising various side issues. On the other hand, the Montagnards were united and uncompromising. In the Convention and at the Jacobins, they insisted that Louis be judged promptly and executed. The sections and Commune of Paris concurred.

In November, for the first time, a great many clubs also discussed the questions of whether the king could be judged, and by whom. At least fourteen made recommendations to the Convention. Only Bourg expressed formal opposition to a trial. It contended, like the deputy Kersaint, that Louis' sins were due to his upbringing, and that he should be confined for life. The remainder desired the Convention to try the king, and most called for the death penalty. Craon and Rennes reasoned that as long as the ex-ruler lived, he would be an encouragement to counterrevolutionaries. Pithiviers, Fontainebleau, Toulon, and Louhans derided the theory of royal inviolability. Toulouse erased the name of the deputy Rouzet from its rolls because he had dared to remind the Convention of the good deeds of the ex-monarch.[4]

Obviously, there was strong sentiment against Louis XVI in the clubs, and it was to intensify in December and early January. Support for the death penalty cut across "party" lines. Béziers,

[3] G. Walter, *Histoire des Jacobins* (Paris, 1946), pp. 265–269. Henriot, *Semur*, p. 161. *JC*, Oct. 13, 18, 1792. PV: Bordeaux, Oct. 30, 1792; Toulouse, Oct. 27, 1792; Pithiviers, Sept. 24, 1792.

[4] Walter, *Jacobins*, pp. 269–272. *JC*, Nov. 29, Dec. 6, 1792. *ArchP*, Nov. 6, 18, 27, Dec. 9, 1792. *AP*, Nov. 26, 1792. Brelot, *Besançon*, p. 108. PV: Pithiviers, Nov. 18–21, 1792; Toulouse, Nov. 22–25, 1792; Bordeaux, Dec. 1, 1792; Lille, Nov. 30, 1792; Lons-le-Saunier, Nov. 18, 27, 1792. Guillemaut, *Louhans*, II, 47. Combet, "Nice," p. 410. Chardon, *Rouen*, p. 100.

Alençon, Morlaix, and Cognac were basically pro-Girondist, yet they wanted to send Louis to the scaffold. Even the Récollets Society applauded when it learned that he was to be tried. Nonetheless, pro-Montagnard clubs tended to be more merciless and intolerant of opposing views. Sezanne was ready to declare anyone who spoke in Louis' defense to be an "enemy of the human race."[5]

Opinion was not unanimous, however. In almost every club that called for the extreme penalty, some members favored lesser punishment.[6] As late as January 11–15, Lectoure was still trying to resolve the question of whether the Convention was competent to try the king.[7] A few societies, because of laziness, disapproval, or caution, refrained from making comments.[8] Ars-en-Ré and Honfleur adhered in advance to whatever the Convention decided, but the latter added the plea that the king's life be spared. Cherbourg said that it did not care whether Louis was imprisoned, exiled, or decapitated. St.-Dié-sur-Loire wanted the monarch to be detained until the war's end, and then exiled. Nuits, on the invitation of the deputy, Marey, polled its members and got these results: for acquittal, 1; for detention, 1; for death, 10; for perpetual banishment, 43.[9]

The cause of clemency was undermined by the discovery, on November 20, of an iron safe in the Tuileries palace, containing incriminating letters of the king. Enraged by this and the pettifoggery of the antiregicides, radicals in Paris turned to coercion. On December 2, delegates from the sections and the Commune appeared before the Convention to demand a trial and to accuse Roland of having destroyed some of the papers in the iron safe to protect his friends. A cowed Convention agreed the next day to judge Louis. It further decreed, on December 6, that the voting in the trial would be by roll-call, thereby exposing antiregicide deputies to hectoring by the sansculottes in the galleries.

---

[5] AN, DXL 18–23. M, Dec. 24, 1792. Wallon, *Fédéralisme*, II, 60–61, 463. ArchP, Dec. 9, 21, 1792, Jan. 11, 1793. PV, Bordeaux, Dec. 8, 1792.

[6] Cf. Lecesne, *Arras*, I, 337–338. PV, Pithiviers, Jan. 4, 1793.

[7] PV, Lectoure.

[8] The trial was not mentioned in the minutes of Montreuil, Châtillon-sur-Chalaronne, Gaillac, Eymoutiers, Guingamp, and Annonay.

[9] Richemond, "Ars-en-Ré," p. 51. Galland, "Cherbourg," p. 383. PV: Honfleur, Dec. 27, 1792; Nuits, Dec. 20–21, 1792. AN, DXL 18, 21.

The next few weeks were rife with dissension. Many of the Girondins wished to spare the king; but they dared not defend him openly, and so, they employed diversionary tactics. For some time they had insinuated that the Montagnards wanted to get rid of Louis in order to put Philippe Egalité (the Duke of Orléans) in his place; and on December 16, Buzot proposed Egalité's exile along with other members of the Bourbon family. The Montagnards at first demanded Roland's dismissal as a quid pro quo; when this motion was defeated, they claimed that Egalité could not be exiled because he was a deputy and, therefore, inviolable. The galleries sided with the Montagnards, jeering and threatening their opponents. After more than an hour of pandemonium the Convention voted to exile the Bourbons, but deferred a decision on Orléans until the nineteenth. On that date, menacing throngs from the sections showed up, and an official of the Commune raised the possibility of an insurrection. The deputies caved in to this intimidation, not only permitting Egalité to keep his seat, but revoking the decree of December 16.

These incidents precipitated a tempest of petitions, resolutions, and letters from the clubs. Thiviers reckoned that Orléans was the evil genius behind the discord in Paris, and it published a speech demanding his punishment. Other societies thought naively that factional fever would subside with the surgical removal of the ex-king. Mont-de-Marsan asserted that the "cause of the troubles is the continued existence of Louis." Langres predicted: "All factions will fall with the head of the king." Lure opined that the beheading of Capet was the "surest way to end the cabals, odious rivalries, jealousies, and intrigues."[10]

Many clubs took the high road, chastening all of the feuding deputies. Gone was the unstinting admiration of September–October; in its place had seeped anger and even contempt. Troyes described the parliamentary infighting as the "principal cause" of public disorders. Poitiers' language was so strong that its deputy-correspondent, Piorry, accused it of sowing disrespect for the Convention. Aix asked the Conventionnels what they had done since proclaiming the Republic, answered "nothing," and com-

[10] AN, DXL 23. Wallon, *Fédéralisme*, I, 474. *ArchP*, Dec. 9, 1792. COR, Montpellier, L 5549. Thiviers' letter was dated December 26 but not published until January 24.

manded them to "judge the prisoner of the Temple." Rochefort, too, charged the deputies with "do-nothingness." Pertuis groused that "personal hatreds and vanity" benefited no one. Marseille commanded the deputies of the Bouches-du-Rhône to be "neither Maratists, Brissotins, Robespierrists, or Rolandists," and to proceed posthaste with the trial of the king. Toulouse told the deputies to end their "scandalous" disputes, to do away with the "bloody despot," and to make a constitution. Condom seethed that four months had been "wasted" and that there was still no decision on Louis. Montauban called for the king's judgment and sobbed: "What will become of the vessel of state, if the pilots who should be preserving it from shipwreck, instead excite storms."[11]

One of the most publicized addresses of this type came from La Rochelle. The Rochellais likened the Convention to a "gladiatorial arena" and ranted about the "criminal slowness" in trying Louis. After declaring their aversion to all parties, however, they gave a backhanded compliment to Marat:

> Roland, hear us! We want neither a Congress nor you as president.
>
> Robespierre! We want neither a dictatorship nor you as dictator.
>
> Brissot! Remember Mirabeau, the Lameths, and Barnave. . . ! You have seen the fall of these intriguers. Let it be an example to you.
>
> As for you, Marat! Whom they have depicted as the most abominable scoundrel. We share not your errors, but neither do we applaud those who cut you to pieces; their fury against you has convinced us that occasionally you may be right.[12]

Most of the wrath of the clubs was concentrated on the sections and Commune of Paris. Once again, a great many voiced support for a law instituting a departmental guard or offered armed aid to the deputies. Dax and Valognes (December 13) called for a guard and, in an apparent allusion to the *événement* of December 2, objected to the "audacious behavior" of the sections and galleries.

---

[11] AN, DXL 18–23. *M*, Dec. 24, 1792.

[12] AN, DXL 19. Wallon, *Fédéralisme*, II, 449. David, *La Rochelle*, pp. 60–61. COR, Poitiers, S 26.

In addresses of December 23 and 25, Alençon exclaimed: "Representatives! You deliberate amid catcalls and murmurs. . . ! Make an appeal to the people, not to those of Paris but to the departments!"[13] About the same date, Tarbes entreated the deputies to surround themselves with a force drawn from the departments and lambasted the "criminals" in the Paris sections, the "rebel" Commune, the "insolent mob" in the galleries, and the "deputy who wants to make so many thousands of heads fall."[14] Rodez (a little before December 23) swore that it was ready to "fly" to Paris, and on December 25 it upbraided the deputies for failing to arrest Marat and for allowing themselves to be put under siege by extremists.[15] Vienne affirmed that it would "never stand for one city to usurp the sovereignty which belongs to the eighty-four departments."[16]

The most important address came from Quimper. Indeed, it set off a movement that was a precursor to the Federalist Rebellions of May–June 1793. On December 12 the Quimper club announced that at its request, the Department of the Finistère was mobilizing an armed force which would leave in a few days for Paris. Quimper summoned affiliates to do likewise, saying that it was up to them to protect the deputies and prevent a renewal of the September Massacres. It also sought legislation creating a guard drawn from all of the departments. "You have brushed aside one proposition of this nature," it told the deputies; "but today there are new problems. . . . Whatever some men say, the judgment of Louis Capet cannot be rushed. We, too, want the king to get the punishment that he deserves, but the honor of France requires that his trial be conducted properly."[17]

At least two clubs of the Finistère (St.-Pol and Brest) joined Quimper in petitioning the Convention to establish a departmen-

[13] AN, DXL 22. PV, Alençon, Dec. 23–29, 1792. Nicolle, *Valazé*, pp. 120–121.

[14] AN, DXL 22. COR, Niort, L 2e M2. Wallon, *Fédéralisme*, II, 462. The deputy Barère was threatened by the people in the galleries on December 16. His brother was vice-president of the Tarbes club.

[15] AN, DXL 18. Combes de Patris, *Rodez*, pp. 177–179. COR, Niort, 3005. The Limoges club decided on January 16, 1793, to draw up a letter "dans le même sens" as Rodez.

[16] AD, DXL 19. *ArchP*, Dec. 31, 1792. *M*, Jan. 3, 1793.

[17] AN, DXL 20–21. Wallon, *Fédéralisme*, I, 395–396, II, 425. *JC*, Dec. 24, 1792. *CD*, Dec. 25, 1792. COR: Poitiers, S 26; Limoges, L 826; Niort, 3003. *ArchP*, Dec. 31, 1792.

tal guard. Moreover, Brest helped recruit cannoneers for the contingent of fédérés that was to march to Paris. After maddening delays, this three-hundred-man force set out on January 23. On route to the capital it was feted by the clubs of several departments. At Auray, on January 26, the president lauded "our brothers of the Finistère who are going to defend our legislators against the bad-intentioned people." Alençon, on February 10, also honored the men of the Finistère for "repairing voluntarily to Paris to fight the evil-doers who wish to trouble the operations of our deputies."[18]

Like Quimper and Alençon, Le Puy was irate about the reports from Paris. In an address of December 23, it shrieked: "There is a plot to discredit the Convention. A violent party wielding a tyrannical dominion over the galleries has pushed its audacity up to the point of menacing the Convention with armed force." Le Puy exhorted the deputies to impeach Marat, Danton, Robespierre, Chabot, and all their associates, to surround themselves with a departmental guard, and if necessary, to flee the capital. A week later, after receiving the Quimper circular, it distributed an edict of the Department of the Haute-Loire ordering the recruitment of five hundred fédérés to go to Paris and put themselves under orders of the Convention. The covering letter to affiliates ended with these words: "What can they do if they are only accompanied by their brothers . . . of the Finistère and a few other departments? What can they not do, if they are seconded by all the departments?"[19]

Much the same thing happened at Perpignan. First, on December 25 the club proffered assistance to the Convention against the "arrogant minority which wants to make the laws." Then, it circulated the proceedings of an assembly of 3,500 citizens held on December 30. This assembly adopted the following resolutions: to demand a constitution; to assure the Convention that the citizens of the Pyrénées-Orientales, if called, were ready to rush to its defense; to put registers in each commune of the department

[18] J. Savina, "Les fédérés du Finistère pour la garde de la Convention," *RF* (1913), pp. 193–224. PV: Auray, Jan. 26–30, 1793; Alençon, Feb. 11, 1793. Maintenant, "Alençon," p. 128.

[19] AN, DXL 21. Wallon, *Fédéralisme*, I, 472–473, II, 279. COR: Reims; Poitiers, S 26. BN, Lb[40] 1064.

on which men who were willing to go could inscribe their names; and to invite other departments to take like measures.[20]

Acting apparently on its own initiative, Bédarieux petitioned the Department of the Hérault, on December 20, to constitute "an armed force to protect the Convention." Montpellier adhered to this petition and sent four of its members to coax departmental officials into adopting it. Not until December 30 did Montpellier receive the Quimper circular. However, it voted immediately to inform the department of the desire of the citizens of the Hérault to emulate their brothers in the Finistère.[21]

The deputy Moreau sent the club of Chalon-sur-Saône a graphic account of the session of December 16, citing it as proof that "there is a party which wants to dissolve the Convention and put Egalité on the throne." Moreau's comments, and the timely arrival of the Quimper circular, primed Chalon for action. On December 27 it broke off affiliation with the Paris club, and it voted to ask the administrators of the Saône-et-Loire to organize "a provisional departmental guard" to be held in a state of readiness to march to the capital and save the Convention from "factionalists."[22]

Quimper's circular was read at Tulle on December 27 (along with one from Saintes suggesting that the heads of the "two odious criminals," Marat and Louis XVI, should fall at once). Tulle promptly approved addresses to the Paris Commune and the Convention and distributed six hundred copies to affiliates. To the Commune it complained about the violence on December 19. The Convention was first chastised for its febrile submission to outside pressure and then offered an escort to a safe place if it was "unfree." Using almost the same language, the Department of the Corrèze, on January 9, blandished the Convention to form a departmental guard and directed communes under its jurisdiction to begin enrolling men who would be willing to serve in it. A little later, the club of Ussel rebuked the deputies for permitting "a criminal faction to besiege their meeting place" and charged that the Commune of Paris, "like Rome of old, aspires

[20] Wallon, *Fédéralisme*, II, 252. AN, DXL 22. COR: Poitiers, S 26; Niort, L 2e M2.
[21] PV, Montpellier, Dec. 20–30, 1792. AN, DXL 20.
[22] Caron, "Moreau," pp. 67–69. *PF*, Jan. 9, 1793.

to universal dominion." The deputies were told that they needed only to cry out, and help would be forthcoming.[23]

The Quimper circular also reached Périgueux on December 27. In the debates that ensued, deep rifts showed up in this club. On one extreme was a small bloc that maintained that the deputies were not under duress, praised the Paris sections, declared that the Finistère had broken the law, and even showed some indulgence toward Marat. At the opposite pole was a somewhat larger element that quoted from Parisian newspapers to prove that the Convention was endangered, claimed to believe in an Orléanist conspiracy, prophesied that new massacres were in the offing, advocated the sending of fédérés, and advanced the idea of moving the nation's capital to a smaller city. The rest of those who spoke generally concurred that the Convention was in peril but had doubts about the legality of sending an armed force. Ultimately, on January 5, the club decided to offer assistance to the Convention, and to be prepared for any eventuality by forming a squad of fédérés. The next day, the Department of the Dordogne authorized the registration of volunteers.[24]

The clubbists of Aurillac adhered to Quimper's circular with more promptitude. On December 30 they declared that death was preferable "to seeing a part of the Republic usurp the rights of representation which belong to all" and asked the Department of the Cantal to muster an armed force to "protect" the Convention. Acceding to their request, the department, on January 11, decreed that two hundred men should be enlisted and made ready to march to Paris within two weeks. The clubs of the Cantal were asked for help. St.-Flour, on January 2, had already written to the Convention to say: "Representatives, if you are not free, tell us; a million arms will come to your defense. If you are free, see to it that your august character is respected."[25]

At the behest of the club of Epinal, the Department of the Vosges decided on January 3 to put a two-hundred-man force at the disposition of the Convention.[26] On January 4, the Republi-

[23] Forot, *Tulle*, p. 244. *CD*, Jan. 4, 1793. AN, DXL 19.
[24] PV, Périgueux, Dec. 27, 1792–Jan. 6, 1793. Wallon, *Fédéralisme*, II, 450. AN, DXL 19.
[25] *CD*, Jan. 10, 15, 1793. AN, DXL 19.
[26] COR, Poitiers, S 33.

can Society of Nîmes told departmental administrators that patriots in the Gard longed "to follow in the traces" of their "brothers of the Finistère." Eight days later the Department of the Gard resolved to create a "departmental force" that would be ready to move at the "first signal." Its number was fixed at 515.[27] At the same instant, Cherbourg importuned officials in the Manche "to levy an armed force which would march to Paris with those of the other departments."[28] And Annonay (January 13) voted to ask the administrators of the Ardèche to send fédérés to Paris to shield the Convention from "anarchists."[29]

In late November Toulon had proclaimed the party strife to be a "public calamity" and had summoned the deputies to cease their quarrels. By January, it was ready to take drastic action. At its bidding, the Department of the Var voted on the eighth to organize an elite battalion of five hundred fédérés. The mission of this battalion was to guarantee that the Convention could "opine freely," and it was to be ready to march by February. Commissars from the club of Draguignan appeared at Callas on January 22 and successfully recruited four volunteers. The battalion of the Var was one of the few that was actually formed and set out for Paris. Before it got there, however, it was diverted to the Vendée.[30]

Given its attitude toward the radicals in Paris, it is not surprising that the Eastern Society of Angers also demanded the mobilization of fédérés to protect the deputies. The Maine-et-Loire Department assented on January 8, ordering 411 guardsmen to assemble at Angers by January 29.[31] On January 18 Angoulême wrote to the Convention to say that "24,000,000 Frenchmen"

---

[27] Rouvière, *Gard*, III, 187–193.

[28] Galland, "Cherbourg," p. 386. On the same day (January 10) the clubs of St.-Lô, Périers, and Avranches sent addresses to the Convention complaining about the excesses of the Parisians and offering assistance. AN, DXL 21. Wallon, *Fédéralisme*, I, 513. M. Deries, *Le District de St.-Lô pendant la Révolution* (Paris, 1881), pp. 126–127.

[29] Rostaing, *Annonay*, p. 190.

[30] Poupé, *Var*, pp. 220–224. Poupé, "Callas," pp. 485–487. AN, DXL 23. *M*, Dec. 24, 1792, Feb. 11, 1793.

[31] Wallon, *Fédéralisme*, II, 11–12, 440–441. AN, DXL 21. The department disbanded this battalion on January 31, believing that order had been restored in Paris.

were anxious to crush the minority that was harassing it.[32] The same day, the Department of the Aude decreed the levy of a three-hundred-man force. The club of Limoux claimed to have instigated this decree. Eleven days earlier, Carcassonne had informed the Convention that the citizens of the Aude were ready to march to Paris to annihilate the "factionalists," and had proposed that another city be made the capital. Narbonne, about the same date, had charged the deputies with pusillanimity: "You allow a handful of agitators and criminals to oppress you. Insolent galleries trouble you and daily impede your march. . . . Legislators! Is this how you justify our confidence in you. . . ? Just say a word, and we will be on our way to Paris."[33]

Surprisingly, the Récollets Society acted somewhat late. On January 19, it finally overcame doubts about the legality of the actions of the Finistère, Haute-Loire, and other departments and decided that the sending of fédérés to Paris was a matter of extreme urgency. The department was asked to organize a force to protect the Convention, and did so on January 21. Once the order of January 21 was given, the Récollets campaigned actively to get citizens to enlist.[34]

Although the number of clubs prepared to send forces to Paris was imposing, some were adamantly opposed to such a venture. As in November, considerable dissension existed in the Gironde. The Club National reprimanded the department for its decree of January 21. Ste.-Foy also carped at the administrators, saying that they had fallen into a trap that would dishonor the citizens of the Gironde. It predicted that the five-hundred-man battalion would be stopped on its way to Paris and forced to return home ignominiously. In fact, the battalion never set off for the capital.[35]

It is safe to presume that Ste.-Foy was greatly swayed by Garrau and Jay, native sons who, practically alone among the delegation of the Gironde, sat with the Mountain. Tonneins had no deputies in the Convention. Its radically Leftist views stemmed largely from the fiery leadership of Jouan le jeune. Under Jouan's

[32] AN, DXL 19. Wallon, *Fédéralisme*, II, 49–50.
[33] COR, Limoges, L 825. AN, DXL 18.
[34] R. Brace, *Bordeaux and the Gironde* (Cornell, 1947), pp. 165–166. Forrest, *Bordeaux* (Oxford, 1975), p. 97.
[35] AD, Gironde, 12 L 40.

tutellage it waged a lonely battle against the moderate clubs of Agen, Clairac, and Villeneuve-du-Lot, and the Department of the Lot-et-Garonne. When the latter, on January 8, ordered that preparations be made to send an armed force to Paris, Jouan accused the administrators of impugning Paris and of being agents of the "vile corruptor, Roland." Over the opposition of the constitutional priest, Jouffret, Tonneins voted to print two hundred copies of Jouan's speech and to purge any members who enlisted in the departmental force.[36]

Rennes and Lorient were exceptions to the rule in Britanny in that both took timorous stands against the dispatch of fédérés to Paris. The Rennes club received divided counsel from the Convention, where two ex-members sat with the Gironde, and two with the Mountain. On this particular issue it sided with the Left. In a published address of December 25 it manifested shock over events in Paris and alarm about the safety of the deputies yet still opposed a departmental guard. "Not even the Amphictions of Greece or the Senators of Rome surrounded themselves with armed men!"[37]

Lorient, which had oscillated to the Right and Left throughout the autumn, discussed the Quimper circular on December 20 and 24. Although some members wished to adhere, it decided to write "fraternally" to Quimper to say that the Department of the Finistère had exceeded the limits of its authority. Further debates occurred on January 3–4, after Lorient learned that the Department of the Morbihan was planning to emulate the actions of the Finistère. This time a few members wanted to rebuke the administrators of the Morbihan, but Lorient again settled for a compromise. In an address of January 9, it begged the Convention to leave citizens in a quandary no longer. "Either decree the establishment of a departmental guard or tell us that you do not need it."[38]

Opposition to the sending of fédérés also materialized in other regions. A little before December 20, St.-Germain printed and distributed a speech of a certain Gourdin. It pointed to the resur-

[36] PV, Tonneins, Dec. 16, 1792–Jan. 25, 1793. COR, Niort, 3005.

[37] COR: Montpellier, L 5547; Poitiers, S 26. St.-Malo, in contrast to Rennes, favored the creation of a departmental guard. AN, DXL 20.

[38] PV and COR, Lorient.

gence of demands for the "infernal proposition of Buzot" as proof that a "terrible faction" existed in the Convention. The ringleaders of this faction were identified as "Guadet, Brissot, and the deputation of the Gironde." On January 6, Strasbourg published a circular accusing the Department of the Haute-Loire of high treason. Not long afterward, Clermont-Ferrand and Argenton declared that the administrators of the Haute-Loire had "raised the standard of civil war" and demanded their execution. After reading Strasbourg's circular, Lille and Tartas went on record as being in opposition to the dispatch of fédérés to Paris. Bayeux announced that it had rejected the invitations of Le Puy and Quimper. Dieppe emphasized that it hated "agitators" but let the public know that it had not called for a departmental guard for the Convention.[39]

GENERALLY speaking, clubs that championed the march of departmental forces on the capital looked with jaundiced eyes upon the "mother society." In response to the criticism that had rained down on it in November, the Paris club had simply become more intransigent. On November 18, it had voted to print a pamphlet entitled *Ni Marat ni Roland*, in which the naturalized Prussian, Anarcharsis Cloots, claimed to have overheard Buzot espouse federalism and Roland say that he wished to transfer the Convention to the Midi. However, the Jacobins appended a note stating that they did not share Cloots's opinions of Marat, that the latter was "pure at heart" and only driven to extremes by the "cruel persecution" of his enemies. This was a significant act, for the Paris club, in effect, rebuffed affiliates calling for the sacrifice of the "friend of the people."[40]

The vote of confidence in Marat was followed by new purges and denunciations. On November 26, Roland, Louvet, and Lanthenas were excluded. Two days later the Paris club printed a speech by Dubois-Crancé linking Pétion, Condorcet, and Carra to the "Brissotin faction." Then, on November 30, an important circular was issued. It defended the Commune and Paris delegation, assailed Roland, Brissot, Barbaroux, Buzot, and Louvet,

---

[39] *CD*, Jan. 10, 1793. *JD*, Jan. 11, 17, 20, 1793. PV: Tartas, Jan. 14–28, 1793; Lille, Jan. 20, 1793. AN, DXL 21. Wallon, *Fédéralisme*, I, 473.

[40] *JD*, Nov. 19–20, 1792.

and declared again that the September Massacres had saved the Republic. Moreover, it shamed members of affiliated societies, "brothers of four years," for letting themselves be deceived by the propaganda of the interior minister.[41]

This circular produced some favorable comment. The Popular Society of Lyon, already a true believer, said it regarded Roland with contempt. Metz adopted a resolution to return his dispatches unopened. Arras published documents that blackened the interior minister. St.-Germain adjudged that the "faction of Brissot" existed, and that Roland was trying to incite hatred of Paris. Lorient, which had been on the verge of breaking off affiliation with the Jacobins, concluded that they were being "wrongly calumniated." From Strasbourg came just the sort of aria one would expect. It thanked the Paris club for the warning of November 30, swore to remain invariably attached, and told it not to worry "about a few misguided societies, or rather the perfidious leaders of these societies." Their defection would purify the network, "separate the good grain from the chaff."[42]

More commonly, the new purges and the November 30 circular disquieted and angered affiliates. Verdun-sur-Garonne asked Toulouse what it thought about the denunciations of Roland; Toulouse replied that it would wait in silence for events to enlighten it. Amiens vouchsafed that its confidence in Roland was mounting daily. St.-Maixent observed that the correspondence of the Paris club had become "a dangerous vehicle of . . . a few factionalists." Le Puy protested the expulsion of Roland and Lanthenas. Grenoble said that it did not follow that Roland had lost the confidence of citizens, just because he was anathematized by "some sections of Paris." Perpignan was "saddened" by the November 30 circular and told the Paris Jacobins: "We have not replied to your letters because we see that you are not the same. We have sworn not to correspond with you until you are delivered from tyranny."[43]

Trouble erupted at Montpellier on December 16, when the

[41] *JC*, Dec. 13, 1792. *JD*, Nov. 22–30, 1792.

[42] *JC*, Dec. 20, 24, 1792. *JD*, Dec. 16, 1792. Heitz, *Strasbourg*, p. 245. COR, Poitiers, S 26. PV, Lorient, Dec. 17, 1792.

[43] PV, Toulouse, Dec. 29, 1792. *ArchP*, Dec. 9, 31, 1792. *PF*, Jan. 2, 1793. Gautheron, "Le Puy," pp. 93–94. COR, Poitiers, S 26. *CD*, Jan. 10, 1793.

society learned via the *Journal du soir* that four members, using its name, had written to Paris to accuse Roland of "corrupting public spirit." After several tumultuous sessions the four were suspended for one year and their names were placed on a "tablet of dishonor." In a formal apology to Roland, the Montpellier club affirmed its "hatred of the Marats and Robespierres." It also described the suspended quartet as "vile factionalists," driven to desperation by their failure to lead the people of Montpellier into "Maratism."[44]

At the club of Marseille on December 10, the Jacobin circular caused an uproar because it impugned Barbaroux, a popular deputy from the Bouches-du-Rhône. Letters from Barbaroux and Roland were applauded on December 12, and in the same session the Marseillais voted to assure Roland that they would "defend liberty to the death against the enterprises of the factionalists." The next day Marseille determined to send a "profession of faith" to the Paris club, and to end correspondence if an appropriate response did not come by a fixed date. Affiliates were notified of this decision.[45]

Without reaching any conclusion, the club of Châtellerault spent a week in late November discussing the situation in Paris and the attitude that it should take toward the "mother society." The arrival of the November 30 circular put an end to its indecision. Referring to this work as an "apology for September 2–3 and a pompous elegy of the Commune," it renounced its allegiance to the Paris society on December 11. Although we are not privy to their debates, it seems that Angers, Quimper, and Quimperlé severed their ties with Paris about the same date.[46]

Like Angers, the Récollets Society had long considered a formal rupture. More debates took place on the subject from December 1 to 13. The issue was never really in doubt. One member who had the temerity to praise Collot and Robespierre was shouted down. A committee assigned to study the subject reported that the Paris club was infested with "anarchists and agitators." The Bordeaux club was also influenced by a letter from Grangeneuve and by Louvet's rebuttal to Robespierre's Novem-

[44] PV, Montpellier, Dec. 16–30, 1792. *PF*, Dec. 30, 1792.
[45] *JDM*, Dec. 6–15, 1792.
[46] PV, Châtellerault, Nov. 22–Dec. 11, 1792. *JD*, Dec. 18, 1792.

ber 5 speech. An address was approved on December 13 and printed four days later. In it Bordeaux announced that it was suspending correspondence with the Paris society until it chased "the Chabots, Merlins, Dantons, Robespierres, and Marats." A covering letter advised affiliates to do "as we have done."[47]

A sizable number of clubs adhered to this circular. Argentat regarded it as a "glorious duty" to follow the Bordelais who, it said, excelled even the "orators of ancient Athens and Rome" in eloquence. Le Puy and Libourne published circulars of their own. Altogether, in late December and early January, twenty-five societies are known to have ceased correspondence with the Paris Jacobins or reaffirmed earlier decisions to do so.[48] In addition, Caen, Loudun, Avallon, Honfleur, Périgueux, Amiens, Laval, Nancy, St.-Affrique, Landerneau, and Toulon issued ultimatums demanding the purge of Marat, the reinstatement of Brissot and Roland, or both.[49] To these "blind daughters" the "mother society" responded with mild reprimands and copies of Robespierre's speeches. With the Récollets Club, it took a harder line, withdrawing affiliation and according this status to the Club National. In a show of defiance the Jacobins also expelled the "triumvirate of the Gironde," Vergniaud, Gensonné, and Guadet.[50]

Although the reading of their correspondence often reduced the Paris Jacobins to "somber silence," some of the news from the provinces was heartening. Montauban, Lille, Tartas, Arles, Beausset, Blaye, and Reims rejected the circulars of the Récollets Society, Le Puy, and Libourne. Strasbourg, Auxerre, Lyon, the Club National, the Popular Society of Nîmes, St.-Chamond, St.-Fargeau, Metz, Fontenay, Fontainebleau, and Tonneins promised "invariable attachment." Rennes and Blois stridently denied rumors that they had separated from Paris. Le Havre begged the Jacobins to send more correspondence. Dieppe,

---

[47] PV, Bordeaux, Dec. 1–13, 1792. *JC*, Dec. 27, 1792. *PF*, Dec. 25, 1792.

[48] The twenty-five clubs were Cherbourg, Bazas, Libourne, Le Puy, Chalon-sur-Saône, Marmande, Chartres, St.-Hippolyte, Beauvais, Coutras, Craponne, Argentat, Meaux, Cadillac, St.-Quentin, Falaise, Montpellier, Fleurance, Brest, Lisieux, Valognes, Niort, Saintes, Pamiers, and Agen.

[49] COR: Poitiers, Reims, Limoges. PV: Périgueux, Jan. 6–8, 1793; Honfleur, Jan. 8, 1793. *JD*, Jan. 22, 25, 27, 1793. *CD*, Jan. 4, 27, 1793.

[50] *JD*, Jan. 2–13, 1793. PV, St.-Cyprien, Jan. 13, 1793.

which had previously threatened a cut-off of communications, decided that it might have been "deceived by the *journaux*." Givet apologized for having been "duped" by Roland. Bayeux announced that it, too, had finally seen the light.[51]

In truth, despite all of the defections, the Paris society had reached the nadir of its fortunes by early January 1793 and had begun a partial recovery. This rebound was due in large part to the trial of the king, which was coming to a dramatic conclusion. On December 27, in a move that is usually interpreted as a last-gasp attempt to save Louis, the Girondist deputy Salle proposed that the judgment made by the Convention should be referred to the nation in the form of a referendum. This motion, called the "appeal to the people," was debated until January 4 and finally defeated in the session of January 15.

Whatever their motives, it is evident that the Girondins blundered in calling for a referendum. Although the motion was made in the name of popular sovereignty and national unity, in fact, it exposed them to charges of royalism and federalism and tarnished their image in clubs that had been howling for Louis' execution. Only one society (Dijon) seemed disposed to favor a referendum; at least thirty-four lodged complaints. Metz stormed that anyone who promoted this idea merited the death penalty. Rennes contended that it was unnecessary since the people had vested sovereign power in the deputies. Auxerre and La Rochelle divided supporters of Salle's proposition into two types, cowards and monarchists. Versailles and the Popular Society of Nîmes feared that counterrevolutionaries would manipulate the primary assemblies. Lyon, Beausset, and Auxerre thought that the motion, if adopted, would foment civil war. It did lead to a nasty riot between Jacobins and royalists at Rouen.[52]

At Marseille, which had been agonizing for two months over

[51] *AP*, Dec. 29, 1792. *JC*, Dec. 27, 1792. PV: Bordeaux, Dec. 29, 1792; Tartas, Jan. 14–28, 1793; Tonneins, Dec. 16, 1792–Jan. 13, 1793. Ligou, *Montauban*, pp. 286–287. COR: Reims, Poitiers, Niort, Lille. *CD*, Jan. 4, 1793. *JD*, Jan. 11–27, 1793.

[52] AN, DXL 18–23. COR: Bordeaux, 12 L 29; Poitiers, S 27, 34. *ArchP*, Feb. 17, 1793. Labroue, *Bergerac*, p. 216. PV: Castres, Jan. 4, 1793; Châteauroux, Jan. 6, 1793; Lons-le-Saunier, Jan. 12–14, 1793. *JD*, Jan. 17, 20, 22, 1793. Hugueney, *Dijon*, p. 138. *AP*, Jan. 15, Feb. 14, 1793. Mazauric, "Rougemaure," pp. 43–52. Chardon, *Rouen*, p. 105.

the schism in Paris, disgust at what was regarded as a ploy to spare the life of Capet finally tipped the scales in favor of the Montagnards. On January 4 the Marseillais "trembled with indignation" over the "incredible discussion in the Convention regarding the traitor Louis." In the January 9 session they listened to reports for and against the "Rolandistes and Jacobins," and "at last discerned the truth." A letter from Barbaroux advocating the "appeal to the people" brought "disapproving murmurs." Fearful that Louis might escape death, Marseille assigned a member to carry a manifesto to the Convention. It described Lanjuinais, Buzot, Rabaud, and Salle as "bad citizens," and Roland and Brissot as "dangerous party chiefs." Barbaroux was warned to recant or be declared a perjuror and traitor. Later (January 18) Marseille published an address urging affiliates to oppose the "appeal to people" and unite behind the Jacobins and sansculottes of Paris. Barbaroux's influence was broken, and on January 23 he and another deputy were expelled for having voted for the "appeal to the people." Henceforth, Marseille was to be implacably anti-Girondist.[53]

Many Provençal clubs quickly lined up behind Marseille. Aix, on January 5, described the "appeal to the people" as a royalist gambit and admonished the Convention to do something about "those unfaithful, weak, and traitorous representatives" who were obstructing its operations. Avignon adhered to Marseille's address of January 18. Arles also veered to the Left. It had announced in December that its fédérés were on their way to Paris "to establish the reign of laws and make factions disappear." In January, however, it pledged undying loyalty to the "mother society" and made some nasty remarks about Roland: "A *virtuous* minister tells us that he knows how to restore order. He means that we need a dictator and that this dictator, without doubt, should be this *virtuous* minister."[54]

Like Marseille, Clermont-Ferrand had a divided delegation in the Convention and was long perplexed about which side to follow. Couthon and Monestier were Montagnards. Bancal des Issarts and Dulaure held Rightist views. Finally, in early January,

[53] Kennedy, *Marseilles*, pp. 116–117.
[54] *JD*, Jan. 11, 22, 1793. Ponteil, "Aix," pp. 467–468. COR: Marseille, L 2075; Bordeaux, 12 L 29.

Clermont committed itself. It opposed the sending of fédérés to Paris and called upon the Convention to reject the "appeal to the people." Bancal, who voted for the "appeal," was disgraced. Clermont notified affiliates that it no longer regarded him as a frère. Riom may have been influenced by Clermont. On January 2, it issued a circular urging other societies to lobby against the "appeal to the people."[55]

Tulle also took a Leftward detour. The reader will recall that in late December it had rebuked the Commune and sections in the affair of Egalité, and had vowed to defend the Convention. But on January 20 it insisted on punitive measures against the deputies of the Right. In a circular to affiliates it said that those who had voted for the "appeal to the people" were unworthy of holding office, and it held up two deputies of the Corrèze, Lidon and Chambon, to public scorn. Tulle's volte-face is understandable if one reads its correspondence from the deputies Lanot and Brival. For they, too, did turnabouts. In a letter of November 4, Lanot had stated that the Paris Commune wanted dominion over other communes, and that there was a party in the "mother society" that "professes dangerous principles." On January 13, however, he warned the Tulle society to "beware of the intrigues of the malevolent men who are seeking to discredit the Jacobins, and by this ruse, to disorganize all of the clubs."[56]

Opinion shifted in Burgundy as well. In October–November the views of most of the clubs of this region seemed to be congruent with those of the Girondins. By January, the pendulum had swung in the other direction. It is true that Chalon-sur-Saône was estranged from the Paris society, but Louhans and Autun criticized the "appeal to the people." And a congress of clubs on January 7 at Mâcon summoned the Convention and Paris Jacobins to stifle the projects of the "few ambitious men who are working with all of their might to federalize the republic." Beaune (January 20) took the trouble to send an address, in manuscript, to the societies of all the departmental seats. It warned them that enemies of the Revolution were using the old strategy

[55] Mège, *Bancal*, pp. 237–255. Couthon, *Correspondance*, pp. 198–213. Baudet, *Dulaure*, pp. 104–106. *JD*, Jan. 17, Feb. 3, 1793. *AP*, Jan. 26, 1793. COR, Bordeaux, 12 L 32. AN, DXL 22.
[56] Forot, *Tulle*, pp. 237–247.

of "divide and conquer." Then it pleaded with affiliates *not* to break with Paris. "Placed at the center of light and the seat of government, the Paris Jacobins ought to be the metropolitan society."[57]

Lons-le-Saunier steered a more or less uncommitted course until January, when it, too, wheeled to the Left. On the fourth, after someone exclaimed that the society was on the verge of a schism, it decided to have a *scrutin épuratoire*. In the sessions of January 13–14, a debate occurred on the "appeal to the people," and the majority voted to demand that Louis be condemned to death and executed within twenty-four hours. On January 20, an unknown member gave a long harangue on the "conspiracies" that had been employed in the trial. The society determined to send a note of thanks to the 424 deputies who had voted against the "appeal to the people" and thereby "saved the republic." Four days later someone moved to drop the names of the "appellants" Brissot and Vernier from the membership rolls.[58]

The execution of the king (January 21) is a sort of halfway mark in the Girondin-Montagnard dispute. Before tracing the story to its tragic denouement, it would be well to sum up the evidence found thus far. From September 1792 to January 1793, 769 clubs are known to have operated, at least briefly. Most left meager records. Some, for which there are relatively abundant sources, seemed to be oblivious to the schism.[59] Others were reluctant to comment on it.[60] Still others wavered or advocated unity.[61] However, 130 societies can be tentatively classified as pro-Girondist; fifty-six (counting those which did about-faces in January) were Montagnard sympathizers. (See appendix F.)

Unless contrary evidence surfaced, the following criteria were used in compiling these figures. Clubs were deemed to be Girondist if they stopped corresponding with Paris or threatened to do so; praised Brissot or Roland; denounced the sections, Commune, or delegation of Paris; called for the punishment of Marat,

[57] *ArchP*, Jan. 4, 11, 1793. *JD*, Jan. 17, 1793. COR, Niort, 3001.
[58] PV, Lons-le-Saunier, Jan. 13–27, 1793.
[59] See PV: Eu, Jonquières, Largentière, Lauris, St.-Roman de Malegarde, Tulette, Montreuil, Thionville.
[60] St.-Cyprien, Guingamp, Orthez, and Semur are examples.
[61] Bergerac, Poitiers, Troyes, Bagnères, Lorient, Rennes, Rouen, and Vesoul are examples.

Robespierre, the "triumvirs," or the "Septembriseurs"; or supported the concept of a departmental guard. Indicators of pro-Montagnard sentiment were antipathy toward the "Brissotins" or "Rolandists"; adulation of Marat, Robespierre, or the Commune; expressions of confidence in the Paris society; and opposition to a departmental guard. Because documentation is so fragmentary, the possibility of error is great. There were also differences of degree. Auxerre and Strasbourg, for example, were more consistently pro-Montagnard than Toulouse or La Rochelle. Still, I believe that the lists printed in appendix F give a fairly good picture of the division of opinion in January 1793.

XXIV

1793

VOTING commenced in the king's trial on January 15 and continued until January 20. On the issue of guilt there was overwhelming consensus: 707 "ouis," 14 abstentions. The "appeal to the people" was defeated by 425 to 286. The margin was narrow on the penalty to be inflicted: 334 for mercy, 361 for death, 26 for death with qualifications. A last-minute attempt to grant a reprieve was overridden by 70 votes.[1] On January 21 Louis was beheaded.

No club (to my knowledge) publicly disapproved of the verdict. Annonay was quite conservative, and its two deputies voted for banishment; but the historian Rostaing may have inferred too much in calling its closure from January 27 to February 17 an "act of mourning." Similarly, one cannot induce that Guingamp's silence was an indicator of disapprobation, even though its correspondent/deputy, Guyomar, voted for the appeal to the people and imprisonment. Guingamp was notoriously laconic. That clubs like Sarrebourg and Dieuze waited until March to applaud the death of the "tyrant" means nothing. They may have been inactive in January and February.[2]

Some clubs were worried about the outbreak of troubles, especially after the assassination of the regicide deputy, Lepelletier, on January 20. At Evreux, the president exhorted citizens not to shed tears for Louis, but for his "victims." And Saintes issued a circular warning affiliates to be on guard. "To play upon the fate of Louis," it predicted, "to interest the hearts of the people in the plight of his family, that will be the game of counterrevolutionaries." But the popular hysteria that often accompanied événements in Paris was largely absent.[3]

[1] Patrick, *Republic*, pp. 83–107. J. H. Stewart, *A Documentary History of the French Revolution* (New York, 1951), p. 385.

[2] Rostaing, *Annonay*, pp. 195–198. Dobet, "Guingamp," p. 101.

[3] Boivin-Champeaux, *Eure*, p. 385. COR: Niort, 3003; Limoges, L 826.

What one does find is broad acceptance of the verdict. At least 212 clubs, ranging from the moderate Récollets Society to the radical Popular Society of Lyon, had written to the Convention by March to endorse the action.[4] Other letters of adhesion, signed by "the citizens" of such-and-such a place, probably emanated from clubs. Certain societies were doubtless afraid that failure to adhere might be construed as a sign of weakness. Ceyzeriat, for one, pontificated that "every republican who is silent after this resounding act of justice is only a coward." Still, when all allowances are made, the show of support was tremendous.

Some of the letters were somber and restrained, describing the sentence as a regrettable but necessary act of justice. Others spitefully referred to the fallen monarch as a "crowned tiger," "Capet the cruel," "a ferocious beast." St.-Jean-de-Luz (which was pro-Montagnard) had the bad taste to call the king a "minotaur" and the deputies "new Theseuses." Issoudun wanted January 21 to be named "equality day." Aix crowed that it had held a fete of thanksgiving. At Libourne a clubbist read an impromptu poem on "L'Amputation de Louis le Dernier." Jouan le jeune of Tonneins composed an opus entitled "Louis in Hell; Lepelletier in the Elysian Fields."[5]

Their thirst for blood unslaked, Cassis, Digne, Nice, and Semur demanded the immediate execution of Marie Antoinette. Limoux, in a published petition, called for the implementation of the decree of December 16 banishing the Bourbon family, and the impeachment of Philippe Egalité if he continued to be a source of disharmony. Castres, Largentière, and St.-Ambroix approved petitions along the same lines.[6]

One point that is evident is that few clubs were, as yet, irrevocably committed to the Girondins or Montagnards. On the contrary, most longed for the cessation of factionalism and the enactment of a constitution. Forcalquier cherished the illusion that with Louis' death "unity will return and the Convention will re-

---

[4] See especially AN, C 247–250, DXL 18–30, and F¹ C III.

[5] Cf. AN, DXL 21. Ponteil, "Aix," p. 463. Besson, *Libourne*, pp. 209–211. PV, Tonneins, March 6, 1793.

[6] Combet, "Nice," p. 419. *JDM*, Jan. 31, 1793. *ArchP*, Feb. 13, 24, 1793. AN, C 247. COR: Limoges, L 825; Niort, 3003; Poitiers, S 33. PV: Castres, Jan. 28, 1793; Largentière, Feb. 10, 1793.

cover its dignity." Meyssac hoped that the deputies would work for the "interests of the fatherland" now that the issue of the "great criminal" had been resolved. "Let his death annihilate all factions," intoned Créon. "No longer waste your time in scandalous debates," sermonized St.-Affrique. "Now only one party exists," exclaimed L'Aigle. "We must all reunite," expounded Montauban; "hatreds must be buried with the king." "Give each other the kiss of peace," piped Nantes. "Crush all factions," commanded St.-Ambroix. "Forget your animosities," homilized Reims. "Abjure your personal hatreds," implored Versailles. St.-Quentin, on the Right, pleaded: "From this moment all divisions ought to cease." From the far Left, Auxerre, cried out: "Representatives! Let the unity so necessary for the welfare of the people be reborn in the French senate."[7]

Unfortunately, the factions were deaf to such pleas. No sooner had the fate of the king been sealed than disputes broke out. On January 20 the deputy Kersaint, who had been an advocate of leniency, submitted a letter of resignation in which he said, in so many words, that he could not bear to sit with murderers. Cambon denounced Kersaint, but Barbaroux defended his colleague and demanded the prosecution of those responsible for the September Massacres. Gensonné seconded Barbaroux's motion; and after fierce debate, it was approved. The justice minister was ordered to begin proceedings. Two days later (January 22), Roland resigned as minister of interior. In a circular to the societies, he defended his administration and asked for their continued support.

These two incidents generated much comment from the clubs. Strasbourg expressed jubilation at seeing the "demi-god" (Roland) dethroned. St.-Chamond and Lyon lusted to see the "poisoner of public opinion . . . dance the carmagnole on the scaffold." But Dunkerque, over the objections of some members, formally commended Roland's ministry. Amiens demanded his reinstatement. Albi, Quillan, and Pau signaled their displeasure at his fall. The Récollets Society congratulated Roland on a job well done. Angers reaffirmed its belief in his virtue; Chartres

[7] AN, C 247, DXL 18. Wallon, *Fédéralisme*, I, 339. Lallié, *Nantes*, pp. 101–103. COR: Reims; Bordeaux, 12 L 38; Niort, 3003; Montpellier, L 5544; Limoges, L 829. *ArchP*, Feb. 2, 1793. PV: St.-Affrique, Feb. 5–8, 1793.

made him an honorary member. And Carcassonne published a circular in which it said: "If we have become better men, more worthy of the republic, it is on account of him."[8]

Positions were reversed on the law of January 20. The Récollets Society proclaimed this act to be the "fulfillment" of its wishes. Perpignan and Fleurance were incensed when petitioners from the Paris Jacobins got the Convention, on February 8, temporarily to suspend its implementation. But St.-Jean-de-Luz did not want any prosecutions and contended that the September Massacres were an "unfortunate necessity." A speaker at Marseille fulminated that the law of January 20 was a maneuver of "frustrated royalists" who wished to exact reprisals against the regicide deputies.[9]

In the same session (January 30) Marseille received a letter from the Popular Society of Lyon in which the latter broadcast its intention of starting a drive to unseat "the representatives who had betrayed the people." Marseille seized upon Lyon's idea. On February 1 it published a circular asking all of the clubs of the Republic to petition for the recall of the "appellants" and the repeal of the law of January 20:

> The massacres were simply one of the unfortunate events which often accompany revolutions, and over which it is necessary to cast a veil. . . . The deputies who foisted this measure upon us are the same ones who were for the appeal to the people. They have gone too far, brothers and friends. Let's remove these traitors and disturbers. Raise a cry in all departments for the convocation of electoral assemblies to recall them and name replacements.[10]

The issue of the recall of the "appellants" came up again at Marseille on February 6. By that date some members had apparently gotten cold feet, for they ventured the opinion that it might be an "impolitic" act and a "provocation to federalism." Mar-

---

[8] *CD*, Feb. 13, 15, 25, 1793. *JD*, Feb. 13, 17, 1793. *ArchP*, Mar. 24, 1793. *PF*, Feb. 5, 1793. Lemaire, *Dunkerque*, p. 363. AN, DXL 21. COR, Limoges, L 825. Wallon, *Fédéralisme*, II, 471.

[9] *PF*, Feb. 9, Mar. 11, 1793. *CD*, Mar. 8, 1793. Wallon, *Fédéralisme*, II, 377. COR, Bordeaux, 12 L 33. *JDM*, Feb. 2, 1793.

[10] *JDM*, Feb. 2, 1793. *JD*, Feb. 3, 13, 1793. Riez Correspondence.

seille decided to ask the Paris club for its opinion on this "important question." However, hundreds of copies of the February 1 address were already in the mail, and the covering letter requested affiliates to pass it along to their sisters.[11]

Marseille's words had the weight of law in the southeast. Within a few weeks, at least nineteen Provençal societies,[12] plus an unknown number of clubs at a congress held in Digne, had adhered to the February 1 circular. Manosque fumed that the decree of January 20 had "revolted the entire Midi." Castellane declaimed that "the days of September 2 and 3 were merely a continuation of those of August 10." Graveson vowed to follow the Marseillais "to victory or to death." The only club of Provence known to have defied Marseille was Draguignan; it regarded the February 1 circular as "incendiary."[13]

Outside Provence support was limited. Beaucaire, St.-Etienne, Bédarieux, Lyon, and the Popular Society of Nîmes applauded Marseille's stand; but Nîmes made its adhesion contingent on approval by the Paris Jacobins. Loudun and Landau merely praised the courage of the regicides. Limoges, Montauban, and the Club National of Bordeaux protested against the decree of January 20 but did not endorse the recall of the "appellants." The Club National expressed the fear to Marseille that if electoral assemblies were convoked in the Gironde, they would sustain the "appellants" and recall the "two or three Montagnards" in the delegation.[14]

On the arrival of Marseille's circular at Montpellier, on February 14, the club opted to send an address to the Convention in the "same sense" and to notify sister societies that it was renewing its affiliation with Paris. Among those assigned to draft these documents were Aigoin and Villaret, two of the members who had been accused of "Maratism" in December, and whose suspensions had just been lifted. Aigoin and Villaret went too far, how-

[11] *JDM*, Feb. 2–7, 1793. AD, Bouches-du-Rhône, L 3037.
[12] Castellane, Aix, Villelaure, Allauch, Lourmarin, Correns, La Coste, St.-Tropez, Ste.-Tulle, Lorgues, Ceyreste, Graveson, Manosque, Cucuron, Peypin, Maillane, Tarascon, Malaucène, and Vaison.
[13] PV: Vaison, Feb. 15, 1793; Castellane, Feb. 17, 1793. *JDM*, pp. 615–643. AN, DXL 18.
[14] *JDM*, pp. 617, 643. *JD*, Feb. 28, 1793. AN, DXL 21. PV, Limoges, Feb. 27, 1793. *CD*, Mar. 8, 1793.

ever, for when the two addresses were presented for approval on February 17, several members voiced concern over "phrases concerning certain personalities" and "impolitic and dangerous" statements. Finding the radicalism of the Left not to its taste, Montpellier banished the "Maratists forever" and reaffirmed its decision not to correspond with Paris.[15]

Tartas referred Marseille's circular to a committee, where it died. Périgueux, Bergerac, and Blaye simply tabled the proposal. Blaye did so on the grounds that "representatives of the people needed to be inviolable so that they would feel free to express their opinions." When Sarreguemines demanded the expulsion of the deputies who had not voted for death, Nancy not only refused to go along but burned Sarreguemines' letter. Salins categorized Marseille's address as a "monstrous" work. Cognac fussed that this initiative "tended to nothing less than the destruction of the Republic and the dissolution of the Convention."[16]

A plenipotentiary of the Marseille club presented a motion to recall the "appellants" at the Paris Jacobins on February 17. It was initially adopted, but finally tabled after Jeanbon St.-André argued that it was "federalist and dangerous." An influx of addresses from Marseille's satellites led to further debates on February 22 and 27. On the latter date, only the intervention of Robespierre prevented the adoption of Marseille's motion. Robespierre contended that the Paris club should not become involved in "a new arena of cabal and intrigue" when the fatherland was in danger. He moved instead that affiliates should simply censure and expel the "appellants." In a letter to Marseille, the Paris Jacobins expressed regret that they could not approve a measure that "traitors might turn to their profit."[17]

On February 15, while the network was mulling over Marseille's radical proposition, the constitution committee of the Convention presented its long-awaited report. The draft constitution of February 15 was primarily the work of Condorcet. In many respects it was more liberal than the Constitution of 1791.

[15] PV, Montpellier, Feb. 14–17, 1793.
[16] PV: Blaye, Feb. 23, 1793; Périgueux, Feb. 19, 1793; Tartas, Feb. 25, 1793. CD, Feb. 24, 1793. Troux, *Meurthe*, p. 246. Le Gallo, "Cognac," p. 416. Labroue, *Bergerac*, p. 220.
[17] JD, Feb. 19–Mar. 1, 1793. *JDM*, p. 654.

For example, all adult men were to have the right to vote. How-ever, there were some undemocratic provisions, including one that would have required voters to sign their ballots. Since the adult male population was only 47 percent literate, this would have greatly truncated the size of the electorate.

For better or worse, the factionalism in the Convention had reached such a pass that the constitution could not be considered solely on its merits. It was sufficient for the draft document to be the work of Condorcet and the Girondins for the Montagnards to oppose it. In a letter of February 16 to Montauban, Jeanbon St.-André remarked: "This unfortunate child of eight or nine Brissotin fathers has against it, in the eyes of men of good will, one essential vice, that of its parentage." As an afterthought, he observed that it was "rachitic, badly formed." Pinet (February 20) grumbled to the Bergerac club that it was "the work of the Brissotins; it is antipopular, petty, and niggardly." The corre-spondence committee of the Paris Jacobins wrote to Niort to say that the proposed constitution was "obscure, impracticable, and lacking in common sense." The Paris club also appointed a com-mittee to draw up a countermeasure. Its spokesman, Anthoine, maintained that Condorcet's draft would "favor the rich at the expense of the poor."[18]

The draft constitution of Condorcet received careful scrutiny from the clubs.[19] Some, like Paris, were instantly hostile. Le Havre said that it was "incoherent and vicious in parts." Laon likewise criticized the project of the Brissotin faction. Lyon wanted all consideration of a constitutional act deferred until the peace. Pithiviers at first approved and then rescinded a motion to remonstrate to the Convention against the provision requiring voters to sign their names. The member who made the motion argued that this article was "contrary to liberty" and gave "to rich and powerful men the means to assure their election to all offices."[20]

[18] Lévy-Schneider, *St.-André*, p. 233. Aulard, *Jacobins*, V, 30. *JD*, Feb. 26, 28, 1793. Labroue, *Bergerac*, p. 223. COR, Niort, 3006 bis.

[19] PV: Tartas, Apr. 12, 1793; Nuits, Mar. 7, 1793; Limoges, Mar. 14, 1793; Montpellier, Apr. 15, 1793; Marseille, Feb. 28–Mar. 4, 1793. COR, Aix, L 2038.

[20] AN, C 249. Riffaterre, *Lyon*, I, 44. PV, Pithiviers, Mar. 1, 3, 1793. *JD*, Mar. 16, 1793.

Before the execution of the king, as we have seen, a host of clubs had cut off relations with the "mother society." In February and early March, many remained unrepentant. St.-Quentin, for example, vowed that it had nothing in common with the "anarchists" in the Paris club. Chartres excised the name of the Montagnard deputy, Chasles, from its rolls and expressed its detestation for the "factionalists and ambitious men" at the head of the Paris society. Perpignan stood behind Birotteau, its deputy, whom the Jacobins accused of preaching "federalism." Libourne refused to open mail that it received from "the malefactors" in the Paris club.[21]

While animosity remained widespread, the gradual *ralliement* to the "mother society," which had commenced in January, continued. Marseille, wishing "to fortify the estimable Mountain," encouraged small clubs of Provence to apply to Paris for affiliation. Moreover, several societies of the southwest, including St.-Jean-de-Luz, La Tremblade, and St.-Macaire, rebuffed the Récollets Society, saying that they planned to remain attached to the Paris club.[22]

Limoges had been clearly leaning toward the Right in January. On the sixteenth, it adhered to an address from Rodez demanding the exclusion of "the traitor Marat" from the Convention. Four days later, it approved a circular to affiliates against "Citizen Egalité." After receiving Roland's letter of resignation on January 28, it gave the ex-minister a vote of confidence. In addition, at an unspecified date, it had ceased to correspond with the Paris Jacobins. However, a metamorphosis commenced on February 2 with a visit from Pontard, Bishop of the Dordogne. Pontard, who was returning from the capital, reported that it was tranquil, that "the attempt to provoke the sending of departmental armed forces to Paris had no other goal than to save the tyrant," and that the Mountain was "the sane part of the Convention." Three weeks later, the Parisian journalist and Montagnard Xavier Audouin paid a call. Audouin, who was a Limousin by birth, brought a letter from the Paris society asking Limoges to resume correspondence. On February 25, the day after Audouin's arri-

---

[21] *PF*, Mar. 2, 1793. *CD*, Feb. 22, 24, 1793. *JD*, Jan. 30, Feb. 28, 1793. PV, Libourne, Mar. 4, 1793.
[22] *JDM*, Mar. 5, 16, 1793. COR, Bordeaux, 12 L 33, 40.

val, a crucial debate took place. One member argued that the club was wrong to have stopped correspondence with the Paris Jacobins. But another riposted that Limoges should have nothing to do with Paris until it purged "the Talliens" and ceased to attack the "estimable Condorcet." Finally, Audouin took the floor and "dissipated all suspicions of the Paris Jacobins and the Parisian people." Limoges voted to reopen correspondence with the "mother society."[23]

Like Limoges, the Périgueux club had tilted toward the Right in January. On the sixth it decided to solicit the formation of a *force départementale* and assigned a member, the Abbé Sirey, to carry an address to the Convention. The next day it voted to demand from the Paris Jacobins an explanation for the purge of Manuel and the "persecution" of Pétion. Continued affiliation was made contingent upon a good response. In the following weeks, however, a transformation took place. It commenced when Sirey reported from Paris (January 17–20) that the Convention had adjourned debate on the question of a departmental force, that the deputies appeared to be "free," and that he had opted not to submit the petition. The club voted to approve Sirey's decision.[24]

Sirey had apparently been influenced by the deputies of the Dordogne, who were overwhelmingly pro-Montagnard. In late January three of them, Peyssard, Pinet, and Lamarque, reprimanded the clubbists of Périgueux for their actions. Lamarque gave his old confrères a veritable tonguelashing: "You have put yourself in a state of sedition and revolt. You want to march against the Left side and the Mountain. Well! Come ahead! You will find that the best patriots are there." Remorseful, and perhaps frightened, the clubbists of Périgueux begged forgiveness in a letter of February 11. They attributed their behavior to reports that they had read in Carra's paper:

> We saw each page of the *Annales patriotiques* filled with references to individuals who soiled the Convention and degraded the great men in it. . . .
> Each page of the *Annales patriotiques* attested that the peo-

[23] PV, Limoges.
[24] For what follows see PV, Périgueux.

ple in the galleries had arrogated to themselves the right to accord or refuse the floor to such and such a deputy.

We discussed the matter for five or six days and put our faith "in the most patriotic papers."

We were wrong.

Citizen representatives! We will never use our arms against the brave Parisians. On the contrary, we vow to support them. We love the good Jacobins and good Parisians.

On February 20 Sirey returned from Paris and gave his observations on the situation there. As his report was well-received, it may be regarded as a reflection of the feelings of the club of Périgueux at that date. Sirey stated that there were "intriguers" on both sides of the Convention, but more on the Right than Left. He expressed his revulsion at the conduct of the Right in the king's trial, and his esteem for Robespierre. He also lauded the zeal of the Paris club, but he was not impressed by the political acumen of all of its members. Nor was he willing to embrace Marat. On the contrary, he depicted Marat as a "madman" to whom the Mountain did not always listen.

Laval, which had disaffiliated itself from Paris, also agonized in February over the wisdom of this act. Debates began on the sixth when a certain Becker, who had been asked to deliver a funeral oration for Lepelletier, refused to do so unless he was given the latitude to speak favorably of the Paris Jacobins whom he believed to have been "unjustly calumniated." He was immediately challenged by three members—Fourdille, Fiquel, and Favrole—who deemed the Paris Jacobins, and Robespierre in particular, to be "agitators, men of blood, and the authors of the days of September."[25]

On February 10, more discussion occurred. Fourdille, quoting from an article in Gorsas, attempted to prove that Danton and Robespierre were responsible for the September Massacres. But Rabaud, who held views similar to Becker's, reminded the audience that Lepelletier had been a Jacobin and that Robespierre had been an incorruptible defender of the people during the Constituent Assembly. Such a man, he said, could not be a murderer. Fiquel combatted Rabaud and moved that the club petition the

[25] For what follows see PV, Laval.

Convention to order the immediate prosecution of the Septem-
brizers. Whereupon, Noyer, in a speech punctuated by boos,
asked for proof of the alleged crimes of the Jacobins. Eventually,
the society decided to approve Fiquel's motion.

After further discord, a bi-partisan effort was made in late February to restore harmony. Fourdille lamented that if there were
many more sessions like the last few, the society would be "lost."
Becker and Rabaud echoed these sentiments, proposing that the
club cease all talk of the Jacobins and parties in Paris. But Leroux,
who thought that Robespierre and Danton were good patriots,
was unwilling for the debate to end. When he asked for an explanation of why the club had broken with the Jacobins, he was
hissed and jeered. Angered by the treatment of Leroux, Becker
forgot his earlier motion, thundered that all members should
have the right to speak, and called for a reunion with Paris. However, the majority still opposed a reconciliation with the "mother
society," and Becker's motion was tabled. The Laval club was
obviously on the brink of a schism. On March 6, two of the pro-
Jacobins, Becker and Noyer, complained of being treated like
"agitators." Fisticuffs almost occurred on March 15 when, on the
reception of a circular from the Jacobins, someone again proposed that correspondence be reopened.

The return to the Jacobin fold was slowed at Laval, and elsewhere, by the outbreak of troubles in Paris. Prices of foodstuffs
and consumer goods had zoomed upward in early 1793, causing
extremists in the sections to become more vocal. They screeched
that the "rich," "speculators," and "hoarders" were to blame and
blasted the prevailing economic system. The result was popular
violence. On February 25–26, more than a thousand shops were
plundered by Parisian mobs. The main victims were big merchants and wholesalers who were thought to be responsible for
driving up costs.

The riot of February 25–26 was a propaganda bonanza for the
Right. The Girondist press accused the Mountain of complicity
in the incident and of preaching anarchism. Much ado was made
over the Commune's negligence in raising an armed force to halt
the looting. The main target for criticism, however, was Marat.
In the Convention Buzot and Salle unsuccessfully demanded his

arrest for counselling Parisians in his paper to "pillage a few stores and hang a few hoarders at their doors."

Placed on the defensive, the Jacobins published a letter of the deputy Garrau justifying Marat's behavior. In addition, they printed and disseminated a report by Robespierre, which endeavored to downplay the significance of the February 25–26 riots. "This event," said Robespierre to the clubs, "would not have been grave enough to write to you about, if it had not been exploited by a dangerous faction that wished to calumny us. Their aim is to destroy the popular societies. They are the same people who wished to spare the life of the king."[26]

Despite these reassurances, many clubs were horrified by the pillaging in Paris. Sète, Morlaix, La Gardelle, and Chambéry yelped for Marat's arrest. Saujon did so, too, likening his works to "the poisonous essence secreted by reptiles who inhabit subterranean dens." Cognac demanded the head of "the eternal provocator of murder and pillage." Pézenas, in an address to which St.-Hippolyte adhered, claimed that "his head must fall to save two hundred thousand others." The Récollets Society warned Parisians to "beware of the birds of prey who lurk in the shadows and provoke rapine and murder."[27]

It should be noted that Bordeaux, like Paris, experienced disorders. On March 7–8, increases in bread prices caused crowds of discontented people to besiege the city hall and threaten the mayor. This incident might have been spontaneous in origin, but city authorities and public opinion in general placed the blame on the Club National. On the night of March 8, a band of men, shouting "Down with the Jacobins," attacked its meeting place. At the same time the municipality ordered that it be closed and its papers seized. This was a foretaste of what was to happen to many pro-Montagnard societies in the Federalist rebellions.[28]

The waves of fury over the February 25–26 riots had not yet subsided when new troubles occurred in Paris. The second out-

[26] *JD*, Mar. 3, 1793.

[27] *PF*, Mar. 19, 22, 23, Apr. 3, 1793. AN, DXL 19–21. *CD*, Mar. 13, 22, 24, 1793. *ArchP*, Mar. 24, 1793. Wallon, *Fédéralisme*, II, 226. PV: St.-Hippolyte, Mar. 30, 1793; Cognac, Mar. 4, 1793.

[28] Brace, *Bordeaux*, pp. 168–169. Forrest, *Bordeaux*, pp. 198–220. *JD*, Mar. 21, 1793. COR, Niort, 3001.

burst was generated not so much by the economic crisis as by the military reverses in the Low Countries. Popular agitators accused the generals of treason and talked of the need for another insurrection. On the night of March 9–10 some of the popular societies and sections of the capital issued manifestos blaming the Girondins for the defeats. Angry mobs ransacked the presses of the *Chronique de Paris* and the *Courrier des départements*. An insurrectionary committee fomented a march on the Convention to expel the "appellants." But a coup d'état was prevented by Parisian national guardsmen with the assistance of fédérés from the Finistère.

Although the Paris society tried to divert attention from this incident and toward the "criminal faction" in the Convention and the "traitorous generals," the riots of March 9–10 intensified anti-Parisian, anti-Montagnard sentiment in certain clubs. Moyrans asked Lons-le-Saunier to join it in censuring the sections and the "mother society." Lesignan demanded that those who "perpetuate anarchy," especially the "so-called friend of the people," be made to pay. Boiscommun implored the Convention to surround itself with an armed force. Châteaulin called for the trial of "the partisans of Robespierre and Marat." Dieppe desired "vengeance against the anarchists." Bayeux wailed: "There should be no more insurrections. The Revolution is finished; the tyrant is dead."[29]

No club was more irate about the events of March 9–10 than Amiens. On March 14 it petitioned the Convention for the following: 1) banishment of the Bourbon house (including Egalité); 2) laws against "those who provoke disorder and murder"; 3) a departmental guard to assure the freedom of the Convention; 4) the arrests of Marat, Robespierre, and Danton; 5) the prosecution of the authors of the September Massacres; 6) dissolution of the Commune of Paris; 7) the rotation of sessions of future legislative assemblies in the principal cities of central France; 8) the reinstatement of Roland; 9) and the abolition of the new "tribunal of blood" (Revolutionary Tribunal).[30]

Amiens circulated this petition to affiliates with an invitation

[29] AN, DXL 19–21, 23. Wallon, *Fédéralisme*, I, 98, 110–111, 410; II, 471. PV: Lons-le-Saunier, Mar. 13, 1793; Boiscommun, Mar. 15, 1793.

[30] *ArchP*, Mar. 24, 1793. *M*, Mar. 26, 1793. COR, Bordeaux, 12 L 29.

for them to adhere. By so doing, it drew hostile fire from pro-Montagnard societies like Lons-le-Saunier, Toulouse, Périgueux, and Montauban. The latter took Amiens to task for fomenting jealousy of a Commune which "up to this point has been the aegis of liberty." It dismissed a departmental guard as being "contrary to republican principles" and accused Roland of "having employed vast sums to corrupt the people." Finally, Montauban vowed eternal fealty to the Paris Jacobins, the "foyer of courage and truth."[31]

One of the planks in Amiens' program was the eradication of the Revolutionary Tribunal, which had been set up on March 9–10 to judge "traitors, conspirators, and counterrevolutionaries" without appeal. Amiens notwithstanding, this action won much support from the clubs, especially those that may be classed as Leftist or Centrist. The Popular Society of Nîmes was euphoric. Condom applauded this legislation. Rouen and Vannes wanted revolutionary tribunals in every department. Strasbourg sought one for the Bas-Rhin.[32]

The formation of the Revolutionary Tribunal was one of several emergency decrees of early March. As far as the clubs were concerned, the most significant was the creation, on March 9, of a task force of eighty-two "representatives-on-mission." Deployed in groups of two, with responsibility for two departments, their principal assignment was to hasten the levy of three hundred thousand men ordered on February 24. But they also had virtually unlimited powers to requisition arms and goods, arrest suspects, and reform local administrations. The length of their missions was not fixed.

The list of eighty-two deputies was top-heavy with Montagnards. Danton, as early as March 10, voiced the suspicion that the Girondins had arranged this to give themselves a free hand in the Convention. The Paris society made similar allegations in a published statement of March 16, describing the March 9 decree as a "public calamity." Initially, some of the pro-Montagnard clubs

---

[31] COR, Limoges, L 829. Lévy-Schneider, *St.-André*, p. 244. PV: Perpignan, Apr. 12, 1793; Vannes, Apr. 19, 1793; Périgueux, Apr. 10, 1793; Lons-le-Saunier, Mar. 27, 1793.

[32] AN, C 252. Rouvière, *Gard*, III, 224. Chardon, *Rouen*, p. 114. PV, Vannes, Apr. 27, 1793.

also reacted negatively. Lille believed the decree of March 9 to be "impolitic" and considered calling for its repeal. Marseille voted to demand that the "brave Montagnards" retake their seats and let the clubs be responsible for recruitment. Tours and Tulle declared that the people wanted the members of the "Holy Mountain" to return to the Convention. Aix, in a published circular, whimpered that the eighty-two commissioners were the men that it "revered and trusted most," and it advocated special elections to name temporary replacements. Rouen adopted an analogous petition.[33]

If the appointment of a predominantly Montagnard slate of representatives-on-mission was the work of the Girondins, it was a prodigious blunder. For it gave the Montagnards a chance to undermine the Girondist base of support in the departments. Marseille, for one, dropped its opposition to the decree when the representative, Fréron, reminded it on March 27 that he was impowered to remove "gangrenous" officials and imprison "suspects." The next day, the Marseille club set up a committee to ferret out traitors. The arrests of the mayor and procurator followed. For about a month, until the sectional revolts, Marseille groaned under a Jacobin tyranny.[34]

Upon arriving in a city, it was customary for the representatives to pay a visit to the club. The clubbists arranged festive receptions. Preparations began days in advance. Honor guards escorted the *pères du peuple* to and from their lodgings. Bells rang, guns were fired, and buildings were illuminated. At the assembly hall the representatives were given bonnets of liberty, bouquets of flowers, fraternal embraces, medals, and other marks of esteem. Club spokesmen pledged to assist them in their labors.[35]

From the podia of the societies some of the representatives engaged in shameless politicking, praising the Left and denigrating the Right side of the Convention. Paganel and Garrau made it

[33] COR, Limoges, L 826. Wallon, *Fédéralisme*, II, 18. PV: Rouen, Apr. 15, 25, 1793; Marseille, Mar. 25, 1793; Lille, Mar. 24, 1793.

[34] Kennedy, *Marseilles*, pp. 121–123.

[35] Cf. Aulard, *Comité*, II, 500, 506; III, 23, 91, 110–111, 261; IV, 76, 554. Dubois, *Ain*, III, 84–85. Lacrocq, "Creuse," pp. 383–384. Forot, *Tulle*, p. 250. Lemaire, *Dunkerque*, pp. 364–365. PV: Pau, Apr. 6, 1793; Orthez, Apr. 9, 11, 1793; Châtillon-sur-Chalaronne, Mar. 26, Apr. 7, 1793; Gray, Apr. 1, 1793; Lectoure, Mar. 29–30, May 15, 1793; Vannes, Apr. 3, 1793.

their special duty to go to the clubs of the Lot-et-Garonne "in order to annihilate the reputations of some men who lead the public astray." Amar and Merlino ended their days at the clubs of the Ain and Vienne "instructing the people and disabusing them of fears . . . of an agrarian law, a dictatorship, and an Orléanist monarchy . . . on which the enemies of the republic play." At Cahors, Jeanbon St.-André and Elie Lacoste took to task the "adherents of a certain party"; whereupon, the club drew up an address cursing "those who have calumnied the Jacobins." At Guéret, Monestier sneered at Girondist charges that the deputies were under duress, pointing out that no "appellant" had yet been harmed, while the regicide Lepelletier had been murdered. Levasseur vaunted to the Nancy society that the "true friends of liberty" were those who had voted for the death of the king. In the Marseille club, Barras concluded that the Convention was in a position analogous to that of the Legislative Assembly before August 10. "The lone thing which can save it is for the people to rise a third time. Paris has need of an impulsion from Marseille." A little later, at Gap, Barras and Fréron accused Roland of being an accomplice of Dumouriez and of embezzling public funds. They urged the Gap society to denounce him to the Convention.[36]

According to the Girondist press and conservatives in the departments, the representatives-on-mission were guilty of preaching anarchy, the agrarian law, and hatred of the rich. Most of these reports were pure smoke, but there may have been some fire as well. Baille and Boisset, in Marseille, definitely instructed the club to take "money and horses from the selfish rich." Fouché, at the St.-Vincent society of Nantes, apparently advocated impositions on "rich merchants, hoarders, egoists, suspects, and self-styled moderates." At Annecy, Simond prophesied that a war of poor against rich was imminent. A representative at Sedan (St.-Just or Deville) supposedly exclaimed: "The Revolution is not over! Rise up, brave sansculottes. Let

---

[36] Aulard, *Comité*, II, 108–112, 532–533, III, 124. Tissot, *Grenoble*, pp. 89–90. Lacrocq, "Creuse," pp. 383–384. *ArchP*, May 6, June 11, 1793. *PF*, May 6, 1793. *CD*, Apr. 21, May 5, 1793. Troux, *Meurthe*, pp. 273–274. PV, Marseille, Mar. 28, 30, 1793. AN, DXL 21. Lévy-Schneider, *St.-André*, pp. 256–259.

your energy be sustained by a salutary mistrust of the rich . . . ! The rich in all times have been scourges of the poor!"[37]

The longer a representative tarried in one place, the more opportunity he had to make his influence felt. Levasseur, Maignet, Maribon-Montaut, and Soubrany turned the club of Metz into their command post and communications center. Similarly, Yzabeau and his entourage practically took over the society of Pau. He was accorded a chair by the president and, in effect, presided. His secretary, Sempronius Gracchus Villate, composed the letters and petitions of the club.[38]

When the representative-on-mission was a native son and club founder, like Duhem of Lille, his personal authority was magnified. One of the first actions of Duhem after his arrival was to wean the society of Lille away from the *Annales patriotiques* of Carra. By the end of May he was advocating the destruction of the Girondist "cabal" in the Convention. And after the fall of the Gironde, he gloated that the "patriotic party" was now in control of Paris.[39]

Duhem may be said to have hardened Lille's views rather than changing them. Much the same thing happened in the Jura where a native son, Prost, was assigned along with Leonard Bourdon. Prost and Bourdon powerfully reenforced the Montagnards who controlled the societies of Dole and Lons-le-Saunier. At their solicitation, Lons-le-Saunier compiled lists of departmental administrators who had "lost public confidence." And they, in turn, purged the District of Dole on the request of the club of that city. Later, in May and early June, when the Department of the Jura embraced federalism and denounced the two representatives, the clubs of Dole, Montmorot, and Lons-le-Saunier rallied to their defense and combatted the federalists.[40]

Some representatives carried out purges in the clubs. Bourges had its first "purification" after the arrival of Fauvre la Brunerie and Forrestier. Fayau and Gaston got the society of Foix to expel

[37] J.-P. Gross, *St.-Just: Sa politique et ses missions* (Paris, 1976), pp. 34–53. PV, Marseille, Mar. 28, 1793. COR, Niort, 3001. Lallié, *Nantes*, pp. 110–111. CD, Mar. 30, May 5, 1793. *PF*, May 4, 1793.

[38] Aulard, *Comité*, IV, 337–341, 375–376. PV, Pau, Apr. 6–May 25, 1793.

[39] PV, Lille, Apr. 16–June 2, 1793.

[40] *JD*, May 12, 23, 1793. COR: Reims; Poitiers, S 33. Libois, *Lons-le-Saunier*, pp. 136–154.

all "aristocrats" and retain only "sansculottes." Julien reported that of 800 former members of the Orléans club, only 130 remained, and their spirit was "Jacobin." According to one report, Mazade filled the Bayonne club with "newcomers" and "strangers." Tallien apparently engineered a purge at Tours, for it became strongly pro-Montagnard and renamed itself the Société épurée et régénérée des sansculottes. The club of Melun informed the Paris Jacobins that Isoré and Mauduyt had thrown out moderates and that now "good sansculottes" were in control. Melun not only resumed correspondence with Paris but wrote to the Convention to praise the "sacred Mountain" and demand the ouster of the "appellants."[41]

The representatives also radicalized the clubs by modifying their reading habits. Wherever he went, Yzabeau harped on the theme of the "corruption of public opinion" by perfidious journalists. Disturbed to find that the Pau society was still reading the *Patriote français*, he declared, in a speech of April 9, that this *journal* was inimical to the public welfare. Chastened, Pau voted to burn the *Patriote* and to send the ashes to Brissot. Again, at Orthez, on May 27, Yzabeau discoursed on the "infidelity" of journalists. The Orthez club voted to cancel all of its subscriptions and read only the official publications of the Convention.[42]

As has been seen, a great many clubs were formed or refounded by the representatives-on-mission. Among them, Lourdes was unique in being pro-Girondist. Most were nonaligned or pro-Montagnard. The first acts of the revitalized societies of Guéret, Aubusson, and Salins were to renew their affiliation with the Paris Jacobins. The new clubs of the Nièvre docilely accepted the arrest of Girondist deputies on June 2. In the Eure, where the Montagnard, Chasles, boasted of having founded "twelve truly patriotic societies," it was probably not coincidental that only Evreux, which was older and under the influence of Buzot, objected to the June coup.[43]

[41] P. Leveel, *La Mission de Tallien . . . en Indre-et-Loire* (Tours, 1958), p. 106. Lemas, *Cher*, p. 220. Arnaud, *Ariège*, pp. 380–381. Galland, "Cherbourg," p. 386. AN, C 255. *PF*, May 24, 1793. *JD*, Apr. 14, 30, 1793.
[42] PV: Pau, Orthez.
[43] LaCrocq, "Creuse," pp. 383–388. Chervy, "Guéret," pp. 435–436. *JD*, Apr. 30, May 10, June 7, 23, 1793. *ArchP*, June 14–July 13, 1793. A. Montier, "Le Dé-

Unquestionably, there were major shifts of opinion in the spring of 1793. In the Manche, where nearly all of the clubs had been anti-Montagnard in late 1792 and 1793, most had become Centrist by May. Movements from the Right to the Center also took place at Agen, Angoulême, Clairac, and Le Puy. Formerly middle-of-the road societies such as Troyes, Tours, Provins, Arcis-sur-Aube, and Le Mans became pro-Montagnard. Unfortunately, it is not always possible to ascertain whether the representatives-on-mission, or other factors, were responsible for these mutations.

The treason of Dumouriez appears to have been the final straw in causing Chalon-sur-Saône to declare against the Brissotins and to resume correspondence with the Paris club. Laval also voted in early April to reaffiliate with Paris, although it was shortly to reverse this decision. Poitiers, too, moved to the Left after Dumouriez's betrayal. Indeed, several pro-Montagnard societies wrote to congratulate Poitiers on a circular that it issued. Said Tonneins: "The route that we follow is truly fatiguing and laborious; but we prefer to scale the heights of the Mountain than run the risk of being sucked down into the muck of the marsh."[44]

The most dramatic and mysterious transformation occurred at Chartres, the home town of Brissot and Pétion. It had been one of the first clubs to cease affiliation with the Paris Jacobins in the autumn of 1792. And for months thereafter, it had been stridently anti-Montagnard. As late as April it congratulated the Convention on the arrest of Marat and accused the representatives-on-mission, Chasles and Guffroy, of "propagating the anarchistic principles of the *Ami du peuple*." But on June 2, at the first report of the coup in Paris, it hailed the Parisians, the Mountain, and the Commune and blew a "fraternal kiss" to Hébert. A little later the representative, Philippeaux, who was visiting Chartres, reported that it regarded Brissot and Pétion with "horror."[45]

One must not conclude from the foregoing that the representatives were uniformly successful in their proselytizing efforts.

---

partement de l'Eure . . . en juin 1793," *RF* (1896), pp. 128–155, 199–222. L. Dubrueil, "Evreux au temps du fédéralisme," *RF* (1925), pp. 244–263, 318–348.
[44] Carraz, "Chalon," p. 186. COR, Poitiers, S 27. PV, Laval, Apr. 1–20, 1793.
[45] *ArchP*, Apr. 24, June 26, July 3, 1793. *JD*, June 11, 1793. *PF*, Feb. 5, Mar. 2, 1793.

On the contrary, they often met stiff resistance. The club of Gap would not denounce Roland as Barras and Fréron had suggested. Vire, which had been warned by its correspondent-deputy, Doulcet, that the representative Duroy was an "imbecilic gosling of the Mountain," gave the latter a cold shoulder. Pocholle and Saladin were quite displeased by what they encountered at Amiens in late March and early April. In reports to Paris they asserted that the club of Amiens was infected by the "poison" of Gorsas. Amiens, in a published reply, stated that it had treated the two representatives with respect but had not tried to conceal its aversion to Marat and the "anarchists."[46]

An interesting confrontation occurred at St.-Flour.[47] When the representatives Faure and J.-B. Lacoste arrived here on April 22, they were honored in a session of the club; but the president let them know in no uncertain terms that the clubbists wanted an end to conflicts in the Convention and the promulgation of a constitution. Faure replied with a short but searing attack upon *gens de plume* and moderates. Then Lacoste crucified the "Vergniauds, . . . Brissots, . . . and especially the traitor Roland," and glorified Robespierre, Orléans, and Marat. The latter was described as "a true friend of the people" whose paper was "read daily by every patriot in Paris." As for the constitution for which so many people were clamoring, he dismissed it as "the work of the Girondins," of the "ignorant" and "devious" Condorcet. Like Barras at Marseille, he concluded that the "people must rise for a third time." And with the aim, perhaps, of cowing the citizens of St.-Flour, he announced that he was going to appoint a committee of six "true sansculottes" to draw up lists of suspects who would be deported or guillotined.

It must have taken great courage, after this, for the clubbist Vaissier to rise and castigate both factions in the Convention. Rather than casting suspicion on each other, he maintained, the deputies should concentrate on writing a constitution based upon the "rights of man." An exasperated Lacoste charged that Vaissier was in correspondence with an "appellant" deputy and de-

[46] AN, C 252. Aulard, *Comité*, II, 523–525; IV, 92–93, 248–249. Nicolle, *Vire*, pp. 232–233. *CD*, May 24, 1793.

[47] For what follows see Wallon, *Fédéralisme*, II, 280–286.

manded the letters so that the said deputy could be sent "to the guillotine." But Vaissier obstinately stood his ground, retorting that he corresponded with deputies of both the Plain and the Mountain and knew how to think for himself.

More pyrotechnics occurred on April 23 when a member named Goyon declared that there was no proof of misconduct on the part of the men whom Lacoste had impugned. He pleaded for an end to the factionalism that was tearing France apart. Thus challenged, Lacoste again expressed his attachment to Egalité, Marat, and Robespierre. Robespierre, he gushed, was as "pure as the light of the sun." He then said that "Moderates, Brissotins, Rolandistes, and Feuillants" had to be "stamped out mercilessly" if the Republic was to survive. Finally, he warned that the commission of sansculottes was already at work and arrests would soon begin of people suspected of "moderatism and Feuillantism." To this, Goyon inquired bravely if he was regarded as suspect simply because he had demanded a constitution. And another member said truculently that the entire society wanted a constitution and an end to dissension. Feigning weariness, Lacoste broke off the argument.

Another mission that had mixed results was that of François Chabot. Chabot, a curious blend of Capuchin monk, Jacobin zealot, and bon vivant, was clearly puffed up with a sense of self-importance at being a representative-on-mission. On route to the Tarn and Aveyron with his colleague, Bo, he stopped at Orléans and Blois to wallow in the adulation of these societies. He also paid a visit to Toulouse, a city where he had lived before the Revolution. On March 22 he persuaded the Toulouse club to denounce the "traitor," Dumouriez. However, as Dumouriez had not yet committed treason, Toulouse reversed this decision soon after Chabot's departure.[48]

When Chabot finally reached his assigned territory, he made up for lost time. In a letter to the Convention he boasted of working eighteen hours a day and visiting numerous clubs to give "instructions to the people." To the Paris Jacobins, he crowed that

---

[48] V. de Bonald, *François Chabot* (Paris, 1908), pp. 178–179. PV, Toulouse, Mar. 23, 1793.

all of the societies of the Tarn and Aveyron regarded the Right as traitors and looked upon Marat, Robespierre, and Danton as "the saviors of the country."[49] The minutes of the clubs attest to his zeal. Arriving at Castres on March 24, he immediately went to the club, lambasted Brissot, Gorsas, and other "perverters" of public opinion, and called for the extermination of "egoists and moderates." On April 1 at his prodding, Castres began a *scrutin épuratoire*, and a few days later it adhered to an address of Marseille against the "appellants."[50] Perhaps Chabot also visited Mazamet, for that society wrote to the Paris club to beg it to "sound the alarm against the Rolandists." Certainly, in late March and early April, he left his mark on the society of Rodez. Shortly after his departure it lobbied to have a public square renamed the Place de la Montagne. On April 14 he gave a demagogic oration at St.-Affrique. At one point he exclaimed: "Only the deputies of the Mountain are concerned about the welfare of the people."[51]

After returning briefly to Castres, Chabot scurried off to the Haute-Garonne, arriving at Toulouse on May 12. During his eleven-day stay the Toulouse club chased "moderates" and "Brissotins" from its midst. In addition, it decided on May 14, with his concurrence, to convoke a congress of all the representatives-on-mission in the Pyrénées region to discuss "measures which needed to be taken to save the Midi." Commissioners were dispatched into twelve neighboring departments to invite affiliates to send delegates to the congress.[52]

Some clubs accepted this invitation. Indeed, there were enough delegates in Toulouse by the twenty-third for the city government to be apprehensive that their presence might cause trouble. On the other hand, many societies refused to send delegates. Montpellier, which was anti-Montagnard, spearheaded the resistance. In a circular of May 17 it expressed loathing for Chabot and pointed out that his powers had been revoked by an April 30

[49] Aulard, *Comité*, II, 311; III, 348–351. *CD*, Apr. 24, 1793.

[50] Rossignol, *Gaillac*, pp. 89–90. PV, Castres, Mar. 24–Apr. 1, 1793. Bonald, *Chabot*, pp. 179–180. Rabaud, *Lasource*, pp. 201–205.

[51] *JD*, Apr. 17, 1793. Combes de Patris, *Rodez*, pp. 184–185. PV, St.-Affrique, Apr. 14, 1793.

[52] PV, Toulouse, May 12–14, 1793. Albert, *Haute-Garonne*, pp. 52–65. Bonald, *Chabot*, pp. 193–195.

decree of the Convention. In response the club of Toulouse circulated an address accusing the clubbists of Montpellier of being in league with the "Brissots, Salles, Rolands, and Buzots." It reissued its call for a congress.[53]

The club of Castelnaudary, which had the Montpellier and Toulouse circulars in its possession, debated the pros and cons of the issue on May 25. It finally decided to decline the invitation to the congress but to refrain from denouncing Chabot or the Toulouse society. In a circular to affiliates Castelnaudary explained that it was not participating because of its "fear of federalism and its desire for a republic, one and indivisible."[54]

Castelnaudary was fundamentally Centrist. Millau, by contrast, held much more conservative views and sharply opposed the congress. The commissar of Toulouse, who arrived there on May 23 and who made some critical remarks about the Récollets Society, was treated as an "apostle of anarchy" and forced to retire. In the discussion that ensued, several clubbists charged Chabot and the deputies of the Mountain with conspiring to place Orléans upon the throne. Ultimately, Millau sent a deputation to the department to demand the arrest of the commissar from Toulouse.[55]

St.-Affrique at first accepted Toulouse's invitation. On receiving the Montpellier circular and learning of the actions of Millau, however, it rescinded this decision and denounced Chabot to the Convention. The Republican Society of Nîmes gloated about the actions of Montpellier and Millau and, like St.-Affrique, accused Chabot of federalism. Auch, in a printed circular, likened Chabot to a "satrap" and expressed its abhorrence of the Paris Jacobins. Carcassonne was vexed that Conventionnels were "promenading about the departments at great cost, only in the hope of gathering sterile applause for themselves." Pau, Mont-de-Marsan, Lacaune, Montastruc, and even Castres, which was repenting its amorous dalliance with the Left, likewise issued anti-Chabot pro-

[53] COR: Poitiers, S 26; Josselin, L 1657; Montpellier, L 5549. PV, Montpellier, May 17, 1793. *ArchP*, May 25, 1793. Labroue, *Bergerac*, p. 254.
[54] COR: Bordeaux, 12 L 30; Niort, 3002. AN, DXL 20. PV, Pau, June 2, 4, 1793.
[55] COR, Montpellier, L 5544. PV, St.-Affrique, May 22–24, 1793.

nouncements. The club of Toulouse came under such criticism that on June 4 it published a "profession of faith" stating that it was "neither Maratist or Girondist."[56]

Clearly, then, in spite of early successes, Chabot's mission ended in failure. Evidence of a backlash against the representatives-on-mission is detectable elsewhere in May. After the departure of Fayau, the society of Tarascon (Ariège) accused him of "unrestrained Maratism." The Club des Capuchins-Mirabeau of Nantes griped that the representatives were behaving like "dictators." Bourg-en-Bresse bade the Convention to order them back to Paris and "avenge their innocent victims." After the June coup, Caen approved of the arrest of two representatives. And Rennes endorsed an address of its sections demanding the recall of the "proconsuls."[57]

[56] COR: Bordeaux, 12 L 30; Montpellier, L 5549. PV: St.-Affrique, May 22–24, 1793; Castres, June 14, 16, 1793.

[57] COR: Poitiers, S 33–34. Dubois, *Ain*, III, 227–229. *CD*, May 21, 1793. *ArchP*, June 13, 1793.

XXV

The Final Crisis

UNRUFFLED by the failure of its first campaign against the "appellants," the club of Marseille was to orchestrate a second movement in the spring of 1793. On March 16 it received letters from correspondents in Paris telling of the defeats in Belgium and placing the blame squarely on the Right wing of the Convention. That evening a series of speakers screamed for the recall of the "faithless deputies," and the club voted to send them an ultimatum. It was published the next day with adhesions from the sections and local officials. So strong was its language that it was censured by the Convention. "For too long," raged Marseille, "you have occupied posts for which you are unworthy. You remain only in the guilty hope of causing the downfall of the republic. . . . We owe the latest reverses to your treason. Depart cowardly and perjurous representatives! We recognize only the tutelary Mountain."[1]

Marseille assigned twenty-four "apostles of liberty" to hand-deliver copies to affiliates and to request adhesions. The greatest support came from the clubs of Provence. Fourteen are known to have adhered.[2] Apt, for example, fretted that if the rotten deputies were not removed, "the fruits of four years of Revolution would be spoiled." Arles professed loathing for the Right side of the Convention. Digne referred to the club of Marseille as the "Mountain of the Midi" and vowed to follow it always. Grasse, however, rejected Marseille's circular; and after weeks of rumination, La Garde-Freinet also decided *not* to give its adhesion.[3]

Outside Provence there was more diversity of opinion. Pre-

---

[1] PV, Marseille, Mar. 16–29, 1793. AN, C 250. *ArchP*, Mar. 21, 1793.

[2] St.-Chamas, St.-Andéol, Forcalquier, La Tour-d'Aigues, Lourmarin, Apt, St.-Tropez, Arles, Digne, Manosque, Aix, Lorgues, Villecroze, La Roquebrussane.

[3] COR: Riez; Marseille, L 2075. AN, DXL 18, 23. *JD*, Apr. 7, 1793. PV, Marseille, Apr. 2–4, 1793. Labroue, "Garde-Freinet," pp. 56–59.

dictably, Lyon, Strasbourg, Auxerre, and the Popular Society of Nîmes adhered; and over fierce opposition, Jouan le jeune persuaded Tonneins to acquiesce. Castres and Grenoble gave their adhesions at the insistence of three "apostles" from Marseille, but Grenoble later recanted. Marseille's address got applause at Lille, but no endorsement. Bergerac gave it two readings, but jettisoned it on learning of the Convention's censure. Tartas and Blaye tabled Marseille's motion without comment. Bourbonne rejected it as "subversive." Toulouse, after three days of debate, opted not to adhere. Vire and St.-Quentin manifested disapproval. Fleurance reaffirmed its respect for the appellants and vowed to "pursue the despots at the Jacobins to the depths of hell."[4]

The Paris Jacobins debated Marseille's motion on March 22 and 24, narrowly deciding against adhesion. There the movement might have stalled, had the treason of Dumouriez not driven the "mother society" to extremes. On April 5, with Marat presiding, it approved a circular to affiliates that was no less than a call to war against the Girondins:

> Friends! We are betrayed. . . . The center of counterrevolution is in the government, in the Convention. . . . Rise up!. . . All popular societies must. . . flood the Convention with petitions manifesting a formal wish for the immediate recall of all its unfaithful members who have betrayed their duty in not wanting the death of the king, and especially those who have led astray a great number of their colleagues. Such deputies are traitors, royalists, or fools.[5]

The publication of this fiery manifesto was followed by demonstrations in Paris. Popular agitators spoke darkly of the need for a "third insurrection." One of the sections called on April 8 for the indictment of the "Vergniauds, Gensonnés, Guadets, Brissots, and other accomplices of Dumouriez." Then, on April

---

[4] *JD*, Apr. 19, 1793. *CD*, May 5, 1793. *PF*, Apr. 1, 1793. Aulard, *Jacobins*, IV, 126. Rouvière, *Gard*, III, 224. Riffaterre, *Lyon*, I, 43–49. Labroue, *Bergerac*, p. 238. AN, DXL 18. PV: Croix-Rousse, Mar. 31, 1793; Castres, Apr. 10–12, 1793; Tonneins, Apr. 10–11, 1793; Lille, Apr. 13, 1793; Tartas, Mar. 25, 1793; Bourbonne, Apr. 3, 1793; Blaye, Apr. 2, 1793; Toulouse, Mar. 27–29, 1793.

[5] *JD*, Mar. 24, 26, 1793. Copies of the circular abound.

15, delegates from thirty-five sections, accompanied by officials from the Commune, appeared at the Convention, accused twenty-two deputies of treason, and demanded their ouster. Although the petitioners were rebuffed, the "twenty-two," as they came to be styled, were marked men.

In the clubs the circular of April 5 added impetus to the drive begun by Marseille. Limoges, which had earlier tabled Marseille's proposition, voted on April 14 to send a letter of adhesion to the Convention. Lyon smote the appellants afresh in a petition of April 11. Auxerre and Tonnerre demanded their recall in printed circulars of April 16. Reims concurred with Auxerre and Tonnerre. Tulle read the Jacobin circular on April 19. The next day it petitioned the Convention to do something about "the perfidious representatives who voted for the appeal to the people and who wish to reestablish the monarchy." La Charité-sur-Loire (April 21) confided to Poitiers that it now believed that the "deputies who voted for the appeal to the people have contributed to the reverses that we have suffered and emboldened the traitor Dumouriez." In late April, the clubbists of Munster, Lons-le-Saunier, St.-Sever, St.-Jean-de-Luz, and St.-Chamond also signified their solidarity with their "brothers from Marseille and Paris."[6]

Throughout May demands for the unseating of the appellants flowed in to the Convention. Sedan referred to them as "traitors" and "cowards." Melun said that they had been "corrupted by the gold of the modern-day Philips." Chalon-sur-Saône declared that at long last it had recognized that "the foyer of counterrevolution is in the Convention," and that the appellants "are traitors or fools." St.-Martory lauded the "unshakeable Mountain" and asked the "twenty-two" to step down voluntarily. Limoux, which now believed that the Mountain should "dominate over all parties," also begged the "twenty-two" to resign for the good of the Republic.[7]

[6] COR: Reims; Limoges, L 825; Poitiers, S 27; Josselin, L 1657. *JD*, Apr. 30, May 1, 3, 1793. Riffaterre, *Lyon*, I, 43–45. Forot, *Tulle*, p. 251. PV: Limoges, Apr. 10–14, 1793; Lons-le-Saunier, Apr. 12–22, 1793; Tonneins, May 1, 1793; Boiscommun, Apr. 18, 1793.

[7] COR: Reims; Bordeaux 12 L 30; Montpellier, L 5538. Carraz, "Chalon," p. 186. AN, DXL 18, 20, and C 255. Wallon, *Fédéralisme*, I, 172, 357. Dubois, *Ain*, III, 231.

For some clubs the unseating of the appellants was not enough. Strasbourg stormed at the Convention: "The sections of Paris have pointed out the partisans of Dumouriez to you; yet, they still breathe! . . . As long as you do not arrest Brissot, Vergniaud, and consorts, you will not have our full confidence." La Rochelle exclaimed: "You have put one on trial because of his exaggerated views [Marat]. Now it is time to judge the others accused of conspiracy. Act on those denounced by the sections." Metz fulminated: "If odious agitators like Brissot, Guadet, Vergniaud, and their consorts persist in blocking your deliberations, send them before the Revolutionary Tribunal." Langres, which recognized only the Mountain, desired "definitive and final measures" against the "corrupt members of the Convention." Moulins and St.-Germain-en-Laye also howled for the prosecution of the "traitorous deputies."[8]

The extreme stand taken by the Paris club in early April provoked a counterstroke from the Right in the Convention. Taking advantage of the absence of the Montagnard representatives-on-mission, Guadet, on April 12, read a copy of the April 5 Jacobin circular and moved that Marat be cited before the courts. After a vigorous debate, Guadet's motion was approved on April 13. On the day of the trial (April 24), however, the Commune and the sections organized huge demonstrations in Marat's favor. The Revolutionary Tribunal, which was packed with Montagnards, unanimously acquitted him; and he was carried in triumph through the streets and back to his seat in the Convention.

One fact made clear by Marat's trial was that, at last, he had a small following among the clubs. Auxerre described his arrest as a "public calamity" and implored the sections of Paris "to preserve the life of the most vigorous defender of liberty." Lons-le-Saunier charged the appellants with trying to silence Marat so that they could carry out their schemes to reestablish royalty. Ingouville looked upon Marat as a "martyr to liberty." Bagnols evinced "sweet satisfaction" at his exoneration. Chalon-sur-

---

[8] COR: Reims; Poitiers, S 34; Niort, 3003. *JD*, Apr. 23, May 1, 17, 1793. Heitz, *Strasbourg*, pp. 259–262. AN, DXL 19. Wallon, *Fédéralisme*, I, 166; II, 402. PV: Pau, May 21, 1793; Lille, May 30, 1793.

Saône and Limoges likewise congratulated Marat on his triumph.[9] It was also apparent, however, that the vast majority of clubs still regarded Marat with abhorrence. Many were jubilant about the indictment of April 13. Libourne said that "all good citizens" applauded it. Bayeux termed it a "magnificent act of justice." Alès chortled that Marat would finally get the penalty that he merited. Sées' only criticism was that the indictment had not come sooner. Châteaulin yearned for the prosecution of the "Duhems and Robespierres" as well. Vannes was upset at the Paris Commune for defending Marat. The Republican Society of Nîmes seethed with fury when "the execrable monster was acquitted by the tribunal of blood." After learning of the verdict, Cherbourg nonetheless praised the Convention for rendering the indictment and urged it to continue to combat the "anarchists."[10]

Even at this late date (April–May 1793), many clubs remained fundamentally moderate. This was evident from the numerous resolutions of support for the beleaguered Girondist deputies. Nancy reassured Salle that he was still "esteemed." La Flotte defended the deputy Dechezeaux. Sées and Alençon expressed confidence in Valazé. Lisieux encouraged Doulcet to "continue to combat the criminals." Evreux reaffirmed its respect for Buzot, Gensonné, Vergniaud, Brissot, and Pétion.[11] Brive, St.-Yriex, and Vire rendered homage to the virtue of the "twenty-two" and the appellants.[12] And several clubs warned that their recall would lead to civil war. One of these, Lacaune, reminded Frenchmen of the fate of Poland. Orgelet contended that the Convention was indivisible, but added that it knew which deputies would be "judged worthy" if the people were consulted.[13]

[9] Carraz, "Chalon," p. 186. *JD*, Apr. 19, May 28, 1793. PV: Ingouville, Apr. 22, 1793; Limoges, May 1, 1793; Lons-le-Saunier, Apr. 19–22, 1793.

[10] AN, DXL 19–23. BN, Lb 40, 1079. Rouvière, *Gard*, III, 243, 251. CD, Apr. 26, May 6, 10, 1793. PV: Honfleur, Apr. 24, 1793; Vannes, Apr. 27–30, 1793.

[11] Troux, *Meurthe*, p. 349. CD, Apr. 29, May, 17, 1793. PF, Apr. 30, May 8, 1793. *AP*, May 8, 1793.

[12] AN, C 258, DXL 19. COR, Poitiers, S 37. Wallon, *Fédéralisme*, I, 168–169; II, 67–68.

[13] AN, C 254, DXL 22. Wallon, *Fédéralisme*, II, 461. *M*, May 23, 1793. Dubois, *Ain*, III, 232.

Defense of the Girondins was often coupled with attacks upon the Montagnards. Evreux asserted that Robespierre must be "wicked" or "insane." St.-Mihiel and Alès shuddered at his "profound villainy" and "excesses." The Club Mirabeau of Nantes accused Danton and Robespierre of distorting the facts: "They say that Brissot and Condorcet are royalists, but Brissot and Condorcet demanded a republic before them. . . . Brissot and Gensonné have been reproached for being friends and correspondents of Dumouriez, but was not Danton also a friend of the perfidious conspirator?" In words reminiscent of those of Nantes, the club of Dax also cautioned affiliates to beware of the deceitful lies of the so-called holy Mountain.[14]

The Paris club was subjected to harsh criticism. On April 10–11, the Department of the Gironde seized some of its letters and published them as proof of a "conspiracy." The Republican Society of Nîmes spun out this thread further after some mail from Paris to the Popular Society fell into its hands by a "lucky chance." In a circular of April 29 it warned affiliates: "You can see that the factionalists of our city . . . hold to the plan of conspiracy formulated by the Jacobins. While the proscribed deputies were to be liquidated in Paris, the same thing was to be done in the departments to those whom the Maratists have designated as counterrevolutionaries, and who are, nonetheless, pure patriots." Beholding the Paris club made the Republican Society "think involuntarily of the Roman Empire overrun by hordes from the north, and the once-flourishing kingdom of China subjugated by Tartars."[15]

Feeling against the Paris Commune and sections likewise ran high. The club of Auvillars referred to the petition of April 15 as a "vile" document. St.-Yriex regarded it as a diversion "to save the head of the most atrocious of men" (Marat). Brive, Is-sur-Tille, Villefranche (Rhône), Oloron, and St.-Girons demanded the arrest and execution of its authors. St.-Ambroix (Gard), Bar-le-Duc, and Moyaux wanted the "evil croakings" from the gal-

---

[14] AN, DXL 20–21. COR, Bordeaux, 12 L 29. *CD*, May 10, 21, 1793. Wallon, *Fédéralisme*, I, 167–169.

[15] Rouvière, *Gard*, III, 180–182, 242–249, 262–264. *CD*, May 5–8, 1793.

leries to be silenced.[16] Lacaune, in a circular of May 15 (to which Bourg adhered), accused the Commune of "actions bordering on tyranny." St.-Quentin scolded the Conventionnels: "Do not allow a rebel Commune to dictate the laws. Forbid the galleries to trouble your meetings. Do not permit Paris to tyrannize." A widely circulated April 19 address of the Commune of Caen, adhered to by the club, sounded once again the theme of the deputy Lasource: "France does not consist of Paris alone. It is made up of eighty-four departments." Caen went on to say that the Convention should leave the "birthplace of liberty" if it could not stifle the "anarchists." Inspired by this circular, Vire, Morlaix, and the Republican Society of Nîmes also advised the Convention to quit Paris.[17]

Another important circular was published on April 22 by "the Commune and united popular societies of Nantes." This circular (which the popular society of St.-Vincent disavowed in early May) demanded nothing less than the suppression of the Commune and sections of Paris. In addition, the Nantais alleged that the authors of the April 15 petition were the same men who had fomented the revolt in the Vendée.[18] The Récollets Society reprinted the Nantes address, and a number of clubs joined Nantes in threatening the "anarchists" with reprisals and offering assistance to the Convention. Alençon, together with local officials, vowed for the "hundredth time" not to let the factionalists intimidate the deputies. Clairac warned the Parisians that they would pay with "their heads" for any harm that befell the Conventionnels. Bras promised to "fly" to Paris if need be. Quimper spoke of raising another contingent of fédérés. Montpellier advised sister societies to be prepared to send forces to Paris at short notice.[19]

[16] AN, C 255, DXL 19–20. Wallon, *Fédéralisme*, I, 521; II, 385. COR, Bordeaux, 12 L 29. *ArchP*, Apr. 27, 1793.

[17] AN, C 254, DXL 18–19, 22. Dubois, *Ain*, III, 232. *PF*, Apr. 30, 1793. *CD*, Apr. 29, May 16, 1793. Wallon, *Fédéralisme*, I, 158–164. Nicolle, *Vire*, pp. 236–239. COR, Josselin.

[18] Lallié, *Nantes*, pp. 112–113. COR: Bordeaux, 12 L 30, 32; Poitiers, S 34.

[19] AN, C 254, 258, DXL 19–20, 23. Wallon, *Fédéralisme*, I, 168–174. *PF*, June 1, 1793. *CD*, May 31, 1793. PV, Montpellier, May 2, 1793. COR: Bordeaux, 12 L 32; Poitiers, S 37.

As in the past, the Récollets Society was the flagship of the pro-
Girondist clubs. At the end of April, it circulated a strongly
worded address of the twenty-eight sections of Bordeaux. Then,
on May 4–5, it received two oft-quoted letters from the deputy
Vergniaud. In the first, datelined "under the knife," Vergniaud
reproached the society for "abandoning" him. The second
begged the Bordelais to be prepared to combat a coup by the Parisians: "Hold yourself ready! If I am forced to, I will ascend to
the rostrum and call upon you to defend us. . . . If we perish,
Bordeaux can still save the Republic."[20]

These epistles caused the sections of Bordeaux to draw up an
address in which they threatened to send fédérés to Paris and
vowed to remain "Girondins . . . up to the tomb." The Récollets
Society circulated copies with a covering letter to affiliates, stating: "Rise up! Rise up! The time has come!" Eight clubs (Caen,
Pau, Libourne, Annonay, Créon, Montpellier, Narbonne, and
Carcassonne) are known to have adhered to this address. However, Agen, which had previously favored a departmental guard
for the Convention, now told Bordeaux that its fédérés would
better serve France in the Vendée. Metz printed a rebuttal, and
Poitiers maintained that Bordeaux's criticism of the Parisians was
unjust.[21]

Moderate clubs like the Récollets Society and the Republican
Society of Nîmes were heartened by news from Marseille.[22] In
that city there had always been a powerful undercurrent of resentment against the club. As the latter became more radical and
imperious, resentment mushroomed into revolt. In March and
April, moderate republicans, secret monarchists, and disillu-
sioned former club members had gradually taken over the sectional assemblies. Then, they had formed a governing body, or
General Committee of the sections, and on April 28 had forced
the representatives-on-mission, Baille and Boisset, to flee. Some
of the club's leaders escaped with the representatives. The re-

<hr/>

[20] Forrest, *Bordeaux*, p. 99.
[21] COR: Bordeaux, 12 L 29–33, 38–40; Poitiers, S 26, 29, 37. *CD*, May 17,
1793. *PF*, May 21, 1793. BN, Lb 40, 908. AN, DXL 18. Wallon, *Fédéralisme*, II,
462, 567.
[22] COR, Montpellier, L 5545. PV, Montpellier, May 19, 23, 1793. *CD*, May
23, 1793. *PF*, May 2, 1793.

mainder were arrested between May 14 and May 20, on orders of the General Committee.[23]

At the first news of the "revolt of the sections," many Provençal clubs rallied to the defense of the "mother society" of Marseille. Salon, for example, convoked a "central committee" of the clubs of the Bouches-du-Rhône. Toulon implored the people of Marseille to close the sections and expel "the selfish rich" who dominated them. And Arles complained to the Convention about the persecution of "true patriots."[24] By the end of May, however, resistance was crumbling. Aix, Digne, and Apt shamefully announced that they had "seen the light" and praised the sectionnaires. Meetings of some societies ceased entirely.[25]

It is possible that the sectional revolt in Marseille and the federalist pronouncements of Bordeaux, Nantes, and Caen inspired the Girondist deputies to make a last effort to defang opponents in Paris. On May 18, Guadet proposed that the Commune be dissolved and that alternate deputies (elected the previous September) be assembled in Bourges so that they could assume direction of the government if circumstances warranted. The Convention did not adopt these motions, but it did vote to create a twelve-member commission to investigate the conduct of the Commune and sections of Paris. On May 24, this Girondist-dominated commission ordered the arrest of Varlet (one of the firebrands at the Cordeliers Club) and Hébert (the assistant procurator of the Commune). These arrests were the immediate cause of the great uprisings of May 29–June 2.

In the departments moderate clubs cheered on the Girondists. During the second half of May, at least twenty societies published and circulated addresses demanding the punishment of the "vultures" in the galleries, the Paris Jacobins, and the "rebel city."[26] Some also announced their intention of forming forces of fédérés.

---

[23] Kennedy, *Marseilles*, pp. 123–127.

[24] COR, Marseille, L 2075.

[25] Ponteil, "Antipolitiques," p. 270. PV: Vitrolles, May 13, 1793; Violès, May 19, 1793; Méthamis, May 19, 1793; Jonquières, May 26, 1793; Malemort-du-Comtat, May 26, 1793. COR, Bordeaux, 12 L 29.

[26] Bourg, Rouen, Caen, Nantes, Angers, Castelnaudary, Carcassonne, Honfleur, St.-Valery-sur-Somme, Annonay, Nîmes (Republican Society), Clairac, Créon, Libourne, Falaise, Briançon, Montpellier, Narbonne, Lourdes, Oloron, Bagnères.

Much attention was given to Guadet's proposal, especially after the Jura Department, on May 24, announced that it would send its alternates to Bourges under military escort. Dole denounced the administrators of the Jura, but Bourg and Nantes praised their courage. Le Vigan and Verdun admonished the whole Convention to go to Bourges and surround itself with an "imposing force."[27]

Several clubs, which had not yet done so, broke off relations with the "mother society." Avallon adopted such a resolution on May 24 after its deputy-correspondent, Boilleau, called the Jacobins "murderers." Auch (May 25) proclaimed that it execrated the Paris club and all "societies which wish to erect tyrannies." Lourdes ended its affiliation on May 28. Blaye, Lorient, and Le Havre seriously considered such action. St.-Hippolyte reaffirmed an earlier decision not to associate with Paris. At the club of Rouen moderates carried out a kind of coup on May 23, securing the approval of an address against the "criminal horde" which was tyrannizing the Convention. The Republican Society of Nîmes wanted to organize an anti-Montagnard network of clubs. "We need more correspondence," it said in a circular of May 24. "We have absolutely ceased all liaison with Maratist societies. . . . We offer to fraternize with all those which speak out energetically against the anarchists. . . . Give us a list of such societies in your region."[28]

Whether the Republican Society was able to obtain a list of the clubs that shared its principles, we do not know. I have compiled such a listing, however; and it indicates that on the eve of the June coup, 126 societies inclined toward the Girondins. In contrast, 195 leaned toward the Montagnards. (See appendix G.) Although no region was absolutely loyal to either "party," Girondist societies predominated in the west-southwest. The southeast, center, and north/northeast were fundamentally pro-Montagnard.

Quite obviously, the Montagnards had won back considerable

---

[27] Wallon, *Fédéralisme*, I, 165; II, 171–172. AN, DXL 20–21. Pionnier, *Verdun*, pp. 328, lxii–lxiii. Dubois, *Ain*, III, 225–233.

[28] COR: Niort, 3005; Bordeaux, 12 L 32; Poitiers, S 34. PV: Le Havre, May 26–30, 1793; Rouen, May 23–26, 1793; Lorient, Apr. 18–May 21, 1793; Avallon, May 24, 1793; Blaye, Apr. 17–May 25, 1793; Lourdes, May 28, 1793; St.-Hippolyte, May 23, 1793.

ground since December. Lest one give too much credence to this data, however, a few caveats are in order. First, the results are based on fragmentary evidence, often only a single letter or petition. Second, many societies did a good bit of waffling, making an accurate placement difficult. Third, most of the Provençal societies were reduced to pulp by the sectional revolt; at the decisive moment of the June coup, therefore, pro-Girondist clubs might have enjoyed a slight numerical advantage. Finally, it should be stressed that "Girondist" societies almost always disclaimed attachment to any party. Only the "Montagnard" clubs were likely to boast of being such.

The nebulosity of Revolutionary party labels is further demonstrated by the fact that some of the clubs listed in appendix G as "Montagnard" and "Girondist" joined sister societies in a massive campaign for unity in April and May. The motivation behind this crusade was the military crisis facing France. Credit for initiating it cannot be precisely fixed. Several clubs (including Gray, Rennes, Brest, Honfleur, and Lodève) printed and circulated letters to the Convention in late March and early April, demanding a rapprochement of all patriots. Oddly, the circular that had the most palpable effect upon the network was published by little Ganges about April 22. The covering letter asked affiliates to urge the deputies to cease their personal disputes and write a constitution. The address itself chastened the feuding parties for causing factionalism to develop "in all the clubs and administrative bodies of the departments. . . . For eight months you have been meeting. We are beginning to think that you want to meet eternally."[29]

In the next six weeks, more than 140 petitions of this type were sent to the Convention.[30] At least 26 were printed and circulated.[31] Béziers voted to send a petition every day containing just the words: "La Constitution!" Nancy got its department to write

[29] *JD*, Apr. 9, 1793. Labroue, *Bergerac*, pp. 240–246. AN, C 252, DXL 20. Wallon, *Fédéralisme*, I, 509. PV: Montpellier, May 2, 1793; Le Havre, Apr. 20–22, 1793; Bourbonne, Mar. 30, Apr. 28, May 1, 1793; Rouen, May 5, 1793.

[30] See AN, C 249–258, DXL 18–23. See also Wallon, *Fédéralisme*, I, II.

[31] Those of Belley, Libourne, Besançon, Epinal, St.-Flour, Le Puy, Castelnaudary, Pau, St.-Germain-en-Laye, Villeneuve (L-et-G), Valence, Anduze, Metz, Castres, St.-Tropez, Rennes, Lamballe, Angers, Nancy, Dunkerque, Périgueux, Carcassonne, Toulon, St.-Malo, Le Trévoux, and Rochefort.

one and to have it delivered by commissioners to the societies of several nearby departments. Three of the most interesting came from Le Trévoux, Libourne, and St.-Germain-en-Laye. These clubs believed that the solution to the party strife was the election of enough new deputies to double the size of the Convention.[32]

It is apparent from a perusal of the unity petitions of April and May, that many clubs were weary of the Revolution and longed for the restoration of order. Moreover, their confidence in the Convention had reached a low ebb. They scored the Conventionnels for "federalizing" the republic with the enemy "at the gates." And a few went so far as to command the deputies to "quit" their posts if they lacked the courage to "save the fatherland." All deplored party spirit, declaring that it had no place "in the Temple of the Laws." Girondin, Rolandist, Maratist, Brissotin, Mountain, Marsh, Plain, Right, Left, Feuillant, and even Jacobin were categorized as "odious" and "ridiculous" denominations. As usual, lessons were dredged from history. The Convention was reminded that internal dissension had destroyed Carthage, and that party spirit had resulted in the restoration of the monarchy in seventeenth-century England. The metaphor of a "gladiatorial arena" remained popular. St.-Jean-de-Luz composed a parable about a "fertile domain" that was taken over by brambles because the farmers could not work in harmony.

A lot of clubs were nonplussed by the charges and countercharges of the rival groups. One that was deeply divided on the subject, Condrieu, decided to write to Joseph Servan, its founder, to ask for his opinion about the "two parties in the Convention which have declared war on each other." Servan, who had become an officer in the Army of the Pyrenees after leaving the Ministry of War, sent a vacillating response from Toulouse on April 14. While admitting that the Mountain had "accumulated damning evidence against Brissot and the deputies of the Gironde," he added that he had been acquainted with the members of this "party" for ten years and was reluctant to believe them guilty of treason. Although he "had never really known the party of the Mountain," he also expressed doubt that it had

---

[32] PV, Pau, June 12, 1793; Béziers, May 30, 1793. Besson, *Libourne*, p. 227. Troux, *Meurthe*, pp. 350–353. Baumont, "Lunéville," p. 351. Denis, *Toul*, p. 25. Dubois, *Ain*, III, 225–230. Wallon, *Fédéralisme*, I, 367.

"planned to assassinate the 'Marsh' on March 10." In other words, he refused to commit himself, and he advised his "brothers" to be cautious and let events enlighten them.[33]

Poor Servan! Once a staunch and self-confident Revolutionary, he was now in an agony of uncertainty. His story (and that of the clubbists of Condrieu) must have been replayed a thousand times in 1793. A decisive moment of the Revolution had come. Jacobins everywhere were being forced to choose between the Mountain and the Gironde. Only the most highly principled and headstrong had already committed themselves; the majority, like Servan, were bewildered and anxious. Instinctively, perhaps, they perceived that their decision might mean the difference between life and death, advancement or disgrace.

[33] COR and PV, Condrieu.

XXVI

Conclusion

THE CLUBBISTS, who were fond of scientific metaphors, sometimes likened the Paris Jacobins to the sun and its affiliates to planets and moons. This is a pleasing analogy, albeit a deceptive one insofar as the period from October 1791 to June 1793 is concerned. The Paris Jacobins, far from being a controlling force, at times provided little direction. Great provincial clubs like the Récollets Society of Bordeaux were autonomous, pulsating centers of influence. And during the Convention the views of some affiliates collided so sharply with those of the "mother society" that the system almost disintegrated.

More than 1,500 clubs filled the Jacobin firmament. They were most numerous in the Midi. But all departments were represented; and societies could be found in the occupied territories, in overseas colonies, and in foreign cities as well. Only a small percentage operated continuously. On the contrary, the network was in a perpetual state of flux as clubs went into and out of operation. There were many factors—including weather conditions, fieldwork, loss of key leaders, local troubles, and "revolutionary burn-out"—that caused societies to function irregularly. But, as a rule, the club movement expanded during national crises and contracted when these crises subsided.

The Legislative Assembly commenced with the clubs sadly reduced in quantity and suffering from budgetary shortfalls, poor attendance, boredom, and low spirits. However, two unpopular vetoes, fears of war, the revitalization of the correspondence committee of the Paris Society, and the appointment of pro-Jacobin ministers acted as stimulants in late 1791 and early 1792. March through August 1792, the crucial period in which war broke out and the monarchy was overthrown, was characterized by intense activity. Scores of societies were born or reformed. Conventions of club representatives took place in many areas, and an interesting, but unsuccessful, attempt was made to establish a system of "central committees," or departmental governing bodies.

In the late summer and autumn of 1792 a downturn in activity occurred. New foundations in certain areas were offset by the near destruction of the club movement in the war-torn north. The correspondence committee of the "mother society" was practically defunct for two months. In France proper, complacency set in with the subsidence of the foreign menace. The party strife in Paris also had ill-effects upon the clubs.

However, the entry of England and Spain into the war, defeats in Belgium, the revolt of the Vendée, and the treason of Dumouriez caused fear to become airborne and dissipated the lethargy that overhung the network. The number of operating clubs in March–May 1793 swelled to totals equalling or exceeding those of the previous spring. Many societies were founded or disturbed from hibernation by the representatives-on-mission. Unfortunately, the network was riven by factionalism, and on the eve of the Federalist rebellions, there were lots of closures.

The number of club members also fluctuated. Much of the expansion of membership in the middle years was due to the foundation and rapid growth of "new" societies. Admissions generally slowed in "old" clubs. Both old and new societies experienced losses of personnel due to enrollments for military service, exclusions, schisms, and purges. Entries and exits, and the common practice of enrolling nonresidents, make it difficult to calculate the degree of citizen involvement. It was probably about 2.5 percent, but the percentage of militants was far smaller.

The first clubs were staffed and run by the bourgeoisie, and as late as May 1793, some remained quite elitist. Toward the end of the Constituent, however, a few began to lower their dues and admit passive citizens. More did so in the "middle years," especially in the egalitarian frenzy that followed the fall of the monarchy. As a result, the percentage of members who were farmers, artisans, and urban workers ascended, while the middle-class professions dropped. The greatest decline was suffered by the haute bourgeoisie. Indeed, in some places the well-to-do largely abandoned the societies. Add to these trends the pressure applied by the "people" who attended the public sessions, and the sum is that the *average* club had changed considerably in composition and comportment by 1793. Even in the most democratic societies, however, the leaders were still likely to be lawyers, doctors, teachers, priests, or small merchants.

Since the 1920s Revolutionary historiography in France has been dominated by Leftists and Marxists who have stressed economics and the class struggle. In propounding and defending the "orthodox canon," they have sometimes gone to extremes and been guilty of a kind of intellectual tyranny. Consequently, scholars like François Furet are to be commended for challenging their dogmas and refocusing attention on politics, psychology, and other factors. It is probable that the revolutionaries were often actuated by motives unfathomable even to themselves. Nonetheless, my own studies of the clubs have led me to the conclusion that there is much truth in the radical-Marxist view of the Revolution, that class conflict was, indeed, a major determinant.

One of the most interesting facets of the middle years was the increase in incidence of antirich pronouncements. In early 1792 a number of societies began to babble angrily about a newly emerging "bourgeois aristocracy." This note, once struck, beat on the air like a hammer-clang. By early 1793 criticism of the rich had become widespread and malevolent. Granted, envy and dislike of the ultra-affluent did not arise *ex nihilo* in 1792–93. But conditions in Revolutionary France aggravated these natural, human emotions. There was a rise in class consciousness. A perception developed that the rich had "benefited most from the Revolution" but were giving little in return. In addition, plutocrats and speculators were thought to be responsible for the country's economic and fiscal woes, and to be profiting from the misery of the people.

Class consciousness was one of the main reasons why there were often two or more prorevolutionary, "Jacobin" clubs in the same township. In 1790–91 numbers of lower-class organizations were formed because of the discriminatory practices of the bourgeois, affiliated clubs. More of these groups appeared in 1792–93 as a result of schisms. Although they went by many names, collectively they may be styled "popular societies." Their leaders were normally lesser men of the "moyenne bourgeoisie" who would have been nonentities in the elite, bourgeois clubs.

Typically, the popular and bourgeois societies became rivals.

During the Convention the popular societies had a definite propensity to be pro-Montagnard. The elitist clubs, where they still existed, were anti-Montagnard. These patterns of behavior, in my opinion, lend credence to the contentions of radical-Marxist historians that there were social as well as political differences between the Girondins and Montagnards.

Class conflict cast a particularly dark shadow over the southeast. Almost invariably, in the small towns of this region, one could find hostile factions which corresponded more or less closely to the social groupings of "bourgeoisie" and "people." Their feuds were envenomed by the brutal interventionism of Marseille. The radicals who dominated the club of Marseille waged a veritable war against the "bourgeois aristocracy" of Provence.

The *crise des subsistances* placed great strains upon the social fabric and deeply troubled the clubs. They seemed genuinely distressed by the plight of the poor, and many feared that shortages and high prices would detonate a popular explosion that would endanger the social order. Thus, they labored mightily to alleviate the crisis. Suspected profiteers were denounced. Money was collected for the purchase of food and fuel. Consumers were urged to restrict their consumption of scarce commodities. Proposals were made to ban "luxury" items. And the cultivation of new crops like potatoes was promoted.

In the palmy days of the Constituent the clubs were nearly unanimous in their endorsement of legislation instituting free circulation of grains. During the Legislative Assembly, despite growing anxiety about high prices, shortages, and the "sortie" of grains, this support generally held. In late 1792, however, gaps appeared in the formerly serried ranks. Some clubs began to seek price controls and other regulatory laws. The most outspoken advocates of regulation, at first, were usually the pro-Montagnard "popular societies." Perhaps they were more closely attuned to the wishes of the people. By the spring of 1793, however, almost all of the clubs had concluded that free trade in grains had not worked, that the gravity of the crisis made price-fixing a necessity.

The clubs also spent countless hours discussing the *crise monétaire* and devising measures to combat it. Up to the spring of 1793 they consistently expressed confidence in the assignats, the paper notes created by the Constituent. Indeed, they called for new emissions of assignats in small denominations as an antidote for the shortage of base coins. Merchants and farmers were encouraged to accept assignats in trade, and members took oaths not to profit from their sale or exchange, or to discredit them.

The monetary crisis, like the crise des subsistances, eventually forced a retreat from economic liberalism. In early 1792 the Lorient club launched a campaign for the repeal of the resolution making the money trade free like all others. During the Convention there was a second flurry of petitions against this resolution. This time, the petitions were rife with attacks upon the rich and demands for the death penalty for those who trafficked in assignats. Support was strong for the decree of April 11, 1793, which specified that trade was to be in assignats alone.

The clubs expressed repugnance for "agrarian laws" and defended property ownership as a sacred right. Yet, they voiced concern about extremes of wealth and poverty in France; and for this reason, they favored the modification of laws and customs relating to inheritance. All approved of the abolition of primogeniture, and the majority endorsed the principle of *égalité des partages*, equal sharing of the parental estate among all children. They rationalized that the head of the household was merely the trustee of the family fortune, and that it was contrary to natural law and to God's law to favor one child over another. Moreover, they cited history to prove that in the long run, French commerce would benefit from the division of estates.

Little of the Church property that had been auctioned in 1790–91 had wound up in the hands of poor peasants or sansculottes—a problem about which the clubs of the Constituent seemed callous. But attitudes differed somewhat in regard to the émigré lands which the Legislative Assembly, after much prodding from the societies, voted to confiscate and sell. A number of clubs demanded that a portion of the properties, or the proceeds of their sale, be given to the families of national volunteers. This idea had radical social implications, for most of the volunteers of 1792 came from lower-class origins. Another sign that the clubs were developing a social conscience was the pressure that they exerted on the Convention to carry out the division of common lands voted on August 14, 1792, and to do so by head.

In 1792–93 the clubs were less assiduous in promoting local economic interests than they had been in 1790–91. This, too, may be a reflection of changing class composition and ethos. Nonetheless, they never ceased entirely to lobby for port improvements, roads, bridges, canals, local industries, governmental offices, and the like. And they behaved in a most selfish and mercenary manner in early 1792, in their elusive pursuit of the lycées, institutes, and secondary schools the Legislative Assembly proposed to create as part of a system of national education.

Enough of class and economics! The Jacobin of the middle years was also powerfully motivated by word and thought. For the provincial clubman newspapers were the elixir of life. The most precious days of the week were those on which the mail coaches arrived with their cargoes of periodicals to which the clubs subscribed. Of paramount interest were Parisian publications. A myriad of papers were founded by departmental clubs or their members, but most were ephemeral or little known outside their regions. The most popular Parisian gazette was the *Annales patriotiques* of J.-L. Carra. Next came the *Moniteur*. Farther down the scale, but still important, were the *Feuille villageoise*, *Patriote français*, *Journal des débats des Jacobins*, and *Courrier des 83 départements*. Generally speaking, the clubbists favored newspapers that contained varied features over those that specialized in news or opinion. They also tended to shun journalists of the extreme Right and Left. That Centrist and moderately Leftist sheets had the largest circulations was of great significance during the Girondin-Montagnard feuds of the early Convention.

As far as the clubs were concerned, the uppermost problem of the first years was the religious schism. And it remained the foremost issue until the advent of the war. Throughout 1791 and early 1792 the societies formulated requests for punitive legislation against nonjuring priests and harried local authorities into instituting repressive measures. Since nuns and monks were suspected of fostering "fanaticism," the societies also clamored for the closure of the remaining convents and monasteries. Their wishes were fulfilled after the fall of the monarchy, when the rump Legislative Assembly approved draconian laws against nonjurors and ordered the emptying of all religious houses.

By and large, the clubs of the middle years continued to sustain the constitutional Church and to make common cause with constitutional priests. In late 1792, for example, when the Finance Committee of the Convention proposed to abolish the budget for public worship, a solitary club raised its voice in assent while a dozen lifted theirs in outrage. Nonetheless, in the course of 1792, disturbing signs appeared. Disbelievers became a little more vocal, and anticlericalism unmistakably increased. Some of the constitutional clergy were accused of greed and acquisitiveness. Proposals were made for the melting down of church bells and silver plate. The liberties of Protestants were upheld with an almost anti-Catholic zeal. The clubs also championed the right of citizens *not* to observe Holy Days, supported the law forbidding priests to wear their garb in public, gave countenance to civil marriage and divorce, and wanted to strip the clergy of the privilege of keeping records of *état civil*. Scattershot criticism of celibacy eventually turned into a campaign to encourage priests to wed.

In early 1793 anticlericalism intensified. Horrified by the murder of a French diplomat in Rome, the clubs charged the pope with complicity. The widening of the war brought new calls for the confiscation of bells and plate, and a demand from Dijon that priests no longer be exempted from military service. For the first time, radicals in some societies declared all priests to be "bad." After the rebellion of the Vendée, Troyes and Auxerre circulated petitions demanding the deportation of every priest who was not salaried by the state or a public official. Auxerre went so far as to say that there was almost no difference between jurors and nonjurors. A few societies agreed with Auxerre; but the majority refused to adhere to its petition. As the Terror approached, most of the clubbists still seemed to be attached to their priests and to the faith of their fathers.

As the great edifice of Catholicism slowly crumbled, a kind of revolutionary religion reared up in its place. Although this religion was not to be fully formed until the Terror, many of its symbols had achieved cult status by 1792. The fantastic popularity of pikes and trees of liberty owed much to the endeavors of the clubs. The societies likewise helped to introduce Frenchmen to the inspirational hymn, the "Marseillaise." A threshold was passed in the spring of 1792, when a few clubs consciously organized civic funeral services, devoid of Catholic rites, for the martyred mayor, Simonneau.

The clubs of the Constituent dreaded a military reaction, and consequently, they tried to have the aristocratic officer corps purged. This aim was to be achieved, not by violence or legislative fiat, but by the mass desertion and emigration of officers that occurred in the second half of 1791. By early 1792, the societies enjoyed, overall, a better relationship with the army leaders, although suspicion lingered of generals like Lafayette.

The decree of April 29, 1791, had finally settled the question of whether off-duty soldiers could attend club meetings; and thereafter, the ties between line troops and societies were knit tight. The clubs recognized the need for military discipline; yet, they preached to soldiers about their rights, sheltered them from "persecution" by their superiors, and opposed nitpicking regulations. During the early Legislative Assembly Brest orchestrated a nationwide movement for the freeing of the soldiers of the Châteauvieux regiment who had been imprisoned following the mutiny at Nancy. Large sums were raised for these "martyrs," and their release was the occasion for celebrations.

From the outset the clubs and the national volunteers were linked by strong bonds. The societies helped to recruit the volunteers of 1791, plied them with gifts, gave them rousing send-offs, corresponded with them, and remained quite concerned about their well-being. However, the volunteers sometimes caused troubles in the clubs of towns where they were stationed or pushed them to extremes. Two levies occurred in 1792, during which the clubs functioned again as recruitment bureaus. The poor responded generously to their patriotic appeals, but the well-to-do often did not. This powerfully nurtured antirich sentiment and caused many societies to make long-term financial commitments to provide for the dependents of volunteers.

Early Revolutionary visions of universal peace faded away in the last months of 1791 as wild rumors circulated about the hostile designs of the Austrians and émigrés, and Brissot and others in Paris began to call hotly for a preventive war. In the departmental clubs, debates on the issue of peace or war commenced in November–December. From the first, a hawkish spirit prevailed, and bellicosity mounted in 1792 as Dijon, Caen, Clermont-Ferrand, Beaune, and the Ambulant Society of the Vendée circulated prowar manifestos. Of 154 societies known to have registered opinions on this subject by April, 141 (90 percent) favored an offensive war. Like the warmongers in Paris, the clubs disavowed conquests and stressed their desire to free oppressed peoples and to punish the "tyrants" and "traitors" beyond the Rhine.

Once war was declared, it became an obsession of the clubs. The thirst for news was unslakable, and there was an orgy of gift giving. Hundreds of thousands of livres and an immense quantity of precious objects were donated for war expenses. The early setbacks stunned the clubs and shattered illusions about easy victory. Under surface bravado swirled fear and hysteria. The triumphs of the autumn, however, restored confidence. A great round of fetes took place in which the clubs played a prominent part. Although orators were careful to distinguish France from conquering nations of the past, it was clear that they looked forward to future conquests.

In the territories occupied by French armies, about fifty clubs were founded by returning exiles, and by French officials and soldiers. They were identical in most respects to the French societies, and they quickly sought affiliation with their French sisters. These "foreign" clubs led the agitation for union with France and won the support of the network for their cause. Yet, outside of Savoy, few natives joined the societies. In Nice and Belgium the bulk of the members were Frenchmen.

Anglophilism, which had been so pronounced during the Constituent, long persisted. In late 1791 and 1792, many French societies ceremoniously installed the flags of the "free" nations (France, England, America, and Poland) in their assembly halls. They also continued to correspond amicably with political groups in the United Kingdom and to advocate a Franco-British alliance. As late as January 1793, some clubs still believed that the majority of Englishmen were kindly disposed toward the Revolution and that war could be averted. When hostilities began in February, however, the clubs made bellicose pronouncements, outfitted corsaires, and responded patriotically to entreaties for assistance from the naval minister, Monge. Henceforth, Anglo-French concord was to be no more than a whimpering ghost.

News that French soldiers were ill-clothed and suffering from the cold caused the societies, in the winter of 1792–93, to collect and send hundreds of thousands of shoes, hose, and other articles of apparel to the fronts. Alas, neither this philanthropy nor pleas to the volunteers could persuade them to stay at their posts. Thousands quit their units and went home. With the number of men under arms drastically reduced, the Convention, on February 24, decreed a levy of 300,000 men. As in past levies, the clubs encouraged enlistment. This time, however, they encountered serious resistance. Troubles erupted in many places, and the societies did much grumbling about shirking by the rich. Several called for the abolition of the provision that allowed well-to-do citizens to buy substitutes. Others demanded that the rich be forced to contribute to the war effort. A petition drive began for a tax on surplus revenues, the proceeds of which were to go to volunteers and their families.

The defeats in the north, the revolt of the Vendée, and the treachery of Dumouriez had an incalculable impact on the clubs. For weeks they lived in a martyrdom of nervous apprehension. Indeed, March–April 1793 is in some respects the most important period in Jacobin history. The machinery of the Terror was put in place, and from this date forward, the clubs became semi-official agents of repression. They nominated members for the surveillance committees, scrutinized magistrates to see if they were worthy of receiving *certificats de civisme*, and drew up lists of suspects to be arrested or disarmed. They also helped to initiate the famous *armées révolutionnaires*.

POLITICALLY, the main theme of the Legislative Assembly was the rise of opposition to Louis XVI. Although Louis had gravely compromised himself by trying to flee the country in June 1791, his acceptance of the Constitution in September 1791 had seemingly restored his popularity. Although a few clubs remained sullenly resentful, the vast majority still regarded the king with benevolent deference and rendered worshipful respect to the "holy Constitution."

The November 12 veto of the decree on the émigrés shocked

and embarrassed the clubs, but did not lead to talk of dethronement or rebellion. On the contrary, criticism of Louis was relatively mild. Some clubs held their tongues out of "respect for the
constitution." Others speculated that the king had been duped by
his advisors or was trying to prove that he was not a prisoner. A
few sought constitutional limitations on the use of the veto. And
a great many begged Louis to change his mind.

The failure of the king to listen to these pleas and the veto of
the decree on nonjuring priests in December had very negative
consequences. Again the clubs covered paper with ink. This
time, however, their epistles and petitions were often menacing
rather than supplicatory. Several clubs warned Louis that he
might lose his crown, and Langres implied that he had violated
article 6, section 1, chapter 2 of the Constitution and thereby forfeited the throne. By February 1792, a few clubs were ruminating
on the need for a "second revolution." However, almost all continued to profess their allegiance to the monarchical constitution,
and none, as yet, called for a republic.

Throughout the late winter and spring of 1792 tales circulated
that counterrevolutionaries were flocking to Paris with the aim of
kidnapping the king and dissolving the Legislative Assembly.
The *Eveil du peuple* of the Récollets Society, one of the most important pamphlets of the period, charged that the conspirators
intended to restore nobility by instituting a hereditary upper
house. The defeats in Belgium in late April accented fears. The
clubs, swallowing the propaganda of Leftists in Paris, concluded
that France had been betrayed by the "Austrian Committee" at
the court.

The rumors of plots and the threat of foreign invasion caused
several clubs to badger the Legislative Assembly to levy a force
from the departments to defend the capital. The Assembly responded on June 8, with a decree ordering the formation of a
camp of twenty thousand fédérés near Paris. The king's veto of
this decree and another on nonjuring priests, together with the
dismissal of the "Jacobin" ministers on June 13, brought screams
of disapproval from the societies. At least forty-nine wrote to
Louis to demand the lifting of the vetoes and reinstatement of the
ministers. Some sought constitutional amendments restricting

royal powers. Others called for Louis' punishment. Much was said, covertly and openly, about the possibility of a revolution.

Many societies defied the king's veto by recruiting corps of fédérés, providing them with money and arms, and sending them to the capital. Let there be no doubt about it—the march of the fédérés to Paris was primarily the work of the clubs. The movement started independently in several regions. Brest initiated it in the west and northwest. In the Midi the impetus came primarily from Marseille and Montpellier. Langres, Toulouse, Nérac, Toulon, Bordeaux, Angers, Le Mans, and Blois also circulated calls to arms. Once under way the march was encouraged by the Paris Jacobins, Leftist deputies, and the radical press. With the exception of the fédérés from the southeast, most did not go to the capital with the intention of overthrowing the monarchy; but some were converted to the cause after their arrival.

A few of the clubs deplored the invasion of the Tuileries on June 20 by a Parisian mob, and in some this incident was the occasion for mass resignations and purges. But the vast majority defended the Parisians, denounced local officials who had condemned the invasion, and criticized the king. Between June 20 and August 10 sentiment against Louis grew rapidly. Scores of societies censured him, and at least eighty-three demanded his dethronement or suspension. Adhesion to the decree of suspension on August 10 was prompt and almost universal. Prior to August 10, however, there was not much public support for a republic. Not until September did republicanism gain sway in the clubs.

Most of the deputies elected to the Legislative Assembly were probably clubmen; and some, during their terms of office, contrived to stay on good terms with the home societies. But the majority lost touch with their Jacobin constituents. Several legislators were scolded in late 1791 for their failure to correspond or to join the Paris Jacobins. More fell from grace by not voting on February 1, 1792, for a motion to censure the naval minister, Bertrand. The real parting of the ways came in the summer of 1792 when the Assembly refused to modify the constitution, dethrone the king, or indict Lafayette. Lists of "good" and "bad" deputies were circulated by the Paris Jacobins after August 10.

The "bad" deputies were passed over in the elections for the Convention and, in some cases, threatened with reprisals.

The degree of club influence on the elections to the Convention is not precisely measureable, but it was sizable, and the societies were generally pleased with the outcomes. Once in office, the Conventionnels, who were mainly clubbists, molded opinion at home with their letters and reports. Clubs with Girondist deputies were likely to be pro-Girondist; those with Montagnard deputies were usually pro-Montagnard; those with split delegations were often divided themselves.

The Girondin-Montagnard schism was bedded on the embers of the disputes that flared up at the Paris Jacobins in late 1791 and early 1792 over the issue of peace or war. At that date, the clubs merely deprecated the fratricidal strife and urged unity. Not until September 1792 were they sucked into the conflict; and in truth, only then did the two groups crystallize into recognizable entities. The Girondins withdrew or were pushed from the "mother society." Bitter exchanges took place in the Convention, and a pamphlet war ensued. As in the Feuillant schism, the clubs were confronted with a Pope and an anti-Pope competing for their allegiance.

Many societies were caught in a net of indecision. Others took a position above the fray, chastising the factionalists and demanding that they do their duty and write France a constitution. Among those that may be said to have taken sides in the schism, the historian is on safer ground with the "Montagnard" societies because they usually boasted of being such. The "Girondist" clubs characteristically disclaimed attachment to any party, although they were critical of the Montagnard leaders and shared many of the views of the Girondins in the Convention.

Initially, pro-Girondist clubs clearly predominated. In October and November, at least thirty-five societies signified their desire for the formation of a departmental guard for the Convention; just eighteen declared against such a guard. At the same time, a great many clubs demanded the expulsion of Marat, Robespierre, and the "anarchists" from the Paris society and threatened a rupture if this was not done. Only a handful—Strasbourg, Auxerre, the Club National of Bordeaux, and the popular societies of Lyon and Nîmes, among others—stood resolutely by the Paris Jacobins.

There are several good explanations for the early Girondist preponderance. First, they had the most popular newspapers. Second, they controlled key governmental agencies through which propaganda was dispensed. Third, the image of the Montagnards was clouded by their association with Marat, who was loathed by the clubs. Finally, few of the deputies with whom the societies corresponded were as yet pro-Jacobin.

Up to January 1793, the tide of opinion continued to run strongly against the Montagnards. On December 12, following menacing demonstrations by the sansculottes in Paris against the Girondins, the club of Quimper announced in a circular that, at its request, the Department of the Finistère was sending fédérés to Paris to protect the deputies. Inspired by this circular, and fearful for the safety of the Convention, clubs in at least seventeen departments adopted resolutions in December and January calling for the dispatch of departmental armed forces to Paris. Although only the battalion of the Finistère reached the capital, this movement was a kind of dress rehearsal for the Federalist rebellions of May–June 1793.

Most of the clubs that, like Quimper, championed the march of fédérés, were by then estranged from the Paris Jacobins. In response to the criticism by affiliates in October and November, the "mother society" had become more intransigent, going so far as to publish statements in defense of Marat and the September Massacres. The upshot was that at least twenty-five societies broke off affiliation in December and early January, and many more threatened to do so.

Just at this dark moment (early January), Jacobin fortunes began to rebound. The proposal of the Girondins to "appeal to the people" to decide the fate of the king was a major turning point in the schism. Although opinion on Louis was by no means uniform in the clubs, most from November onward had called for his trial and execution by the Convention. Rightly or wrongly, some concluded that the Girondins were trying to save the life of the ex-monarch and threw in their lot with the Montagnards. The most significant convert was the mighty club of Marseille. When Marseille became pro-Montagnard, most of the clubs of the southeast queued up behind her. However, at the time of the execution of the king, the only other region that was pro-Montagnard was the north. Nationwide, pro-Girondist clubs still had a two-to-one edge.

The clubs resoundingly approved of the king's execution. Many fancied that his death had removed the primary source of discord, and in their letters of adhesion they admonished the deputies to cease their quarreling. Instead, the party strife escalated. In a circular of early February, Marseille urged affiliates to petition for the recall of the deputies who had voted for the "appeal to the people." Many of the Provençal clubs adhered, but outside Provence, this proposal fanned controversy. And it died when the Paris Jacobins failed to endorse it. Another divisive issue of February was the draft constitution written by Condorcet. The Paris club denounced it as being undemocratic, and some societies shared this opinion.

The trend that had begun in early January continued after the execution of the king. Some of the "Girondist" or Centrist clubs reforged their bonds with the "mother society," or considered doing so. The return to the Jacobin fold was slowed, however, by riots that occurred in Paris in late February and early March. Many clubs blamed Marat for these incidents and demanded his arrest and execution.

Another turning point in the schism was the decree of March 9 sending eighty-two representatives-on-mission into the departments. The bulk of those appointed were Montagnards. If the Girondins engineered this to get their enemies out of Paris, they grievously erred. For the representatives used their formidable powers to further the Montagnard cause. They were not uniformly successful. Some clubs were as immovable as granite. Nonetheless, as a result of their proselytizing efforts, many societies gravitated from the Right to the Center or Left.

By April–May the ratio of pro-Montagnard to pro-Girondist societies was three to two. Montagnard strength was greatest in the north/northeast, southeast, and center, but Leftist clubs could also be found elsewhere. When Marseille, backed this time by the Paris Jacobins, started a second petition drive for the recall of the "appellants," societies in almost every region adhered.

Despite the Montagnard gains, Girondist societies were still numerous and vocal, and they predominated in the west and southwest. They refused adamantly to associate themselves with the Paris club, villified Robespierre and the Paris Commune, applauded the arrest of Marat, lamented his acquittal, and defended the twenty-two deputies whose ouster from the Convention had been demanded by the sections. As in December and January, they offered aid to the Convention and began preparations to send fédérés to Paris. They were greatly cheered by the sectional revolts in the southeast that led to the closure of the club of Marseille.

Up to the very eve of the Paris coup, however, the majority of societies were nonaligned or at least not irrevocably committed to any faction. Proof of this was provided by a massive petition drive in April and May. In it, the "parties" were subjected to scathing criticism and commanded to stop their bickering and give France a constitution. The uncommitted clubs watched anxiously as the crisis in Paris moved toward a denouement. After the purge of the Girondins on June 2, they were to be forced against their will to make a decision.

An Essay on the Sources of
Jacobin History
in the Departments

For the Jacobin historian, research in the National Archives is obligatory. In this vast repository of documents, three series warrant special mention. The first is series C, the *procès-verbaux* of the Legislative Assembly and Convention, with attachments. It holds an enormous quantity of pieces from the clubs, classed in chronological order. Only a fraction are printed in the *Moniteur* or the *Archives parlementaires*. The second is series DXL, the Petitions Committee of the Legislative Assembly and the Convention. It is especially helpful in tracing the evolution of political opinion. The third, and perhaps the most bountiful, is series F^{1}C III, Public Spirit. It is ordered by department.

Before quitting Paris, the researcher ought to pay a call on the Bibliothèque nationale. It has colossal numbers of speeches and pamphlets printed by the clubs, and a huge horde of Revolutionary newspapers. Among the Parisian papers four stars go to the *Journal des débats/correspondance* of the "mother society"; but the *Annales patriotiques*, *Courrier des 83 départements*, and *Patriote français* also printed lots of club news.

Hundreds of books, articles, theses, *diplômes*, and *mémoires* have been written on individual clubs. And the number of local histories that touch upon the societies runs into the thousands. A multitude of these works are cited in the notes to this book and in the first volume of this series.

Much information on the societies may be distilled from local newspapers, from the diaries, memoirs, and letters of revolutionaries, and from the deliberations and correspondence of departmental, district, and communal administrations. With all due respect to these sources, however, they are poor substitutes for the archives of the societies themselves.

Only debris of club archives remain. Most of the membership lists, as noted, date from the Thermidorean Reaction. It is extremely rare to come across the files of committees. In all of France scarcely a dozen sizable collections of loose correspondence subsist. The number of clubs for which there are registers of minutes is about 170; but many of the registers that appear to be gems from thumbnail descriptions in catalogs turn out on closer scrutiny to be paste. Parts are illegible. All too often they begin late in the middle years or end early. And the vast majority have lacunae. Pages were ripped out by clubbists who wanted to eradicate the record of their dark pasts. Whole sections were left blank because secretaries were too lazy to transfer their notes from looseleaf into the official record. Frequently, the club simply stopped meeting.

What follows is a survey of the wreckage. Those departments that are unnamed are, to the best of my knowledge, devoid of minutes or significant assemblages of correspondence. I make no claim to know of everything that is extant. Rather, I plead to scholars, as I did in volume one, to point out documents I have overlooked. With your advice, I might one day be able to write a definitive essay on the sources of Jacobin history in *province*.

Pyrénées-Atlantiques

St.-Jean-de-Luz

Two fires near the turn of this century laid waste to the papers of the clubs in this department. From notes taken before the burning of the minutes of St.-Jean-de-Luz (November 1791–1793), J. Annat published a synopsis of its history in the *Revue de Béarn* (1910), pp. 71–76, 118–129, 168–175, 200–213.

Orthez

And happily, the minutes of Orthez (May 27, 1792–frimaire an II), which were consumed in the same blaze, had already been printed by A. Planté in "Les Jacobins d'Orthez," *Bulletin de la Société des sciences de Pau* (1901), 263 pp. Three breaks occur in the Orthez minutes in early 1793; the longest is thirty-seven days.

Pau

The two extant registers of minutes of Pau (AD, 29 L 1–2), are disappointing insofar as the middle years are concerned. The first concludes on October 15, 1791, just two weeks into the Legislative Assembly. The second begins on December 2, 1792, when the society was reorganized by fifty-seven citizens, goes to December 13, then skips to February 20, 1793.

LANDES, HAUTES-PYRÉNÉES

Tartas

The minutes of Tartas (AD, Landes, 67 L 3) desist on March 1, 1791, just after the club had moved into new quarters. Save for four meetings in September–October 1792, no more are mentioned until January 14, 1793. Like Pau, however, Tartas was very active in the spring of 1793.

Lourdes

Compared to the minutes of Lourdes (AD, Hautes-Pyrénées, L 1181), those of Tartas and Pau are splendid. Lourdes convened just twice between September 1791, and May 6, 1793, when it was reestablished by representatives-on-mission.

ARIÈGE

Foix

The minutes of Foix (AD, 7 L 5) span the period from December 1789 to June 30, 1793, but up to 1793 its meetings were widely spaced and largely uneventful. Its register of correspondence (AD, 7 L 8) starts on May 17, 1793.

Le Mas-d'Azil

At the beginning of the present century, the minutes of Le Mas-d'Azil and Saverdun were in the municipal archives of those places. It would hardly be worth the trouble to search for those of Le Mas-d'Azil, since this club was defunct from May 1791 to May 23, 1793. But Saverdun's (January 9, 1792–July 19, 1793) were apparently fairly newsy.

Saverdun

PYRÉNÉES-ORIENTALES

Perpignan

The registers of the central committee of the society of Perpignan (AD, L 1449–51, January 26, 1791–May 4, 1792, July 24–October 25, 1792, April 6–August 24, 1793) are little more than a listing of matters discussed and correspondence received.

HAUTE-GARONNE

Toulouse

From the great club of Toulouse we have a kingly bequest of documents. The portions of the minutes that encompass the middle years (AD, L 4543–44, 4546–47) are crowded with information. The recorder, who was a paid scribe, even put a gloss in the margin.

TARN

Castres

Gaillac

Two clubs of the Tarn left minutes that span our period: Castres (AD, L 1531) and Gaillac (AM, Gaillac). Castres was the leading society of the Tarn and met continuously. Gaillac was relatively petite and went into occasional swoons, but it piques one's curiosity because of its ardent royalism in 1792. Someone has conveniently indexed its minutes.

Briatexte

From the other clubs of the Tarn we have pitifully small testaments. The minutes of Briatexte (AD, L 1521) commence tardily, on May 9, 1793. Scraps of correspondence and extracts of meetings of the clubs of Albi, Labruguière, Lavaur, Lombers, Mazamet, Rabastens, and Valdéries are deposited in the AD, cartons L 1515, 1548, 1553, 1558, 1562, 1574, 1585.

AVEYRON

Rodez

The second book of minutes of the club of Rodez (May 1791–November 1793) vanished during the Restoration. Thus, B. Combes de Patris' *Les procès-verbaux des séances de la société populaire de Rodez* (1912) was of minimal assistance to me. In Combes de Patris' time, a register of minutes of the society of Marcillac (February 17, 1793–July 1795) was in existence. Its present resting spot is a mystery.

St.-Affrique

The Abbé Raylet printed the "Procès-verbaux de la Société . . . de St.-Affrique" in the *Mémoires de la Société des lettres d'Aveyron* (1942). They are complete except for one space from June 5 to September 5, 1792, when St.-Affrique met just three times. Alas, even when it assembled regularly, St.-Affrique spent most of its time reading newspapers and electing officers.

TARN-ET-GARONNE

Montauban

Two able historians, F. Galabert and D. Ligou, have mined the rich seam of documents left by the club of Montauban. These include lists of members and deliberations of committees (AD, L 385–387, 407–409), and a book of minutes (L 403, September 1791–October 14, 1792). A register of outgoing letters (L 412) adds tidbits on the period after October 14, 1792.

Moissac

In 1901 the AM, Moissac, had a volume of minutes of the club of Moissac. L. Levy-Schneider, in *Le Conventionnel Jeanbon St.-André*, refers to incidents that occurred in sessions of early 1793 at the Moissac club.

LOT-ET-GARONNE

Tonneins

During the Terror the records of the clubs of the Lot-et-Garonne were burned because they were "tainted with federalism." But the minutes of the militantly pro-Montagnard society of Tonneins were spared. They are inscribed in notebooks, or *cahiers*, at the departmental archives. The relevant ones are: no. (4) August 19–November 11, 1791; (5) November 13, 1791–February 1, 1792; (6) February 5–May 17, 1792; (7) May 20–August 25, 1792; (9) December 16, 1792–March 27, 1793; (10) March 28–July 18, 1793. Cahier 8 is missing. Tonneins' minutes were written in a sprightly style, probably by the articulate schoolmaster, Jouan le jeune.

GERS

Lectoure

The best source in the Gers is the register of minutes of Lectoure (AD, L 697, May 1791–pluviôse an II), but that is not saying much. Some sessions of the autumn of 1791 were so poorly attended that no business was transacted. Only nine meetings took place from January 15 to May 15, 1792, and just one between May 15 and October 14, 1792.

Estang

Paul Tallez had the minutes of Estang in his possession when he wrote "Une Société populaire en Bas-Armagnac," *Revue de Gascogne* (1920), pp. 97–112.

The Estang club met forty-seven times between September 2, 1792, and July 28, 1793.

Gondrin

The initial date of the register of minutes of Gondrin (AD, L 696) is April 29, 1793.

GIRONDE

Bordeaux

The AD, Gironde, has one of the most voluminous collections of club correspondence. Five cartons (12 L 29–33) are packed with mail from the clubs of the departments to the societies of Bordeaux. They are classed alphabetically. Cartons 12 L 38–40 hold letters from the clubs of the Gironde. The general correspondence of the Récollets Society and Club National is filed under 12 L 15–20, 25–26. There is also a folder at the AM, Bordeaux, I 74, containing 166 pieces of correspondence sent to the Surveillant Society.

Registers of minutes of four clubs of Bordeaux have been preserved. The most meaty, those of the mighty Récollets Society (AD, 12 L 13–14), begin on August 31, 1792, and proceed to the summer of 1793. The Récollets Society met almost every day and, as we have seen, was staunchly pro-Girondist. The minutes of the Club National (AD, 12 L 23) run for about a year, from December 1791 to December 1792. But part of that time it was not very active. Those of the Surveillant Society (AM, Bordeaux, I 72–73, July 1791–frimaire an II) are intact. The Patriotic Society of La Merci was basically a reading circle. Its minutes end in 1792.

Pellagrue

Pellagrue met four to five times per month from October 2, 1791, to April 15, 1792. No further meetings are reported in its register (AD, 12 L 40) until 1 brumaire an II. Blaye's register of minutes (AD, 12 L 38, February 1791–an III) is infinitely more interesting to the generalist and has no significant breaks. Better still are the minutes of Libourne conserved in four volumes at the AM, Libourne. The tomes that concern the middle years are:

Blaye

Libourne

No. 5—June 1791–February 1792
No. 6—January 1792–January 1793 (mostly blank)
No. 7—February 1792–May 1793
No. 8—May 1793–May 1794

DORDOGNE

Périgrueux

The Dordogne also has a weighty store of documents. Périgueux, a large and vocal society, met five to six times a week in 1792. Its excellent minutes (AD, 13 L 12³–12⁴) flow from October 1791 to June 1793 without a significant break.

Bergerac

Bergerac's minutes, preserved at the AM, Bergerac, in three registers, were published and edited in 1913 by H. Labroue. Although they have one gaping fissure (March 2, 1792–February 5, 1793), they still make good reading. Labroue, who was a fine scholar, also summarized the correspondence of the society (AM, Bergerac, U 43, 46). It consisted in 1913 of 117 letters from Pinet, a deputy in the Legislative Assembly and Convention, together with dozens of items from affiliated societies.

St.-Cyprien

The remaining registers in the Dordogne come from small clubs that met irregularly. St.-Cyprien was founded on October 23, 1792, and averaged twelve assemblies per month to April when it began to have attendance problems. Its minutes (AD, 13 L 13) halt temporarily on May 12, 1793.

Beaumont

At Beaumont short busy periods were sandwiched between extended recesses. The second register of minutes (AD, 13 L 3) commences on January 31, 1792. But L. Testut had access to summaries of the first register (April 1791–January 30, 1792) when he wrote *La Ville de Beaumont . . . pendant la Révolution* (1904).

Monpazier

Monpazier met only eight times from October 2, 1791, to February 2, 1792, mainly to elect officers. Then, save for one session in September, it did not reconvene until January 11, 1793. After that date its minutes (AD, 13 L 6) are slightly more interesting.

CHARENTE-MARITIME

Marennes
Tonnay-Boutonne

In the Charente-Maritime remains are skeletal. Interred at the departmental archives are a few minutes of the club of Marennes (L 1323) dating from 1791, a slender book of sessions for Tonnay-Boutonne (L 1329, March 4, 1792–prairial an III), and, in ascending

Ars-en-Ré order of importance, the deliberations of Ars-en-Ré (L 1322, June 3, 1792–vendémiaire an III). The latter were published by Meschinet de Richemond in the *Archives historiques de la Saintonge at de l'Aunis* (1934), pp. 1–253. The Ars-en-Ré club was isolated and weak and met infrequently up to 1793. It had no sessions from September 23 to December 1, 1792.

CHARENTE

Cognac

Confolens

Montbron

The best source in the Charente is the register of minutes of Cognac (AM, Cognac, C 7 G, April 1791–messidor an II). Cognac remained fairly active throughout the middle years. Babaud-Larivière utilized the minutes of Confolens in 1863 when he wrote his *Etudes historiques et administratives*. Confolens suspended its meetings in the summer of 1792, but apparently resumed them in the following spring. The minutes of the society of Montbron survive at the departmental archives.

CORRÈZE

Tulle

Uzerche

Donzenac
Allassac

As in the Constituent, the fundamental source in the Corrèze is V. Forot's *Le Club des Jacobins de Tulle* (Tulle, 1912). Forot's work is a résumé of the minutes rather than a reprint, but it is very complete. Tulle met continually throughout the Legislative Assembly and early Convention.

One register of minutes of the club of Uzerche (August 3, 1792–prairial an II) is stored at the AD, Corrèze, L 1152. A. Ulry's "Les clubs révolutionnaires de Donzenac and Allassac," *Bulletin. Société scientifique de la Corrèze* (1920), pp. 153–177, was hewn from two registers which were then in private hands. Donzenac's began on May 1, 1791, but ran to only thirty-five written pages. Allassac's went from June 1791 to the Terror; however, Ulry states that the session of November 25, 1792, was the first in a year.

CREUSE

Guéret

At times the Creuse had no functioning clubs. The society of Guéret, the departmental seat, died in mid-

1791 and was not resurrected until March 1793. Its minutes, such as they are (AD, L 733, March 21, 1793–April 23, 1793), were printed by L. Lacrocq, "Notes sur les sociétés populaires de la Creuse," *Mémoires. Société des sciences . . . de la Creuse* (1901), pp. 197–205.

CANTAL, PUY-DE-DÔME

Aurillac

The premier source in the Cantal is the register of sessions of Aurillac (AD, 259 F, July 1790–messidor an II). In the papers of the local erudite, Jean Delmas, is an inventory of references to the societies of the Cantal in series L of the departmental archives.

Artonne

The lone register of minutes in the Puy-de-Dôme, that of tiny Artonne, was published by F. Martin in *Les Jacobins au village* (1902). But Artonne met only ten times in the middle years, mainly to transact routine business.

LOZÈRE, ARDÈCHE

Largentière

Except for crumbs on Mende, Villefort, and Meyreuis (AD, L 532, 533, 533 bis), the fare in the Lozère is unappetizing. The menu of source materials in the Ardèche is scarcely more tempting. The Largentière book of minutes, which begins on October 20, 1792, may be studied first-hand at the AD, L 1052. And A. Mazon summarized some of its meetings in "La Société populaire de Largentière," *Revue du Vivarais* (1903), pp. 248–281, 305–314. It is also possible that the minutes of Annonay (March 1791–germinal an III) still exist. L. Rostaing had them when he wrote *Les Anciennes loges maçonniques d'Annonay et les clubs* (Lyon, 1903). In any event, Rostaing says that Annonay avoided taking stands on issues and held just twenty sessions from September 1791 to January 1793.

Annonay

HAUTE-LOIRE

Le Puy

Le Puy had a noteworthy club, and detritus from its archives is clustered at the AD, 3 J 9–18, and BM, Le

Puy, Fonds Cortial, ms. 10, 22, 151. After December 10, 1792, the first date for which minutes are available, it assembled three to six times per week. A sixteen-day void from March 19 to April 4, 1793, appears to have been due to secretarial negligence.

Montfaucon

Some papers of Montfaucon survive from the years 1791–1793 (AD, L 1328).

ALLIER, NIÈVRE, INDRE

Moulins

Moulins had an energetic and opinionated club, but its minutes (AD, Allier, L 900) are disheartening. Only two sessions (December 30, 1792, and January 6, 1793) are recorded. The register of minutes of Varzy (Musée de Varzy) stands in isolation in the Nièvre, and it does not start until May 3, 1793. The Varzy club was the subject of a recent study by R. Baron, *Annales de Bourgogne* (1968).

Varzy

Châteauroux

Compared to the aforementioned sources, the minutes of Châteauroux (AD, Indre, L 1581) are superb. They commence on August 11, 1792; the longest hiatus is twenty-one days (August 26–September 16, 1792).

LOIRET

Montargis

The preeminent club of the Loiret, Orléans, left few memorials. Montargis, although a town of only seven thousand, also had an active society; but its minutes (AD, L 1212) start late, on May 3, 1793. The best registers that we have are from smaller societies. Boiscommun (AD, L 1202), with only twenty-five to thirty regulars, met a stunning 123 times from September 22, 1792 to June 30, 1793. Pithiviers (AD, L 1215), which was about the same size, averaged a respectable nine sessions per month from its founding on September 9, 1792, to March–April 1793, when its zeal waned.

Boiscommun

Pithiviers

LOIR-ET-CHER

Blois

Blois' minutes at the BM, Blois, are quite good until they stop on November 2, 1792. O. Petit utilized a book of sessions of Contres (May 1791–September

Contres

1795) in his *Contres pendant la période révolutionnaire* (1926). At that date it was in the AM, Contres.

YONNE

I would give much to have the archives of the radical Auxerre society at my disposal. Unfortunately, they are nonexistent. M. Giraud printed the minutes of Avallon (June 1791–October 1794) in "La Société des *Avallon* amis de la constitution à Avallon," *Société d'Etudes d'Avallon* (1914). Pages 131–162 encompass the middle years. M. G. Prévost published résumés of the *Villeneuve-le-Roy* minutes of Villeneuve-le-Roy (October 1790–November 3, 1792) in "La Société populaire de Villeneuve-le-Roy," *Bulletin de la Société des sciences historiques de l'Yonne* (1913), pp. 508–523. Giraud does not reveal the location of Avallon's minutes. Villeneuve's were in the AM, Villeneuve.

HAUTE-VIENNE

Limoges Some of the papers of Limoges disappeared shortly before they were transferred to the AD, Haute-Vienne in 1888. Yet, what remains is extremely valuable. There are admission lists and committee records (L 813–14, 819), and a five hundred page register of minutes (L 816, April 26, 1792–messidor an II). Fray-Fournier summarized the contents of this register in *Le Club des Jacobins de Limoges* (1903). For the generalist, however, the most precious items are the loose pieces of correspondence. Cartons L 820–21 contain letters from diverse groups and persons. Folders L 822–829 hold correspondence from other clubs.

The registers of two smaller clubs also exist. But *Eymoutiers* Eymoutiers (AD, L 831) had just twenty-six recorded meetings in the middle years, most after February 22, *Magnac-Laval* 1793, and Magnac-Laval (L 834) shut down from September 1791 to April 11, 1793.

VIENNE

Poitiers On a scale of 1 to 10 the records of the club of Poitiers merit a 10. They are conserved intact at the BM, Poitiers. In addition to the minutes of the sessions and committees, there are over one thousand pieces of correspondence catalogued by year. These folders are especially important:

S 19—1791, handwritten, from towns and clubs of the departments

S 20—1791, printed, from Paris (including the Paris club)

S 21, 22—1791, printed, from towns and clubs of the departments

S 23—1792, handwritten

S 25—1792, printed, from the Paris Jacobins

S 26—1792, printed, from the departments (mostly the clubs)

S 27—1793, handwritten

S 29—1793, printed, from the Paris Jacobins

S 33, 34—1793, printed, from the departments (mostly the clubs)

Châtellerault This monstrous collection overshadows the register of minutes of Châtellerault (AD, L supplement 2). It is, nonetheless, a good source.

DEUX-SÈVRES

Niort Most of the papers from the Revolutionary epoch were destroyed in a fire of 1805 at the departmental archives. But segments of the archives of Niort, which were then in the AM, Niort, escaped damage. These include a detailed register of minutes, which unfortunately ends on February 14, 1792 (AD, L 2e suppl. M/5). Most notable, however, is the correspondence. It is filed in the following cartons (L 2e suppl. M/1–3, 3001–3006 bis).

VENDÉE, MAINE-ET-LOIRE

Sables-d'Olonne

Durtal From feast we go to famine. In the Vendée all that remains is one morsel, the minutes of Sables-d'Olonne (AD, L 1369, April 12–September 24, 1793). Pickings in the Maine-et-Loire are even more skimpy. Durtal, for which we have a register of minutes (AD, 1 L 1311), met only once in the middle years.

LOIRE-ATLANTIQUE

Paimbeouf

Paimbeouf's register of minutes, which is unique in the Loire-Atlantique (AD, L 1342, January 1791–pluviôse an II), is more pithy. Nonetheless, an afternoon's work will exhaust the folios (35–68) that chronicle the meetings from October 1791 to June 1793. In Paimbeouf's register of outgoing correspondence (L 1343), just six folios (9–14) are accorded to our period. A smattering of club correspondence is cached in folders L 3338, 3341, and 3343 of the AD, Loire-Atlantique.

MORBIHAN

Lorient

The Morbihan has extensive holdings. Lorient has passed down the fullest minutes (AD, L 2000–01, September 1790–vendémiaire an III). The Lorient club met consistently about eight to ten times per month. It was also quite outspoken and instigated several petition drives. For this reason its register of correspondence (L 2002, letters sent) is very instructive.

Vannes

Although the original minutes of Vannes (February 1791–April 22, 1793) are missing, three copies exist at the AD, Morbihan. The most complete is catalogued under the call letters L 1530[4]. Copy L 1646 contains some useful data not given in the first. The third copy is L 1997. A six-month break in the meetings occurred from June 2 to December 6, 1792.

Auray

Auray's minutes (AD, L 1476) start on November 20, 1791. Up to March 1792 it convened twice weekly, but only once a week thereafter. The sessions cease on April 18, 1793. Two folders of correspondence of the club of Josselin also survive (L 1657–58).

Josselin

Most of the letters, however, date from the Terror.

CÔTES-DU-NORD

Guingamp

The one book of minutes in this department (Guingamp, October 1790–July 1793) is in private hands. I know of it strictly from F. Dobet's "La Société des amis de la constitution de Guingamp," *Bulletin. Société d'émulation des Côtes-du-Nord* (1951–52). By 1793, the Guingamp club seems to have been in decline. Meetings were discontinued for forty-one days beginning on April 27.

ILLE-ET-VILAINE

St.-Malo

St.-Servan

The minutes of St.-Malo (AD, LL 153, November 1789–May 6, 1793) are rather cursory. Its register of correspondence (LL 155) halts on April 22, 1792. Three volumes of minutes of the club of St.-Servan (March 1791–94) rest at the AM, St.-Malo.

MAYENNE

Laval

Mayenne

Laval's minutes (AD, Mayenne, L 1628) do not begin until February 3, 1793. Nonetheless, they are well worth examining. Mayenne, for which we also have minutes (L 1631), was inactive from the late Constituent until April 17, 1793.

SARTHE, EURE

Le Mans

Bernay

The best source in the Sarthe, by far, is the register of minutes of Le Mans (AD, L 1006, March 1790–September 2, 1792). Le Mans met continually throughout this period, although it was bedeviled in late 1791 by budgetary woes and indifference. Its folders of correspondence (L 1005, 1007) contain only one or two letters from the middle years.

Two volumes of minutes of the Bernay club have been recently transferred to the AD, Eure (L supplement). The second bridges nearly four years (August 1791–May 1795).

ORNE

Argentan

Alençon

Two stops are necessary at Alençon. A nearly five-hundred page register of minutes of the club of Argentan (April 1791–frimaire an II) is held by the BM, Alençon (Ms. 612, Collection La Sicotière, 10195). The minutes of Alençon are lodged at the AD (L 5095, May 1791–March 10, 1793) and have only one lacunae, late August to late September 1792. The Alençon club was the subject of an article by

G. Maintenant, "Les Jacobins d'Alençon," *Société historique et archéologique de l'Orne* (1976), pp. 79–147.

MANCHE

Cherbourg

I have twice been foiled in attempts to see the three registers of minutes (April 1790–ventôse an II) and the book of correspondence of Cherbourg. On the first occasion the Municipal Archives was being moved; on the second, the archivist could not locate them because they had not yet been reclassified. Judging from the remarks of A. Galland, "La Société populaire de Cherbourg," *Bulletin du comité des travaux historiques* (1906, 1908) and M. Le Loup, "La Société populaire de Cherbourg" (University of Caen, D.E.S., 1956), they are quite good.

Valognes

J.-L. Adam made use of the minutes of Valognes, since obliterated, in his *Etude sur la ville de Valognes* (Valognes, 1912). Unfortunately, he did not quote from them often.

CALVADOS

Honfleur

In the Calvados, at any rate, the minutes of Honfleur (AD, Honfleur, I 60–61, January 1791–nivôse an II) are peerless. Although the Honfleur club teeter-tottered several times on the brink of extinction, it always contrived to right itself. The longest interval between meetings was just eighteen days.

Vire

The minutes of Vire were casualties of the Normandy invasion in 1944, but we know a lot about them from the works of M. Butet-Hamel, "La Société populaire de Vire . . . ," *Bulletin. Comité des travaux historiques* (1900), and especially P. Nicolle's *Histoire de Vire pendant la Révolution* (1923). Gutted by mass resignations, the Vire club stopped meeting from November 4, 1792, to March 17, 1793.

Falaise

The minutes of Falaise (AM, Falaise, January 1791–germinal an III) leave the impression that the Falaise club was closed except for two or three sessions, from December 1791 to June 1792, and from December 1792 to July 1793. But we know from other sources that it operated during parts of these periods. Responsibility for the gaps must rest with the secretaries.

SEINE-MARITIME

Rouen

Rouen had a populous and active club. We are lucky, therefore, that four of its seven registers of minutes from the "middle years" have been saved (AD, L 5692–95). The missing ones are: May 14–December 19, 1791; April 20–July 16, 1792; and January 31–March 3, 1793. The extant portions have been ably summarized by E. Chardon, *Cahiers des procès-verbaux des séances de la Société populaire de Rouen* (Rouen, 1909).

Le Havre

The three volumes of minutes of the club of Le Havre (AD, L 5641–43, February 1791–August 3, 1793) are also of sterling quality. They have one protracted intermission, however, from August 1792 to January 1793.

Fécamp

Fécamp was essentially a reading circle, although it was occasionally galvanized into action by outside currents. At one point in its minutes (AD, L 5626), a secretary noted that he had not bothered to record a month of sessions (March 25–April 29, 1792) "seeing that almost nobody had come." The minutes stop totally from May 10, 1792 to May 23, 1793.

Eu

Eu held its inaugural meeting on September 21, 1792. Thereafter it averaged about six per month (AD, L 5624), but it engaged in little meaningful activity until February–March 1793. Ingouville was founded much later, on March 9, 1793; but its advanced social views make its minutes (L 5662) more engrossing.

Ingouville

SOMME, PAS-DE-CALAIS

Amiens

Miserable fragments of the archives of the affiliated club and popular society of Amiens are conserved at the AM, Amiens, (2 I 4, 5).

Aire

In the Pas-de-Calais the residue of club documents is larger. All in all, the best source is the four-volume set of minutes of Aire (AD, 4 L 2–3, Provisional no. 149, May 1790–floréal an II). The Aire society was

Hesdin

Montreuil

Boulogne

closed for brief spells in the late summer of 1792 and
the winter of 1792–93. Hesdin's registers of minutes
and correspondence (AD, Provisional no. 4, January
1790–May 1793) are often illegible. Montreuil's minutes (AD, 4 L 6) commence on December 1, 1791,
and go to March 8, 1793, without a serious breach.
Montreuil, however, whiled away its time reading
newspapers. J.-B. Holuigue printed extracts from the
minutes of Boulogne (August 1790–July 27, 1792) in
Les promoteurs de la Révolution en Boulonnais (Boulogne, 1892). At that time they belonged to a
"friend."

NORD

Bergues

Bourbourg

Douai

Lille

Source materials in the Nord are not as daunting as
they appear to be at first glance. The AD, Nord, has
nearly three hundred cartons of papers (L 889–989, L
10113–10301) classed alphabetically and by commune, but the bulk of the pieces in this collection date
from the Terror. Moreover, the four registers of minutes in municipal archives have huge holes. Bergues'
meetings (AM, Bergues) arrest on April 30, 1792, and
do not resume until October 1793. G. Lefebvre, *La
Société populaire de Bourbourg* (1913) tells us that Bourbourg's minutes are mute from July 22 to November
1, 1792, and from May 9, 1793, onward. At Douai,
records of the sessions (AM, Douai, D 4 12bis) break
off from June to mid-September 1792, and again
from November 1, 1792 to June 2, 1793. Two gaps in
the minutes of Lille (AM, 18.328–329) in early 1792
(January 30–February 27, April 22–June 3) appear to
have been due to secretarial laxity. For it is evident
from the register of correspondence (18.332, March
1791–an II) that the club continued to function. Lille's
meetings definitely stopped, however, from August
26 to November 3, 1792.

OISE

Compiègne

The mid-nineteenth-century historian A. Sorel cited
the register of minutes of Compiègne in several articles, and it is possible that this register still exists. According to Sorel, the Compiègne society disbanded

on March 1, 1792, and was refounded on September 21.

Beauvais

The principal surviving source in the Oise is the second book of minutes of Beauvais (AD, 4 L unclassified, August 1791–September 14, 1792). It fills 276 written pages. Some facts of interest may also be

Senlis

gleaned from the minutes of Senlis (AD, 4 L unclassified, July 1791–October an II).

YVELINES, SEINE-ET-MARNE

Versailles

As far as they go, the minutes of Versailles (BM, Versailles, Ms 568–69) are unmatched for clarity and detail. Regrettably, they terminate on March 12, 1792.

In the Seine-et-Marne the main sources are also in communal libraries. They are the registers of minutes

Fontainebleau
Provins

of Fontainebleau (BM, Fontainebleau, May 1791–1793) and Provins (BM, Provins, no. 183, January 1791–frimaire an II). Synopses of Provins' sessions were published by J. Bellanger, *Les Jacobins peints par eux-mêmes* (1908). There is one major lacuna, December 1791–May 1792.

MEUSE

Bar-le-Duc

There are three registers of minutes at the AD, Meuse. The best comes from the club of Bar-le-Duc (L 2188); unfortunately, its terminal date is July 28,

Ligny

1792. Ligny's minutes (Lp 2197, 1791–94) have recently been moved from the AM, Ligny. Unfortu-

Verdun

nately, I have not had them in my hands. Verdun's (L 2192) do not start until April 14, 1793.

MARNE

Reims

One of the treasures of the AM, Reims, is the virtually complete corpus of papers of the club of Reims. It includes committee records and four registers of minutes (L 11, 13–15, November 1790–pluviôse an III). The correspondence with other societies, in cartons L 37–51, surpasses one thousand pieces. The

Châlons-sur-Marne

AD, Marne, has some dossiers of the correspondence of Châlons-sur-Marne (E 5837–5846).

AUBE

Research is difficult in the Aube. Series L of the departmental archives is not classified, and the papers of the societies (such as they are) have been mixed with those of the departments and districts. In the AM, Troyes, I 2, carton 1, are a few copies of letters from that club.

HAUTE-MARNE

Bourbonne-les-Bains

Judging from the minutes of Bourbonne (AD, L 2212, September 1790–October 1793), the number of societies in the Haute-Marne was small. The most radical and outspoken, Langres, seemingly left no records. Bourbonne itself was not a mover or shaker. It was defunct from August 28 to December 11, 1791, and met just four times between September 5 and December 30, 1792.

St.-Dizier

St.-Dizier's minutes (AD, L 2019) start on April 18, 1793. Folder L 2017 contains bits of correspondence of the Joinville society.

Joinville

MEURTHE-ET-MOSELLE, MOSELLE

Lunéville

In the Meurthe-et-Moselle there are apparently no registers of minutes anterior to 1793. Lunéville's (AD, L 3130) initiates on April 22, 1793. In 1895, when A. Denis published his book, *Le Club des Jacobins de Toul*, the minutes of Toul (January 23, 1793–prairial an III) were housed at the AM, Toul, in series JJ.

Toul

The Revolutionary holdings of the AD, Moselle, were turned to rubble in 1944. After World War II, however, the Archives acquired the papers of the Canon Lesprand, a noted local historian. In these papers is a copy of the minutes of Thionville (18 J dépôt 58, July 1791–March 1795). N. Dicop's recent monograph, *Le Club des Jacobins de Sierck* (1975), is based on the diary of a member of the club of Sierck.

Thionville

Sierck

BAS-RHIN

F.-C. Heitz's fine work, *Les sociétés politiques de Strasbourg*, is drawn primarily from newspapers and Rev-

olutionary pamphlets. The minutes fizzle out in
March 1791. The only other society about which we
have extensive knowledge is Saverne. Three registers
of its minutes (April 1791–messidor an III) are conserved at the AM, Saverne. Like many other clubs,
Saverne was inert in the first months of the Legislative Assembly, but it was revived in the spring of
1792 by the future Conventionnel Bentabole.

Saverne

HAUT-RHIN

P. Leuilliot, the author of *Les Jacobins de Colmar*
(1923), has christened 1792 in the Haut-Rhin as the
year of "la crise des clubs." Except for a brief flurry of
activity at the beginning of the war, the Colmar club
dropped almost completely from view from October
1791 until May 23, 1793, when its minutes (AM, Colmar, B 36) start afresh. Just a smattering of letters sent
to it in late 1791–92 have been preserved (AM, B 34).
Belfort's minutes (AD, Haut-Rhin, L 765) are rid-
dled with holes. Delle's (AD, Territoire de Belfort, 33
E dépôt, série 1Z) have an initial four-month break
(December 1791–April 1792) and cease altogether
from May 18, 1792, to December 1793. Thann convened just three times from May 1791 to March 25,
1793, when its minutes start up again. Thann's minutes are summarized by H. Poulet, *L'Esprit public à
Thann pendant la Révolution* (1919).

Colmar

Belfort
Delle

Thann

HAUTE-SAÔNE

If not jam-packed with data, Gray's minutes (AD,
361 L, 1–3, April 1791–nivôse an III) are nonetheless
quite useful. The other register of minutes in this department is that of Jussey (AD, 363 L 1, April 6,
1793–pluviôse an III).

Gray

Jussey

DOUBS

La Vedette, the *journal* of the Besançon club, is the op-
timum source of information in the Doubs. Ornans
has transmitted the longest run of minutes (AD, L
2360, January 1791–frimaire an II), but in parts they
are barely legible. The *délibérations* of Quingey (AD,

Ornans

Quingey

Belvoir L 2362, March 7, 1792–frimaire an III) and Belvoir (L 2352, February 3, 1793–frimaire an III) are sketchy.

JURA

Lons-le-Saunier H. Libois has published full summaries of the meetings of Lons-le-Saunier in his *Délibérations de la Société populaire de Lons-le-Saunier, du novembre 1791 au 25 juin 1793* (1897). The originals are at the AD, Jura.

SAÔNE-ET-LOIRE

Chalon-sur-Saône The minutes of Chalon-sur-Saône (AD, Fonds Canat de Chizy) are among the finest that I have run across. Folios 196 to 326 of volume one cover the period from September, 29, 1791 to August 29, 1792. R. Carraz of the University of Dijon evidently tapped a second volume of minutes for his article, "Girondins et Montagnards: Le Cas Chalonais," *Actes du Colloque Girondins et Montagnards* (1980), pp. 167–192. But archivists could not locate it when I made inquiries in 1982 and 1986.

Louhans A notebook of minutes of the club of Louhans (June 19–December 9, 1792) was "communicated" to L. Guillemaut just before he wrote the *Histoire de la Révolution dans le Louhannais* (1879). Several pages

Charolles were missing. The AM, Charolles, has three registers of the sessions of the club of Charolles (April 1790–frimaire an III).

CÔTE-D'OR

Semur The papers of the club of Semur (AM, Semur), which were the bedrock for M. Henriot's book *Le Club des Jacobins de Semur* (1933), seem to be the richest in the Côte-d'Or. The register of minutes does not start until September 18, 1792, and has a two-and-a-half-month lacuna. But there are two registers of correspondence and a dossier of 124 letters from affiliates.

Vitteaux Three sets of minutes are preserved in the AD, Côte-d'Or. Vitteaux's (L IVb 21², February 1791–ventôse an II) are more or less a record of admissions with references to a few letters from Dijon and Semur. I count only thirty-seven meetings from Octo-

Montbard

Nuits

ber 1791 to June 1793. Montbard (L IVb 14[1], September 1791–July an II) met one less time, but recessed for four months and two-and-a-half months. Nuits was more dynamic. Its minutes (L IVb 14bis, 1, 2, August 1791–ventôse an II) are uninterrupted in the middle years. *Mémoires* on these three clubs have been written by students of R. Carraz.

AIN

Châtillon-sur-Chalaronne

Bourg

For most of the Legislative Assembly, the register of minutes of Châtillon-sur-Chalaronne (AM, Châtillon, LL 8, April 1791–ventôse an II) is the lone source of its kind in the Ain. The Châtillon club met about once a week and was so minuscule that it set its quorum at seven. It was inactive in the early Convention. Bourg's minutes (AD, L 937) are spotty. Seventeen meetings are recorded in July–August 1792; then, excluding two sessions in November, silence reigns up to March 8, 1793.

RHÔNE

Lyon

Neuville-sur-Saône

Condrieu

Two sectional branches of the Popular Society of Lyon have willed us their minutes: Bellecordière, AD, 34 L 1, August 1791–May 16, 1793; and Croix-Rousse, AD, 34 L 3, January 1791–May 12, 1793. A few pieces of correspondence of the sectional societies also exist (AD, 34 L 4–6).

The book of minutes of Neuville-sur-Saône (AD, 34 L 23, November 1790–June 24, 1792) is half-sized. Neuville closed in disgust after the June 20 attack on the Tuileries. Condrieu met just a few times per month in the middle years, and its minutes (AD, 34 L 29, March 1791–ventôse an III) have three gaps of a month or more in the second half of 1792. But its register of correspondence (34 L 30) contains some interesting letters.

ISÈRE

Bourgoin

L. Fochier published "the most salient" parts of the minutes of Bourgoin in *Souvenirs historiques sur Bourgoin* (1880). The Bourgoin club closed for about fifty days in August–September 1792 and met infrequently in early 1793.

Drôme

Valence   Of the two clubs of Valence, only the Surveillant Society left accounts of its sessions in the middle years (AD, L 1085–1086). Between October 1, 1791, and April 8, 1793, the date of its merger with the Friends of the Constitution, it met just fifty-six times and got little correspondence. The longest breaks in its meetings were August 5–September 30, 1792, and February 17–April 8, 1793.

Tulette   Tulette was inoperative at the end of 1791 and for most of the remainder of the period averaged about 1.5 sessions per month. In the late summer and autumn of 1792, however, it was very active; and its minutes (AD, L 1099) are filled with news on the

Tain   clubs in its vicinity. Tain's register (AD, 1103) halts on October 23, 1791, vaults to May 27, 1792, and thence to September 1, 1793. In the early twentieth century, two registers of minutes rested in municipal archives. When I checked in 1982, archivists could

St.-Vallier   not locate St-Vallier's (June 1791–germinal an III).

Etoile   Etoile's (February 1791–fructidor an III) may still be at the AM, Etoile.

Vaucluse

Apt   In the BM, Marseille (Ms 1373), are ten cahiers of minutes of the club of Apt (February 1791–messidor an II). Cahiers 4–6 deal with the middle years.

The AD, Vaucluse, boasts fourteen sets of minutes.

Courthézon   The best are those of Courthézon (6 L 24–25, February 1791–prairial an III). Courthézon met continuously and occasionally became involved in national movements. The minutes of Lauris (6 L 22, Novem-

Lauris   ber 1790–nivôse an III, in seven cahiers) stop on October 18, 1792, and do not resume until the Terror; but its register of letters and petitions (6 L 23) goes a little farther. Most of the 148 items in this register

La Coste   concern local matters. La Coste (6 L 15, August 1791–messidor an II) met just once a week when it was active and was preoccupied with the condition of roads,

Grambois

Vaison

the public fountain, the salary of the schoolmaster, and other gripping issues. From Grambois there is a fragmentary transmission: 6 L 19, November 10, 1791–June 15, 1792. Vaison's minutes (6 L 12) proceed from April 10, 1792, to vendémiaire an III; but it was idle from July 22, 1792, to January 25, 1793.

The other registers of minutes begin after the fall of the monarchy:

Malemort

Malemort, 6 L 3, September 18, 1792–germinal an III

Méthamis

Méthamis, 6 L 17, September 16, 1792–frimaire an III

Lioux

Lioux, 6 L 21, September 22, 1792–March 11, 1793

Piolenc

Piolenc, 6 L 16, April 11, 1793–pluviôse an II

Vitrolles-les-Luberon

Vitrolles-les-Luberon, 6 L 20, October 25, 1792–fructidor an II

Cheval-Blanc

Cheval-Blanc, 6 L 13, April 21, 1793–vendémiaire an III

Violès

Violès, 6 L 9, October 10, 1792–prairial an II

St.-Roman-de-Malegarde

St.-Roman-de-Malegarde, 6 L 8, August 17, 1792–frimaire an III

Jonquières

Jonquières, 6 L 10, September 30, 1792–messidor an III.

Of these nine documents Jonquières' is the most complete. The AD, Vaucluse, also has the deliberations of the "secret committee" of Jonquières and registers of receipts and expenses of the Surveillance Committee of the club of Orange (6 L 11, 1, 2).

Orange

Any student of the clubs of the southeast would also be well-advised to consult the Fonds H. Chobaut at the Musée Calvet in Avignon, especially numbers 5992–5994.

HAUTES-ALPES, BASSES-ALPES

Serres

The archives of the Hautes-Alpes have little to offer. But two books of minutes of the club of Serres are conserved at the National Archives (F[7] 4552, dossier 1).

Digne

The AD, Basses-Alpes (Alpes-de-Haute-Provence today), has an ample fund of minutes dating mainly from 1792. Most of the information in them pertains to the region. The register of Digne (L 848), the departmental seat, runs from June 22 to November 28, 1792. The call numbers and opening dates of the *Castellane, Riez* others are: Castellane (L 851, May 4, 1792); Riez (L *Senez* 856/1, May 14, 1792); Senez (L 857, May 24, 1792); *Thorame, Valernes* Thorame-Haute (L 859, September 2, 1792); Valernes *Volonne* (L 861, April 11, 1792); and Volonne (L 862, May 20, 1792).

Of special note in this department is the dossier of correspondence of the society of Riez (L 856/2). It contains 128 printed and manuscript pieces, and many date from 1792.

ALPES-MARITIMES

J. Combet got most of the material for "La Société populaire de Nice," *Annales. Société . . . des Alpes-Maritimes* (1909), from two volumes of minutes of the *Nice* Nice club (October 2, 1792–floréal an III) at the BM, Nice. According to Combet, they are in general quite readable but are marred by numerous lacunae in late 1792 and early 1793. Interspersed in the first register are the minutes of the Surveillance Committee and Central Committee of the club.

VAR

In the Var, one need only follow the trails blazed by E. Poupé and H. Labroue. These two early-twentieth-century historians thoroughly scoured the department for club papers and published their results in books and articles. The premier source in the Var, in *St.-Zacharie* my opinion, is the dossier of correspondence of St.-Zacharie (AD, L supplement). It is comparable in size *Villecroze* to the correspondence of Riez. Villecroze has left the most complete register of minutes (AD, L 2037). It *Callas* opens on November 11, 1792. Callas' minutes (L supplement, December 10, 1792–brumaire an III) are rather boring and have empty spaces. The first date in *La Garde-Freinet* La Garde-Freinet's register (AM, La Garde-Freinet) is April 21, 1793.

BOUCHES-DU-RHÔNE

Marseille Less than two months of the minutes of Marseille survive (AD, L 2071, February 28–April 18, 1793); but there is a published record of its meetings in the *Journal des départements méridionaux* (March 6, 1792–May 7, 1793). And many letters from affiliates are conserved at the AD, L 2072, 2075–77).

Aix

The archives of the Antipolitiques of Aix have come down to us whole. Of prime importance are three registers of minutes (AD, L 2026–28, November 1790–frimaire an II) and two folders of correspondence (L 2038–39). The minutes of Eguilles and Martigues (AD, L 2064, 2080) are less helpful.

Eguilles
Martigues

GARD

Nîmes

F. Rouvière printed many sources relating to the clubs of Nîmes in volumes two and three of his *Histoire de la Révolution française dans le Gard* (1887–89). For those who want more data, the AD, Gard, has ten months of the minutes of the Popular Society (11 L 2, November 13, 1791–September 9, 1792) and a collection (on microfilm) of some of its letters. The original letters are in the AM, Bar-le-Duc (Fonds Colson).

St.-Hippolyte

St.-Hippolyte left the most complete minutes of any of the small-town clubs (AD, L 2130–31, June 1791–September 1793), with over 220 sessions in the middle years. St.-Julien-de-Peyrols (AD, L 2133) had just ten uneventful sessions from December 12, 1792, to May 19, 1793. The minutes of Aiguesvives (AM, Aiguesvives, July 1790–fructidor an II) are not much more informative. Just two meetings took place from August 31, 1792, to February 26, 1793. But Aiguesvives has provided us with a record of letters sent and received.

St.-Julien-de-
Peyrols

Aiguesvives

HÉRAULT

Montpellier

The Hérault is a fitting place to end this essay, and a must stop for historians of the clubs. Montpellier's papers are excelled by none and only rivaled by those of Poitiers and Reims. In the AD are six cartons of correspondence from the clubs of the Hérault (L 5531–36) and fourteen (L 5537–50) from clubs outside the department. The only break in its minutes (AD, L 5498–5501, February 1790–October 1793) is from April to September 1792. For Montpellier we also have the records of committees, lists of newspapers received, and the like.

Béziers

Béziers and Sète, clubs of some consequence, also left minutes. Béziers' (AM, Béziers, register 2, July 1791–pluviôse an II) have no breaks during the middle years. Sète's (AD, L 5601) stop on January 31, 1792. Sète has also given us a register of correspondence and the deliberations of its Economic Committee (AD, L 5605, 5609).

Sète

Marsillargues

Marsillargues, for which we have the minutes (AD, L 5493, September 1791–nivôse an II) and a register of incoming correspondence (L 5494), convened weekly to read newspapers.

Appendix A

Geographical Distribution of Towns with Clubs

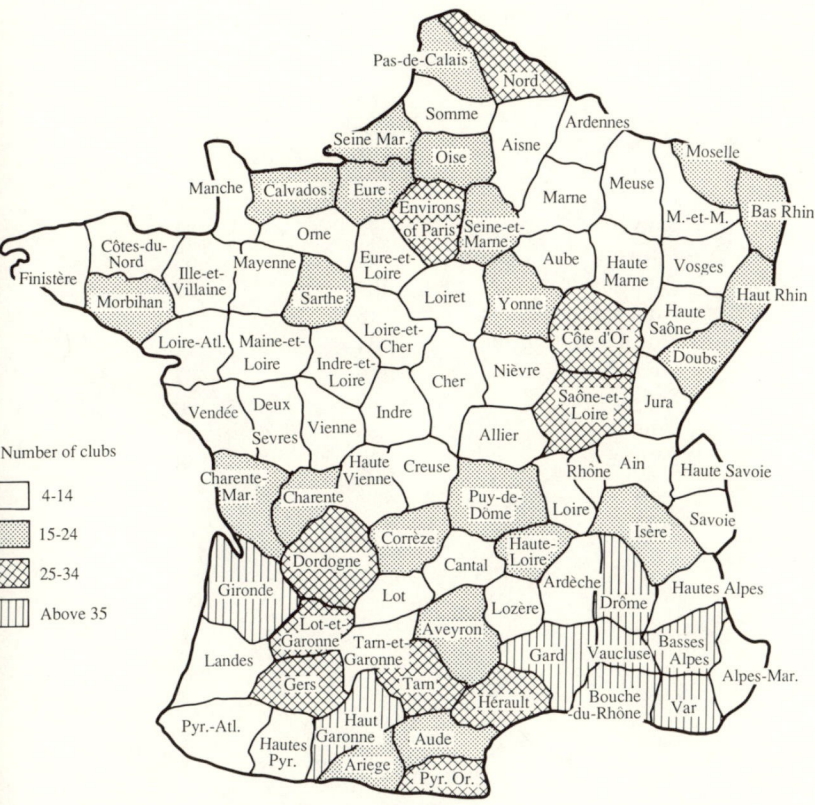

NOTE: The names and boundaries on this map are those of modern departments. Belfort, however, is considered to be part of the Haut-Rhin. The area called the "Environs of Paris" is roughly equivalent to Paris and the old Seine-et-Oise.

Appendix B

ADMISSION OF NEW MEMBERS INTO THE CLUBS

Club	1789– September 1791	October 1791– May 1793
Sauveterre	72	23
Vauvert	99	65
Alençon	105	55
Bourbourg	18	17
Villeneuve-le-Roy	34	12
Grenoble	186	37
Semur	89	50
Toul	66	43
Vitteaux	70	58

Appendix C

Club	Population of City	Number of Members
Marseille	110,000	3,000
Bordeaux (Récollets)	100,000	2,000
Lille	60,000	270
Strasbourg	50,000	500
Orléans	33,000	800
Montauban	29,000	1,749
Aix	22,500	1,200
Dijon	21,000	800
Le Havre	20,500	600
Douai	18,000	250
Colmar	12,700	624
Alençon	12,000	160
Boulogne	11,300	169
Toul	9,400	109
Vire	9,000	254
Cherbourg	8,700	300
Guingamp	5,200	199
Riom	5,000	165
St.-Dizier	4,900	50
Semur	3,750	126
Tonneins	3,500	300
Bourbonne-les-Bains	2,860	108
Ars-en-Ré	2,750	68
Mayenne	2,500	51
St.-Zacharie	1,500	195
Villecroze	1,200	108
Vitteaux	1,000	128

Appendix D

PROFESSIONS OF CLUB MEMBERS

Profession	1789–September 1791	October 1791–May 1793
Ecclesiastics	6.5%	4.4%
Servicemen	4.8%	4.0%
Farming	2.8%	9.4%
Shopkeepers, retail merchants	14.8%	14.7%
Salaried employees	8.4%	7.5%
Government officials	7.2%	6.9%
Liberal professions	13.3%	9.9%
Wholesale merchants, rentiers	15.8%	11.1%
Artisans, petty tradesmen	25.4%	29.8%
Manual laborers	.03%	1.6%
Miscellaneous	.9%	.7%

Appendix E

THE TOP 28 NEWSPAPERS

Newspaper	Number of Subscribers Oct. 1791– May 1793	Number of Subscribers 1789– Sept. 1791	Rank in 1789– Sept. 1791
Annales patriotiques et littéraires	52	41	1
Moniteur	34	35	3
Feuille villageoise	23	36	2
Journal des débats des Jacobins	17	9	14
Patriote français	17	12	9 tie
Courrier des 83 départements	14	11	12 tie
Courrier de Strasbourg	11	—	—
Gazette universelle	10	16	6
Chronique du mois	10	—	—
Sentinelle	9	—	—
Logographe	9	11	12 tie
Chronique de Paris	8	8	15 tie
Journal général de l'Europe	8	—	—
Mercure universel	8	8	15 tie
Révolutions de Paris	8	12	9 tie
Ami des citoyens	7	—	—
Journal des débats et des décrets	7	17	5
Journal de Perlet	7	5	25
Journal du soir	7	—	—
Courrier du Midi	6	—	—
Argus du Nord	5	—	—
Père Duchesne	5	—	—
Paquebot	4	6	20 tie
Journal de Paris	4	13	7 tie

APPENDIX E (*cont.*)

Newspaper	Number of Subscribers Oct. 1791– May 1793	Number of Subscribers 1789– Sept. 1791	Rank in 1789– Sept. 1791
Journal des hommes libres	4	—	—
Courrier de l'égalité	3	—	—
Défenseur de la constitution	3	—	—
Journal des départements méridionaux	3	—	—

Appendix F
Political Alignments in
January 1793

WEST

Girondist tendencies: Brest, Landerneau, Morlaix, Quimper, Quimperlé, St.-Pol, Auray, Pontivy, Port Louis, Dinan, St.-Brieuc, Lannion, St.-Malo, Vitré, Avranches, Cherbourg, Coutances, Granville, Périers, St.-Lô, Valognes, Louviers, Alençon, Argentan, Caen, Falaise, Honfleur, Lisieux, Fécamp, Laval, La Flèche, Le Mans, Angers, Nantes, Sables-d'Olonne, Niort, St.-Maixent, Châtellerault, Loudun, Angoulême, Aigre, Cognac, Marennes, Saintes, St.-Pierre (Char.-Mar.).

Montagnard tendencies: Bayeux, Dieppe, Le Havre, Fontenay, Civray, La Rochelle.

SOUTHWEST

Girondist tendencies: Bazas, Bordeaux (Récollets), Cadillac, Coutras, Langon, Lesparre, Libourne, St.-André-de-Cubzac, Périgueux, Villamblard, Agen, Clairac, Marmande, Villeneuve-du-Lot, Cahors (Friends of Liberty), Moissac, Castelsarrasin, Rodez, St.-Affrique, Villefranche (Avey.), Castres, Fleurance, Beaumont (H.-Gar.), Carcassonne, Limoux, Narbonne, Perpignan, Pamiers, Dax, Meilhan, Tarbes, Bayonne, Pau.

Montagnard tendencies: Blaye, Bordeaux (Club National), Ste.-Foy, Tonneins, Cahors (Defenders of Liberty), Montauban, Lavaur, St.-Jean-Pourge, Montrejeau, Toulouse, Tartas.

SOUTHEAST

Girondist tendencies: Bédarieux, Béziers, Montpellier, Alès, Nîmes (Republican Society), St.-Hippolyte, Sommières, Grasse, Callas, Draguignan, Lorgues, Ollioules, Toulon, Villefort (Loz.), Orange, Viens, Annonay, Ampuis, Bois-d'Oingt, Condrieu, Villefranche (Rhône), St.-Bonnet-le-Château, Grenoble, Vienne.

Montagnard tendencies: Nîmes (Popular Society), St.-Avançon, Aix, Arles, Marseille, Salon, Beausset (Var), Avignon, Lyon, St.-Chamond, Crémieux.

CENTER

Girondist tendencies: Craponne, Le Puy, Maringues, Aurillac, St.-Flour, St.-Yrieix, Limoges, Argentat (Corr.), Brive, Ussel, Nevers, Chartres, Orléans, Beaugency, Boiscommun, Courtenay, Pithiviers, Avallon, Villeneuve-sur-Yonne.

Montagnard tendencies: Riom, Clermont-Ferrand, Tulle, Bort, Argenton, Châteauroux, Blois, Châteaudun, Auxerre, St.-Fargeau, St.-Florentin.

NORTH

Girondist tendencies: Bar-sur-Seine, Meaux, Provins, Beauvais, Amiens, Péronne, St.-Quentin, Nancy, Epinal, Chalon-sur-Saône.

Montagnard tendencies: Fontainebleau, St.-Germain, Versailles, Senlis, Aire (P.-d.-C.), Arras, Lille, Givet, Reims, Metz, Sezanne, Strasbourg, Beaune, Autun, Louhans, Mâcon, Lons-le-Saunier.

Appendix G
Political Alignments in
March-May 1793

West

Girondist orientation: Alençon, Angers (Eastern Society), Angoulême, Argentan, Bayeux, Caen, Châteaulin, Cherbourg, Dieppe, Evreux, Falaise, Granville, Honfleur, Lamballe, Landerneau, Laval, Lisieux, Lorient, Marennes, Morlaix, Moyaux, Nantes (Mirabeau), Niort, Pontivy, Quimper, Rennes, Rouen, St.-Brieuc, St.-Malo, St.-Maixent, St.-Pierre (Char.-Mar.), Saujon, Sées, Vannes, Vire.

Montagnard orientation: Angers (Western Society), Bernay, Chaumont, Fontenay, Gisors, Ingouville, Jarnac, L'Aigle, La Rochelle, La Tremblade, Le Havre,[1] Le Mans, Loudun, Mamers, Nantes (St.-Vincent), Poitiers, Pont-de-l'Arche, Roquefort, Ruffec, Valognes, Vernon, Yvetot.

Southwest

Girondist orientation: Agen,[2] Albi, Auch, Auvillars, Bagnères, Bazas, Bergerac, Blaye, Bordeaux (Récollets), Caraman, Carcassonne, Clairac, Cognac, Coutras, Créon, Dax, Fleurance, Gaillac, Lacaune, La Gardelle, Langon, La Teste-de-Buch, Lézignan, Libourne, Lombez, Lourdes, Marciac, Millau, Mirande, Moissac, Montastruc, Mont-de-Marsan, Narbonne, Nogaro, Oloron, Perpignan, Plaisance, Queyrac, Quillan, Rauzan, St.-Girons, Ste.-Bazeille, Sauveterre, Tarascon, Tournon (L-et-G).

Montagnard orientation: Bayonne, Bordeaux (Club National), Cahors,[3] Casteljaloux, Condom, La Caussade, Lavaur, Lesparre, Limoux, Lusignan, Mazamet, Montauban, Montbasens, Negrepelisse, Périgueux, Rodez, St.-Affrique, St.-Jean-de-Luz, St.-Macaire, St.-Martory, Ste.-Foy, Tarbes, Tartas, Tonneins, Toulouse.

[1] Le Havre wavered at the end of May and considered breaking off relations with the Paris club.

[2] Agen became almost centrist in April–May.

[3] Cahors made some pro-Montagnard pronouncements in the period from March to May, but it also issued a statement strongly opposing the June coup. Perhaps there were two clubs here, as in the previous autumn.

SOUTHEAST

Girondist orientation: Alès, Anduze, Annonay, Bras, Briançon, Chambéry, Draguignan, Gap, Grasse, Grenoble, Montpellier, Nîmes (Republican Society), Pézenas, Roanne, St.-Ambroix, St.-Hippolyte, St.-Jean-du-Gard, Sète, Sommières, Le Vigan, Villefranche (Rhône).

Montagnard orientation: Aix,[4] Allauch, Annecy, Apt,[5] Arles, Avignon, Bagnols, Beaucaire,[6] Bédarieux, Béziers, Boen, Bourg-St.-Andéol, Carpentras, Castellane, Ceyreste, Correns, Crémieu, Cucuron, Cuges, Digne,[7] Forcalquier, Graveson, Lacoste, La Tour-d'Aigues, Le Beausset, Lorgues, Lourmarin, Lyon, Maillane, Malaucène, Manosque, Marseille, Nice, Nîmes (Popular Society), Pertuis, Peypin, La Roquebrussane, St.-Chamas, St.-Chamond, St.-Etienne, St.-Germain-Laval, St.-Rémy, St.-Tropez, Ste.-Tulle, Salon, Sisteron, Tarascon, Toulon, Trets, Uzès, Vaison, Velaux, Villecroze, Villelaure.

CENTER

Girondist orientation: Avallon, Brive, Champlitte, Chartres,[8] Gannat, St.-Yrieix.

Montagnard orientation: Ambert, Argenton, Aubusson, Auxerre, Blois, Châteauroux, Clamecy, Clermont-Ferrand, Cosne, Effiat, Guéret, La Charité, Limoges, Massiac, Meyssac, Montargis, Moulins, Nevers, Nogent-le-Rotrou, Orléans, Riom, Saillant, St.-Fargeau, St.-Florentin, St.-Sauveur (Yonne), Tonnerre, Tours, Tulle, Ussel.

NORTH/NORTHEAST

Girondist orientation: Amiens (Friends of Republic), Bar-le-Duc, Beauvais, Belley, Bourg-en-Bresse, Châlons-sur-Marne, Gueux, Is-sur-Tille, Maraye, Moirans, Nancy, Orgelet, Pontaillier, St.-Mihiel, St.-Quentin, St.-Valery, Salins,[9] Verdun, Vezelise.

Montagnard orientation: Abbeville, Aire, Amiens (Popular Society), Arcis-sur-Aube, Arras, Autun, Auxonne, Beaune, Cambrai, Chalon-sur-Saône, Champagnole, Compiègne, Dijon, Dole, Dormans, Ferney-Voltaire, Fontainebleau, Givet, Givry, Joinville, Jougne, Landau, Langres, Laon, Lille, Lons-le-Saunier, Louhans, Lure, Luxeuil, Mâcon,

---

[4] Aix made obeisance to the sections in late May and denounced the Montagnards.

[5] Apt did the same as Aix.

[6] There were several clubs at Beaucaire.

[7] Digne emulated Aix and Apt.

[8] Chartres was pro-Girondin up to April. By early June, however, it was fiercely pro-Montagnard.

[9] A new club was founded at Salins in April or May. It immediately aligned itself with the Paris society.

Mantes, Melun, Metz, Montcenis, Montdidier, Montmorot, Morteau, Munster, Nuits, Orbais, Ornans, Pernes, Porrentruy, Provins, Reims, St.-Avold, St.-Denis, St.-Germain-en-Laye, St.-Pol (P-d-C), Ste.-Menehould, Sarrebourg, Sarreguemines, Sedan, Senlis, Sezanne, Soissons, Strasbourg, Talmay, Tournan (S-et-M), Troyes, Valenciennes, Vaucouleurs, Versailles, Wissembourg.

Index

Castellane, 14, 333
Castelnaudary, 351
Castillon-sur-Dordogne, 19, 24
Castres: and congress, 16; meetings
  at, 6, 27; and grain trade, 75-76; and
  Albi, 102; and volunteers, 163; and
  levy of 300,000, 165; and Parisian
  press, 178, 180; and local press, 193;
  and Legislators, 237; and Day of
  June 20, 1792, 275; and dethronement, 278; and elections of 1792,
  287; relations with Paris club, 297;
  and departmental guard, 299; and
  Duke of Orléans, 330; and Chabot
  mission, 350-351; and appellants,
  354
Cereste, 14
Ceyzeriat, 330
Chabot, F., 105, 230, 251, 292, 296,
  314, 349-352
Chalier, M.-J., 47
Chalon-sur-Saône: zeal of, 4; and
  March 1, 1792 circular, 12; congress
  at, 16; and subsistances, 72; and
  grain trade, 77-78; and assignats,
  81-82; and billets de confiance, 85-
  86; and émigré properties, 95; and
  public schools, 105; and Beaune circular, 129; and postal system, 175;
  and Parisian press, 178, 180, 186;
  and local press, 193; and monastics,
  200; and anti-clericalism, 203; and
  pikes, 218-219; and Legislators,
  231; and first vetoes, 245, 247; and
  Eveil du peuple, 253; and fédérés,
  264; and Moreau, 290; relations
  with Paris club, 305-306, 315, 326,
  347; and appellants, 355; and trial of
  Marat, 356-357
Châlons-sur-Marne, 18, 23, 165
Chantilly, 129
Charleston, 4
Chartres: and line army, 112; and
  Phrygien bonnet, 221; and Pétion,
  229; relations with Paris club, 306;
  and Roland's resignation, 331;
  purges Chasles, 336; moves Leftward, 347
Chasles, P.-J.-M, 28, 336, 346-347
Château-du-Loir, 287
Châteaulin, 341, 357
Châteauneuf-du-Pape, 14
Châteauroux: and Feuillant schism, 7,
  53; and elections of 1792, 23; mem-
  bership, 34; schism in, 53-54; and
  grain trade, 74; and volunteers, 163;

and revolutionary army, 170-171;
  and Day of June 20, 1792, 275-276;
  and overthrow of king, 283; and
  departmental guard, 298
Château-Thierry, 17, 278
Châteauvieux, Swiss regiment of,
  115-117
Châtellerault: and Parisian press, 183,
  185; and Phrygien bonnets, 222;
  and Legislators, 230, 237; relations
  with Paris club, 322
Châtillon-sur-Chalaronne: attendance
  at, 6; and billets de confiance, 86;
  and foreign regiments, 117; and Parisian press, 178; and celibacy, 210;
  and Dijon circular, 216
Chaumont, 167
Chef-Boutonne, 163
Cherbourg: frequent meetings, 22;
  and port facilities, 100; and volunteers, 135; and war victories, 137;
  Anglophilism at, 154-155, 157; and
  war with England, 157-159; war
  gift of, 162; and Parisian press, 178,
  180; and local press, 195; and mo-
  nastics, 200; and dethronement,
  278; and elections of 1792, 287; relations with Paris club, 293, 305; and
  Marat, 303; and trial of king, 310;
  and departmental guard, 317; and
  trial of Marat, 357
Cheval-Blanc, 27
Chinon, 105
Cholet, 6, 7
Chronique de Paris, 182, 292, 341
Chronique du mois, 182, 292
Civrai, 293
Clairac, 72, 165, 319, 347, 359
Clamecy, 29
Clarensac, 268
Clavière, E., 17-18, 182, 250, 256, 306
Clermont-Ferrand: zeal of, 4; found-
  ing of clubs, 13; and congresses, 16;
  schism in, 53; and public schools,
  105; for war, 128; and Parisian
  press, 182; and Protestants, 205; and
  Dijon circular, 216; and Phrygien
  bonnet, 221; and Legislators, 230,
  232; and first vetoes, 245; and sec-
  ond vetoes, 257; and Convention-
  nels, 290; and departmental guard,
  319; and trial of king, 325-326
Cloots, A., 320
Cognac: and congresses, 14; and grain
  trade, 71; and volunteers, 119; and
  Chambéry, 142; and pikes, 218; and

Library of Congress Cataloging-in-Publication Data

Kennedy, Michael L.
 The Jacobin clubs in the French Revolution. The middle years / Michael L.
Kennedy.
p.   cm.
 "This is the second of a proposed trilogy of works on the Jacobin clubs during
the French Revolution"—Pref.
 Includes index.
 ISBN 0-691-05526-2   (alk. paper) : $49.50
 1. Jacobins 2. France—History—Revolution, 1789-1799—Clubs.
I. Title.
DC178.K47 1988
944.04—dc 19   87-22298
                                                                    CIP